EXPLORING
COLLABORATIVE
RESEARCH
IN
PRIMARY
CARE

EXPLORING
COLLABORATIVE
RESEARCH
IN
PRIMARY
CARE

EDITED BY

BENJAMIN F. CRABTREE
WILLIAM L. MILLER
RICHARD B. ADDISON
VALERIE J. GILCHRIST
ANTON J. KUZEL

SAGE Publications
International Educational and Professional Publisher
Thousand Oaks   London   New Delhi

For information address:

SAGE Publications, Inc.
2455 Teller Road
Thousand Oaks, California 91320

SAGE Publications Ltd.
6 Bonhill Street
London EC2A 4PU
United Kingdom

SAGE Publications India Pvt. Ltd.
M-32 Market
Greater Kailash I
New Delhi 110 048 India

Printed in the United States of America

Library of Congress Cataloging-in-Publication Data

Main entry under title:

Exploring collaborative research in primary care / edited by Benjamin
    F. Crabtree . . . [et al.].
        p.   cm.
    Includes bibliographical references and index.
    ISBN 0-8039-5489-1.—ISBN 0-8039-5490-5 (pbk.)
    1. Interdisciplinary research—Congresses.   2. Primary care
(Medicine)—Research—Congresses.   I. Crabtree, Benjamin F.
R853.I53D49   1994
362.1′072—dc20   94-9470

94 95 96 97 98   10 9 8 7 6 5 4 3 2 1

Sage Production Editor: Diane S. Foster

CONTENTS

PREFACE

The core of this book results from events prior, during, and following the Conference on Multimethod Research that was convened in Omaha, Nebraska, in May 1993. Our goal in both the conference and the book has been the development and furtherance of a collaborative, cross-disciplinary research community in primary care.

The book is divided into four sections. Part I explores the basic tools required to build multimethod research. It includes chapters on traditional quantitative methods that have defined primary care research (epidemiology, psychometrics, econometrics, clinical trials, and statistical analysis) and qualitative methods that are increasingly recognized as necessary (participant observation, interviewing, interpretive analysis, human document research, and critical analysis). The chapters in Part I were written to minimize disciplinary jargon.

Part II is about the perspectives and disciplines that have formed the core of research in the area of changing provider behavior. It includes chapters on theories of provider behavior and discusses models and techniques of study. The chapters provide an opportunity to see how a problem area has been investigated by researchers from diverse disciplines and look not only at how these disciplines overlap but also at how they individually fail to account for critical pieces covered by other perspectives. These chapters were initially developed prior to the conference to provide a basic understanding of research in health care provider behavior to someone with little background in the area. They were subsequently expanded to provide insights for readers with little or no familiarity with the topic and for content area experts.

Part III follows the authors of the chapters in Parts I and II, researchers from widely diverse disciplines and perspectives, as they worked in a conference format to develop collaborative projects around an assigned content area. The chapters examine the process and lessons of the conference by looking at the conference as stages in community development and focusing on the process by which a group of expert researchers with extremely diverse areas of expertise came together to work on common tasks. The first chapter tells the story of our aspirations, experience, and learning. Other chapters look at four case reports in which conference participants worked together in four different problem areas to develop research questions and designs. A final chapter reflects on the conference through the eyes of our conference commentators: the practitioner, the researcher (both quantitative and qualitative), and the funding agency.

Finally, Part IV provides a summary of past and current efforts toward cross-disciplinary research and searches for a future based on past successes and failures and the lessons learned from the conference.

Acknowledgments

The editors of this volume gratefully acknowledge the Agency for Health Care Policy and Research for their support of the "Conference on Multi-methods in Primary Care Research." This publication was made possible in part by grant number 7 R13 HS07291-02. We also acknowledge the assistance of the Department of Family Practice at the University of Nebraska, especially the efforts of Marlene Hawver who helped coordinate the conference and helped to make the figures.

INTRODUCTION

Benjamin F. Crabtree

A powerful and dominating army with a vast arsenal of weapons approaches a small, lightly equipped community protected only by a wall. A messenger for the army is sent to the gate and demands surrender; the messenger can't imagine any possible alternatives. Behind the wall, in a language unknown to the forces outside, the tiny community grieves, talks, and envisions new possibilities. With refreshed faith and hope, they turn and go to the wall and, using a common language, converse with the enemy. Through the resultant dialogue, the community is preserved and those outside (and inside) the wall are transformed.

This narrative might represent researchers from many disciplines focusing on their own disciplinary perspectives while looking out through the ivy at the dominating landscape held by other researchers, but it is the story of Jerusalem under siege by the Assyrians in 701 B.C.E. as told in 2 Kings 18-19. Walter Brueggemann, an Old Testament scholar and hermeneutist, highlights the two places where the drama unfolds. There is the "conversation behind the wall" and the "conversation at the wall" (1991, pp. 41-42). This book is about not only the need for the research community to have conversation behind the wall—the internal discourse that disciplines and traditions have about who they are and what they do—but also the need to have transformation and translation at the wall. It is at the wall where, in a language understood by all participants, a space for more expansive imagination can be created, where tools for listening and seeing must be shared, and where transforming stories should be enacted.

STIMULATING CONVERSATIONS AT THE WALL

Why is there a need for conversing at the wall? For primary care research, the need is clear and simple. It stems from a number of interrelated changes that have occurred in health care in the United States over the past several decades. Both primary care practice and the needs of practitioners and patients have significantly diverged from much of traditional biomedical research. The Report of the Task Force on Building Capacity for Research in Primary Care (University of Minnesota, Dept. of Family Practice, 1993) states:

> The inadequacy of existing medical research for primary care is in a large part the result of the differences between problems and interventions studied in university settings compared with the problems that people bring to primary care settings in the community and the processes that primary care practitioners must employ. (p. 10)

We maintain that primary care research is not working because it has been stuck in a technological mode of thinking that is specialist dominated. Thinking about primary care problems in specialist language—for example, in terms of individual illnesses and disease models—has produced solutions of limited utility. It cannot be assumed that if the "egg of knowledge," like Humpty Dumpty, is broken into pieces, it can be put together again. It is becoming more and more apparent that there are limits to the utility of technological solutions.

As primary care has diverged from tertiary care centers, solo practices have given way to group practices, and public health centers and managed care organizations have increased, the old standard research approaches have become outmoded. Collaborative research conversations and multimethod research approaches may facilitate this primary care paradigm shift while still being consistent with the nature of inquiry (see Dzurec & Abraham, 1993).

Of course, a major assumption in this argument is that a paradigm shift is underway; however, considerable evidence supports this assumption. There are some fundamental changes in the world leading to doubt in *enough people* that a particular worldview can be assumed; thus there is an erosion of legitimacy of the existing modes of power and dominance. Montuori and Conti (1993) discuss factors that have contributed to this erosion: (a) global/transglobal diversity, (b) complexity and multiplicity, (c) the rapid rate of change, and (d) an unmanageable information explosion. The primary care research of the past spoke to a different time and structure and is often no longer relevant.

It is increasingly difficult to comfortably assume that the world is lawful, ordered, functionally related, and measurable in a value-free closed system (Cook, 1985). The indigenization of knowledge serves to undermine notions of generalizability (Easton & Schilling, 1991). The need to communicate in words creates a cultural specificity of language that also serves to erode a universal approach to research. The methods currently in use reflect one particular historical experience (see Lather, this volume).

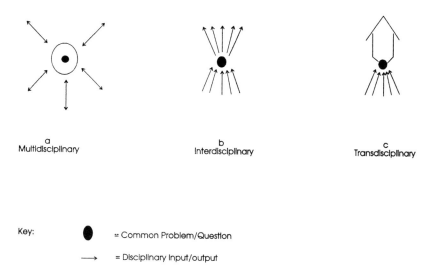

Figure I.1. Types of Cross-Disciplinary Research

As stated by the Report of the Task Force on Building Capacity for Research in Primary Care (University of Minnesota, Dept. of Family Practice, 1993), "although primary care practitioners can use some of the knowledge generated by this [biomedical] research, in fact, most of it is not relevant to primary care because of its focus on singly developed diseases, carefully selected patients, and the reporting of strictly physiological outcomes" (p. iii). Thus it should not be surprising that primary care provider behavior has not changed as hoped (see Borkan, this volume). To improve relevance, research needs to have broader ownership of the data and findings.

A TYPOLOGY OF CROSS-DISCIPLINARY RESEARCH

To begin addressing the complexities that make up primary health care practice, an expanded imagination that includes multimethod collaboration becomes essential. Taking off from the work of Rosenfield (1992), we see three ways to expand the research imagination, or three types of collaborative research: *multidisciplinary, interdisciplinary,* and *transdisciplinary* research. These collaborative research strategies are illustrated in Figure I.1.

Multi means "many." In multidisciplinary research many disciplines contribute their piece to solving the problem (Figure I.1a). Each person comes to his or her wall, gets a question, and then returns to his or her own confines to work on that question. The researchers have a conversation behind the walls on a common topic. This is like an edited volume or like hearing separate presentations from many content experts. It may all come together, but often it doesn't. This is the traditional approach to policy issues.

Inter means "between" and "among." In interdisciplinary research, each contributor comes to the gate and talks from his or her expertise, so there is a conversation at the wall between and among participants from different disciplines (Figure I.1b). One such interdisciplinary group might be a collaborative health team consisting of a psychologist, a social worker, a physical therapist, a physician, and a nurse who jointly focused on a common topic, problem, or patient. This is what we had planned for our conference described in Part III.

Trans means "across" and "beyond." In this research the conversation takes place beyond the wall in a new common space and goes beyond and across what any one discipline offers (Figure I.1c). The idea is to create a new shared language. Examples of transdisciplinary efforts include the emergence of family systems medicine, some farming research, and conservation biology, each forming out of several different disciplines.

In order to develop cross-disciplinary research, particularly transdisciplinary research, it is necessary to build a research community and a language for conversation. This is not an easy task. This book examines the process of developing such a community by looking at some of the disciplines that contribute methodologically to primary care research (Part I), reviewing a particularly vexing primary health care research area and identifying important questions (changing primary care provider behavior) (Part II), and attempting to create collaborative research designs to address these questions (Part III). We conclude with a discussion of critical issues in developing collaborative research and recommendations (Part IV).

I

Methodological Perspectives in Primary Care Research

A fundamental assumption on the part of the editors as they constructed the Conference on Multimethods Research in Primary Care and produced this volume was that research designs are a function of the goals of the research and the research question. Thus a central tenet of developing multimethod research should be that *the question and context are primary; methods must adjust to the setting and the question.* Researchers should mix and match methods as driven by particular questions.

For researchers to make space for multimethod research, and certainly for transdisciplinary research (see Introduction and Chapter 23), it is essential that they make clear distinctions among paradigms, research styles, research traditions, and research methods. Habermas (1968/1971a) differentiates three major paradigms. *Materialistic inquiry* or *logical positivism* seeks to uncover objective truth. This is currently the dominant paradigm operating in the health care field. *Interpretive, constructivist,* or *naturalistic inquiry* seeks to understand, in a circular fashion, the meaning of context, history, and assumptions of both the researcher and the people being studied. A third major paradigm uses *critical/ecological inquiry* and seeks to understand larger systemic and structural issues by focusing on the distribution of power and elements of domination. Researchers working within any one of these paradigms see the world differently from those working within the other two. However, it is important to note that using any one of these paradigms does not necessarily dictate what methods are employed.

1

For example, interpretive inquiry and qualitative methods are sometimes confused, and the concepts are used interchangeably. *Although interpretive inquiry often utilizes qualitative methods, the two are not synonymous.* Furthermore, both quantitative and qualitative methods may be used in any of the three paradigms. For example, researchers operating from within a materialistic paradigm can use a qualitative method such as focus groups to help design research instruments and enhance the survey style of research (see K. O'Brien, 1993). Conversely, those operating under an interpretive paradigm can use the results of a survey to assist in sample selection and to better define the topical areas for focus groups or other qualitative methods (see Stange, Miller, Crabtree, O'Connor, & Zyzanski, in press).

From a multimethod perspective, "the choice of research style for a particular project depends on the overarching aim of the research, the specific analysis objective and its associated research question, the preferred paradigm, the degree of desired research control, the level of investigator intervention, the available resources, the time frame, and aesthetics" (Miller & Crabtree, 1992, p. 6). Thus the actual research methods employed are not a driving force and become subservient to the research goals, the immediate research questions, and the research context.

If the question concerns "how many," "how much," "how often," "what size," or numerically measurable associations between phenomena, then a survey research style using the designs and methods of observational epidemiology is appropriate. If the question asks "if————, then————" or "is———— more effective than————," then an experimental style is reasonable. Many questions, however, concern experience, meaning, patterns, relationships, and values; these questions refer to knowledge as story. How do insurance practices and workers' compensation laws constrain the possibilities of patients and doctors? These questions weave the clinical concerns into a holistic narrative and call for the designs and methods of the qualitative clinical researcher.

As researchers begin to broach more and more complex issues, they need to conceptualize a continuum of research (Zemke, 1989) that incorporates paradigm and methods according to the question at hand and fully integrated research methods. Texts describing such an integration are beginning to emerge (e.g., see DePoy & Gitlin, 1993). To this end, we have gathered some of the top methods experts in primary care research to present their particular area of expertise.

The first five chapters are devoted to quantitative methods. Thomas Newman and John Stanfield, an epidemiologist and a sociologist, combine to talk about observational epidemiology in Chapter 1. Psychologist Lee Sechrest and nursing student Souraya Sidani give an outline of measurement issues in

Chapter 2, and in Chapter 3, Curt Mueller, an economist with Project Hope, introduces the application of econometrics to primary care research. Catherine Gilliss, an accomplished nurse researcher, presents randomized controlled trials, the gold standard of biomedical research, in Chapter 4, and David Katerndahl, a family physician researcher, provides an excellent discussion of statistical concepts and meta-analysis in Chapter 5.

The last five chapters in this section are dedicated to qualitative methods. In Chapter 6, Stephen Bogdewic and P. K. Jamison provide a succinct overview of participant observation. Jaber Gubrium, a sociologist and gerontologist, discusses issues in interviewing in Chapter 7 and includes commentary by Lee Sechrest and Souraya Sidani, who reviewed his chapter. John Stanfield, a sociologist, and David Katerndahl, a family physician, collaborate in Chapter 8 to describe the applications of written documents to primary care research. Sociologist Norman Denzin offers a clear summary of interpretive interactionism in Chapter 9. And finally, in one of the more radical chapters in this volume, Patti Lather, an educational researcher, provides an excellent synopsis of critical inquiry in qualitative research.

1

OBSERVATIONAL EPIDEMIOLOGY

Thomas B. Newman
John H. Stanfield, II

This chapter discusses the observational epidemiologic approach to clinical research. It begins with some definitions and an assumption, then reviews four basic epidemiologic study designs, and last discusses how to determine whether observed associations are causal. Throughout, the examples will be of studies in which the goal is to predict the occurrence of a disease, because epidemiologic methods are easiest to understand when applied to predicting disease. However, these same methods and designs may sometimes be applicable to predicting other outcomes, such as provider behaviors. The chapter concludes with a discussion by Dr. John Stanfield of ways in which qualitative—"subjective"—methods can be utilized to expand the scope of observational epidemiological research.

DEFINITIONS

The epidemiologic approach generally involves making measurements on a *sample* of individuals from a *population* and then trying to infer causal relationships between *predictor variables* and *outcome variables*. None of these terms is very difficult, and all are discussed at greater length in standard epidemiology texts (e.g., see Hulley & Cummings, 1988; Kelsey, Thompson, & Evans, 1986). It is probably easier to illustrate them with a couple of examples than to go through a series of boring definitions.

So here is an example: you want to know whether passive smoking by infants might be a cause of otitis media (earache). The population of interest is all infants, but clearly you can't study all of them, so you will choose a sample—say, the infants coming to one of three primary care clinics whose parents are willing to enroll them in the study. Clearly, as will be discussed later, how you choose your sample will determine how confident you can be that the results are generalizable.

Now that you have your sample, you are going to make some measurements. We will divide these into two types: *predictor variables* and *outcome variables*. The predictor variables are the things you think may cause the outcome variable. Often there is one predictor variable in which you are particularly interested (in this case, passive smoking), and there are other *covariables* (in this case, perhaps breast-feeding or social class) that you also need to measure to separate their effects from those of the variable of interest. Predictor variables can be risk factors, as in this example, or interventions, as in a clinical trial. The outcome variable is the thing you are trying to predict (or in an interventions study, to affect); in this example it is the occurrence of otitis media.

ASSUMPTIONS

There may be more assumptions than I realize, but there is one major assumption: that the phenomena of interest can be measured. If we can't accurately tell which infants have otitis media, it will be very hard to tell what causes otitis. And in order to tell whether passive smoking might be a cause of otitis, we need to be able to measure not only passive smoking but other potential causes of otitis (covariables) as well.

The harder it is to obtain valid quantitative measurements of the phenomena of interest, the less likely these epidemiologic methods are to be helpful. Phenomena may be difficult to measure for many reasons: some are multidimensional, with different observers likely to disagree on the relative importance of different dimensions (e.g., quality of life); others are behaviors that are difficult to observe and may not be accurately reported (e.g., certain sexual practices); still others may relate to group interactions or feelings that are difficult to quantify (e.g., empathy). Of course, numbers can still be attached to all of these concepts or phenomena, but the investigator and reader need to be aware that the numbers may not tell the whole (or even the most important part) of the story.

STUDY DESIGNS

There are many ways to classify study designs (prospective, retrospective, etc.), but because we are going to review only four of them very briefly, it is probably easier just to describe them.

Cohort studies are conceptually very easy (see Kelsey et al., 1986). In a cohort study, measurements of the level of the predictor variable are made on subjects free of the disease at the beginning of the study. The subjects are then followed over time to see whether the proportion who develop the outcome variable varies according to the level of the predictor variable. Thus parents of infants at risk of otitis media might be questioned as to their child's level of exposure to smoke, and then the children could be followed over time to see if the number of ear infections was higher (or lower) in those exposed to cigarette smoke.

Cross-sectional studies look at both predictor and outcome in a single slice of time (see Hulley & Cummings, 1988; Kelsey et al., 1986). Cross-sectional studies tell you about prevalence of disease (how many people have it at a particular point in time) rather than incidence (how many people get it over a period of time). If the outcome itself does not last a long time (as in the case of an episode of acute otitis media) it is hard to study with a cross-sectional study. Thus cross-sectional studies are good for looking at chronic conditions, such as high blood pressure and HIV seropositivity.

Question 1: Can you think of a chronic condition related to acute otitis media that might lend itself better to a cross-sectional study? [Answers on p. 11.]

Case control studies are just a bit trickier than the preceding two designs (see Kelsey et al., 1986; Schlesselman, 1982). In case control studies, we begin with a group of subjects who already have the outcome of interest (infants with acute otitis media), measure their level of the predictor variable (passive smoking), and compare it to the level in a comparable group of subjects without otitis media.

Case control studies are tricky, so I will give just a few more famous examples. A case control study found that children with Reye's syndrome (cases) were much more likely to have taken aspirin during an immediately preceding episode of chicken pox or flu than children who had chicken pox or flu but did not develop Reye's syndrome (controls) (Hurwitz et al., 1985). That is why there are now warnings about Reye's syndrome on baby aspirin packages, leading to the near-disappearance of Reye's syndrome in the United States. A case control study also found that women who developed toxic shock syndrome (cases) were much more likely to use Rely tampons than their friends (who were the controls) (Herbst, Ulfelder, & Poskanzer, 1971).

Ecologic studies are different from the three study designs mentioned above because the sampling unit and unit of analysis are a geographic area (or other defined group of people) rather than individuals (see Kelsey et al., 1986). For example, if there were good population-wide data on tobacco use and frequency of otitis media, we might ask whether countries (or states or counties) with higher per capita tobacco consumption had more recorded episodes of otitis media per child.

Ecologic studies are appealing because they generally make use of existing data (making them very inexpensive to do) and at first glance seem to make possible studies of enormous sample size. However, the data available are often only very rough surrogates for the variables of interest (e.g., higher overall tobacco consumption in a state may not necessarily mean greater tobacco exposure to infants), and the actual sample size is not the number of subjects living in the areas studied but the number of geographic units that were sampled.

Furthermore, ecologic studies are subject to the ecologic fallacy: associations present at the level of geographic areas may not hold among individuals. For example, counties with higher levels of condom use may also have higher levels of sexually transmitted diseases (STDs) (because both probably are related to the county's level of sexual activity). But this does not suggest that use of condoms by individuals increases their risk of STDs; among individuals, those who use condoms may be at lower risk than those who do not.

INFERRING CAUSALITY

As stated previously, a common goal in epidemiologic research is to identify causal relationships. Observed associations can be distorted by *chance* or *bias*; in either instance the observed association may not actually exist. In addition, true associations may exist but not be due to a cause-effect relationship. This could be either because the outcome caused the predictor (*effect-cause*) or because both are due to some extraneous, third factor (*confounding*). We will briefly review each of these bases for associations in observational studies.

Just by chance (bad luck), we might happen to select a group of infants exposed to smoke that was more or less likely to develop otitis than the general population of passive smoking infants. In that case, the estimate of association between passive smoking and otitis media found in our study would be incorrect, even though we might not have done anything wrong.

By definition, what we are talking about here is bad luck. If we were to repeat the study several times, the average answer given by the study would be the right answer, and very wrong answers would become progressively less likely. There are two important characteristics of errors due to chance: (a) they can be reduced by increasing the sample size or repeating the study, and (b) their probability of occurrence can be quantified statistically. In fact, quantifying the possible contribution of random error (chance) is one of the major tasks of statisticians.

The other type of error, bias, is a bit more pernicious. Unlike chance, bias persists with larger studies or with replications of the same study because it is due to faults in study design rather than bad luck. And unlike chance, its importance cannot be quantified statistically; it takes careful (nonstatistical) thought about what could have gone wrong. (It pays to do that thinking at the time the study is designed, to prevent the bias from occurring in the first place.)

The easiest way to think about bias is to realize that the process of doing research is full of compromises between feasibility and validity. Although the most valid approach might be to study everyone, this is not feasible, so we select a sample instead. If the sample is a random sample of the population, it will differ only by random error, and there will be no bias. But much more commonly, nonrandom samples are selected. For our convenience, we chose to sample volunteers from three primary care clinics. Is the association between passive smoking and otitis media likely to be different among infants attending such clinics? This is the type of question we need to ask to address the possibility of bias.

Question 2: What do you think about the possibility of sampling bias in this study?

We can think of the measurements of predictor and outcome variables as compromises as well. If the infant's exposure to components of cigarette smoke is the actual predictor variable of interest, the ideal measurement of it might involve sampling the air the infant breathed. What we will probably have to settle for is a self-report of exposure from a questionnaire. This type of self-report is subject to bias: for example, smoking parents may underreport the extent of their child's exposure to their own smoke. Similarly, if the true outcome of interest is acute otitis media, the measurement of that outcome that we are likely to have to settle for is a diagnosis of otitis by an intern or resident, who may not be very good at looking at eardrums, particularly in crying infants.

Once we have considered spurious causes of an association between predictor and outcome (chance and bias), we should consider whether the association might be real but not causal. One such basis for an association is effect-cause: that is, the outcome is causing the predictor variable. Could the stress of having a child with frequent ear infections cause parents to smoke more? The best way to rule out effect-cause is to show that the predictor variable temporally preceded the outcome: did the passive smoking begin before the first ear infection? In addition, as in this example, one direction for the causal relationship may be more biologically plausible than the other.

A more challenging possibility is effect-effect (also called confounding): could both otitis media and passive smoking be related to some third factor? For example, breast-feeding seems to protect against otitis media. If (as seems plausible) women who smoke are less likely to breast-feed, babies exposed to passive smoke will be more likely to get otitis, even if the passive smoke did not actually cause the otitis, simply because they are less likely to be breast-fed. Similar concerns might apply to social class.

There are several methods for dealing with confounding. All try to look at the effect of the predictor on outcome, while holding potential confounding variables constant. The simplest is *specification,* in which the investigator specifies that only subjects with a single level of the confounder will be studied. For example, if the study were restricted to bottle-fed infants of poor women, neither feeding nor social class could be responsible for any association observed. The trouble with specification, though, is that it will limit both the generalizability of the findings and the sample size available for study.

Another sampling strategy is *matching,* in which subjects are matched according to their levels of the confounder and comparisons are made only between matched pairs. For example, in a cohort study, each infant exposed to passive smoke could be matched to an unexposed infant of the same social class being fed the same way. In a case control study, infants with otitis (cases) could be matched to infants with no otitis (controls), so that members of each case control pair had the same social class and feeding method. Then any difference in passive smoking between cases and their matched controls could not be due to feeding method or social class (to the extent that we are able to measure these two variables accurately).

Stratification is similar to matching, except that it is done after the study has been completed, at the time the data are being analyzed. Thus we could stratify by breast-feeding, looking for an association between passive smoking and otitis separately in breast-fed and bottle-fed infants. Stratification allows the ability to detect interaction or effect modification, in which the relationship between predictor and outcome varies according to the level of a third variable. That is, stratifying could allow us to notice if passive smoking were a risk factor in bottle-fed but not breast-fed infants.

One trouble with stratification is that control of only a few levels of only a few confounders can lead to sample sizes within some strata that are too small. One way around this problem is to model the association between predictor variables and outcome using *multivariate statistics*. Models typically make simplifying assumptions about the way the predictor variables relate to outcome. For example, the model may assume that there is no effect modification: that is, that the effects of each variable on outcome do not depend on the levels of the other variables. Multivariate methods also often use a specific mathematical model to relate each predictor to outcome; linear and logistic models are the most popular. The model can then examine the effects of each predictor variable, with the effects of the others held constant statistically.

But multivariate models have limitations too. The most important of these is that the model may not fit (i.e., the simplifying assumptions may be false). Unfortunately, the ready availability of software packages offering multivariate statistical methods has frequently led to inappropriate use by investigators not familiar with the underlying assumptions. A parallel problem is that many readers of medical journals are not familiar with these models and cannot interpret the highly derived statistics generated therefrom. It is therefore a good idea to begin with stratified analyses and use multivariate methods second, preferably with the help of someone with statistical expertise.

ANSWERS TO QUESTIONS

1. How about either serous otitis media (otitis media with effusion; persistent fluid in the middle ear) or a history of recurrent otitis?
2. Although the prevalence of passive smoking and otitis is probably different in clinics than in private practices or other settings, the association between passive smoking and otitis seems a bit less likely to vary from one setting to another. Perhaps the biggest problem is the bias that might arise from those who decline to participate. If parents are invited to participate in a study of passive smoking and ear infections, it seems plausible that parents who smoke and whose children have had many ear infections might be less likely to volunteer to be in the study because it could lead to guilt about their children's illness.

COMMENTS—JOHN H. STANFIELD, II

Observational epidemiological approaches are invaluable in medical research, but the narrow focus of this approach leads to important limitations. What is missing are attempts to find creative ways to integrate broader social, political, and cultural contexts into observational epistemological research designs.

For example, until very recently, medical researchers ignored the impacts of sexism and racism on the physical and mental well-being of patients. This is because the oppressive experiences of women and people of color were considered moral or political economic issues with no place in medical diagnosis. This view in medicine is beginning to change slowly. In addition, it is becoming increasingly apparent that certain aspects of human development, such as spirituality, which used to be considered as nonissues in sciences, are important issues in physical and mental health.

Although thanks to epidemiological research we know a great deal about the distribution of a large array of diseases, we do not know very much about how people experience and define disease. How people feel about disease and how diseases make them feel as human beings may be at least as important as understanding the causes of diseases and their distributions. Thus epidemiologists would do well to incorporate qualitative dimensions into their observational research designs.

Each of the research designs discussed earlier could integrate qualitative methods that would generate subjective data of great benefit to epidemiological studies. Depending upon the research focus, any number of human documents could be collected along with statistical information to enhance the multidimensionality of data collection and interpretation. In cohort designs, for instance, perhaps the researcher could examine diaries, personal correspondence, physician charts, and other qualitative data to grasp the multidimensionality of diseases as human experiences over time. Using qualitative data in ecologic study designs could be an effective preventive measure against ecological fallacies because the researcher would be collecting and analyzing not only aggregate data but also experiential data drawn from individuals. Individual experiential data collection in ecological locations preserves the rich variation of status, institutional, community, and psychological definitions of and responses to diseases.

Qualitative data collection and analysis can also be important checks and balances in the conventional reporting of disease distributions in populations. Documents such as diaries and personal correspondence, as well as in-depth interviews and oral histories, can sensitize researchers about the process through which disease reporting is shaped by social, political, economic, cultural, and historical contexts. In a word, the statistical numbers used to represent patterns and trends in disease distributions in populations are human inventions that become most meaningful when we can grasp the conditions under which they were created.

The use of qualitative approaches to sensitize epidemiological researchers in this fashion is particularly important in historical studies. The further the historical distance from the epidemiological issue, the more the use of statistical data becomes problematic because the data come from eras with alien climates of opinion (taken-for-granted cultural assumptions, language, etc.). Epidemiologists tend to impose contemporaneous social categories on events occurring in the distant past rather than reconstructing the ontological particulars of the era in which the epidemiological event occurred.

What I am proposing in this section is, I am afraid, a time-consuming, expensive venture. Being interdisciplinary always is much more cumbersome and even frustrating than remaining within the narrow procedures and practices of one's discipline. But if knowledge is to advance in significant ways, researchers across numerous fields must begin to find ways to cross-fertilize their logics of inquiry because, after all, the world is complex. The intricacies of the realities we are drawn to investigate require that we develop multidimensional logics of inquiry found to be adequate more because of their isomorphism with an empirical problem under study than because of their conformity with longstanding professional traditions. It is in this spirit that I suggest that researchers with quantitative and qualitative methodological preferences work together to find common ground to improve knowledge bases in medical research areas such as observational epidemiology.

2

MEASUREMENT

Lee Sechrest
Souraya Sidani

Trying to define measurement in any technical way would probably not be productive because we all understand well enough what measurement means and what the idea entails. Measurement is the assignment of quantitative values to observations according to rules that result in a relationship between the assigned values and some presumed underlying magnitude. It is only at the margin that we would disagree at all. Therefore it is worth discussing at least one marginal issue. Specifically, we believe that the process of declaring the presence or absence of some object, property, or characteristic is a form of measurement. Such declarations can be expressed in binary form, 0 or 1, and they therefore constitute measurement, however crude, as we understand it. In principle, then, *any* set of observations can be converted into measured form by being expressed in binary form.

Binary measures can be treated like any others: they can be added, subtracted, multiplied, and divided. That is not to say that just any sort of treatment of binary measures is a good idea, but they do not have any special status or restrictions on their use. For example, one could examine a manuscript, code all favorable adjectives as 1 and their absence as 0, and then calculate the mean across all nouns, if one thought that would be meaningful.

Measurement theory is well developed and fairly extensive. In fact, several approaches to measurement theory exist and are useful for different purposes. For the sake of this presentation, classical test theory and generalizability theory are both relevant. A convenient reference is Crocker and Algina (1986).

CLASSICAL TEST THEORY

Classical test theory begins with the assumption that any test score, for which we may substitute a more generic term, *observation,* is determined by *true score* plus or minus error. Thus, for example, if a group of people are asked to state their incomes, the resulting "observed" income for any one person is a function of the true income of the person plus or minus some error. In this case, error might arise from the person's failure to recollect some items of income, from counting a reimbursement check as income, from an error in multiplying biweekly income by 26, and so on. Across persons these and any other errors are assumed to be random: that is, not correlated with actual income. Moreover, errors are assumed to be random over occasions so that a person who errs by overestimating income on one occasion is just as likely to underestimate it on some other occasion.

Exactly the same thinking may be applied to other, even qualitative, observations. Thus one might ask a person to name his or her favorite color. From the standpoint of classical measurement (test) theory, we assume that the response, say "blue," reflects the person's true disposition to like blue plus error. But what would error be in this case? Well, that particular person might have been thinking for the moment of his or her wardrobe, whereas another person, who said "yellow," might have been thinking of the warmth of a Van Gogh painting. Still another person might have been thinking, "This is a tricky psych question; blue is probably a safe answer." If, in general, responses are determined by what is on people's minds momentarily, the error in assessing "favorite color" is large.

Error

A word should be said about the component of many observations that is also often referred to as *error.* Specifically, many sets of observations are characterized by *bias,* a systematic distortion of observations. For example, one person may tend to exaggerate his income in order to create a favorable impression on others, and another person may understate his income because of concern for losing welfare benefits. If bias is known to exist and its extent can be estimated, its effects can be allowed for—for example, by subtracting an amount from a person's estimate of income. If bias is not known or cannot be estimated, then it is indistinguishable from the true score. Absent other sources of information, for example, it may be impossible to determine whether a person's highly favorable self-description represents self-aggrandizement or sainthood.

All measures must be assumed to be in error; we would have no way of recognizing a given estimate as absolutely correct. If a table is measured 10 times with a sufficiently finely graded tape measure, the measurements are virtually certain to vary. We can estimate a true length for the table by using the mean of all 10 measures, but we must assume that even the mean, the best estimate of the true length, is in error in some degree. Somewhat paradoxically, statistics uses the variability, the errors, in measurement in order to increase precision of estimates of true values.

Random, which is to say otherwise unexplained, variability in measures can be better estimated and thus eliminated from our considerations by use of multiple, independent observations or measures. It is common, and understandable, for carpenters, especially cautious amateurs, to measure boards twice or three times before they cut them. It would be even better if those carpenters used two very different tape measures, and better still if two different carpenters did the measuring. That is what is meant by independence of measures. What independence does is maximize the randomness of errors and hence the likelihood that errors will cancel each other out. Errors of measurement can be reduced by using multiple measures, even if they are individually fallible, as long as they are independent in the sense of having errors that are uncorrelated.

In fact, aggregation of measures, even if they are not particularly reliable when taken alone, can have remarkable effects on dependability of measures (Rushton, Brainerd, & Pressley, 1983). The Spearman-Brown prophecy formula, well known in psychometrics (see Crocker & Algina, 1986), can be used to forecast the effects of aggregating measures. If, to take one example, ratings by different raters correlate only .30, a level much too low to make single ratings acceptable, the use of five raters would result in an estimated reliability for ratings of about .70. Ten raters would result in a reliability of .81. Increases in dependability of measures from aggregation arise from the fact that errors, because they are uncorrelated, do not accumulate, but the variance in true scores does accumulate, resulting in an increasingly large proportion of reliable variance as the number of observations increases.

Eliminating bias is not so simple, as will be discussed later under the heading *reactive measures.* Essentially, though, bias in measurement can be reduced by using measures that do not share the same sources of error. If we have a measure that seems susceptible to self-aggrandizement (self-serving bias), we need to find one or more other measures that are less susceptible to that source of bias. Using multiple measures that all share the same tendencies does not help the problem at all. Using two or more different measures, however, may reduce the average amount of bias and help triangulate in on a better estimate of the true score. At the very least, the use of two or more measures that are quite different in their sources of error may serve a sentinel function of alerting us to potential problems of interpretation with respect to a measure we may favor as a best estimate. The importance of multiple measures should be familiar to qualitative researchers, who, for example, would recognize that the perspectives of both management and workers probably need to be taken into account if one is to have an adequate picture of an organization, or who would be alerted to the possibility of something wrong if an agency claimed to be open on Saturdays but phone calls on that day were always connected to an answering machine.

Reliability

Classical test theory places heavy emphasis on the concept of reliability of measures, by which is meant, roughly, that measurements obtained under the same conditions should result in the same scores. Reliability of a measure is not a monolithic construct; separate reliability indexes are required for different conditions of measurement. The most readily understood notion of reliability, often referred to as *test-retest reliability,* is that observations should remain consistent across occasions of measurement. Of course, observations should not be expected to be consistent if real trait changes occur over occasions. We do not expect a high level of consistency between table manners used while eating alone at home and table manners used while eating in company at a posh restaurant. We do not even think that measures of mood *should* be consistent over occasions. *Internal consistency* is the most often calculated and referenced form of reliability, and it is intended to indicate the degree to which an observed score is attributable to the particular set of test items that is used. Put another way, internal consistency estimates the extent to which it may be supposed that the items used can be considered to have been drawn from a hypothetical, homogeneous pool of items. The concepts of test-retest reliability and internal consistency are easily, and usefully, extensible to a wide range of measurement or observational situations. Thus, if one observes a physician to have been abrupt with patients on a given day, one may wonder whether on some other day that same abruptness would be found. Or if one observes a physician to have been abrupt with two patients, one may wonder whether that same abruptness would be found with most other patients: that is, each patient is an "item" by which the physician's behavior may be tested, and one may look for consistency across items.

A reliability problem of wide relevance has to do with agreement between observers (or scorers, or judges). If a physician is being observed and is judged to be abrupt with patients, one wants reasonable assurance that another observer would reach the same conclusion. A critical question, one that can be answered only conceptually, not in terms of measurement theory, is whether by "same conclusion" one means on an absolute scale or only on a relative scale. Two observers may agree that Dr. A is more abrupt with patients than Dr. B, but one observer may regard Dr. A's abruptness as offensive, whereas the other may consider it only mildly troublesome. Agreement calculated by means of correlation will show only that observers order targets in the same way, not necessarily that they agree with respect to the level of the trait being observed.

Validity

A second important characteristic of measures dealt with by classical test theory is validity. Again, roughly, *validity* may be defined as the extent to which tests measure what they purport to measure. Many different validity concepts or types might be distinguished, but four will be mentioned here: face validity, predictive validity, construct validity, and discriminant validity. Of these, face validity is ordinarily the least important, but it often cannot be ignored.

Face validity refers to the extent to which a measure *appears* to measure what it is supposed to measure. To have face validity, a measure of depression ought to include items that appear to be assessing depression. A measure of mathematical ability ought to be made up of mathematical problems; even if a test of knowledge of grammar correlated well with math ability, it would not be regarded as face valid. Face validity is often important in gaining acceptance in the group in which a measure is to be applied. That is, people may resist having measures applied to them that lack face validity; they may refuse to cooperate. If a researcher appears to draw too many conclusions from the nature of the furnishings and decor of an executive's office, those conclusions may be rejected as not appearing to be related in any clear way to the observations made.

Predictive validity is an indication of the extent to which one may predict standing on an unmeasured characteristic, often regarded as a "criterion," from a measured characteristic (Cohen, 1990). Admissions test scores (an observed variable) are used to forecast college grades (as yet unmeasured). A vocabulary test may be used as a proxy for (i.e., predictor of) verbal intelligence if the vocabulary test has been shown to predict scores on a full verbal intelligence measure. An interviewer who guesses that the person she is waiting for must be tall because his adjustable chair is elevated to its full height is invoking predictive validity: tall chair = tall person.

Our interest in many measures we use cannot easily be reduced to questions about just what it is they predict. Rather, we have an idea that the measures get at (reflect) some underlying construct of interest. To the extent that we believe we can trust that a measure assesses some construct, it is said to have *construct validity* (Cronbach & Meehl, 1955). A measure of anxiety, for example, may not stand or fall on its relationship to any particular other measure (criterion) but rather is to be judged on the pattern it shows of relationships to other variables. It will be accepted as having construct validity if it is plausible that anxiety is the construct responsible for that pattern of relationships: for example, anxiety is assumed to cause a person both to complain of frequently feeling "nervous" and to have sweaty palms while working on a demanding task. Construct validity cannot be summarized by any single statistic such as a validity coefficient but is established more or less by consensus of those working in a field as the measure in question accrues more and more evidence of its theoretical and empirical consistency.

If a measure is to have construct validity, not only must it correlate with other measures related to the construct, but it must *not* correlate too highly with measures of other constructs (Sechrest, 1963). A way of referring to that idea is that a measure must have *discriminant validity* (Campbell & Fiske, 1959). A measure of depression, for example, must, if it is to be regarded as valid for measuring that construct, correlate with other measures and phenomena of depression. But a measure of the construct of depression should not correlate too highly with measures of anxiety, with measures of general psychological distress, with measures of current life stress, and so on (see Craik, 1986). If a measure of depression correlates too highly with measures of other constructs, then it lacks discriminant validity and is of no specific value for the measurement of depression.

GENERALIZABILITY THEORY

An alternative, or better, a complementary approach to measurement is generalizability theory (Shavelson & Webb, 1991; Shavelson, Webb, & Rowley, 1989). Instead of thinking of each object of measurement as having a "true" score—a real, if idealized, standing on some trait—one may think of each object as potentially yielding a "universe" of values for any set of measurement conditions. For example, a friend may have told you that she ate at the Elite Cafe recently, and she would rate her meal there as an 8 on a scale of 10. Classical test theory would try to relate that rating of 8 to some "true" quality of the restaurant plus or minus an "error" component reflecting a conglomeration of variables related to the particular conditions of the observation. Generalizability theory, however, attempts to address an observation and question such as, "Now, here we have a rating of 8 for this restaurant, obtained under a particular, specifiable set of conditions. To what other 'performances' of this restaurant would this rating of 8 generalize?" Generalizability theory would ask whether the rater is a good representative of a population of raters of interest, whether the particular meal the rater ate is representative of the fare offered by the restaurant, whether the day of the week and the time of day may be regarded as representative of the circumstances under which other persons, for example, you, might want to eat there, and so on. If your friend reveals that she ate sweetbreads *financiere*, you might wonder whether her rating, perhaps quite justified, would generalize to your more ordinary favorite entree of grilled pork chops. Or if she went to the restaurant at 5:00 in the afternoon on Wednesday, you might wonder whether her rating would generalize to your more likely dining time of 7:30 Friday evening.

The thinking underlying generalizability is straightforward, and the approach is of great potential value. Generalizability analyses are not easy to do because they require systematic designs and complex analyses. Certainly they are not as easy as running off a little internal consistency study yielding a single alpha coefficient. On the other hand, they are usually highly informative because they yield a set of coefficients describing the generalizability of an observation, whether from a test or an experiment, across whatever facets (conditions) of measurement that have been allowed to vary and have been measured.

TWO MEASUREMENT TASKS

Measurement operations and problems can be distinguished according to two reasonably distinct aims: establishing absolute levels of performance and differentiating between individuals. These two tasks are often related to the concepts of criterion-referenced and norm-referenced tests. A *criterion-referenced test* involves a measure for which one can set a standard of performance standards that represents an acceptable level. Persons who do not achieve the criterion level are judged to have "failed" the test, and those who exceed the criterion will have "passed" it. The test does not attempt to differentiate between persons in any way except at the cutting score; exceeding the cutting score by a large margin is no better than barely exceeding it. A "reliable" criterion-referenced measure is one that yields the same decision—pass or fail—every time a person takes it. A *norm-referenced test* or measure is one that judges the performance of any individual against performance of a normative sample and that emphasizes ordering of individuals in a consistent way. Thus, if a test were given on two occasions, and a criterion of 70% correct responses had been established as satisfactory, a decline in the number of persons reaching the criterion would probably be regarded as a problem for a criterion-referenced test. In contrast, if individuals maintained their relative order across the two testings, the reliability would be regarded as high: that is, individuals would be sorted out in the same way over time.

If one were studying problems of sexual harassment in organizations, a normative approach would be to try to determine whether the organizations differed dependably in occurrences of sexual harassment. This would mean that one could say with some confidence that one organization had more such problems than another. It would not mean, necessarily, that the worst organization would be very bad by some outside standard, although that could be determined if data (norms) were available from other studies. Even in that case, however, one might only be able to say that an organization had a worse sexual harassment record than 85% of similar organizations. Is that bad? A criterion-referenced approach would be to decide, perhaps using something like a Delphi panel (Delbecq, Van de Ven, & Gustafson, 1975), what would be an intolerable level of sexual harassment in an organization and then determine which organizations exceeded that threshold. One would not have to suppose that of two or more organizations with intolerably bad records one could be dependably described as worse than another.

LATENT VARIABLES

A fairly recent development in psychological measurement, although one with a long but unappreciated history, is the growing recognition of the gains to be achieved by putting greater emphasis on latent variables that may be presumed to underlie the observed variables that we represent initially by our tests and observations. *Latent variables* are hypothetical variables that are presumed to give rise to the variables we actually observe. Thus we observe a score on an anxiety measure, a score on a measure of palmar perspiration, and a rating by a peer on "nervousness," and we presume that the latent variable anxiety may be the source of all our observations in the sense that anxiety level determines the scores or values that are observed for the measures.

The use of latent variables as constructs to substitute for observed measures means, first, that observed values may be analyzed for their common variance and added in a way that potentially simplifies a data set by reducing the number of variables to be dealt with. A second advantage is that the relationships between the several observed variables may be used in order to estimate the reliability of the measure of the latent trait (variable). That reliability estimate may then be incorporated into our analyses in order to correct estimates of parameters of the data for unreliability. This process is one of incorporating measurement models into our analyses.

Researchers often use a variety of sociodemographic variables in their analyses to aid in the search for meaning, usually by including moderating variables in their analyses. For example, they may determine whether results of some intervention differ by sex of subject. More often than not, however, researchers who use demographic variables are not interested in those variables in their own right. That is, researchers are not actually interested in biological sex, years spent in school, or literal number of dollars someone earns per year. Rather the researchers are interested in the residue of experience that is generally different for males and females, the greater opportunities that are available to someone with more education, or the increased stress that is associated with not having enough income. In all cases, however, the sociodemographic variables are quite imperfectly correlated with the underlying (latent) variables of interest. Some males may have had experiences that resemble those of females and vice versa, education will have rubbed off more on some people than others, and income-related stress may vary from family to family because of other aspects of the family's circumstances and existence. The fact that variables such as sex, education, and income can be measured reliably does not mean that any variables for which they are proxies are well measured. To the extent that observed variables are imperfect proxies for the variables of real theoretical interest, statistical analyses such as multiple regression will underestimate the effects of the theoretical variables. No easy solution to the problem posed here exists, but the first step is to realize that observed variables are often used as proxies and then to allow for that in one's analyses, perhaps by doing sensitivity analyses that will bracket the likely values for reliability estimates.

SCORES AND METRICS

Measures do not score, or otherwise attach values to, themselves. Values for observations may be derived in different ways (Fiske, 1978). One of the most common ways is simply to count the number of relevant observations and take the total as the score. For example, an investigator might state that Organization A had 10 incidents of sexual harassment in the past year and that Organization B had 15 incidents. Several potential problems exist with such scoring, one being that such counts constitute only a numerator of a variable that ordinarily must have some denominator. If Organization B had three times as many employees as Organization A, then 1.5 times as many incidents of sexual harassment would not seem so bad in comparison. Problems may also arise from the fact that all of the instances of sexual harassment in one organization may arise from the acts of one or two employees. Moreover, such counting treats all observations as equal, which may or may not be reasonable.

A second method of obtaining a score, one slightly more sophisticated, is to define in advance a set of relevant observation points—for example, items or subjects—and then to count the number of critical responses. For example, by dividing the number of individuals in an organization involved in sexual harassment by the number of employees, one in effect defines each employee as a relevant observation and equates the two organizations for opportunities. Probably most tests are scored in that way: that is, every subject has the same number of opportunities (items) to respond in a particular way, and the score is the number of opportunities realized. In that type of scoring system, however, it is still true that all observations are treated as equal. Verbal harassment is treated as the same as physical contact, for example. Or an anxiety item such as "I am often nervous" is treated the same as "Sometimes I panic in stressful situations."

A still more complex approach to scoring is to weight responses in some manner so as to produce a scale. Likert-type scales are one example, with responses weighted according to strength of endorsement of each item: for example, *strongly agree* might be weighted 5, *agree* weighted 4, and so on, down to *strongly disagree* weighted 1. It is also possible to have responses weighted by means of expert judgments by one or another of various procedures for scaling. In the study of sexual harassment, the act of "occasionally telling offensive jokes" might be weighted 5, "inappropriate touching on the hands, arms, or shoulders" might be weighted 10, and "unwanted embrace" might be weighted 20. If the weighting system is to be used, it implies that four incidents of telling offensive jokes is equal to one unwanted embrace. Under some circumstances, a score may be assigned based on the most extreme response noted. Thus a score of 20 might be assigned to an office in which one incident of unwanted embrace occurred, whereas in another office a score of 10 might be assigned because the most extreme response that occurred was inappropriate touching, even though the offense was repeated many times. In criminal cases, for example, an offender is usually judged by the most serious of his or her crimes, not by the average or even the total.

Many measures used in social science end up expressed in metrics that have no inherent meaning. A score on a depression measure, for example, usually indicates the number of items answered in a "depressed" manner. What is one to make, then, of information that the mean depression score in a group decreased by five points? One has a sense of what it might mean to change the probability that a woman might, in the course of a week, be subjected to unwanted sexual advances. That sense is lacking for the finding that attitudes of male employees toward females improved by an average of 0.75 points on a 5-point scale. Behavioral scientists need to work toward better calibration of their measures and the development of metrics that are directly meaningful.

Many, perhaps most, behavioral science measures are *reactive* in some ways and to some degree (Webb, Campbell, Schwartz, Sechrest, & Grove, 1981). Reactivity is the change that occurs in response to the act of measurement. For example, one cannot test the taste of a cake without destroying some of the cake—eating it. Some changes produced by measurement are relatively enduring, as when eating the cake changes it permanently. Other changes are temporary, as when asking to measure a person's height causes that person to stand taller. Personality and attitude measures are particularly reactive because when people know they are being evaluated, it is relatively easy for them to respond in a socially desirable way so as to create a favorable impression. Ability measures are less reactive, at least in a positive direction, but if someone taking an ability test does not believe it important, his performance may suffer.

A variety of stratagems exist by which reactivity may be reduced, ranging from administering tests anonymously or telling respondents that the results will not be used in any way to make decisions about them to using measures not dependent on voluntary responses, for example, physiological measures of arousal. A particularly useful approach is to devise ways of observing behavior that do not require the knowledge and cooperation of the person(s) being measured. Such measures are called *unobtrusive* and often have the advantage of not sharing many of the biases characteristic of many self-report measures (Webb, Campbell, Schwartz, & Sechrest, 1966).

CONCLUSION

This brief overview of measurement covers a wide range of issues of central concern in the development of quantitative measures of behavior. Although the discussion has focused on types of measurement problems that are more or less standard in quantitative areas, the concepts and at least some of the potential solutions apply equally well to qualitative research efforts. Like their quantitative colleagues, qualitative researchers must be concerned for the reliability, validity, and generalizability of their observations. They must be concerned for how they weight the diverse materials they assemble and the responses they record. And they must be concerned for the possible reactivity they and their methods produce in the systems, situations, and persons they study. Quantitative and qualitative researchers have much to learn from each other.

3

ECONOMETRICS AND PRIMARY CARE RESEARCH

Curt D. Mueller

A typical problem in primary care research is to quantify relationships between a dependent variable, such as a health outcome measure, and factors that are hypothesized to affect the dependent variable after controlling for other factors that may also affect the relationships of interest. For example, suppose a researcher is interested in modeling relationships between functional health status, use of primary care, and severity of a chronic condition. The researcher has obtained quantitative measures of health status, medical care use, and severity of condition for a random sample of persons with the chronic condition. What functional status is expected for given levels of severity? How much is functional status affected as the disease progresses? How does use of care affect functional status, and how much does functional status affect use of care? Are age and lifestyle factors related to functional status for persons with the condition, holding severity of the condition constant?

Health economists, clinicians, and other policymakers often use the tools of econometrics in research and policy analyses to help answer such questions. There are a number of definitions of *econometrics,* but for purposes here it refers to the development of a quantifiable model and an array of statistical tools that are used to analyze the model and its implications.[1] The objective of this chapter is to briefly describe econometrics and its history of applications to health services and policy research questions for primary care researchers; the theme is that econometric methods can be fruitfully used in primary care research.

A brief overview of econometric modeling and estimation methods is provided in the first two sections. The role of the classical linear regression model in econometrics is summarized.[2] Ordinary least squares regression is not appropriate in certain situations, including when the dependent variable is qualitative and in many instances when the underlying model is a simultaneous, multiple-equation model. A historical overview of the application of econometrics to health services and policy research is presented in the third section. Extensive application of econometric methods postdates the development of health economics as a subdiscipline of economics. Major contributions of econometrics to health economics and health policy research have occurred as a result of analyses of large, person-level databases.

FEATURES OF ECONOMETRIC MODELS

An econometric model may be defined as a set or system of mathematical equations that is used to describe or investigate a theory or phenomenon. A model may consist of one or more equations, some of which must describe relationship(s) between endogenous variables—those determined by the model— and other independent, or exogenous, variables. Although econometric models may be developed in part for purposes of clarifying a complex phenomenon or theory, models of interest to primary care researchers are generally ones that can be estimated using data from the real world. This means that the model's dependent variables and key independent variables must be quantitatively measurable. This may be a severe limitation to the applicability of econometrics to certain types of problems confronted by the primary care researcher. Other quantitative and qualitative research tools may be required to help develop quantifiable measures, such as factor analysis, focus groups, and case studies.

Estimation of econometric models also requires that sufficient data be available to support application of relevant econometric and statistical methods. The number of observations (sample size) that is required depends on the nature of the model and the number of parameters to be estimated. Estimation of multiple-equation models may require considerably larger sample sizes than for case studies to ensure that estimates of sufficient power are available to test hypotheses. The extent to which data are available may depend on the level of analysis. Some models are designed to describe behavior of persons representing a population, so person-level data for individuals with specific characteristics within the population may be required. For example, a representative sample might require significant numbers of blacks and Hispanics to model behavior. Other models are designed to describe geographic areas, such as health care markets. For the latter, data may include measures that are aggregates for populations residing in the geographic areas of interest.

Econometric models serve several functions. First, they are developed to help explain phenomena—especially phenomena that are complex and involve a number of interrelationships between endogenous variables (i.e., variables determined *within* the model). Specification of the relationship is often based on an underlying theory, such as economics or sociology. For example, the economic theory of consumer demand applied to medical care suggests that the "demand" for primary care, which might be measured by the number of physician contacts, depends on the monetary and nonmonetary costs of care confronting the family: factors influencing demand include income, insurance coverage, and needs as measured by a person's health status. In the same way, a person's demand for health itself depends on the price of medical care and personal and family characteristics, such as education (Grossman, 1972). Econometric estimates of demand models have been used to "test" predictions of economic theory.

Sometimes models are specified not according to a particular theory but as part of a general data exploration strategy (Hartwig & Dearing, 1980). Estimation methods can be used to identify exogenous and endogenous factors that are important determinants of the model's key endogenous variables, after controlling for other factors that affect observed relationships between dependent and exogenous factors (some of which might be controlled for automatically if an experimental design were employed). Results can be used in conjunction with other quantitative and qualitative research methods to help formulate theories, hypotheses, or explanations of phenomena.

Second, econometric models are used to predict. Estimates of key behavioral parameters of econometric models can be used to simulate effects of changes in exogenous variables—such as factors that can be manipulated by public policies—on the model's endogenous variables. For example, models are being used to help predict impacts of providing insurance coverage to the uninsured.[3] Models can also be used to predict impacts for a standard or specific population by holding population characteristics constant from experiment to experiment.

TYPES OF ECONOMETRIC MODELS

Numerous econometric studies have been conducted by health care researchers. The complexity of the modeling effort varies considerably, depending on the specifics of the application and its purposes. The most commonly used econometric model—and the building block of more sophisticated models—is the single-equation model.

The Single-Equation Model

A single-equation model is a mathematical relationship between a dependent variable and independent variables that are hypothesized to affect or "determine" the value of the dependent variable. For example, a model that relates the dependent variable H with independent variables S and X might be represented by

$$H = h(X,S) \qquad [3.1]$$

where $h(X,S)$ represents a functional relationship. Specification of $h(X,S)$ may be dictated by theory but more often is chosen by the researcher.[4] Although there are a number of ways to estimate a single-equation model, the method that is used most often is ordinary least squares (OLS) regression. An algebraic representation of this model can be written as follows:

$$H = b_1 + b_2S + b_3X + u \qquad [3.2]$$

The *coefficients* b_1, b_2, and b_3 are values that describe the relationships between H and the independent variables S and X; the *disturbance term,* represented by u, is the error that characterizes relationships that are not exact. The disturbance term reflects sampling error, errors in the data, and errors in specification of the model. Econometric analysis is used to estimate the model's parameters (b_1, b_2, and b_3) from data on H, S, and X, to examine the nature of the disturbance terms, and to examine other implications of the model.[5]

Under certain conditions, OLS estimates have special characteristics.[6] The most important is that OLS estimates are unbiased. An unbiased estimate is one that lacks systematic distortion and therefore is the best point estimate of the value that describes the true relationship between the dependent and independent variable.[7] When OLS is not appropriate—that is, when the special conditions do not hold—other estimation strategies may be needed.

One situation that often occurs in health services research is that the dependent variable is categorical or qualitative. For example, a regression model might be used to help identify patient characteristics that are associated with hospitalization. In this instance, the dependent variable might be "0" for patients that have not been hospitalized, and "1" for patients with at least one hospitalization. OLS regression estimates can be used to predict values of the dependent variable for each person in the sample; each prediction is like a probability that the person would be hospitalized, given his or her characteristics. A problem, however, is that results may be nonsensical. Predicted values of the dependent variable for combinations of reasonable values of the independent variables may be outside the range of 0 to 1, and therefore outside the range of feasible probabilities. A solution is to use an alternative regression strategy, such as logit or probit regression (Aldrich & Nelson, 1984). Both are nonlinear models. Estimates ensure that predicted values of the dependent variable are constrained between 0 and 1.

Multiple-Equation Econometric Models

In certain situations, the primary care researcher may be interested in studying relationships that require more sophisticated modeling efforts. Single-equation models may not be suitable for examining the structure of a phenomenon, complexities of behavior, complex relationships between members of a population, and interrelationships among members of a population or among phenomena. In a multiple-equation model, there must be one equation for each endogenous variable, although there may be additional equations in the model that impose certain mathematical conditions or constraints that affect endogenous variables; and each equation contains one or more exogenous variables, some of which may be in more than one equation.

The *recursive model* is the simplest type of multiple-equation model. In a recursive model, a number of factors determine or influence a dependent variable, which in turn is one of several determinants of yet another variable. A third dependent variable may be determined by the first and second endogenous variables, but the third does not affect the first and second, and so on. Using algebraic notation, an example of a three-equation recursive model is as follows:

$$V = f(Z) \tag{3.3}$$

$$D = g(V, X) \tag{3.4}$$

$$H = h(V, D, Y) \tag{3.5}$$

In this model, factors represented by Z "determine" V through the functional relationship $f(Z)$, and V and X determine D; the two endogenous variables V and D determine H, along with the exogenous variable Y. "Higher-level" endogenous variables do not appear in "lower-level" equations, so D doesn't affect H in Equation 3.3, and H doesn't affect D in Equation 3.4.

This model might be used, for example, to model the impacts of prescription drugs and ambulatory care on health status. Health status (H) is hypothesized to depend on ambulatory care (V), use of prescription drugs (D), and other factors (Y). Prescription drug use depends on the use of ambulatory care and other factors (X). The use of ambulatory care depends on a variety of other factors (Z). According to this model, both ambulatory care and drug use affect health, and some ambulatory care is necessary prior to prescription drug use, but the level of drug use is not hypothesized to affect utilization of ambulatory care. The health outcome measure in this model does not affect use of ambulatory care and drugs.

In the more general simultaneous-equations model, endogenous variables may affect any other endogenous variable. The following model is an example:

$$V_t = f(D_t, Z, H_{t-1}) \qquad\qquad [3.6]$$

$$D_t = g(V_t, X) \qquad\qquad [3.7]$$

$$H_t = h(V_t, D_t, Y) \qquad\qquad [3.8]$$

The subscripts t and $t-1$ represent time periods. In contrast to the recursive model above, D and V are determined simultaneously: D affects V in Equation 3.6, and V affects D in Equation 3.7. This version is a refinement of the simpler recursive utilization model above. It recognizes not only that ambulatory care can lead to use of prescription drugs but that use of drugs may affect ambulatory care use, as when laboratory tests or consultations are required to monitor effects of drugs; the model also recognizes that use of medical care and health status during the current period depends on health status during the preceding period.

The researcher faces several choices concerning the estimation of multiple-equation models. The researcher may be interested in the "total effect" of exogenous variables on particular endogenous variables. For example, suppose that use of ambulatory care is a positive function of family income (a Z-type variable in Equation 3.3) and the use of pharmaceuticals (in this case, income is an X-type variable in Equation 3.4). Thus income affects drug use directly and through its effect on ambulatory care in Equation 3.7. The total effect of income on drug use is the sum of these "partial" effects: the effect of income on drug use for a given level of ambulatory care plus the effect of income on ambulatory care. When the researcher is interested in total effects, the model can be estimated using OLS; each endogenous variable of interest is regressed against all independent variables in the full model.[8]

If, on the other hand, the researcher is interested in relationships among endogenous variables and "partial" effects of exogenous variables, simple OLS regression may not be sufficient. More sophisticated methods are necessary to investigate the structural equations of the model. In a simultaneous-equations model, an endogenous variable or lagged endogenous variable that is also a regressor (that is, an independent variable in the equation for another endogenous variable) is likely to be correlated with the disturbance term of the equation. This correlation will result in simultaneous-equations bias if OLS is used. For example, ambulatory care use (V) and health status during the preceding period (H_{t-1}) are probably correlated with the disturbance term in the drug use equation (Equation 3.7). OLS estimates will be biased because a change in the disturbance term in Equation 3.7 will affect drug use, which in turn will affect ambulatory care use in Equation 3.6, which will also affect drug use in Equation 3.7. Special estimation methods, such as indirect least squares, instrumental variables, or two-stage least squares methods, may be necessary to overcome the bias problem and other problems associated with simultaneity.[9]

A HISTORICAL OVERVIEW OF THE USE OF ECONOMETRICS IN HEALTH SERVICES RESEARCH

Following the explosive postwar growth in private health insurance and the introduction of Medicare and Medicaid in the mid-1960s, economists and health care policy experts began econometric investigations of the markets for medical care. A number of research projects focused on forces underlying the demand for and supply of medical care, and how money prices were determined in health care markets as a result of demand and supply forces. One of the early lessons from the application of the tools of econometrics was that health markets differ fundamentally from many other markets in the U.S. economy.

In the textbook example of a competitive market, producers do not have any control over the level of demand. Competitive market theory predicts that an increase in the number of suppliers of a service will decrease the market-clearing price of the service and increase the amount purchased by consumers. This occurs because an increase in the number of suppliers increases the quantity of services that are available at every price. The level of demand is not affected, so market price falls and the number of services provided to consumers increases.[10] By contrast, empirical evidence suggested that health care providers exercised some control over the level of demand. Some evidence suggested that physicians could use their market power to set prices so as to achieve a target level of income for themselves (Feldstein, 1970).

Estimation of a multiple, structural equation model of the market using state-level data also provided additional support for supply-side influences on demand (Fuchs & Kramer, 1973). A body of literature on the role of the physician as a decision-making agent for the patient and implications of this role on econometric modeling developed during the 1970 and 1980s (e.g., Auster & Oaxaca, 1981; Evans, 1973; Rossiter & Wilensky, 1983).

The econometric applications by Feldstein and Fuchs and Kramer employed aggregate data: that is, the unit of analysis was not the individual but the market as an aggregate of many individuals. For Feldstein, the market was the United States, spanning several years during the 1960s; for Fuchs and Kramer, the unit of analysis was the state. Other econometric applications with aggregate data include the Davis and Russell (1972) analysis of the market for hospital care and Feldstein's (1973) estimation of a simultaneous-equations model of the market for dental services.

Beginning in the 1970s, health services researchers began to rely much more extensively on the use of person-level data in econometric applications. There were a variety of reasons for this shift in focus, including the recognition that aggregate models sacrificed predictive accuracy that was needed in discussions of the effects of policies on specific parts of the health care sector or industry (Newhouse, 1987); improvements in computer technology that made analysis of large, person-level data sets easier; technological progress in sampling and administration of large surveys; recognition that more aggregative, structural models might not be appropriately estimated given peculiarities of the market (e.g., the physician's controls over demand, and difficulties in defining the outputs of "health" and "medical care" when physicians' services were so heterogeneous); and the recognition that many person-level attributes affected health care decisions.

A number of different lines of research employing econometric methods began during the 1970s. Areas of analysis included efficiency in medical practice, based on survey data collected from physicians' offices (e.g., Kushman et al., 1978; Reinhardt, 1975), and analyses of the economic rates of return to physicians, based on surveys of physicians and other professionals (e.g., Langwell, 1980). Many econometric studies focused on access to care and utilization of medical services (e.g., Berk, Bernstein, & Taylor, 1983; Mueller & Monheit, 1988) and models to help anticipate responses to policy changes (Schur, Berk, & Schoenman, 1992). Data were patient- and consumer-level survey data. Person-level data that were used in these and other econometric studies were from the 1977 National Medical Care Expenditure Survey and 1987 National Medical Expenditure Survey (directed by the Agency for Health Care Policy Research, U.S. Public Health Service) and the 1980 National Medical Care Use and Expenditures Survey, periodic National

Nursing Home Surveys, and periodic National Health Interview Surveys (directed by the National Center for Health Statistics).

Analyses of data from the Health Insurance Experiment, which began during the mid-1970s, have been especially influential. The Health Insurance Experiment is one of the largest social experiments ever undertaken. Over 7,700 participants were selected from six geographic areas. Persons were assigned in an unbiased manner to one of several health insurance plans that differed with respect to cost sharing but covered similar services. The experiment was designed in part to estimate a key economic parameter, the *elasticity of demand*. This elasticity refers to the responsiveness of changes in the amount of medical care used when money price changes.[11] Estimates of elasticities are important to policymakers' assessments of changes in benefits packages and cost sharing.[12] The experiment has contributed substantially to our understanding of the roles of insurance and cost sharing (Manning et al., 1987; Newhouse et al., 1982). Benefits from the experiment have not been limited to the results of econometric analysis. Results have also contributed to an understanding of how econometrics can be used to further improve the quality of quantitative analysis in policy research (Newhouse, 1987).

The Medical Outcomes Study (MOS) is a more recent project that has produced data for econometric analysis. It was designed to examine how components of the health care system affect health outcomes and to develop tools for monitoring outcomes (Riesenberg & Glass, 1989; Tarlov et al., 1989). Samples of physicians from different types of practice settings were selected. Patient samples included a general cross-section sample of the clinicians' patients and special samples of patients with diabetes, hypertension, coronary heart disease, or depression for prospective and longitudinal data collection and analysis.

Many of the research tools and econometric models that were first applied to health services research as part of the Health Insurance Experiment are now being used to analyze MOS data (Greenfield et al., 1992; Kravitz et al., 1992; Stewart et al., 1989). Each patient was in one of five systems of care, ranging from an HMO to solo practice/single specialty fee for service.[13] The effects of chronic conditions on physical functioning were examined. An index measuring physical functioning was constructed from six patient-reported data items that assessed the patient's capacity to perform a variety of physical activities, including carrying groceries, climbing stairs, and walking. The index measures functioning on a 0- to 100-point scale, with higher values corresponding to higher levels of functioning. Key independent variables in the physical function model are categorical variables that indicate the presence of nine chronic conditions, including diabetes, hypertension, arthritis, and chronic lung problems. A negative, statistically significant regression coefficient for diabetes, for example, would suggest that persons with diabetes are less able to function than persons in the control group: that is, persons with no chronic conditions. Regression analysis was used to compare physical functioning of persons with each condition to that of average patients with no chronic conditions; estimates were used to predict functioning index values for the control group and then for each of the nine conditions, holding all other variables in the regression constant at the mean values for patients included in the analysis. This ensured that the difference in the predicted mean values of the functional index for control patients and for each chronic condition reflected *only* the effects of the chronic condition, and not other factors that had already been controlled for.

Logistic regression was used to determine the effects of health delivery system characteristics on whether the patient was hospitalized during a given time period (Greenfield et al., 1992). Independent variables included indicators for system of care and sociodemographic patient characteristics. Predictions of the likelihood of hospitalization were obtained,

> assuming that all patients were in the HMO, then assuming that everyone was a prepaid patient in the multispecialty group, and so forth for each of the five systems. . . . Thus we achieve comparisons of rates of utilization for the mix of patients that is equivalent across all specialties and systems of care. (p. 1626)

Predicted probabilities were tabulated by system (Table 2, p. 1627), and results indicated that the average probability of admission for HMO patients was 0.049, which is 29% less than the point estimate of 0.069 for patients of solo/single specialty, fee-for-service physicians. Although these results are consistent with the hypothesis that resource use is less in HMOs because the incentive structure is cost-saving, qualitative research methods could be used to generate as well as test other hypotheses concerning the likelihood of hospital admissions for patients in alternative systems of care.

CONCLUSIONS

Econometric methods are used extensively in health services research applications. Models have been developed to explain aggregate phenomena, such as determination of prices and expenditures, and to understand and predict individual behaviors. Econometric techniques are among a number of quantitative research methods that can be used in primary care research. These techniques can supplement qualitative methods in the development of research questions and theories, and they can be used to extend analyses that began with qualitative methods of inquiry. Although estimation of multiple-equation econometric models may not be possible in some areas of primary care research because data on sufficient numbers of persons are lacking, it is often possible to estimate abbreviated simpler models.

NOTES

1. See the beginning sections of Kennedy's (1989) brief, very readable, and thoroughly referenced guide to econometrics for practitioners who do not have significant backgrounds in economic theory or statistics.

2. A comprehensive review of regression is beyond the scope of this brief overview. However, many good econometrics references are available. Lewis-Beck (1980) provides a brief introduction to regression analysis. Draper and Smith (1966) is a standard reference for applications of econometric methods. Kmenta's text (1986) begins with to-the-point introductions to probability and statistics, sampling theory, and hypothesis testing that are important to econometrics and applied researchers but are not necessarily well covered in other econometrics texts. Kennedy's book (1989) is an excellent "field guide" and "road map" to more technical discussions.

3. Parameter estimates from econometric models are also used in microsimulation models. The latter are developed for policy analysis. At present, several microsimulation models are being used by the administrative branch of the federal government to estimate costs of various health reform policy options.

4. For example, $h(X,S)$ might be specified as a simple linear relationship as in Equation 2, or as a relationship that is linear in the natural logarithms of X and S.

5. The value of b_1 is referred to as the *intercept,* which is the value of H when the other variables (X and S) are zero; the numerical values of b_2 and b_3 can be interpreted as *slopes* of lines or three-dimensional planes. If the estimated value of b_2 in the above example is 3.5, then a one-unit increase in S is associated with an increase in H of 3.5 units; in other words, the regression line that depicts the relationship between H and S, holding X constant, has a slope of 3.5. See Lewis-Beck (1980) and Wonnacott and Wonnacott (1977) for an introduction to interpretation of regression results. When the estimated coefficients are used to predict values of H from patients' values of S and X, the predicted values will generally not equal the observed values of H. The difference between the predicted value and the observed value for each patient is the *error,* an estimate of the unobservable disturbance term u. In fact, there is a probability distribution for u "around" the regression line at each value of X, given S (or S, given X). This emphasizes that the relationship between H and the independent variables S and X is "stochastic": that is, the relationship is inexact, in part because it is subject to selection of the specific sample of patients who represent the population of interest in the study. Estimates of the regression coefficients from a different (but similarly random) sample of patients would not exactly equal those coefficients obtained from the original sample because of the stochastic nature of the model. Analysis of residuals is analysis of the model's observable error.

6. Conditions that must hold for OLS to yield unbiased and efficient estimates are the following: (a) the dependent variable is expressed as a linear relationship of the independent variables; (b) the disturbance term is normally distributed with a mean of zero; (c) all disturbance terms have the same variance; (d) disturbances are not correlated with each other; and (e) values of the independent variables are fixed in repeated samples. The first condition restricts the nature of the hypothesized relationship. In certain situations, nonlinear regression is desirable. Violations

of conditions (c) and (d) are common. Condition (c) is violated when the level of the independent variable is related to the residual. For example, the disturbance term in a model of ambulatory care expenditures may be directly related to family income, an exogenous variable in the model, because when income is relatively large, relatively more discretion can be used in consumption decisions. Condition (d) is violated, for example, when data describe multiple family members because individuals' behaviors within the family are correlated. The last condition states that the regression could be reestimated with other samples if desired, using values of independent variables that are predictable and not stochastic in nature. See Kennedy (1989) for discussion of these conditions and the effects of violations.

7. A second property of OLS estimates is efficiency. Each regression coefficient is from a probability distribution of values. Application of the OLS method is, in essence, "optimal" selection of regression coefficients from their probability distributions. *Efficiency* refers to the variances of the distributions. OLS regression estimates are from distributions that have variances that are no larger than variances associated with other methods. An unbiased estimate is an estimate of the mean of the probability distribution.

8. These equations are the model's *reduced form* equations, obtained by solving the system of equations that comprise the model for the endogenous (dependent) variables. The equations that make up the model (Equations 3.6-3.8) are called the model's *structural equations* because they convey the structure of relationships described by the model. The requirements of OLS, of course, must hold for the reduced form equations. Condition (e) in note 6 above is usually violated when a lagged endogenous variable is a regressor, so OLS would not be appropriate in estimation of the reduced form equations for the model given by Equations 3.6-3.8.

9. The researcher interested in structural relationships needs to be concerned with the problem of identification. *Identification* refers to mathematical requirements that must be met if unique structural estimates of the model's parameters can be obtained. See Kennedy (1989) and Kmenta (1986) for discussions of the identification problem.

10. In terms of economic theory, the market supply curve shifts outward along a fixed demand curve. Equilibrium price falls and quantity increases.

11. For example, if the quantity demanded by the market increases by 1% when money price falls by 5%, the elasticity is 1% divided by −5%, or −0.2. When the elasticity is less than 1 in absolute value, demand is inelastic; a decrease (increase) in price results in a less than proportionate increase (decrease) in the quantity demanded by the market.

12. As Newhouse argues, over 14% of the Gross Domestic Product is spent on health care. Hence the rewards for accurate empirical assessments of policy effects are considerable. Econometrics contributes point estimates as well as hypothesis tests to the policy debate (Newhouse, 1987).

13. The three other systems include multispecialty group/prepaid; multispecialty group/fee-for-service; and solo practice/single-specialty group prepaid.

4

RANDOMIZED CLINICAL TRIALS

Catherine L. Gilliss

- What is the most effective drug to use in treating breast cancer in women under 30?
- Is early family intervention an effective approach to facilitating school readiness in children?
- Can a program of nurse-initiated telephone calls facilitate the at-home recovery of postcardiac surgery patients?
- Can episodes of childhood illness among child day care center children be reduced through a program of center staff education?

These questions are among those best addressed through the research design known as the *randomized clinical trial* (RCT). Known for its ability to address precise scientific questions, the RCT is a planned experiment designed to test the efficacy or effectiveness of treatment by comparing one or more groups of patients experiencing an experimental treatment to another receiving a control, or usual, treatment. This design assumes that real and generalizable differences can be detected and that those differences can be replicated so as to permit prediction of outcomes in other situations.

In the RCT, contrast groups may be established by random selection or random assignment, and therefore are presumed to be not significantly different from one another on important characteristics. The test of the experimental treatment involves a comparison for some predetermined outcome criterion or criteria. Thus three characteristics distinguish the RCT, or true experiment, from other experiments: (a) experimenter *manipulation* of some treatment variable; (b) control over the experimental situation, including introduction of a *control group;* and (c) *randomization* used for selection of the sample or assignment of the sample to contrast groups, or both (Polit & Hungler, 1989). Many scientists believe the RCT to be the ideal study design in that it limits the amount of unintended variance (from extraneous variables and measurement error) and maximizes the variance expected to be due to the treatment itself.

Although often used interchangeably, the words *efficacy* and *effectiveness* are not synonymous in reference to RCTs. *Efficacy* is assessed in the conduct of an explanatory trial. Such trials are undertaken to compare two or more programs that differ in their theoretical foundation. The trial aims to determine, with a high degree of certainty, that a theoretically based treatment works, thus contributing to a theoretical explanation. In contrast, *effectiveness* is assessed in a pragmatic, or management, trial. These trials examine whether implementing a program or treatment in a variant pattern or with different personnel changes the outcome (Buck & Donner, 1982).

HISTORICAL PERSPECTIVE

Although some historians date the RCT back to the Book of Daniel (verses 12-15), Avicenna, an Arabian physician and philosopher (980-1037) established seven rules for the evaluation of drugs on diseases in his *Canon of Medicine* (Meinert, 1986). Examples continue throughout scientific history and are punctuated by the introduction of untreated control groups (Lind, 1753/1953), the use of the sham procedure (Haygarth, 1800), the introduction of randomization in the 1920s, and the notion of the multicenter trial in the 1940s. The introduction of the Nuremberg Code for Human Experimentation in 1946 and the 1966 publication of the U.S. Public Health Service regulations requiring Institutional Review Boards for research involving humans introduced an ethical component into the design and implementation of trials.

PRINCIPLES OF DESIGN

To be considered a true experiment, three conditions must be met: (a) subjects must be either randomly selected from the population group under study or randomly assigned to the test conditions, or both; (b) a contrast "no treatment" group must be employed (ideally with similar baseline characteristics), and the experimental treatment group's outcomes must be compared to the control group's; and (c) a treatment or experimental condition must be administered in a controlled fashion. Generally, the analysis involves a comparison of the final outcome variables (dependent variables) for the control and the experimental groups. More than one experimental condition may be evaluated, and measures can be taken at several intervals to evaluate the rate of change or whether effects created are sustained (e.g., see Spilker, 1991).

Variations on the Design

For some experiments, it is desirable to offer the treatment to both groups but at differing times. A treatment can be offered to one group and the outcomes compared to those of the untreated control group. After a period of time/treatment/measurement, the treatment can be offered to the control group. Results of the second treatment group are compared to that group's own pretreatment results, as well as the results from the first treatment group. In the meantime, the first treatment group, whose treatment is now completed, may be evaluated another time to determine whether the changes observed are being sustained. This approach is known as a *lagged design* because both groups receive the treatment, but one "lags" behind the other.

The lagged design was used in a study by Gilliss, Lewis, Holaday, and Pantell (1989) designed to evaluate the effectiveness of an educational program for child day care providers aimed at reducing the spread of infectious illness. The educational program was not believed to be harmful and was expected to be helpful. After the first group received the protocol, the results were compared to those of the untreated group. Then the second group received the teaching protocol, and results were again compared.

A *cross-over trial* is appropriately matched to situations in which the conditions are constant and only temporarily affected by the treatment (Bulpitt, 1983)—for instance, hypertension or diabetes. In these designs, a series of treatments is presented to subjects in varied order. That is, one group receives treatments A,B,C,D, and the next receives C,A,D,B. When interpreting results, the investigator must be cautious that carryover does not create observed differences.

A *trial to detect an interaction* involves administering at least two treatments and a combination of the two treatments, and then comparing these three conditions to that of the control group. This design permits direct observation of the interactive effect that the combined treatments might have.

Combining the above variations, *a cross-over trial to detect an interaction* employs the repeated administration of treatments, including a combined treatment, in varying sequences.

A *run-in design* (Hulley & Cummings, 1988) aids in reducing the noncompliant subjects from the study at the outset. All inducted subjects are placed on a placebo treatment for an initial period to establish who will be compliant with the treatment. After a set period of time, random assignment of the compliers occurs. Experimental subjects begin the experimental treatment, while control group members remain on placebos and noncompliers are excused. This enables the initial effect of any treatment (halo effect) to be established before the experiment begins. In addition, the effect of the treatment is enhanced by including only those who are participating in the protocol.

PRINCIPLES OF IMPLEMENTATION

Although the design itself appears rather straightforward, implementation of a trial requires close attention throughout to avoid problems in several key areas. Chief among these are sample selection and size determination, developing a plan for randomization, selection of appropriate treatments, limiting contamination, and maintaining the control group.

Sample

Sampling procedures are critical to establishing the level of generalizability of the study's findings. Samples must be representative of the groups to which the researcher wishes to generalize (ethnic groups, socioeconomic status, gender, healthy or at-risk groups). Historically, this has been problematic because many trials omitted female subjects to avoid the intervening variable of the menstrual cycle. Despite the exclusion of women from these samples, research on exclusively male samples was incorrectly generalized to the case of women.

The sample size determination is critical to approximating a probability sample and correctly finding real differences in the study results. Two types of errors must be avoided. *Type I* or *alpha error* involves the probability of finding a statistically significant difference that is not real. Generally, an alpha level is investigator determined prior to selection of a sample size, with an eye toward limiting the probability of a false-positive finding (alpha < .05). Alpha errors often are made when multiple comparisons are undertaken. In such cases, the probability of finding statistically significant results increases as the number of contrasts are examined. Some are statistically significant by chance, and the likelihood understandably increases with the number of tests.

Type II or *beta error* involves the probability of not detecting a real difference that is present. The probability of missing a real difference is reduced when *power* (defined as 1 − beta) is increased. Power, then, is the probability to detect real differences. It is desirable to have a high probability to detect real differences (high power) and small alpha and beta errors. Effect size is a term used to describe the size of the difference the treatment is expected to create. In studies in which the size of the real difference is expected to be small (as opposed to medium or large), a larger sample is required to detect the effects.

In addition to selecting the sample, in studies in which random assignment is employed the investigator must take precautions to ensure that subjects are not promised a particular treatment during recruitment. In fact, to avoid creating a halo effect of being in "the special group," subjects should be told that several conditions are being evaluated and that their assignment is contained within a preexisting list, unknown to the recruiter/inductor. If subjects are aware of their status prior to consenting, the recruiter is recruiting for the condition, which theoretically biases the recruited group. For similar reasons, those who have contact with subjects during a trial should be "blind" to the subjects' status in the investigation.

Randomization

Although many approaches can be used to systematically assign subjects to groups, many of these tip off the recruiter to the potential subject's status. For instance, plans that rely on dates of birth (odd/even), or dates of admission (odd/even) easily become known to the induction personnel. Presealed envelopes that identify the status ensure that no one has prior knowledge of the subject status. Such packets can be drawn up in advance with the aid of a study statistical consultant. Periodically, an assessment should be made of the balance between controls and experimental subjects. Imbalances can be corrected throughout the induction period.

Selection of Appropriate Treatments

Although difficult to imagine, the selection of an inappropriate treatment can produce disastrous results in an RCT. The selected treatment(s) must have some theoretical or empirical relevance to the outcome measures to be gathered. For instance, in a study of health promotion behaviors among male firefighters who have completed a 10-week class on diet, exercise, smoking, and safety, why would their female partners be evaluated for changes in health promotion behavior? Only with adequate theoretical justification would this treatment be seen as related to the planned outcomes.

Limiting Contamination

In studies in which subjects from different treatment groups are likely to come into contact with one another, it may be necessary to take steps to limit this contact. In a report by Gortner et al. (1988), hospitalized patients and their family members were randomized to receive a psychoeducational treatment or usual care. After receiving the treatment, patients and their family members returned from the ward visiting room to their four-bed rooms, and those in the experimental groups told their untreated roommates all about the treatment. Such "contamination" of the control group can limit the expected difference between the two groups. In a follow-up study, the same team reported having reduced contamination by implementing a randomized cluster design (Gilliss et al., 1993). In this design, a series of control subjects was inducted, and, once discharged, a series of experimental subjects was inducted. This procedure ensured that subjects from the two conditions never came into contact with one another.

Maintaining a Control Group

Because subjects in a control condition can have little or no contact with investigators in a study that lasts over a period of time, controls can be lost to follow-up. In an effort to retain controls, some cautious contact is recommended; this contact should vary from the treatment in content and intensity so that contact does not become an "unintended intervention."

Monitoring for Untoward Effects

Throughout the conduct of a trial, particularly trials of medical treatments with unknown effects, the condition of the subjects must be monitored. If data suggest that the experimental treatment is deleterious to the subjects, or if the positive effects of treatment are overwhelming, premature conclusion of the trial should be considered. Making a decision of this nature should be undertaken with institutional review boards and funding agencies. Often "stopping rules" are established at the outset of the study, forcing investigators to monitor their results. Unfortunately, some investigators manipulate their data to avoid the impact of established stopping rules.

PRINCIPLES OF ANALYSIS

To correctly plan the analysis of trial results, each investigation must clearly specify the appropriate *unit of analysis.* If families were randomized to a condition, then the unit of analysis is the family. Similarly, if five hospitals are in the control group and five others are in the experimental group, then the analysis should address outcomes for the hospitals. The same principle applies when looking at practice groups. If the intent of the study is to examine outcomes for all individual experimental subjects who were randomized by groups, then an additional cluster analysis must be performed.

Cluster analysis takes into consideration the likelihood that the members of the cluster are intercorrelated and adjusts for this group intercorrelatedness before examining subjects across groups (see Hauck, Gilliss, Donner, & Gortner, 1990).

Dealing With Sample Attrition

Because a sample is difficult to retain, most studies do lose some subjects. In planning the study, researchers should oversample to avoid subject loss that jeopardizes power. In addition, steps must be taken to describe who or what was lost from the sample. Wherever possible, those subjects lost to follow-up should be compared to those who remain in the study. Ideally, the comparison is made for final outcome variables. However, when this is not possible, baseline data should be compared. Regardless of the data available, the final analysis should include available data for all those subjects inducted and randomized into the trial. This holds true even when subjects did not receive the treatment. The conservative approach is to analyze all subjects for whom the researchers had the "intention to treat."

Establishing Comparability Between Groups

As soon as the treatment and control groups have been established, their comparability can be evaluated on variables of interest. No statistically significant differences should be seen. When present, such differences should be controlled for in subsequent analyses by evaluating the variance in light of the original differences. In some instances, the differences are so great as to threaten the integrity of the experiment.

The remaining analyses are a function of the questions at hand; however, in a trial with repeated measures of variables, an *analysis of variance* (or analysis of covariance) is often used to determine whether there are changes between (or among) groups that are due to the treatment, time, or a time-by-treatment interaction. In the general case, the analysis asks whether there is more difference within subject groups or between subject groups, and how much of the difference is due to unexplained factors (such as errors in measurement).

LIMITATIONS OF THE RANDOMIZED CLINICAL TRIAL

Although trials are held in the highest regard by those who believe the role of science is prediction, they are severely limited in their ability to improve understanding of the human experience. Why something works is usually less clear than whether it works. In addition, trials offer little insight into the process of how and when things change, as would a time series analysis.

In some cases ethics might prevent or otherwise influence the use of the RCT. Marquis (1983) describes the ethical dilemma of designing clinical trials wherein enough must be known to establish that the two arms of the trial are not equivalent and that at least one must be effective. In addition, ethics influence decisions about when to release preliminary results from the trial. Once the public learns that results of a drug or treatment are potentially beneficial, subject recruitment may be biased. Public demand for the treatment must be balanced against the need to establish sufficient scientific evidence to support use of the treatment. The influences of politics on science emerge in such cases, as they have over the access to trials and treatments for persons with AIDS.

Sloppy trials (those in which the treatment is not well controlled) add little to our understanding of the treatment's effect. Only those trials that clearly specify the treatment so that it is replicable add to our knowledge of therapeutic efficacy.

Although other approaches are better suited to understand and describe the human experiences of patients in primary care settings, the RCT serves as a useful and important strategy for evaluating the effect of specific treatments.

5

STATISTICAL CONCEPTS AND META-ANALYSIS

David A. Katerndahl

STATISTICAL CONCEPTS

Quantitative research relies heavily on statistical concepts. Its results are typically defined in statistical terms: means, p values, and so forth. The validity of a quantitative study is often dependent upon its statistical underpinnings. Although we cannot know reality, statistics serves to minimize our chances of deviating from it. Any discussion of quantitative research methods must consider the statistical concepts at issue. In this chapter, we will discuss sampling concepts, probabilistic thinking, and statistical analysis (also see Moses, 1985; Riegelman, 1981).

Sampling Concepts

If the goal of a study is to generalize results, then the distinction between *sample* and *population* is important for any study. The *sample* is the group of subjects that participate in the study. The *population* is the group to which the investigator wishes to generalize the study results. For example, because we cannot study all of the hypertensive patients in the U.S. population, we draw a sample of them for our research study. We hope to take our study results and apply them to all of the hypertensive patients in the U.S. population. Rarely can we study all the individuals of interest. We must rely upon a sample of them. Generalizing results to a study population will be appropriate only if our sample is representative of that population. *Representativeness* means that the important characteristics in the study are present to the same degree in sample and population. The dilemma that arises is that we cannot access the population and can thus never be certain of our sample's representativeness. However, if study results are to be used for treatment or policy decisions, we are forced to generalize results.

The first step in determining sample selection is to determine our study population. We then choose the best method for obtaining a sample representative of that population. Therefore, to study factors in help-seeking behaviors, we must use a community-based sample. We cannot use a tertiary clinic sample to generalize results to our population. On the other hand, to study drug effects in a rare malignancy, the use of tertiary care patients would be appropriate.

Unfortunately we may not always have access to the ideal sample. We may have to use available clinic patients—a *convenience* sample—or volunteers. These samples are far from ideal, because they are not selected from the population and differ significantly from the population. Volunteer samples may differ from nonvolunteer samples in motivation and baseline characteristics.

The use of *randomized samples* is often best because individuals in the population have an equal chance of being included in the study. In addition, randomization helps control for unknown confounding variables that may alter results. The method of randomization is important to ensure true randomization. The use of coin tossing or random number tables is appropriate. Assigning subjects based upon the day of the week that they present may not be appropriate. Hence the method used must be evaluated against potential confounding variables.

Because certain conditions may not be evenly distributed among the study population, sampling methods to compensate may be necessary. In *stratified sampling,* the population is segregated into groups based upon a key variable and then a random sample of each group is taken. Similarly, in *probabilistic sampling,* segments of the population may be oversampled to adjust for distribution inequalities. The above methods rely upon knowing a potential confounder before data collection. Frequently, the confounders are not discovered until later. The best that can be done after data collection is to adjust for the confounder through statistical means such as stratified analysis, Mantel-Haenzel tests, or regression analysis. The only way to deal with unknown confounders is through random selection of our sample.

Once the sample is selected, there are other threats to representativeness. Dropouts and excluded subjects may distort the sample and bias results. Documentation of the subjects' reasons for dropping out or being excluded is important. Surveys are cross-sectional descriptions of a population. The validity of survey results depends upon the response rate, and confounders may affect response. Although some authors recommend a response rate of at

TABLE 5.1 Comparison Between Reality and Study Results

	Reality	
Study Results	Difference	No Difference
Difference	Agreement	Type I Error
No Difference	Type II Error	Agreement

least 95%, surveys frequently produce response rates considerably lower, particularly if sensitive issues such as sexual behavior or illicit drug use are involved. The only method for estimating representativeness in a low-response survey is to compare respondents and nonrespondents on key variables to assess differences that may have affected response.

Probabilistic Thinking

Statistics cannot prove or disprove anything. It provides a probabilistic frame of reference for judging results. It is up to the reader to make the final interpretation (see Brown, 1985).

We have access to the study results; we do not have access to reality. Table 5.1 presents the comparison between reality and study results.

As long as the study results agree with reality, we will make the correct conclusion. A *Type I error* exists when we conclude there is a difference when, in fact, none exists. The chance of this happening is called the *alpha level*—an a priori experiment-wise level. It is determined from the data through statistical analysis and reflected in the *p* value—a post hoc test-wise value. A *p* value of .05 means that if the study was repeated 100 times, we would falsely conclude that a difference existed five times. Conversely, a *Type II error,* falsely concluding that no difference exists when indeed there is one, occurs with a probability termed the *beta level.* Subtracting beta from 1.0 gives us the *statistical power*: the ability to detect accurately a difference. Sample size determination should be based upon our desired alpha and beta levels as well as the magnitude of the difference between groups *(effect size).*

Analysis

Although special cases exist, the interpretation of most quantitative research depends upon statistical analysis. Statistics provides a framework for our interpretation based upon our theoretical constructs, hypotheses, and judgments. Although a wide variety of tests are available, the selection of a particular test should follow from the nature of the data and the research question. The particular test(s) to be used should be identified before data collection.

Statistical tests consist of two groups: parametric and nonparametric. Nonparametric tests make fewer assumptions about the data and are less powerful than parametric tests. Therefore, if appropriate, it is wise to use parametric tests. However, these tests can be used only if certain conditions exist. In addition to assuming that subjects are selected independently, parametric tests can be used only with *interval-level* data. This means that the data are continuous, not categorical or *nominal,* and that the interval between adjacent points is equal along the continuum. For example, blood pressure is interval level but flavor preference is not. *Ordinal* data have order to them but do not require equal spacing along the continuum—for example, class ranking data. Parametric tests also assume that the data come from a normally distributed population and that the variability among subgroups is similar. If these assumptions are violated, nonparametric testing is a more appropriate approach.

In addition to the parametric-nonparametric issue in test selection, the level of the data—nominal, ordinal, interval—is also important. A test is only appropriate for one level of data. An interval-level analysis is more powerful than a nominal-level analysis.

The type of sample is the third factor considered when selecting a test. How many groups are there? Are you comparing two groups—for example, males and females? Are you comparing the sample against a model—for example, is age normally distributed? Are you comparing many groups—for example, groups based upon ethnicity? Are the groups independent of each other or paired? Paired analyses are preferred if appropriate because they are more powerful than unpaired tests.

Finally, the purpose of the study is important. Different tests allow the researcher to answer questions of association, difference, and prediction. Table 5.2 provides examples of particular test selections based upon these factors.

After choosing the test one wishes to use, one must determine whether the data meet the unique requirements of that particular test. For example, if one is comparing two nominal variables looking for differences, one will most likely use a chi-square test. This test compares actual frequencies against expected frequencies. If any cell has an expected frequency of less than 5, one should consider using an alternate analysis, such as Fisher's exact test.

Similarly, use of a Pearson correlation to measure association is based on the assumption that the data are interval level, that the variables are independent of each other, and that the data are normally distributed, with similar variances within groups. Although Pearson correlations are *robust*—violation

TABLE 5.2 Relationship Between Characteristics of the Research Design and Statistical Test

Level	Para-metric vs. Nonpara-metric	Association	Purpose of Study				
				Difference			
			One-Sample Case	Two-Sample Case		Many-Sample Case	
				Independent	*Related*	*Independent*	*Related*
Nominal	Nonpara-metric	Contingency coefficient	Chi-square, binomial test	Chi-square, Fisher exact	McNemar test	Chi-square	Cochran Q test
Ordinal	Nonpara-metric	Spearman rank	Runs test	Mann-Whitney test	Wilcoxon test	Kruskal-Wallis ANOVA	Friedman ANOVA
Interval	Nonpara-metric		KS test	Randomiz-ation test	Randomiz-ation test		
Interval	Parametric	Pearson correlation	Z-test, Student's *t*-test	Student's *t*-test	Paired *t*-test	ANOVA	ANOVA with blocking, ANCOVA

of assumptions rarely affects the validity of the conclusions—if these assumptions are not valid, one should consider using the Spearman correlation. Whenever measuring associations, one must not confuse association with causation. Although encouraged by readers and editors to use causational terms, one must refrain from such overinterpretation. The plotting of the data can often provide insight into the exact nature of the relationship between two variables.

The *t*-test is used to calculate the standardized difference between means in two groups. The *t*-test actually has three important forms. Each form uses interval-level data and assumes a normal distribution. The *first form* compares two group means using a pooled variance—a standardized measure of the dispersion of data—of the two groups. If the variances are dissimilar—determined with an *F*-test—then the *second form* is used, and the separate variances are applied. These two forms are helpful in comparing (a) two group means, (b) two post-tests when the pretests are similar, or (c) two measures of change—pretest minus post-test—when pretests are dissimilar. The *third form* of the *t*-test is the paired *t*-test, comparing (a) the pretest with the post-test in one group or (b) the means of two matched groups. The paired *t*-test is preferable if appropriate because it is more powerful than the unpaired forms.

In conclusion, statistical concepts are essential to issues of sampling and representativeness. However, if practicality forces one to use a less than ideal sample, statistics can be helpful in controlling for confounding variables. Statistics also leads one to employ a probabilistic approach to analysis and interpretation while determining the appropriate sample size. Finally, the selection of a particular test for analysis should be done before data collection, based upon data characteristics and the study question. Particular test assumptions must be considered when conducting the analysis.

META-ANALYSIS

The technique of *meta-analysis* continues to grow in popularity as its clinical usefulness is discovered (see Hedges & Olkin, 1985; Katerndahl & Cohen, 1987; Lau et al., 1992; Light & Pillemer, 1984; P. C. O'Brien, 1993; Rosenthal, 1984; Smith & Glass, 1977). Meta-analysis is the quantitative counterpart to the traditional qualitative literature review, which summarizes a body of literature based upon the author's subjective interpretation. It seeks to summarize a body of literature by combining results of individual research studies in a similar fashion to the combination of subjects in a traditional study. Here the results of each study constitute a separate data point. By coding for study features as well, we can determine the effect that study characteristics have upon the results. Such pooling of results may not be appropriate in experiential studies due to their heterogeneity. In fact, some meta-analysts feel that this procedure should be used only to combine results from randomized clinical trials (Sacks, Berrier, Reitman, Ancora-Berk, & Chalmers, 1987).

The three basic concepts in meta-analysis are inclusiveness, calculation of a standardized effect size (ES)—the magnitude of the difference between treatment and control groups—and pooling of results. Inclusion criteria are established to ensure that all studies deal with the subject matter, have an appropriate control group, and meet minimum study quality criteria. Next, *all* studies must be sought. Although some authors feel that unpublished studies should not be included, the presence of publication bias and the observation that unpublished studies may be of equal quality to published studies make the search for unpublished studies essential. Not only should computer searches and bibliographic reviews be pursued, but dissertations should be sought as well. A quantitative review cannot be complete without inclusion of *all* available, relevant studies. Hence the meta-analyst should seek such studies until all avenues have been exhausted.

A standardized ES must be calculated to combine study results. This usually takes the form of the difference between group means divided by the pooled standard deviation—the average variance—but may take other forms as well. Meta-analysis differs from data pooling techniques in which individual subjects from different studies are pooled together into one large data set. The pooling of subjects is appropriate only if the study protocols are similar, the study results are similar, and the studies are randomized trials. The pooling of results in a meta-analysis usually involves the calculation of an average ES with its corresponding confidence interval—the range in which the "true" ES can be expected. Often individual study results are weighted based upon their sample size so that large studies contribute more to the overall ES. To place meta-analysis in perspective, we will discuss its assumptions, applications, and limitations.

Assumptions

For meta-analysis to produce a valid summarization, certain conditions must be true. First, the studies must deal with a similar outcome, provide enough information to compute an effect size, and use appropriate control groups. Second, the analysis must include *all* relevant studies. If a portion— for example, unpublished studies—is not included through lack of identification, then the investigator must address the chance of publication bias. Finally, because important variables often rely upon a subjective coding, a meta-analysis assumes interrater reliability in coding. Although consensus methods are often used to reach a final coding, measures of interrater reliability are preferable.

Applications

Meta-analysis is a labor-intensive procedure. Therefore it is not useful in summarizing a body of literature in which the studies agree in conclusion among themselves. However, meta-analysis is valuable in three situations. If a literature has found conflicting results, meta-analysis can suggest the best overall trend in the literature. In addition, by assessing the relationship between effect size and study characteristics, such as design variables and sample characteristics, meta-analysis can help explain a conflicting literature based upon differences in study characteristics. Finally, because many studies have insufficient power to detect significant differences, a body of literature may require many studies before the true conclusion is obvious. Meta-analysis effectively increases the statistical power of the individual studies such that a group of nonsignificant studies may produce a significant meta-analysis. In fact, the application of meta-analyses sequentially to a body of literature has been advocated as a method to identify the earliest point at which the literature has answered a research question so that further studies are unnecessary.

Limitations

Meta-analysis is simply another tool in the investigator's arsenal. It is not the ultimate truth. Because it purports to give the "true" overall effect, it is tempting to use meta-analysis for policy decisions. However, we must recognize its limitations. First, the comprehensiveness of the meta-analysis is based upon including every relevant study. Selection bias may result in excluding relevant studies, and publication bias can also limit access to relevant work. The studies themselves can vary widely. Investigator bias may have biased individual study results, and the heterogeneity of study designs may invalidate the combinability of results. Hence meta-analysis has important limitations and should be interpreted cautiously. These potential limitations should be addressed in any meta-analysis, and failure to resolve these issues should cast doubt upon its conclusions.

6

PARTICIPANT OBSERVATION

Stephen P. Bogdewic
P. K. Jamison

Participant observation is a qualitative research technique that reveals information about and stresses the significance of "the meanings (realities) people use to make sense out of their daily lives" (Jorgensen, 1989, p. 15). In participant observation the everyday setting, in which behavior gives meaning to beliefs, acts as the frame of reference or "context" for the research study.

Therefore participant observation sets out to uncover and discover the "culture" of a group or organization. In this chapter, *culture* refers to those behaviors and beliefs that signify and are representative of the disposition of individuals in a particular setting: their values, beliefs, attitudes, experiences, and histories. The focus of participant observation, then, is on "the way we do things here" (Pheysey, 1993, p. xiii), or how the activities and interactions (communications and practices) of individuals in a setting give meaning to their behaviors and beliefs.

BACKGROUND

Rooted in social and cultural anthropology, the origin of participant observation is generally attributed to Malinowski's fieldwork among the Trobriand Islanders (Malinowski, 1961). Malinowski is credited as being the first to use this unique way of collecting data to generate specific anthropological knowledge (Ellen, 1984). Lindemann (1924) first used the term *participant observation* to distinguish between "objective observers" and "participant observers." Through the use of interviewing, "objective observers" approach a culture from the outside, whereas "participant observers" use observation to research a culture from within (Friedrichs & Ludtke, 1974).

Despite the different purposes of social science, the value of observation as a research method is not so unusual. Observation is drawn from everyday life. Although "we can only see what we look at," as a result of observation "what we see is brought within our reach—though not necessarily within arm's reach" (Berger, 1972, p. 8). As Bogdan (1972) suggests, participant observation requires "a prolonged period of intense social interaction between the researcher and the subjects" in order to record and systematically collect field notes (p. 3). More importantly, sustained participation over a period of time is required if a researcher is to gather critical data and discover the meanings of a culture beyond a single event. In other words, participant observation should attempt to "observe" more than events; it should consider the relation between events and people. In this way, participant observation discovers the ways in which individuals construct their definitions of reality, and the manner in which they organize their world (Goetz & LeCompte, 1984).

In the study of provider behavior, and in particular the study of primary care medicine, participant observation may increase understanding of the assumptions and aspirations of those persons who provide primary care service and education in a particular health care setting. By gaining entry into a health care setting and taking part, a researcher can observe the different activities and interactions of a culture that tend to influence the provider-patient relationship and give meaning to the concept of primary care. Observation provides data about a culture that quantitative measures, such as questionnaires, cannot because "organizational data are often qualitative, rich in detail, and full of subtle and unique events" (Cunningham, 1993, p. 131). The following provides an overview of the need for participant observation in understanding provider behavior, a description of the salient features of participant observation and how these can reveal the characteristics of provider behavior, a discussion of the methodology of participant observation, an exploration of the value of ethnographic records in conceptualizing primary care, and a brief examination of the associated problems of participant observation.

A NEED FOR PARTICIPANT OBSERVATION: GAINING A RICHER UNDERSTANDING OF PROVIDER BEHAVIOR

In recent years, there has been a heightened interest in primary care medicine, provider behavior, and primary care education and service. This interest has raised important issues and questions. For example, it is important to ask, "Is primary care beneficial for patients and the medical field?" and "What kind of training will future primary care physicians require?" Furthermore, the addition of primary care programs in medical schools, hospitals, and community centers raises questions such as "What organizational and administrative issues arise during the implementation of primary care medicine programs?"

Despite the well-intentioned and earnest desire of those involved to address these questions, the more critical questions are often overlooked. Two such questions are, first, "What is primary care?" and, second, "What does the term refer to?" These last two questions address the need to examine further the assumptions that underlie primary care medicine and provider behavior.

The concept *primary care* is immediately problematic. The term is frequently used to refer to the actual providers, those persons who have received specialty training in primary care medicine (family medicine, general pediatrics, and general internal medicine). However, with increased attention being given to the role of primary care in the health care system, a growing number of health care providers have begun to identify themselves also as being "primary care." Alternatively, *primary care* may refer to the setting itself, where a particular type of medicine is practiced, such as a community health center. And lastly, *primary care* may refer to a specific level of care, one that is part of a larger system of health care.

Movements to promote the study of provider behavior and primary care medicine also pursue the study of organizational and cultural change in the health care professions. When attempting to implement change in a culture, the critical area of change (such as primary care) is often fuzzy. Yet there is still a reliance on predetermined criteria or measures of change that provide limited data. In addition, such data do not reflect the dynamic relationships and naturally occurring change that are a part of every culture. As a result, in large cultures such as medical settings, it becomes increasingly difficult to influence or alter provider behavior in the area of primary care medicine if the particular context in which individuals work is not accurately described. The need for participant observation, and its ability to enable greater understanding of the variety of behaviors and practices that take place in a setting, is therefore better recognized when it is used as a way to reveal the unique and critical behaviors occurring and constructed in a culture. Situated within the health care setting context, a researcher is able to observe the ways in which the setting and people influence individual and group behavior. Hence the participant observer is able to describe provider behavior as a result of a direct relationship with a setting in which knowledge is "finally more than the explanation of objects. It is always a knowing with the other" (Sullivan, 1983, p. 316).

Participant observation derives meaning from the social knowledge and practices of a culture. It provides understanding of a culture, not through alteration or intervention strategies, but from active participation with the existing culture and thoughtful observation of its participants, policies, and practices.

> Participant observation allows the observer to take on, to some extent, the role of a member of the group and participate in its functioning. The observer is asked to experience the problem practically and personally. This is an opportunity to see the conflicts and miscommunications which might never have been recognized by asking questions in an interview. (Cunningham, 1993, p. 132)

To more fully understand provider behavior and primary care medicine, the study of primary care culture through direct observation is an imperative. Participant observation can reveal a greater understanding of the current conceptualizations and practices termed "primary care" and provider behavior. Observation becomes the vehicle through which a way of seeing

> establishes our place in the surrounding world; we can explain that world with words, but words can never undo the fact that we are surrounded by it. The relation between what we see and what we know is never settled. . . . The way we see things is affected by what we know or what we believe. (Berger, 1972, pp. 7-8)

The following assumptions further outline the need for participant observation:

- Providers and patients in a health care setting have an understanding of that setting, and each is an active participant and interpreter of that setting.
- Meanings are constructed within the setting that in turn contribute to a shared understanding of the cultural context of the setting.
- Health care settings are complex webs that defy definitive measurements.
- The complete phenomenon known as "provider behavior" is embedded within an intricately connected, and often changing, lived experience.
- Only over time, and through participating and interacting in a health care setting with multiple persons, can an in-depth understanding of provider behavior be obtained.
- Provider behavior can be best understood by observing the social and cultural meanings of a practice environment and observing how such meanings inform behavior.

Given these assumptions, there are situations in primary care in which participant observation could prove useful. The business of primary care takes place in different organizations, and all have their own unique cultures. How many conceptualizations of "primary care" are there? There are various occupational groups involved in the delivery of primary care, and each functions in accordance with particular norms, language, customs, and rituals. Consequently, how do these groups interpret and carry out what they each define as primary care? How do their conceptualizations differ? What values dominate the training of members of these occupations? If an understanding of these research questions requires a conceptualization of the interpretations, processes, events, and relationships that individuals and groups construct in a social situation, then participant observation is the most appropriate method.

FEATURES OF PARTICIPANT OBSERVATION

It is clear (to all except some mystics) that if the aim of science is to establish bodies of knowledge about the world, then somewhere in the process of doing science the world must be studied or observed. (Philips, 1990, p. 33)

Participant observation offers several distinct features that provide insight into the everyday realities of provider behavior. In Table 6.1, the features of participation observation are applied to provider behavior and primary care medicine using the framework offered by Jorgensen (1989) and the description of ethnography outlined by Schwandt (1990).

METHODOLOGY OF PARTICIPANT OBSERVATION

In placing the meaning of everyday life first, the methodology of participant observation differs from approaches that begin with concepts defined by way of existing theories and hypotheses. (Jorgensen, 1989, p. 15)

Participant observation stresses the significance of observing daily experience in a particular context and how it influences provider behavior. The "findings are literally the creation of the process of interaction" between the participant and the setting (Guba, 1990a, p. 26). Because meaning is assumed to be actively derived through experience on the part of the participant observer and the other participants of the study, it is the interaction that provides an understanding of the natural phenomena occurring in a setting. This is unlike most traditional scientific studies, in which the focus of the study is predetermined, created, or set up. For example, in contrast to quantitative studies (such as drug studies), participant observation discovers the socioculturally constructed web in which the participants are active interpreters of meaning, interacts in that web, and then describes that web. Over time

TABLE 6.1 Features of Participant Observation and Applications to Primary Care Research

Key Features of Participant Observation (Jorgensen, 1989, pp. 13-14)	Key Concepts of Ethnography (Schwandt, 1990, p. 266)	Application to Provider Behavior and Primary Care
Insider's viewpoint	Understanding as nearly as possible some aspect of human experience as it is lived or felt or undergone by the participants in that experience.	Describes the context of the primary care setting from the interpretation of individuals in the setting.
Here and now of everyday life	Procedures for bounding an inquiry within a particular context, for it is only within some context that the experience has meaning.	Depicts routine and unique qualities and interactions within the primary care context.
Development of interpretive theories	Contexts naturally occurring as opposed to contrived or fabricated.	Builds theory about primary care medicine and provider behavior from within the primary care context.
Open-ended process of inquiry	The inquirer follows procedures for considering the context and experience as a complex temporal, sociocultural, and geographic whole.	Inquires into primary care context (through observation, and informal and formal interviews).
In-depth case study approach	Inquiry is conducted using the investigator-as-instrument, who employs ordinary fieldwork methods.	Simultaneously describes and questions the context that gives meaning to "primary care" and provider behavior.
Researcher's direct involvement in informants' lives	Inquirer disavows a hypothetico-deductive paradigm in favor of forms of inductive analysis.	Connects primary care providers' and related individuals' lived experiences to the primary care context.
Direct observation as a primary data-gathering device	As a result of inductive analysis, produces not a technical report but a type of narrative, text, or case report.	Data collected are descriptive and contextually related to individuals and primary care setting.

and through multiple contacts with individuals in the setting, a more holistic description of the culture and its setting can be derived and a more in-depth understanding recorded. Although some aspects of provider behavior may be measured by quantitative studies (such as numbers of patients seen daily, demographics of patients, types and numbers of clinical tests ordered), an understanding of social and cultural complexities defies objective measured outcomes. Instead, the intricacy of provider behavior is better discovered through observation of the complex and perhaps contradictory practices and beliefs present in real settings. The challenge, then, is to appreciate the need for embracing the "big picture" when trying to understand behavior in areas such as primary care. When the intent of a study is to see the whole picture that informs each piece of the primary care setting and persons, then participant observation is an appropriate research method.

PROBLEMS OF PARTICIPANT OBSERVATION

Particular types of problems arise in participant observation that stem in part "from being present and visible as an observer" (Cunningham, 1993, p. 133). First, if a researcher adopts the position of onlooker rather than participant (especially when he or she is only going to be present in a setting for a brief time), it will be difficult to gather data about the complex meanings and interactions of a culture. Furthermore, if individuals suspect that a researcher will be present only for a brief period of time, they may not cooperate if they are concerned that he or she will interrupt the daily events and then leave. Or perhaps it is believed that the researcher's presence will interrupt the natural setting and dynamics of the environment. Whenever possible, it is preferable for a researcher to go beyond the position of onlooker and "become accepted and respected as a researcher in a way which encourages people to be as natural as possible" (p. 134).

Second, although a participant observer does discover events and meanings in a setting, he or she must be careful not to act as a change agent. This is difficult, due to the approach itself and its underlying assumption that the data of the study will act, in the end, to inform individuals in the setting. However, this is different from the researcher's acting as a change agent in the setting, drawing on his or her assumptions about the future direction of a culture. Although in some instances a participant observer may be faced with a situation that requires him or her to confront the culture, generally participant observers would not.

Third, a researcher during his or her observation of events and experiences and collection of data may be attracted to exaggerated events and exotic data. Likewise, he or she may focus on data that support viewpoints different from his or her own. Shifts of perspective such as these bias field data and reporting.

Fourth, records used to support field notes and data should be carefully examined. Records are saved by organizations and cultures for different purposes, and such records are not value-free. It is worth finding out the purpose of such records before using them to support or counter research findings.

Finally, participant observation can be very time consuming. It can take a year or even more to complete the fieldwork portion of a study. In contrast, it is possible to conduct traditional research in only 1 to 3 months (Bernard, 1988).

THE VALUE OF ETHNOGRAPHIC RECORDS IN CONCEPTUALIZING PRIMARY CARE: CONSTRUCTION OF AN ETHNOGRAPHIC RECORD

Several prior articles on participant observation (Guba, 1990a; Jorgensen, 1989; Muller, 1992) suggest that one area of discussion critical to recognizing the need for and the features of participant observation in understanding provider behavior is the "ethnographic record." A review of four of the primary contributions of participant observation to an understanding of provider behavior (in particular, primary care provider behavior) will enhance an appreciation for such records.

Direct Observation of Events and Interactions

Muller (1992) makes a distinction between the "participant-observer" study and the "observer-participant" study. The first is the more active approach. In a related argument, Becker (1993) stresses the difference between the descriptive mode and the discovery mode in research outcomes, suggesting that many research studies, like participant observation studies, describe what is going on but never address how and why events occur. An individual who is skilled and knowledgeable in a specific area, such as primary care medicine, has more potential to be an active, informed participant observer. Alternatively, an individual who does not possess such knowledge and skills is more likely to act as an observer participant, carrying out a participant observation but from a more distanced position. But over time, as familiarity, confidence, and the focus of the study begin to shift, the researcher may find that he or she does indeed become a participant observer. Although this may appear difficult, the actual mechanics of a participant observation study are intended to foster such an evolution (Bogdewic, 1992).

The importance of this distinction for understanding the construction of the ethnographic record is that knowledge of primary care medicine may provide more informed pictures of study in particular areas such as diagnosis, doctor-patient relationships, and doctor-to-doctor relationships. Yet a more (initially) distanced researcher might collect in-depth information in areas such as patient-doctor communication, patient interpretations and beliefs of doctor knowledge and practices, and doctor-to-administrator relationships. Both positions, the descriptive and the discovery modes, provide information that is integral to comprehending the "big picture" of provider behavior in primary care medicine. But as Becker (1993) argues, a study that wants to pursue in depth the cultural themes associated with behaviors that come from interactions in the setting must understand that "the meaning grounded in social interactions requires a sensitivity to cues and subtle pattern and the ability to find patterns in seemingly unconnected occurrences" (p. 259). Again, participant observation is extremely useful for describing social and organizational life through the construction of an ethnographic record. But the value of an ethnographic record derives from its depiction of meanings and interpretations based on intense and continuous observation of a culture.

Informal and Formal Interviews

The ethnographic record of participant observation is commonly associated with obtaining spoken records. Stories—verbal interpretations of the meanings and events in a setting that provide narrative, contextual, chronological, and often contradictory information—though shunned by most quantitative studies, provide valuable data for participant observation. Such stories emanate from events in a setting, but they also shape events within the setting. Therefore the encounters in which such stories are embedded provide the researcher with a rich discourse from which he or she can begin to discover both the subtle and overt social, cultural, and political relationships being continuously constructed in a setting. Initially, such stories are spoken and shared through the eyes of the individual actively situated in the setting. A careful and responsible researcher ensures that aspects of these original stories, whether factual or exaggerated, become a part of the final description of the culture (Dingwall, 1977). Although such stories might be shared for a variety of reasons (including the intent to alter the outcome of the study) and through a variety of formats and texts (such as moral, mystery, historical fact, and legend), an individual must feel comfortable in order to share personal or organizational stories with the researcher. "Although participating as a researcher places the observer on the margins of human action, it rarely is possible to remain uninvolved with insiders. People have a tendency to involve you. . . . Involvements with people indicate that you are being accepted to some extent as a part of the setting" (Jorgensen, 1989, p. 58).

The methodology of participant observation ensures that the stories of everyday life are given in-depth attention and meaning as well as value in the final study report.

Collection of Documents and Artifacts

Documents and artifacts are important to understanding the relationship between a setting, individuals, and the construction of meaning. Although at one level a document or artifact may be read within its own frame of reference, the greater value of documents and artifacts may come from discovering what meaning each has outside that frame of reference.

In health care settings, many documents and artifacts (e.g., medical records) are covered by specific laws, both national and state, that prevent the sharing of medical information. But again, other documents (e.g., schedules, minutes, newsletters) can provide important clues to the beliefs and behaviors of individuals in a setting. Such documents and artifacts might represent the views of the administration or of doctors, or the policies and desires of others (such as federal review boards) who are not necessarily engaged in the setting on a daily basis. In participant observation, a researcher can observe the ways in which a document or artifact affects the setting and the roles that one or the other plays in communicating ideas and developing policy. Alternatively, a document or artifact can be used as a point of discussion in an interview and can help the researcher understand how individuals interpret the meaning of such materials in the setting. Again, participant observation incorporates the meaning of documents and artifacts into the final report, particularly if the materials are relied upon by individuals to assist their construction of meaning in a setting.

Open-Endedness in the Direction of the Study

In a culture, there are both practical and personal activities regularly taking place that interact and contradict. Despite this insight, traditional research studies focus on the outcomes of activities in a setting and engage in the analysis of these behaviors in order to determine their quantitative value. This method of research relies on maintenance and control of activity in order to describe a culture. In contrast, participant observation acknowledges personal activity and interpretation as integral processes to the construction of cultural settings. In participant observation, the value of "change" is represented in the "open-endedness" of a study. Through observation and interviews, the researcher is able to inquire into the daily movement and alterations that make up the whole picture of a living and dynamic setting. In this way, the researcher is better able to follow the more subtle directions or aspects of change in a culture that only a full participant might recognize. In essence, participant observation minimizes rigid adherence to a priori concepts.

CONCLUSION

In summary, participant observation, as it is described here, enables the observation of

- behaviors in action
- decision-making effectiveness in a particular context
- individuals' reliance on the context of a setting
- organizational behavior within a context
- unique occurrences or deviations from the norm in a setting
- culture of a provider environment
- group dynamics
- provider and patient expectations
- different stories about illness/wellness experience
- cultural belief systems about illness and therapy

Furthermore, in the areas of provider behavior and primary care, participant observation may enrich the knowledge of visible and/or hidden behaviors that are present in a particular setting and that influence the cultural activity. Examples of behaviors that might be influenced by context are beliefs, values, practices, ethics, decisions, assumptions, attitudes, skills, knowledge, motivations, patient-provider relationships, performance, transformations/learning, avoidance mechanisms, interactions, management/supervisory skills, lived experiences, expectations, commitments, priorities, organizational skills, reliance on others, adaptation mechanisms, resistance, and monitoring and evaluation skills. In addition, participant observation may reveal greater understanding of the unique manner in which primary care providers employ critical skills: problem solving, listening, observation, and empathy.

Short of actually conducting a participant observation study, anyone interested in learning more about this methodology would benefit from reading a quality work such as Mizrahi's (1986) *Getting Rid of Patients: Contradictions in the Socialization of Physicians.* Mizrahi spent one year observing 102 internal medicine house staff (residents) who were in training during that year. She was able to function as a participant observer in all aspects of the residents' daily life. Her conclusions were fascinating. She discovered that the house staff learned a set of techniques for distancing themselves from patients. This distancing, which was accomplished either physically or psychologically, was termed *getting rid of patients,* or GROP behavior. House staff learned techniques such as "transferring." Someone skilled in this technique knew how to work the system, how to pass responsibility down the medical hierarchy or across to social workers and other nonmedical staff. To psychologically distance themselves from patients, house staff quickly learned how to avoid or objectify patients. Mizrahi further concluded that her findings corroborated the existence of a strong house staff culture throughout the academic setting, one that faculty could affect in only a very limited way.

Mizrahi's study of resident socialization addresses that question that drives all participant observers, "What is happening here?" Ask anyone in the setting and he or she will give you the unexamined answer that he or she has come to accept. Stick around for a while, question the assumptions, record what you are learning in some meaningful way, and the answer to your question may provide a unique insight and understanding.

7

INTERVIEWING

Jaber F. Gubrium

Commonly, standard social research textbooks describe interviewing as a survey technique for gathering information from individuals about thoughts, sentiments, and activities. As I address this technical side of the enterprise, I aim to raise contrasting and increasingly pertinent epistemological questions about who the interviewer is, what it means to question, and who the respondent is claimed to be. I do so from the standpoint of someone who conducts interviews as part of interpretive, ethnographic research in a variety of therapeutic settings.

Textbook discussions of the interview as a social research technique describe it as a process whereby (a) someone usually called the interviewer, (b) asks questions, (c) of someone else referred to as the interviewee or respondent, who in turn (d) answers the questions out of his or her experience. The ideal interview is one in which the respondent's answers are not artifacts of interviewer characteristics or the question format, but rather accurately represent the respondent's experience.

WHO IS THE INTERVIEWER?

Much discussion in the methodological literature has centered on whether and how the interviewer's personal characteristics and demeanor affect outcomes. The conventional wisdom has been that the least threatening, most neutral and inviting interviewer is the middle-aged woman. This now raises the epistemological question of whether all the social research founded on the assumption has generated glosses on experience rendered to a friendly, middle-aged female. Broadly, the question is whether the best interview is one in which the personal characteristics of the interviewer and interviewee match. The idea is that when they match, interview responses address the experiences under consideration rather than other matters, such as to whom experience is being conveyed.

As far as primary care practice is concerned, this would suggest that, other things being equal, such as the degree of acquaintance between physician and patient, the most honest responses would be obtained when the physician's and patient's personal characteristics were similar. I take it that this would be a technical rationale, say, for female physicians treating female patients.

Rarely, if ever, is there more than one interviewer in an interview session. This seems rather strange, given the many circumstances in everyday life in which individual attitudes and sentiments are interpreted and rendered by the respondent in relation to multiple correspondents. Silverman (1987) has shown in his studies of doctor-patient encounters that the presence of a mother in physicians' encounters with insulin-dependent, diabetic children makes a good bit of difference in how the child's compliance is represented. Mothers consider their children's compliance to be part of mothers' moral responsibility and thus speak of and for their children in relation to that understanding. One might guess that what the child says to the physician, if much at all when his or her mother is present, may not be what the child says alone with the physician. I don't mean to suggest that the latter would be a more authentic version of the child's attitudes and sentiments. It could be argued that the mother best represents what the child actually feels and does, as in the idea of "interlocutorship" (see Gubrium, 1992, 1993b). The methodological issue here in general is whether the one-on-one interview arbitrarily privileges a particular communication format and, in turn, a particular type of knowledge of experience.

The strangeness of the one-on-one interview format is underscored when we ask whether experience is ever conveyed to an exclusive, individual correspondent. The questions "Who is this individual interviewer?" and "What does he or she want to hear?" are potentially present throughout interviews and, as such, can ongoingly engage the respondent with the various attributed personas of the "single" interviewer.

An alternative view of the interviewer follows from a vastly different approach to communication, founded on the assumption that experience is constituted in and through the communication process (see Filmer, Phillipson, Silverman, & Walsh, 1972). From this standpoint, the interview is a meaningful encounter in its own right, with its attendant roles, its preformed and emergent agendas, and its manifold narrative contexts. There is no reason to think of the interviewer as at best a neutral interrogator and at worst "biased" (cf. Moser, 1958, chap. 13; Selltiz, Jahoda, Deutsch, & Cook, 1959, Appendix C).

Rather than working from a preformed set of questions or inquiries, the interviewer aims to help the respondent to ask the types of questions the respondent deems pertinent to matters under consideration. The interviewer orients to the question of how the respondent frames experience and what the relevant concerns of that framing are, aiming to make both framework and concerns part of the interview process.

This is an interviewer who not only searches for the frameworks of experience from the respondent's point of view but suggests ways of viewing the matters under consideration, in the manner that respondents themselves do in relation to others in daily life. The format resembles the more conversational design of the focus group, in which the respondents are taken to be not so much vessels of answers for questions about experience, but as actively putting together and conveying attitudes and sentiments in relation to manifold horizons of meaning.

WHAT IS A QUESTION?

The standard textbook understanding is that the interviewer asks questions of, but does not provide answers to, the respondent. If questions are to be asked about charged issues, they should at least be neutralized, that is, set narratively in a context that accepts all responses as communicatively suitable, even if they prove to be morally unacceptable. A common technique is to preface such questions with options that convey a broad range of feelings about the matter, such as stating that some people feel one way and others differently. Least of all should questions be "loaded" or cause the respondent to answer in a particular way because of how the question is formulated. The comic classic is the question "When did you stop beating your wife?"

The idea of the neutral question is at odds with the possibility that the question-and-answer format itself, as neutral as it might technically seem to be, might be a manner of communication "unnatural" to some respondents. I've lost the specific reference, but I recall reading a review a few years ago of a study of Australian aboriginals' encounters with their country's criminal justice system. In court proceedings, the aboriginals tended to answer yes to everything out of respect to the occasion and its participants, incriminating themselves in the process. However neutral the questions put to them, to the aboriginal defendants the questions signified a way of acting, not a neutral mode of inquiry into their actions.

The idea that a question-and-answer format may be a way of acting and not a neutral mode of inquiry is also suggested by feminist researchers, who argue that men and women convey experience in different ways (see Abel, 1991;

Gilligan, 1982; Harding, 1987). It is said that question-and-answer formats are less evident in the natural conversations of women than in those of men. Women are likely to explore their attitudes, their sentiments, and the meaning of their actions, whereas men tend to convey them in discrete units if they speak of sentiments at all. Whether the difference is learned or essential, it nonetheless suggests that questioning may be an inappropriate means of accessing women's experiences, which raises the possibility that the interview is not neutral by design.

Of course, standard textbooks do present various interview formats, from open-ended to fixed choice. Social researchers who do surveys tend to work within more structured formats, whereas those concerned with personal meaning and everyday life tend to work more open-endedly.

But the Australian aboriginal material and feminist criticism are raising a more fundamental concern, about whether we can suitably know by means of asking lists of questions. Is it possible that for some people or contexts of experience, the communication of experience is a constant search for new ways (new questions) to reveal the meaning of self, others, and everyday life? My own work in support groups for caregivers of Alzheimer's disease sufferers shows that participants are as much attuned to the types of questions that could be raised about matters such as familial and personal responsibility as they are concerned with getting answers. For one thing, certain answers implicate them in undesirable ways, which lead them to search for alternate ways of posing questions about what it means, say, to "be family" or "be a dutiful husband [or wife]" in caregiving (Gubrium, 1986a, 1988b, 1993b).

WHO IS THE RESPONDENT?

Textbook discussions usually assume that the respondent is interviewed alone, not in the presence of others such as a spouse, parent, child, or acquaintance, although there has been some recent work, in family sociology for example, in which spouses are interviewed together (see Gilgun, Daly, & Handel, 1992, chaps. 7-11). Needless to say, multirespondent interviews do not lend themselves to the individualized form of data analysis that single-respondent interviews do. In multirespondent interviews, data must be analyzed as social interaction, not as more or less representative of individuals' experiences.

In principle, especially in one-on-one interviews, the respondent is looked upon as a vessel of answers to questions about his or her experience. Somewhere in his or her background lie answers to relevant questions. If answers do not, the experience under consideration is technically nonexistent. The vessel-of-answers view of the respondent means that at best he or she accurately represents attitudes and sentiments, and of course at worst he or she does so inaccurately. If the respondent doesn't know the answer, then he or she simply doesn't know. In this view, the respondent ideally is passive, scanning his or her experience, conveying it accurately and, it is hoped, concisely. (Needless to say, a respondent who doesn't get to the point can be a source of inefficiency, if not irritation, in surveys.)

Despite the evident bodily presence in the interview of a single respondent, we might still ask whether there is a single self providing answers to the matters under consideration. It has been my experience as a fieldworker doing both participant observation and ethnographic interviewing in settings where attitudes and sentiments come under careful scrutiny, that respondents may ask in what personal capacity a question is to be answered, or they simply state the capacity. For example, in the Alzheimer's disease caregiver support groups I studied, it was not unusual for participants to preface a remark about their caregiving experience by stating, say, "Speaking as a wife, I feel . . ." or "Putting my caregiver's hat on, I think. . . ." They then would go on to describe how they felt or thought in that capacity. Some would eventually turn about to convey sentiments and thoughts in a different capacity. Indeed, the different capacities could have their own perceived thoughts and feelings, as when a participant stated, "Right now, I prefer to think of myself as his wife, not his caregiver, because a wife naturally feels more."

The point is that the respondent is not a mere body voicing experience but a set of voices that takes account of who she or he is to be in the interview process. This is complicated by accompanying understandings about what is preferred at the moment, not to mention ideas about who one should be for particular questions, despite one's own sentiments. Seen in this way, respondents are quite active and diversely personified in the interview process. They become outrightly inventive when they accompany responses by remarks such as "I've never thought about that before" and go on to think about it and convey their thoughts.

The respondent need not be treated as an isolated individual. He or she may be interviewed either with others present or alone. My own experience in support groups indicates that the manifold and complex "interviewing" in which participants engage one another can shed much light on a particular matter. It was not uncommon in the groups for one caregiver, following the testimony of a second caregiver, to address his or her own caregiving experience with new questions and subsequently constitute its meaning as opposed to revealing its meaning differently. The appropriate term of reference here is *constitute;* the term *reveal* would imply that the respondent was a vessel of answers and that there was an available answer that could be revealed.

A more decidedly social format can be introduced into one-on-one interviews. For example, interviewed alone, the respondent might be apprised of how other named or unnamed persons framed a particular matter and thereby encouraged to consider whether alternative points of view make matters look different. I've undertaken to do this in my latest project on what I call "the horizons of meaning" for nursing home residents. After listening to respondents speak about the personal meaning of being nursing home residents in the context of their lives as a whole, I selectively informed them of how others saw it and then asked the respondents what they now thought and felt in comparison. Some said it made no difference to them. Others began to entertain the possibility that there might be another way of thinking about what had become of their lives, particularly what it meant to grow frail and leave home or one's family and significant others, perhaps forever.

Another option, especially for health care practitioners, is to systematically interview various parties to an event or problem, such as the members of a family who might enter into a care decision (see Gubrium, 1992). It is important not to privilege a priori any particular respondent's answers but rather to orient to responses as various perspectives on the matter under consideration. Equally important to keep in mind is that respondents have their own senses of who the privileged voices are in their affairs, which may or may not agree with each other.

The popular use of focus groups as a way of turning the interview into a social occasion reflects many of these considerations and options. Of course, support groups have many similar features. Each challenges the one-on-one interview as a neutral occasion for studying experience.

FROM TECHNIQUE TO MEANING

The epistemological scenario of standard textbook discussions of the interview presents the problems of interviewing as technical. If answers to questions about experience lie in individual experience, they are retrievable in principle from the respondent. When answers are not retrievable, either there is no correspondence in experience, the appropriate question has not been posed, the interviewer is incompetent, or the interview situation has been contaminated. The idea that experience is constituted in and through the interview process is not given serious consideration.

If the interview is reconceived as an occasion for meaningfully constituting experience, textbook ideals are technically reversed. The interviewer becomes less a formal role than a point of entry to a conversation about experience. Questions are less set or formatted than serving all participants as sources of discussion, converging on answers in practice. Respondents are active interrogators in relation to both answers to and questions about their experience. All are implicated in making meaning.

COMMENTS—LEE SECHREST, SOURAYA SIDANI

We are unsure whether interviewing is being proposed as a technique for data collection or as an alternative method of inquiry (strategy). As a technique for data collection, interviewing could be used by proponents or practitioners of virtually any other method. In fact, interviewing *is* used by practitioners of virtually every method: phenomenology, ethnography, grounded theory, survey research, experimental intervention.

If interviewing is being put forth as a potential candidate to the array of methodological strategies, then we think that it needs further elucidation and rationalization. For example, we wonder whether any proposal to employ interviewing as a strategy should not address such issues as the proper content of interviews, specifications for identifying potential interviewees, and like specifications for selecting (certifying) interviewers. All that would point in the direction of spelling out a conscious, structured methodology for the conduct of interviews. We are not certain whether Gubrium has in mind the codification of a method of inquiry.

We are also uncertain about just what constitutes an interview, when one may affirm that an interview has taken place. How is an interview different from a simple conversation? For example, if one converses with one's airplane seatmate about his or her views of health care in the United States today, is that an interview? What if one has a professional interest in the views of the public about health care? Would that interest convert the conversation into an interview? What if one uses responses from the conversation in formulating one's own thinking about the views of the public? What if one happens to quote one's seatmate in a talk or article? Can one "inadvertently" interview someone? Or must an interview be teleological in nature, have a structure (even if only of sorts) that is aimed at achieving some aim? Must interviews be intentional, planned, and directed?

Such issues raise, for us, interesting questions, which we do not pretend to answer, about ethics of interviewing, about the meaning of informed consent in informal research methods, and so on. What happens if neither the interviewer nor the interviewee quite understand that an "interview"—that is, a research procedure—is taking place?

Gubrium states that the interviewer must be aware of the role being enacted by the interviewee. How is that awareness to be achieved and verified—especially since it is likely that the role of the interviewee will shift often, perhaps nearly continuously, during the course of the interview? And is it not equally required that the interviewer be aware of his or her role to the same degree and at all times? Must the interviewee be equally aware of the role, the shifting role, of the interviewer? How is such awareness to be achieved without interfering with the flow of the interview, and how is awareness to be assessed on both sides of the interchange?

A clear advantage of the interview as a technique is that it permits the interviewer to "dig in" when necessary and advisable, justifying the cliche of the "in-depth" interview. But it seems to us that "digging in" implies a substantial familiarity of the interviewer with the subject matter of the interview; otherwise the interviewer might miss any number of subtle but critical points and dig in at the wrong places. (Indeed, we have known that to happen frequently, even among experienced interviewers.) Is it intended that interviewers should be well informed on the subject matter of the interview topics? Beyond familiarity, however, is the potential problem of bias, the risk that the interviewer will dig in at points of critical interest to him or her. The instance that comes readily to mind is the current concern for the false memory phenomenon, involving the apparent creation of memories of such childhood events as sexual abuse, by interviewers who "dig in" at critical moments.

The problem of bias worries us a lot with respect to interviewing. It is worrisome as an inverse function of the number of interviewers and the number of interviewees. It is frequently the case, or seems so to us, that the term *in depth* is taken to justify a very small number of interviewers (e.g, ethnographers) and a not much larger number of informants. (Margaret Mead comes to mind.) Gubrium expresses interest in the possibility of making use of multiple interviewers, but, seemingly, all at once. Such a procedure would not represent the kind of independence that we think necessary to reduce the threat of bias. Moreover, interviewing is labor intensive, and efforts to deal with bias issues may come a cropper on cost issues.

If interviewing is to be used either as a procedure for data collection or as a strategy for inquiry, some method of processing (analyzing) the data obtained in the interview should be specified. What is one to do with the large pile of material that comes from the digging in characteristic of the in-depth interview? We are not even sure what the unit of analysis should be. William Stiles (1992), a psychologist, has devised a method for coding interview content that consists of breaking everything down into single "utterances" that can then be coded into several discrete categories for subsequent analysis. At the other extreme, some interviews are treated as intact units, and the "sense" of the interviews is in some manner abstracted by the interviewer and conveyed in a few words or sentences of prose.

We surmise that Gubrium views the interview as a type of transaction between the interviewer and interviewee and assumes that the transaction will be translated by the former into a narrative of some kind, an account that will "tell a story" about what went on in the interview. That prospect introduces again the issue of bias on the part of the person who gets to tell the story, but it also points to thc fact that storytelling ability may become a paramount skill in the research strategy. Those who win may be the best storytellers whether they have, in the long run, the best stories to tell or not.

Finally, we are uncertain as to whether the idea of the interview is meant to be part of the phase of exploration or the phase of justification (using Popper's [1959] terms) in the research process. We are enthusiastic about a wide array of methods in the process of exploration. We can, and should, be fairly free and daring in formulating and advancing hypotheses for further exploration and testing. That managed competition will help to control health care costs without reducing quality of care is a reasonable hypothesis. We cannot think of any combination of qualitative methods that would justify it as a solution to health care cost problems, and we cannot think of a combination of qualitative methods that would be persuasive in ruling out managed care as a possibility. It will require empirical, quantitative testing. Interviewing, perhaps even as a tentative strategy for conducting inquiry, may be a useful addition to our armamentarium of research methods, but we are dubious that the strategy will often produce results that will be persuasive to those who are doubters in the first place, and those are the only ones who count.

REJOINDER—JABER F. GUBRIUM

The issues raised in response to my discussion of interviewing are important and I believe need to be answered at two levels: technical and philosophical. I'll try to combine the two in this rejoinder, but I don't promise to always give them equal treatment. Bear in mind that I work in a vein that foregrounds the ineluctable relationship of the subjective and objective in human experience, orienting to the two as never entirely separable. Their inseparability has crucial implications for how we proceed in doing research, how we present what is "found," and what is to be made of it all.

The "How" With the "What"

Perhaps one source of confusion is that, from the start, I set up the standard textbook description of the interview as my straw person. I moved back and forth between what the standard conveys and how we might rethink some of its assumptions to take account of the ordinary communicative complications of the interview, especially from the standpoint of the interviewee, seeing him or her as theoretically astute.

The standard suppresses the view that findings are at least partially artifacts of the interview situation and its constructs. (I don't take the more radical view that interview data are totally products of interview situations.) The interview is an occasion for considering matters that crop up on other occasions, even though they might come up for the first time in some interview situations. I'm interested in the "how" of the process by which interviewees respond and the "what" that they convey to us, and I insist that the two questions must not be separated. (Radically reflexive ethnomethodologists would dissolve it all into the "how" side.)

In my view, which has roots in ordinary language philosophy, we can ask reasonable questions about the relationship between experience and research artifacts only when we see how the "how" and the "what" questions are related in practice. It's not so much that the relationship needs to be dealt with and resolved, as that the relationship needs to be documented as a very part of the research process. The goal is to show, perhaps by means of what anthropologists call "apt illustration," how the data are produced in the communication between the interviewer and interviewee—that is, how communication figures into what is said. (An important issue arises here because the focus is so much on communication, namely, what is not said is ignored. I feel that this requires us to keep a theory of social structure at hand as we proceed.)

Multiple Interviewers and Interviewees

What I had in mind in suggesting the use of multiple interviewers and interviewees is something similar to what would be provided by a focus or a support group. My image is a collection of people—both "interviewees" and "interviewers"—who collaborate to answer a shared agenda of questions centered on pertinent aspects of experience. I worry that the standard one-on-one interview, in its own right, sustains the researcher's framework in the interview process. I am especially concerned with the understanding in survey research that interview data are principally about the interviewee's experience, not what is construed about experience in the context of the interview. I prefer a research format that makes visible the practical conditioning of what we know or come to know about interviewees' experiences.

The question of the consistency of responses across interviews is one that can be answered in two ways in relation to the viewpoint I take. Consistency can be taken to be a worry about methodology as much as a worry about data—a position that could be used to argue that consistency of responses in the standard, one-on-one interview is as much a product of consistent interrogation as of consistent responses. In other words, the format itself works to produce consistency.

Procedurally, there is a useful middle ground here, derived from the less radical position noted earlier. It might be interesting and quite theoretically significant to compare the information gathered in one-on-one interviews with the reactions of the "same" respondents in a focus group. Such comparison would not privilege any one interrogation format but would diversify formats in order to highlight both the hows and whats of communicated experience.

The "Objective" Interviewer

As far as the one-on-one interview is concerned, the issue of the "objective" interviewer or researcher involves a prior question: On what grounds do we claim objectivity? If the grounds are procedural, we can set standard technical criteria for what comprises an objective interview. This would involve strictures against the interviewer leading the interviewee, among other so-called biasing actions. My own preference is to link the objective to the interviewee's subjectivity, to argue in principle that whenever our attention is being diverted from interviewees' worlds and how those worlds are constituted we are not being sensitive to the worlds' "objects," that is, we are not being "objective."

How this principle translates into practice is as difficult as it is for any other methodology; it means that the interviewer must constantly be alert to how the interviewee frames his or her responses and how this process is linked with the interviewer's own framing. Although the interview may begin with an agenda of questions, say, an interview schedule or interview guide, the agenda is viewed as a point of departure, not a fixed communicative format. In practice, the idea is to alter the agenda to suit the frameworks from which the interviewee is responding.

This means fewer interviewees but more interview sessions with each interviewee, a procedure that is suitable for research focused on subjective meaning. The results of an initial interview are analyzed for that session, suggesting frameworks before a framework-sensitive agenda of questions is formulated for a second session. In turn, the results of the second session are analyzed for its leading frameworks before further interviewing is undertaken, and so on. In this way, questions and answers are systematically tied to interviewees' emerging frames of reference for responding, linking the how with the what and providing interviewee-sensitive contexts for interpreting results.

This systematic movement back and forth between question agendas and frames of reference ideally is an ongoing coding procedure, not one confined to an ostensible, pretesting phase of research. Just as frames of communicative reference are not necessarily fixed on first encounters, they are not necessarily fixed following initial research encounters. Instead of the interview material being precoded or coded after interviews are completed, leading frames of reference become the basis of procedural coding. (See Glaser & Strauss, 1967, for a similar coding strategy based in ethnographic research.) The working question is, "From what standpoints does the interviewee respond to interview questions?" The standpoints comprise the leading set of coding categories, with more specific response codes following.

The Biographically Active Interviewee

I am sympathetic with the view that memory—in this case, the interviewee's memory—is an active, constructive process. Based on an interest in narrative and interpretive practice, my instinct is to call memory "biographical work" and to see the activity less as a matter of constructing memory than as a matter of mediating memory with talk and interaction. I see this activity as embedded in the many ordinary language games (a là Wittgenstein) within which communication takes place (see Gubrium, 1988a).

Interviewees are biographically active because they have stories to tell in their own right, to which research is expressly attuned. Stories, of course, are not just data points but harbor horizons of meaning and have themes and authors (Gubrium, 1993a). If we think of the active interviewee as engaged in biographical work, the interviewee's storytelling is not just another way of seeing the same thing that constructively oriented psychologists call memory. Rather it reveals the narrative contours—partly factual and partly inventive—of conveying experience for research purposes.

Indeed, as stated in my initial comments, formal questioning may not be an appropriate vehicle for investigating all experience. This was noted in relation to many feminists' view that the asymmetric format of the one-on-one interview may be a gendered form of communication and validly convey men's not women's experiences. In other words, the interview format mediates biographical activity along gender lines. For example, Ann Oakley (1981), a prominent feminist social scientist, has written an article entitled "Interviewing Women: A Contradiction in Terms." My own work (Gubrium, 1986b) on the means by which caregivers for Alzheimer's disease sufferers communicate "what it's like" to witness the mental demise of a loved one suggests that no form of ordinary communication can tell what it's like; only nonprosaic forms such as poetry can.

In general, the idea of the biographically active interviewee should get us to thinking theoretically about what we know of experience in relation to the interview process. This is especially important because the voices of gender, ethnicity, and class can take serious issue with the very methods by which we have customarily gathered the data of experience.

8

USING HUMAN DOCUMENTS

John H. Stanfield, II
David A. Katerndahl

This chapter discusses the value of human documents in health provider-service recipient research. Historical documents can reveal much about the values, beliefs, attitudes, social skills, philosophy, linguistics, motivation, and behavior of their producers. In this sense, historical documents are cultural artifacts (Bennett, 1981; Blumer, 1946; Erikson, 1975; Heller, 1991; Henige, 1982; Stanfield, 1993, 1994; Stanfield & Rutledge, 1993; Tonkin, 1992).

Cultural artifacts are material representations of human thinking and behavior. In the case of historical documents, cultural artifacts are the material fragments of how human beings construct and interpret their realities. Those realities can vary from the development of concepts of self and others to the formation of institutions, communities, societies, and world-systems. Human documents can be used to understand how human beings interpret who they are and who others are in various levels of reality interpretation. The critical issue is whether there are enough reliable and verifiable human documents to reconstruct a valid reality interpretation.

Human documents come in numerous forms. Archival materials include personal correspondence, diaries, financial statements, organizational and institutional records, newspapers, and other printed media. Oral histories, autobiographies, photographs, art, music, folklore, literature, and obituaries constitute the biographical class of human documents.

Whose Reality?

When the appropriate historical documents are collected, it is possible to develop a narrative describing a reality interpretation such as how a patient or a health care provider feels about his or her self, the ways in which fire rescue workers interact with victims, or the ways in which a community responds to an epidemic. The purpose of the narrative is to tell the subjective story of those who produced the documents. This is a critical point because researchers have mistakenly used historical documents to interpret the lives of those other than the producers of the materials. This often happens in status-related research. For instance, records of male mental health care providers have been used to interpret the self-concepts of women when such records actually reveal male interpretations about women. White male and female physician records have often been used to interpret the physical and mental health of nonwhite patients when in fact it is the social and cultural perceptions of people of color being interpreted by the constructors of the records.

Hence a guiding principle is: *Historical documents should be used to reconstruct reality interpretations of those who produced the records.* The extent to which records articulate the views and lives of those who did not produce them is controversial. Care must be exercised to ensure that what is found is not confused with the subjectivity of the investigator.

If a health care provider is interested in using historical documents, the meaning of his or her own records must be kept distinct from the meaning of records collected from patients as clients or customers. The provider's own records are valuable resources for understanding past and present institutional attitudes, beliefs, and behavior in regard to the operations or changes in his or her organization or his or her impressions of service recipients. If health administrators wish to understand the reality interpretations of their clients or customers, they must collect and analyze the human documents their service recipients produce. One way to do this is to ask recipients of health services to keep journals of their daily experiences that may assist institutional administrators in diagnosing a problem. Another way is to conduct in-depth exit interviews or oral histories of service recipients, thus providing contextual information valuable for understanding the clients' perspectives on a problem.

Validity and Reliability

When one is collecting and analyzing human documents, validity and reliability are extremely important. *Validity* in this context means the quality and adequacy of data needed to construct interpretations. Basically, the human documents must be authentic. Authenticity is a problem in human documents research for several reasons. First, it is possible for human beings to unintentionally create things due to overly active imaginations, anger, faulty memory, or a sense of historical importance. Second, people can get confused about facts or allow their social biases to distort or exclude information. Third, human documents producers or their heirs may alter or destroy materials in an effort to protect or preserve personal reputation. Finally, a lucrative industry exists in the production of fraudulent documents of famous persons. Trying to determine whether a record is accurate or falsified is perhaps the most difficult validity problem a human documents researcher will face. No matter what the social status of the service recipient is, health and medical researchers will encounter patient records with faulty information regarding age, educational level, occupation, and so forth, created unintentionally or intentionally by the service recipient or by health care provider or staff record keepers. Certain information may be excluded or even altered on physician charts in attempts to protect the reputation of the service recipient or of the health care provider.

Moreover, truthtelling is a social and cultural construct shaped by historical context and politics, making the issue of how valid human accounts and impressions are even more complex. Truth is in the "eye of the beholder" and is therefore actually a personal opinion. This means that especially in culturally pluralistic nation-states such as the United States, ethical issues such as truth and its connotations (professionalism, honesty, fairness, etc.) are quite problematic. One issue that is ripe for future research is the ways in which the different cultural foundations of ethical behavior, such as truth telling, in the United States influence the ways in which culturally different health care providers and service recipients structure relationships within medical and health care practices. Given the growing politicization of cultural pluralism in the United States, international problems in medicine and health generated from intercultural miscommunications and social stereotypes are increasing. This is because we have yet to identify ways of adequately sensitizing doctors-in-training or practicing physicians about the normality of cultural differences. Until this happens, there will be persistent difficulties in research efforts such as assessing the validity of human documents derived from the lives of culturally different health care providers and service recipients.

Reliability deals with whether the analyzed documents can be generalized to other human cases and settings. In some cases, collected human documents are adequate for interpreting the reality of only one individual or one human category (such as class, age, race, ethnicity, nationality, or gender). This is because there can be something about the personal history, personality, social role, or cultural background of an individual or social category that is so unique that generalization would be a gross misapplication of assumptions.

The issue regarding unique cases is compounded by contextual factors, such as history, geography, politics, economics, technology, and life-cycle phases, that can make generalization particularly hazardous.

For instance, the cultural and class limitations of the case studies that Sigmund Freud used to develop "generalized concepts" of mental health and illness are problematic. Some of his ideas may be relevant to understanding only the mental health and illnesses of upper-middle-class Austrian patients at the turn of the century. How relevant are his ideas for understanding the mental health and illnesses of middle-class Afro-American patients in the late 20th century?

Unless there is an interest in a particular individual or social category, it is prudent to collect human documents that can be used to adequately interpret the realities of people across historical eras, cultures, and social categorization. Attempts to generalize are not efforts to find laws of human behavior because such laws are assumed not to exist. Universals are only "similar patterns" and "general tendencies." These phrases imply that there is the potential to discover common qualities among human beings across time, space, and cultures without compromising the realities of human differences, paradoxes, and contradictions.

The major dilemma in the "similar patterns and general tendencies" approach to human understanding is that it involves inductive reasoning. Thus "certainty" becomes "uncertainty" when we step beyond the boundaries of the last collected case. In other words, even though we may observe a similar pattern in a sample of 20 cases, the 21st case may be so different that it could invalidate the standing explanation. The best way of dealing with the inevitable dilemma of inductive reasoning is to learn to live with ambiguity as a normal state of affairs in research by always viewing what is found as tentative.

Particularly in a culturally plural (race, ethnicity, immigrant status) nation-state with tremendous social diversity (age, gender, class, sexual orientation, etc.) such as the United States, it is imperative that health care administrators collect data detailing the human experiences of various types of people. In the case of human documents, this could mean doing oral histories or archival research on people drawn from various categories in a particular health care consumer market, such as males, females, young people, mature adults, Euro-Americans, Afro-Americans, Latinos, the rich, and the poor. The problem is how to sample.

SAMPLING

An example of stratified sampling is the act of identifying all the different populations or categories of people in a particular health care market and then using a formula to select representatives from each population or category.

One method would be to calculate the percentage of each population or category in the area to be sampled and then to use these percentages to determine the sampling percentages of each subgroup.

The sampling could be done through either a randomized method—for instance, a random numbers table—or snowball sampling. The use of random numbers tables is appropriate if population or category characteristics are more than likely to be scattered throughout the general sampling area. Snowball sampling is a networking method of developing a pool of people to be studied. It involves asking each person interviewed who should be interviewed next. Snowball sampling is appropriate when population or category characteristics are relatively rare (e.g., interracial couples) or when one is interested in a reputational (e.g., informal network membership) rather than a random representation.

DESIGN

The quality of any data—survey, census, laboratory, or human documents—depends upon the skill of the collector and interpreter. Only through developing an adequate research design that includes validity checks and effective sampling procedures can there be assurance that data are collected and interpreted appropriately. When using human documents, the basic question is: *Do the collected documents allow the researcher to develop an adequate narrative about a pertinent issue such as the human experience of illness or wellness?* Of course, this question is best contextualized through trying to understand illness and wellness issues within the broader framework of quality of life matters such as place of residence, family and significant other dynamics, work, leisure, religion, and civic involvements.

Validity and reliability questions do not get at the various technical "how to do" issues regarding interpreting the numerous types of human documents. For instance, how does one initiate an oral interview? How does one do a proper content analysis on a diary or journal? The answer to both questions is "with open-mindedness." It is important to stay aware of the fact that the whole purpose of a human document is to provide a window into someone else's life. It is inappropriate to impose one's own personal views onto the text. If a letter writer says something "offensive" to us, it is important to distance ourselves enough to prevent getting personally offended. Only then can we proceed to ask analytical questions.

In conclusion, human documents bring to light the thoughts, values, and attitudes of their creators. A document tells us just as much about the creator as about the object of focus of the text. When crafted carefully, the collection and analysis of human documents can provide an important source of information for institutional administrators interested in learning more about their organizations and their clients or customers.

TECHNIQUES

Before proceeding further, we should discuss a few examples of how to apply human documents approaches to health care provider-recipient issues. Most fundamentally, the use of human documents involves content analysis. After archival or other human documents are collected, the investigator must develop a systematic method of searching for patterns and unique occurrences in the materials. Such *text patterns* and *text idiosyncracies* are called *textual themes*.

Teasing textual themes out of archival materials is an intricate and sometimes tricky business. An investigator must ascertain several things before content analyses of archival materials are both valid and reliable. First, the investigator must make sure that the archival material is "deep enough." There should be more than one or two archival items such as letters or journal statements articulating a textual theme. The question of how deep archival materials should be to make an accurate assessment is a hard one to answer. But certainly the more textual materials available to establish a textual theme, the better. There is also the problem of tracking and recording textual themes. Before the days of content analysis software computer packages, human documents investigators had to track and record textual themes by hand. For those without access to a computer or to content analysis software, it is, of course, still necessary to use index card systems to track and record textual themes. Using index cards involves simply jotting down trends as one reads through materials. Needless to say, it is a very tedious and time-consuming task.

Something should also be said about oral history and journal writing techniques. Oral histories and journals have one thing in common as qualitative methodologies: namely, the recording of human events is an open-ended experience. The investigator using oral history techniques should develop a loosely structured set of open-ended questions that allow the interviewee an opportunity to articulate a detailed story of life events such as wellness or illness. The investigator's questions should be asked to encourage more detail or more clarity about issues the interviewee raises. Questions should not be asked to overly influence the direction of the interview or to substantiate the biases of the investigator. A tape recorder should be used if at all possible. If that is impossible, the investigator should take detailed notes and write up a summary after the interview is over—*as soon as possible.*

Oral history interviews should not be more than 4 hours in length per setting and should have brief breaks every 50 minutes. They should be conducted in a private, comfortable place such as a kitchen or a study where both the investigator and the interviewer can unwind with ease. Outdoor interview settings such as parks and backyards are also nice settings for oral histories.

Journal writing, at its best, is undertaken when the recorder feels secure enough to divulge confidential and potentially embarrassing thoughts about self, others, and surroundings. It is important to assure potential journal keepers that the utmost care will be taken to protect their confidentiality. Because people tend to really let go and get deeply involved in keeping a journal once they start, enough time and space should be allocated to allow for extensive commentaries. Three handy ways to get someone to begin writing a journal are to (a) ask them to write a detailed autobiographical statement as the first entry, (b) ask them to write commentaries on current events and how such issues relate to daily experiences, and (c) encourage them to write first thing in the morning or just before they turn in at night (or vice versa if they are working night shift!).

One of the most amazing and rewarding discoveries about conducting oral history interviews and journal projects is that the investigator finds out that people enjoy talking about themselves. Under the right conditions, feeling secure in particular, people will open up and say the most candid things. This observation applies to children as well as to adults, who can, and will, express themselves in the most profound ways when given the opportunity.

METHODOLOGICAL WEAKNESSES

Like all methodologies, human documents research has its share of weaknesses. We have already pointed out a number of validity and reliability problems. We have also discussed the ways in which we can misinterpret records by not paying attention to who created them and for what reasons. There are the persistent problems of information incompleteness and possible fraud.

A most important weakness in human documents research is that we often forget the implications for human documents research that achieved status (class) and ascribed status (race, caste, tribe, gender) and ethnic culture are universal characteristics of human beings. Every human document is culturally constructed and is a culture-bound artifact defined through status filters such as class, age, ethnicity, religion, race, and gender. When we forget that, we fall into serious bias problems that tarnish our ability to reach adequate understanding of human beings. One of the frontier questions in human documents research and in qualitative research in general is how to check the generic cultural and social status origins of those who use and produce the documents under scrutiny. Until we develop the intercultural and social sensitivities that make us empathetic human beings in a culturally plural and socially diverse nation-state and world, we will continue to skirt issues and give superficial responses to such pressing qualitative methodological questions in health care and in the other human sciences.

HEALTH CARE APPLICATIONS

It is important for health care providers to utilize human documents approaches for two reasons. First, the increasing entrenchment of consumer rights in health care delivery requires that health care providers pay greater attention to subjective characteristics that may be barriers to their ability to compete for "customers." Also, given the increasing entrenchment of managed health care practices and policies in which employers and/or employees select physicians, health care providers have to become more in tune with human relations interaction techniques. The idea that people go to certain health care providers because they have no other choice is a bygone assumption accurate only in the most rural or inner city areas. Thus it is within the economic interests of health care providers to treat their service recipients with much more respect than in past eras and to seek out their impressions about the quality of service delivery. The use of qualitative techniques to seek service recipient experiences and suggestions is a possible way in which health care providers can compete successfully for the patient as consumer. Although the subsequent collection and analysis of such data is critical, what is more important is that qualitative feedback from service recipients to health care providers humanizes a social relationship known for its asymmetrical distance.

Second, the changing ethnic and racial demographics of the United States require that health care providers develop methods for understanding and respecting the cultural backgrounds and interpretations of their service recipients. Giving service recipients the opportunity to freely express their views in writing or verbally is a major way to close the growing ethnic-cultural gap between health care providers and service recipients. Trying to fit non-Euro-Americans into Eurocentric notions of wellness, illness, and quality of life has resulted in distorted diagnoses and treatments, leading to problems in the health status and the general quality of life of nonwhites in the United States. Only recently has the American medical establishment begun to recognize that the possible impact of racism on physical well-being is a legitimate aspect of diagnosis. The unawareness or superficial awareness many health care providers have about the subjective worlds of the culturally different will continue to frustrate the administration and distribution of health care resources and will contribute to the growing crisis in organized American health care.

We do not mean to approach the health care provider sector as a homogenous entity. To the contrary, we are mindful of the great variation in forms of traditional and Western health care and medical practices in the United States. We are also quite sensitive to the fact that there is considerable variability in medical and health care and between medical subspecialties. This heterogeneity of health care and medical practices has profound implications for human documents research. Needless to say, different types of practices and subspecialties produce different types of records. One would not expect a hospital to keep the same records as a private practice, and there are distinct differences between the record keeping of a gynecologist, an ophthalmologist, and an advanced practice nurse provider. Record access and accuracy varies across and within types of practices and subspecialties due to political and ethical considerations as well as professional traditions and structural attributes. A practice experiencing management problems may be more difficult to access than a successful one. Different practices and subspecialties lend themselves to different human-documents-based research methodologies. Oral histories, for instance, require significant verbal skills on the part of service recipients, and recipient journals work only when patients are literate.

In the health care and medical field, human documents could be used in creative ways to assess the attitudes, beliefs, perceptions, and values of providers and service recipients. We have discussed numerous ways in which such research approaches can be utilized. There are certainly other sorts of human documents that can be used to explore provider-recipient relations. For example, before malpractice suits became a pervasive problem in medical practice, charts and other records kept by physicians were invaluable sources of information about the subjective views they had concerning service recipients. Owing to the malpractice suit climate, even though patient records are still the subjective constructions of physicians, they may now reflect a more cautious, objective perspective on illnesses, treatments, and the medical procedures to be strictly followed in order to avoid possible legal action.

One line of research could examine how the record keeping of physicians has changed over time and determine its implications in terms of the changing value and relevance of such records for assessing the ways in which physicians respond to patients. An extension of this could study the probable consistency over time of mental health professionals' use of subjective interpretations of patients in their records due to the more subjective nature of their work.

We also emphasize the importance of health care providers' gaining quality of life perspectives on the illness and wellness of their service recipients through using oral history and journal techniques. For instance, in order for health providers to accurately assess how patients define wellness and illness, and the ways in which health states are related to other areas of their lives such as work and family relations, providers could ask patients to keep time-bound journals. Service recipients could be asked to keep a journal beginning 2 weeks prior to their appointment or during their hospital stay. In addition, the time spent in waiting rooms could be utilized by patients to write a brief overview of their activities over the course of a month or two. For those patients unable to keep journals or write overviews due to health reasons or literacy problems, periodic in-depth telephone interviews could be conducted, tape recorded, and transcribed for analysis. The interviews, like the journals and brief historical overviews, would provide information that could paint a total picture of a patient's quality of life as a context for understanding wellness and illness.

Given the tendency to divorce illness and wellness issues from the contexts of everyday life, perhaps the greatest advantage of the use of qualitative methods in health care and medical practices is the needed construction of holistic—quality of life—analyses of the health status of service recipients. It is through such quality of life approaches that health care providers will be able to become much more effective and competitive in a more and more consumer-driven, plural nation-state and world.

9

INTERPRETIVE INTERACTIONISM
THE INTERPRETIVE PROCESS

Norman K. Denzin

Interpretive interactionism represents an attempt to make the world of problematic lived experience directly accessible to the reader (Denzin, 1989). The research methods of this approach include open-ended, creative interviewing; document analysis; participant observation; and the collection and analysis of self- and personal experience stories. The focus of interpretive research is on those life experiences that radically alter and shape the meanings persons give to themselves and their experiences.

My argument proceeds in four stages. Beginning with a brief review of the major assumptions of the interpretive approach, I then examine two types of interpretive researchers, discussing in some detail applied, interpretive evaluation. I then turn to the major research strategies associated with interpretive interactionism, concluding with a discussion of the criteria that can be used to evaluate research in this tradition. Although my examples will be taken from my own and my students' research, I believe that the approach I advocate has high relevance for primary care medicine.

WHEN TO USE THE INTERPRETIVE APPROACH

Interpretive interactionism is not for everyone. It is based on a research philosophy that is counter to much of the traditional scientific research tradition in the social sciences. Only persons drawn to the qualitative, interpretive

AUTHOR'S NOTE: This chapter draws from Denzin (1989, Chap. 3; 1993).

approach are likely to use the methods and strategies I discuss in this chapter. Not all qualitative researchers will use the methods I propose. The approach advocated in this chapter should be used only when the researcher wants to examine the relationship between personal troubles—for example, wife battering, AIDS, or alcoholism—and the public policies and public institutions that have been created to address those personal problems. Interpretive interactionism speaks to this interrelationship between private lives and public responses to personal troubles.

At the applied level, the interpretive approach can contribute to evaluative research in the following ways (see Becker, 1967, p. 23). First, it can help identify different definitions of the problem and the program being evaluated. It can show, for example, how battered wives interpret the shelters, hotlines, and public services that are made available to them by social welfare agencies. Through the use of personal experience stories and thick descriptions of lived experiences, the perspectives of clients and workers can be compared and contrasted.

Second, the assumptions, often belied by the facts of experience, that are held by various interested parties—policymakers, clients, welfare workers, on-line professionals—can be located and shown to be warranted or unwarranted (Becker, 1967, p. 23). Third, strategic points of intervention into social situations can be identified. In such ways, the services of an agency and a program can be improved and evaluated. Fourth, it is possible to suggest "alternative moral points of view" from which the problem, the policy, and the program can be interpreted and assessed (see Becker, 1967, pp. 23-24). Because of its emphasis on lived experience, the interpretive method suggests that programs must always be judged by and from the point of view of the persons most directly affected. Fifth, the limits of statistics and statistical evaluations can be exposed with the more qualitative, interpretive materials furnished by this approach. Its emphasis on the uniqueness of each life and each situation holds up the individual case as the measure of the effectiveness of all applied programs.

A basic thesis drives the applied focus of interpretive interactionism: the importance of interpretation and understanding as key features of social life. In social life there is only interpretation. That is, everyday life revolves around persons interpreting and making judgments about their own and others' behaviors and experiences. Many times these interpretations and judgments are based on faulty or flawed understandings. Persons, for instance, mistake their own experiences for the experiences of others. These interpretations are then formulated into social programs that are intended to alter and shape the lives of troubled people—for example, community services for the mentally ill or the homeless, treatment centers for alcoholics, or medical services for AIDS patients. But often the understandings that these programs are based upon bear little relationship to the meanings, interpretations, and lived experience of the persons they are intended to serve. As a consequence there is a gap or failure in understanding. The programs don't work because they are based on a failure to take the perspective and attitude of the person served. The human disciplines and the applied social sciences are under a mandate to clarify how interpretations and understandings are formulated, implemented, and given meaning in problematic, lived situations. Ideally, this knowledge can also be used to evaluate programs that have been put into place to assist troubled persons. The perspectives and experiences of those persons who are served by applied programs must be grasped, interpreted, and understood if solid, effective applied programs are to be created. This is the argument that organizes interpretive interactionism.

TYPES OF INTERPRETIVE RESEARCHERS

There are two basic types of interpretive researchers. Those like Geertz (1983), Strauss (1987), and Becker (1986) engage in theory-building interpretation for the purposes of building meaningful interpretations of social and cultural problematics. These scholars aim to construct interpretations that are grounded in social interaction. For example, Strauss's work on chronic illness and medical technology has as its goal a grounded theory that "accounts for a pattern of behavior which is relevant and problematic for those involved" (Strauss, 1987, p. 34). Becker's studies of how schools fail to teach students to learn are examples of pure interpretation that becomes evaluation (see Becker, 1986, pp. 173-190). This type of work (Strauss's and Becker's) can inform the second type of interpretive work, which is interpretive evaluation. Such researchers engage in policymaking research. They conduct research on "a fundamental social problem in order to provide policymakers with pragmatic, action-oriented recommendations for alleviating the problem" (Majchrzak, 1984, p. 12). Interpretive evaluation research is conducted from the point of view of the person experiencing the problem; it sides not with policymakers but with the underdog that policymakers make policies for (Becker, 1967). This does not mean, however, that the point of view of the policymaker cannot be considered. This can be the case in those situations in which others are criticizing and forming policy for policymakers (Stake, 1986).

WHAT INTERPRETIVE RESEARCHERS CAN DO

Interpretive research can produce meaningful descriptions and interpretations of social processes. It can offer explanations of how certain conditions came into existence and persist. Interpretive evaluation research can also furnish the basis for realistic proposals concerning the improvement or removal of certain events or problems (see Becker & Horowitz, 1986, p. 85). This mode of research may also expose and reveal the assumptions that support competing definitions of a problem (Becker, 1967). Here interpretive interactionism aligns itself with critical theory and critical ethnography (see Quantz, 1992, p. 473). There is a commitment to those "emancipatory interests" that transcend the practical interests of everyday life, which stress harmony and integration (Quantz, 1992, p. 473).

TAKING SIDES

Interpretive evaluation researchers who do this type of work are often partisans (both implicitly and explicitly) for one point of view (radical, conservative), and some become state counselors (work for the government). Silverman (1985, p. 180) has discussed the problems with this latter approach, for often the sociologist becomes an agent of the state and is unable to conduct his or her research in a completely free fashion.

All researchers take sides or are partisans (knowingly and unknowingly) for one point of view or another (Becker, 1967; Silverman, 1985). Value-free interpretive research is impossible. This is the case because every researcher brings preconceptions and interpretations to the problem being studied (Gadamer, 1975; Heidegger, 1927/1962). The term *hermeneutical circle* or *hermeneutic situation* (Heidegger, 1927/1962, p. 232) refers to this basic fact of research. All scholars are caught in the circle of interpretation. They can never be free of the hermeneutical situation. This means that scholars must state beforehand their prior interpretations of the phenomenon being investigated. Unless these meanings and values are clarified, their effects on subsequent interpretations remain clouded and often misunderstood. It is never possible, however, to be free of all of these preconceptions.

INTERPRETIVE CRITERIA FOR EVALUATIVE STUDIES

When the research project is an evaluation study, the following steps are advised. They are based on my study of the termination of an employee assistance program (EAP) at a large midwestern university (Denzin, 1988, in press). Among other benefits, this program had paid up to 80% of the cost of psychiatric treatment for university employees. Under new regulations this figure dropped to 50%, and in many cases disappeared if the employee did not use the services of a certified treatment provider. Because of new certification procedures, 95% of the local psychiatrists and psychologists refused to participate in the new program. This meant that a significant number of the employees in need of services were now forced to pay for this treatment. Houses were mortgaged, bank loans were taken out, and many families experienced high levels of stress and anxiety because of the procedures.

The evaluation researcher begins by collecting personal experience stories from the persons in charge of the program (volunteers, caregivers, paid professionals) and from the persons served by the program. These stories are used as a way of identifying the different local and scientific definitions of the problem and the program under evaluation. As these materials are collected and analyzed, the investigator seeks to identify the moral, political, and economic biases that structure the definitions of the problem and the program.

In my study, I learned that there had been a long history of resistance to an EAP. High-ranking state and university administrators felt that universities were not in the business of supplying such services to their employees. Thus there was a moral bias against the EAP, which was countered by vigorous support from a local faculty union. At the same time, individuals who had been served by the EAP now found themselves in a situation of having to justify the need for services on new moral grounds.

As differing definitions of the problem are identified, the researcher also seeks to isolate the competing models of truth (rationality and emotionality) that operate in the setting. Administrators in my study used a model of truth based on the standards of formal bureaucratic rationality. They argued that the program had been abused by persons who did not need the services they had been receiving. Proponents of the EAP held to an emotional theory of truth that justified the EAP on humanitarian grounds.

As the investigator moves more deeply into the inquiry, efforts should be made to collect thick descriptions of client and caregiver experiences. These materials allow the researcher to present the phenomenon to be evaluated in the language, feelings, emotions, and actions of those being studied. I collected stories from clients who had been forced out of the program because of new regulations. I interviewed local psychiatrists who told stories of being forced to break the rule of client confidentiality in order to receive money for services delivered.

From these stories and accounts, the evaluator formulates analytic and thick interpretations and understandings of the program on the basis of the local theories of each of the categories of persons in the situation. Thus state officials argued that the new program was working because now only qualified persons in need were being served. They thus interpreted the changes in positive ways, in light of a bureaucratic theory of fiscal savings. Clients and critics of the new program felt they were being discriminated against and not receiving the services they thought they had paid for.

In the next stage it is necessary to compare and contrast the local and scientific interpretations and understandings of the program in question. Thus I was led to compare the accounts of clients and bureaucrats, noting that the state officials displayed little compassion or understanding for the situations employees were now forced to address. In supporting the new program, administrators furnished statistical analyses to justify the program changes. These materials could be read as distorting and glossing the actual work of the program.

After conducting the foregoing steps and reviewing the appropriate materials, the researcher makes proposals for change based on the fit between lived experiences (successes, failures) and the possibilities for change that exist within the program being evaluated. I was led to recommend, for example, that the new program be terminated and that employees be reimbursed for the costs they had incurred as a result of the changes.

These criteria and steps are value laden and take the side of the client in any setting.

THE STEPS TO INTERPRETATION

There are six phases or steps in the interpretive process. They may be stated as follows:

1. Framing the research question
2. Deconstruction and critical analysis of prior conceptions of the phenomenon
3. Capturing the phenomenon, including locating and situating it in the natural world and obtaining multiple instances of it
4. Bracketing the phenomenon, reducing it to its essential elements, and cutting it loose from the natural world so that its essential structures and features may be uncovered
5. Construction, or putting the phenomenon back together in terms of its essential parts, pieces, and structures
6. Contextualization, or relocating the phenomenon back in the natural social world

A discussion of each of these steps follows.

Framing the Research Question

The research question is framed by two sources: the researcher and the subject. The researcher with the sociological imagination uses his or her life experiences as topics of inquiry.

Interpretive Interactionism 93

The Sociological Imagination

The person with the sociological imagination thinks historically and biographically. He or she attempts to identify the varieties of men and women who prevail in a given historical period, such as the late 1980s and early 1990s in the United States (see Mills, 1959, p. 7). Such scholars attempt to examine "the major issues for publics and the key troubles for private individuals in our time" (Mills, 1959, p. 11). Persons with the sociological imagination self-consciously make their own experience part of their research. The sociological imagination is not just confined to sociologists. There is the "clinical imagination," the "psychological imagination," the "anthropological imagination," the "historical imagination," and the "journalistic or literary imagination" (see Mills, 1959, p. 19). What matters is the ability to think reflectively, historically, comparatively, and biographically.

The researcher is led to seek out subjects who have experienced the types of experiences the researcher seeks to understand. The subject in the interpretive study elaborates and further defines the problem that organizes research. Life experiences give greater substance and depth to the problem the researcher wishes to study. Given this interpretation of subjects and their relationship to the research question, the task of conceptualizing the phenomenon to be studied is easily given. It is contained within the self- and personal experience stories of the subject. The researcher seeks to uncover how the problematic act or event in question organizes and gives meaning to the persons studied.

The question that is framed must be a "how" and not a "why" question. Interpretive studies examine how problematic, turning-point experiences are organized, perceived, constructed, and given meaning by interacting individuals.

Framing the research question is a time-consuming process. It cannot be rushed. Once formulated, it structures every subsequent phase of the research process. It tells the researcher what to look for, what questions to ask, what literature to examine, what empirical materials to collect, and what evidence to use in writing up interpretations.

Formulating and asking the "how" question involves the following. Working outward from their own biographies, investigators locate within their personal history the problematic biographical experience to be studied. Having identified the experience to be studied, they then attempt to discover how this problem, as a private trouble, is or is becoming a public issue that affects multiple lives, institutions, and social groups. This will involve locating the institutional formations or sites where persons with these troubles do things together. The investigator now begins to ask how these experiences occur, attempting to formulate the research question into a single statement.

Exemplars: Emotional Experience and the Alcoholic Self

In *On Understanding Emotion* (Denzin, 1984), I focused on a single "how" question. I asked: "How is emotion, as a form of consciousness, lived, experienced, articulated, and felt?" This led to an examination of classical and contemporary theories of emotion, an extended analysis of the essence of emotional experience, and two case studies dealing with family violence and emotionally divided selves. I attempted to answer my "how" question by going to concrete situations in which persons interactionally displayed violent emotions.

In *The Alcoholic Self* (Denzin, 1987a) and *The Recovering Alcoholic* (Denzin, 1987b), I asked two "how" questions: "How do ordinary men and women live and experience the alcoholic self active alcoholism produces?" (Denzin, 1987a, p. 15), and "How is the recovering self of the alcoholic lived into existence?" (Denzin, 1987b, p. 11). These two questions led me to A.A., to alcoholic families, and to treatment centers for alcoholism, where I found persons interactionally grappling with the problematics contained in my two "how" questions.

Implementing the "How" Question

The "how" question is implemented in four ways. First, persons may be brought to a research site—for example, the scholar's office or laboratory. Once they are at the site, their stories and accounts of the processes in question are solicited. Second, researchers, as suggested above, may go to those places where persons with the experience naturally interact. Third, investigators may study their own interactional experiences. Fourth, the scientific, biographical, autobiographical, and fictional accounts that persons have given of their own or others' experiences with the "how" question may be examined. It is advised that the researchers use as many of the above strategies as possible when they begin to implement their "how" question. I turn now to the task of deconstruction.

Deconstruction

A deconstructive reading of a phenomenon involves a critical analysis of how it has been presented, studied, and analyzed in the existing research and theoretical literature. Deconstruction has the following characteristics. It lays bare prior conceptions of the phenomenon in question. This includes how the phenomenon has been defined, observed, and analyzed by previous scholars. A critical interpretation of previous definitions, observations, and analyses is then offered. The underlying theoretical model of human action implied and used in prior studies is critically examined. The preconceptions and biases that surround existing understandings are then presented.

Exemplar: Battered Wives

Cho's (1987, 1993) social phenomenological analysis of Korean family violence provides an example of how deconstruction works. The major theory in the area is based on social exchange theory. This theory argues that violence is a normal part of family life and that husbands and wives seek to maximize rewards and minimize costs in their exchange relations. It argues that when the husband perceives an imbalance of exchange, he becomes violent and uses physical force as a resource to restore equity in the relationship. This theory has been operationalized with a severity of violence scale that measures eight forms of violence: (1) throwing things, (2) pushing and shoving, (3) slapping, (4) kicking and hitting, (5) hitting with something, (6) beating up, (7) threatening with a knife or gun, and (8) using a knife or gun.

The theory predicts that wives stay in violent relationships when the rewards are greater than the punishments. Wives leave when punishments are greater than the rewards. Cho argues that this framework has the following flaws: (a) it is tautological—there are no independent measures of rewards and costs, other than leaving and staying; (b) it contains no objective measure of the ratio of rewards and punishments; and (c) it contains no way of measuring a wife's subjective definition of the situation. Hence the theory has no predictive or explanatory power.

Methodologically this theory rests on the assumptions of positivism. It assumes that family violence has an objective existence in family life that can be measured on a scale. It assumes that observations can be made free of temporal and situational factors. It presumes a linear model of causality. The theory does not address subjective experience or the interpretive process that structures violent interaction (Denzin, 1984). It views the wife as a passive agent in the violent marriage.

Cho's deconstructive reading of this literature followed the steps outlined above. She developed an interpretive interactionist view of family violence that built from the accounts battered wives gave of their experiences.

Capture

Capturing the phenomenon involves locating and situating what is to be studied in the natural world. Deconstruction deals with what has been done with the phenomenon in the past. Capture deals with what the researcher is doing with the phenomenon in the present, in his or her study. In this phase multiple cases and personal histories that embody the phenomenon in question are secured. The crises and epiphanies of the lives of the persons being studied are next located. Multiple personal and self-stories from the subjects in question concerning the topic or topics under investigation are then obtained (Thompson, 1978).

Exemplar: Battered Wives

Cho (1987, 1993) collected personal experience stories from 64 battered Korean wives. She obtained her stories from an organization in Seoul, Korea, called the Women's Hotline, which received calls from battered wives from 10:00 to 6:00 on weekdays and from 10:00 to 2:00 on Saturdays. Cho worked as a volunteer in the organization. She took calls from battered wives, with whom she later held conversations concerning their battering experiences. (She received permission to do these interviews, and her respondents signed informed consent forms.) From these conversations emerged the personal experience stories that she analyzed in her study.

Bracketing

Bracketing is Husserl's (1913/1962, p. 86) term. In bracketing, the researcher holds the phenomenon up for serious inspection. It is taken out of the world where it occurs. It is taken apart and dissected. Its elements and essential structures are uncovered, defined, and analyzed. It is treated as a text or a document: that is, as an instance of the phenomenon that is being studied. It is *not* interpreted in terms of the standard meanings given to it by the existing literature. Those preconceptions that were isolated in the deconstruction phase are suspended and put aside during bracketing. In bracketing, the subject matter is confronted, as much as possible, on its own terms.

Exemplar: Battered Wives

Cho developed an interpretation of the centrality of resentment (*ressentiment,* see Scheler, 1912/1961) in the Korean family, based on her bracketed reading of the personal experience narratives of battered Korean wives. Her interpretation argued that there are seven stages to resentment once violence enters a marriage. These stages are (a) craving for genuine conjugal love, (b) rejection, (c) feelings of hatred, (d) feelings of revenge, (e) repression of revenge, (f) deep resentment, and (g) a secret craving for revenge. When a wife reaches this last stage, she harbors desires to kill her husband. A wife speaks: "Until he comes back at night, I can't sleep. I can't eat, I can't rest. I hate and hate. . . . For 14 years of our marriage, this feeling has built up. My nerve is so weak that I take a pill to rest. . . . I just want to kill him" (Cho, 1987, p. 250). Cho's bracketed reading of stories like this led her to develop the interpretation of resentment given above. Each of the above terms (craving, love, hatred, revenge, desire to kill) was carefully defined by Cho on the basis of actual statements made by Korean wives.

Construction

Construction builds on bracketing. It classifies, orders, and reassembles the phenomenon back into a coherent whole. If bracketing takes something apart, construction puts it back together, showing how the structures and parts of the phenomenon cohere into a totality.

Exemplar: Resentment in Violent Marriages

Cho's (1987, p. 249; 1993) seven features of resentment (*ressentiment*) in the violent marriage, which were identified and defined through the process of bracketing, were then contextualized in the following way. She states that in the beginning

> the wife craves . . . love. . . . It is rejected by the husband's adultery. . . . The incident of battering happens. . . . [She] begins to feel hatred toward the husband. . . . The hatred increases as the battering continues. She wants revenge. . . . The feelings of revenge are repressed. . . . Ressentiment arises out of this situation. . . . Her craving for revenge never stops. . . . The revenge plan . . . [she] has in mind is not to end the relationship . . . but to restore it with the punishment. (Cho, 1987, p. 262)

In this contextualizing statement Cho has created a processual definition and interpretation of resentment in the violent marriage. She has reassembled each of the elements in a sequential manner, indicating how each builds on and influences the other.

The Goal of Construction

The goal of construction is to recreate lived experience in terms of its constituent, analytic elements. Merleau-Ponty (1964) describes this process in the following words. He is discussing the phenomenological study of emotion: "One gathers together the lived facts involving emotion and tries to subsume them under one essential meaning in order to find the same conduct in all of them" (p. 62). Replace the word *emotion* with the phenomenon in question—battered wives, alcoholism, sexual stories, murders, 12-step calls, leaving home—and Merleau-Ponty's injunctions still apply. The interpretive interactionist, in the phase of construction, endeavors to gather together the lived experiences that relate to and define the phenomenon under inspection. The goal is to find the same recurring forms of conduct, experience, and meaning in all of them. Construction lays the groundwork for the next step of interpretation, which is contextualization.

Contextualization

Contextualizing begins with the essential themes and structures disclosed in bracketing and construction. It attempts to interpret those structures and give them meaning by locating them back in the natural social world. For example, Cho located the resentment Korean wives felt toward their husbands back in their violent marriages. Contextualizing takes what has been learned about the phenomenon through bracketing and fits that knowledge to the social world where it occurs. It brings phenomena alive in the worlds of interacting individuals. Contextualizing locates the phenomenon in the personal biographies and social environments of the persons being studied. It isolates its meanings for them. It presents it in their terms, in their language, and in their emotions. It reveals how the phenomenon is experienced by ordinary people. It does this by thickly describing its occurrences in their world of interaction.

The intent of contextualization is to show how lived experience alters and shapes the phenomenon being studied. Whether the process is of being battered or receiving treatment for alcoholism, the structures of the experience will be altered and shaped as they are experienced, described, and given meaning by their participants. Contextualization documents how this occurs.

EVALUATING INTERPRETIVE MATERIALS

Deconstruction, capture, bracketing, construction, and contextualization bring into sharper focus the phenomenon under investigation. The goal of these interpretive activities, as indicated earlier, is to create a body of materials that will furnish the foundations for interpretation and understanding. Interpretation clarifies the meaning of an experience. Interpretation lays the groundwork for understanding, which is the process of interpreting, knowing, and comprehending the meaning of an experience. Understanding, by locating meaning in the experiences of interacting individuals, is the goal of interpretive interactionism.

Ascertaining Meaning

The meaning of an experience or event is established through a triadic, interactional process. It involves the person interpreting and acting toward an object, event, or process. This interpretive process brings the event or object into the person's field of experience, where it is acted upon and defined. These interpretations are reflected against the person's ongoing self-definitions. These definitions of self are emotional, cognitive, and interactional, involving feelings and actions taken in the situation. Meaning is biographical, emotional, and felt in the streams of experience of the person. Locating meaning in interaction involves uncovering how a person emotionally and biographically fits an experience into his or her emerging, unfolding definitions of self. It is assumed that this is done through the production of personal experience and self-stories. Meaning is anchored in the stories persons tell about themselves.

The following story is an example. The speaker has been sober and free of drugs for nearly 8 months. He is speaking to a group of A.A. members.

> I used to use drug and drink with my old friends. We'd picnic and party. One time it went on for 5 days over the 4th of July. Now I don't drink or drug anymore, and it's like we haven't got anything in common. I mean, now that I'm in recovery, recovery means more than anything else to me. So it's like I don't have these old friends anymore. I've only got friends in recovery now. I've got this customer. He tends bar. He keeps asking me to come by and have a drink. I can't tell him I'm an alcoholic and don't drink any more. It's like I've lost this friend too. But man, I stand back and look at these people and look at me. It's like they're standin' still, goin' nowhere, and I'm movin' forward. They're back where I used to be. I'm glad I'm a recovering alcoholic and don't have to do that stuff anymore.

The meaning of recovery for this person is given in the above statements. He connects recovery to the loss of old friends and the gain of new ones. He connects his recovery as an alcoholic to his statements concerning where he is going and where his friends are. Meaning is given in his experiences.

Interpretive Criteria

Interpretive materials are evaluated in terms of the following criteria:

1. Do they illuminate the phenomenon as lived experience?
2. Are they based on thickly contextualized materials?
3. Are they historically and relationally grounded?
4. Are they processual and interactional?

    5. Do they engulf what is known about the phenomenon?
    6. Do they incorporate prior understandings of the phenomenon?
    7. Do they cohere and produce understanding?
    8. Are they unfinished?

Each of these questions requires brief discussion.

Illumination: An interpretation must illuminate or bring alive what is being studied. This can be done only when the interpretation is based on materials that come from the world of lived experience.

Thickly Contextualized Materials: Interpretations are built up out of events and experiences that are described in detail. Thickly contextualized materials are dense. They record experience as it occurs. They locate experience in social situations. They record thoughts, meanings, emotions, and actions. They speak from the subject's point of view.

Historical and Relational: Interpretive materials must also be historical and relational. That is, they must unfold over time, and they must record the significant social relationships that exist between the subjects being studied. Historically, or temporally, the materials must be presented as slices of ongoing interaction. They must also be located within lived history.

Process and Interaction: These two dimensions should be clear. An interpretive account must be processual and interactional. Each of the exemplars that has been discussed above meets these two criteria.

Engulfing: Engulfing involves including all that is known to be relevant about the phenomenon in question. This means that the interpreter must be an "informed reader" of the phenomenon in question. Engulfing expands the framework for interpretation. It attempts to exclude nothing (including anomalies and negative or deviant cases) that would be relevant for the interpretation and understanding that is being formulated. Because understanding and interpretation are temporal processes, what is regarded as important at one point may at a later time be judged not to be central. Interpretation and understanding are always unfinished and incomplete (see below).

Prior Understandings: Engulfing merges with the problem of incorporating prior understanding into the interpretation of a segment of experience. Prior understandings would include background information and knowledge on a subject; concepts, hypotheses, and propositions contained in the research literature; and previously acquired information about the subject and his or her experiences. Nothing can be excluded, including how one judged the phenomenon at the outset of an investigation. This is the case because prior understandings shape what is seen, heard, written about, and interpreted. Hence prior understandings are part of what is interpreted. To exclude them is to risk biasing the interpretation in the direction of false objectivity.

Coherence and Understanding: These two criteria ask if the interpretation produces an understanding of the experience that coalesces into a coherent, meaningful whole. A coherent interpretation includes all relevant information and prior understandings. It is based on materials that are historical, relational, processual, and interactional. A coherent interpretation is based on thickly described materials. The reader is led through the interpretation in a meaningful way. The grounds for the interpretation are given. The reader can then decide whether to agree or disagree with the interpretation that is offered.

Unfinished: All interpretations are unfinished, provisional, and incomplete. They start anew when the researcher returns to the phenomenon. This means that interpretation is always conducted from within the hermeneutic circle. As one comes back to an experience and interprets it, prior interpretations and understanding shape what is now seen and interpreted. This does not mean that interpretation is inconclusive, for conclusions are always drawn. It only means that interpretation is never finished. To think otherwise is to foreclose one's interpretations before one begins. That is, individuals should not start a research project thinking that they will exhaust all that can be known about a phenomenon when they end their project.

CONCLUSIONS

I have discussed the major assumptions of this interpretive approach to research. Pure and applied interpretive research were also discussed. The personal, biographical, critical nature of interpretive interactionism was stressed. The steps and criteria of interpretation were presented. Because the subject matter of interpretive studies is always biographical, the lives of ordinary men and women play a central place in the research texts that are created. It is, after all, their lives and their problems that are studied.

In a certain sense, interpretive studies hope to understand the subject better than the subject understands him- or herself (Dilthey, 1900/1976, pp. 259-260). Often interpretations are formed that subjects would not give of their actions. This is so because the researcher is often in a position to see things the subject cannot see. The full range of factors that play on individuals' experiences is seldom apparent to them. The interpreter, as a critical ethnographer, has access to a picture of the subject's life that the subject often lacks. The interpreter also has a method of interpretation that the subject seldom has (Denzin, 1984, p. 257). However, the interpretations that are developed about a subject's life must be understandable to the subject. If they are not, they are unacceptable.

But investigators are always enjoined to locate within their personal history the problematic biographical experience that is to be studied. Thus is this

interpretive approach defined by its recurring emphasis on personal experience, on caring for others who may have also experienced the same personal
troubles as the researcher.

10

CRITICAL INQUIRY IN QUALITATIVE RESEARCH

FEMINIST AND POSTSTRUCTURAL PERSPECTIVES: SCIENCE "AFTER TRUTH"

Patti Lather

Across the social sciences, unsettlement and contestation permeate discussion of what it means to do inquiry. For much of the 20th century, field-based "paradigms"[1] have been articulated and developed. Rooted in the research traditions of interpretive sociology and anthropology, such alternative practices of social research focus on the overriding importance of meaning-making and context in human experiencing (Mishler, 1979). Over the last two decades, advocacy approaches to research that are openly value based have added their voices to this methodological ferment. For example, "critical ethnography" of education is constructed out of interpretivist anthropology and sociology as well as neo-Marxist and feminist theory (Anderson, 1989). Making an epistemological break with the positivist insistence on objectivity, "openly ideological" research argues that nothing is outside ideology, most certainly the production of social knowledge (Lather, 1986a, 1986b). As the concept of "disinterested knowledge" implodes and collapses inward, social inquiry becomes, in my present favorite definition of science, a much-contested cultural space, a site of the surfacing of what it has historically repressed (Hutcheon, 1988, p. 74).

In terms of my focus in this essay, a "critical social science" is intended to work toward *changing* as well as *understanding* the world (Fay, 1987). What Van Maanen (1988) calls "critical tales" ask questions of power, economy, history, and exploitation. In the words of Poster (1989), "critical theory springs from an assumption that we live amid a world of pain, that much can be done to alleviate that pain, and that theory has a crucial role to play in that process" (p. 3). Doing critical inquiry means taking into account how our lives are mediated by systems of inequity such as classism, racism, sexism, and heterosexism. Of late, such work has been profoundly challenged by postmodernism/poststructuralism/deconstruction.[2] Hence what follows will attempt to note these challenges as well as to delineate the parameters of critical inquiry.

CRITICAL INQUIRY: PARADIGMATIC ASSUMPTIONS

Science is in crisis in both the natural and the social sciences. Quantum physics and chaos science have created a physics very different from the one the social sciences have aspired to in their quest for legitimate scientific status. This questioning of what science is and what role it plays or might play in our lives is within a larger context of what Habermas (1975) terms a "legitimation crisis" in cultural authority.

Hence it is both a dizzying and an exciting time in which to do social inquiry. It is a time of openness and questioning of established paradigms in intellectual thought. At some level, we're moving out of the cultural values spawned by the Age of Reason, the scientific revolution of the 16th and 17th centuries, and the Enlightenment and its material base, the Industrial Revolution. We're well into an age of late capitalism in which knowledge is increasingly configured in electronic language in a way that deeply affects our relation to the world (Poster, 1990). Furthermore, the profound effect that electronic mediation exerts on the way we perceive ourselves and reality is occurring in a world marked by gross maldistribution of power and resources.

Within such a context, the orthodox consensus about what it means to do science has been displaced. A proliferation of contending paradigms is causing some diffusion of legitimacy and authority. This situation is often characterized by the term *postpositivism*. This term refers not to the loss of positivism but rather to the end of its claim to being the only way of doing science. Within postpositivism, paradigms of disclosure are vying for attention with paradigms of prediction/prescription, and advocacy paradigms are competing with "neutral" paradigms. In the postpositivist paradigm chart in Table 10.1, I have added deconstruction to Habermas' (1971b) thesis of the three categories of human interest that underscore knowledge claims: prediction, understanding, and emancipation.[3] This chart is but one way to present the proliferation of paradigms that so characterizes contemporary social science. Like any conceptual map, it has many problems. For example,

TABLE 10.1 Postpositivist Paradigms of Inquiry

Prediction	*Understanding*	*Emancipation*	*Deconstruction*
positivist	interpretive	critical	poststructural
	naturalistic	neo-Marxist	postmodern
	constructivist	feminist	postparadigmatic
	phenomenological	race-specific	diaspora
	hermeneutic	praxis-oriented	
	symbolic interactionist	Freirean	
	microethnographic	participatory	

NOTE: *Diaspora*, as used by Jewish and African-American historians, refers to the forced relocation of people from out of their homelands. Caputo's (1987) "post-paradigmatic diaspora," then, refers to the proliferation of frameworks for understanding contemporary social inquiry as well as to the incommensurability of these frameworks. The contesting discourses about inquiry force a researcher both to relocate away from secure, "one best way" approaches and to negotiate the resources of different inquiry problematics.

feminist work goes on across the paradigms. Despite such problems, such a chart helps to distinguish how each paradigm offers a different but not necessarily exclusive approach to generating and legitimating knowledge. I, for example, place my work in the emancipatory column with great fascination for the implications of deconstruction.

Positivism is not dead, as anyone knows who tries to get published in most journals, obtain grants from most funding agencies, or have research projects accepted by thesis and dissertation committees. What is dead, however, is its theoretic dominance and its "one best way" claims over empirical work in the human sciences. Philosophy and history of science, sociology of knowledge, the various voices of marginalized people, and developments in physics have combined to make positivism's dominance increasingly shaky. *Postpositivism,* then, refers to the great ferment over what is seen as appropriate within the boundaries of the human sciences. Postpositivist philosophies of science turn more and more to interpretive social theory, where the focus is on *constructed* versus *found* worlds in a way that increasingly focuses on the role of language in the construction of knowledge (Rorty, 1967).

In sum, there are many ways to do science. Positivism, with its claims of methodological objectivity and mathematized procedures, is one way. Critical inquiry, with its belief that there is no transhistorical, culture-free, disinterested way of knowing, is another way. Foregrounding the politics of knowing and being known, examples of critical inquiry are especially visible in the fields of anthropology, qualitative sociology, semiotics, and poststructural linguistic theory as well as the transdisciplinary fields of feminist and cultural/communication studies (e.g., Clifford & Marcus, 1986; Fine, 1992; Grossberg, Nelson, & Treichler, 1992). In the rest of this essay, I position critical inquiry methodologically within the "uneasy social sciences" in what is generally referred to as "the postpositivist intellectual climate of our times" (Fiske & Shweder, 1986, p. 16). My particular focus is the challenge post-structuralism offers to the development of critical approaches to empirical research in the social sciences.

CRITICAL INQUIRY: METHODOLOGICAL ASSUMPTIONS

Critical inquiry views both method—techniques for gathering empirical evidence—and methodology—the theory of knowledge and the interpretive framework that guide a particular research project—as inescapably tied to issues of power. Methods are assumed to be politically charged "as they define, control, evaluate, manipulate and report" (Gouldner, 1970, p. 50). The point of the above is that "the role of ideology does not diminish as rigor increases and error is dissipated" (LeCourt, 1975, p. 200). Such a recognition of the pervasiveness of ideology provides the grounds for an openly value-based approach to critical inquiry. The central issue is how to bring scholar-ship and advocacy together in order to generate ways of knowing that interrupt power imbalances.

Oriented toward the interests of marginalized social groups, an emancipa-tory, critical social science develops out of the social relations of the research process itself, out of the enactment of research praxis that uses intellectual effort to work toward a more just society. Given poststructuralism's warnings that nothing is innocent, including intellectuals with change aspirations, Foucauldian (Foucault, 1980) questions come to the fore: How do practices to discover the "truth" about ourselves influence our lives? How can we learn to track the play of power across intendedly "liberatory" approaches to inquiry? What would it mean "to grow up in our attitudes toward science" (Fine, 1986, p. 2) in an era characterized by the loss of certainties and absolute frames of reference?

To explore such questions, I first sketch the characteristics of critical research designs and then call on a handful of exemplars [4] to flesh out those characteristics. I deliberately use feminist work in order to situate it as a fertile site for the generation of new research methods that take into account the growing lack of confidence on the part of social scientists regarding ways of portraying a world marked by the elusiveness with which it greets our efforts to know it.[5] This lack of confidence in the taken-for-granted patterns of Western science is often coded with the term *the crisis of representation,* and it has profound implications for rethinking the practices of the social sciences (e.g., Rosenau, 1992; Van Maanen, 1988).

CHARACTERISTICS OF CRITICAL RESEARCH DESIGNS:
FEMINIST POSTSTRUCTURAL EXEMPLARS

Critical research designs are characterized by the following: (a) they explore more interactive, dialogic, and reciprocal research methods that work toward transformative action and egalitarian participation; (b) they connect meaning to broader structures of social power, control, and history; (c) they work toward open, flexible theory building grounded in both confrontation with and respect for the experiences of people in their daily lives and profound skepticism regarding appearances and "common sense." Finally, given poststructuralism's cautions regarding the researcher as "The Great Liberator" (Foucault, 1980), (d) they foreground the tensions involved in speaking *with* rather than *to/for* marginalized groups. Rather than speaking *to* or *for* those struggling for social justice, the goal is to proceed in a mutually educative way that works against the central danger to praxis-oriented empirical work: "emancipating" people in a way that imposes a researcher's agenda. The following exemplars both embody and problematize this listing as they explore the implications of the critical paradigm. I begin with an example from medical anthropology and then turn to feminist poststructural inquiry.

Nancy Scheper-Hughes (1992), in *Death Without Weeping: The Violence of Everyday Life in Brazil*, presents an ethnographic portrayal of mothers, children, and child mortality among the poor in a Brazilian shantytown. Drawing on extensive fieldwork into people's daily lives, Scheper-Hughes works within the framework of critical medical anthropology to challenge standard biomedical and social definitions, particularly the Western notion of maternal love. As infant mortality among the poor is related to larger political and economic forces, distinctions between official diagnostic definitions of disease and illness and patients' experience of them are positioned as cultural constructions and probed for whose interests they serve. Returning to give the shantytown residents copies of her book, she speaks of becoming involved in the lives of those she has studied: "They become closer to us [anthropological fieldworkers], more intimate to us sometimes, than sisters and brothers" (Scheper-Hughes, cited in Coughlin, 1992, p. A9). Exploring how the political and medical establishments have transformed the social problem of hunger into medical problems in ways that serve class interests, this example of critical medical anthropology demonstrates how critical ethnography connects meaning to broader structures of social power. As critical ethnography, it works to build theory in a way that is grounded in respect for disenfranchised people's everyday lives.

A first example of feminist critical work that takes the crisis of representation into account is Richardson's (1992) essay about her interview with

"Louisa May" as part of her study of unmarried mothers. "Consciously self-revelatory" in probing the lived experience of the researcher (p. 125), Richardson cheekily hopes that she has not "ventured beyond Improper" as she "breache[s] sociological writing expectations by writing sociology as poetry" (p. 126). First presenting "a transcript masquerading as a poem/a poem masquerading as a transcript" (p. 127), her primary goal is "to create a position for experiencing the self as a sociological knower/constructor—not just talking about it, but doing it" (p. 136). Speaking autobiographically in order to provide "an opportunity to rethink sociological representation" (p. 133), Richardson evokes her need to break out of the "dreary" writing of "'straight' sociological prose" (p. 131) as the part of her that has written poetry for 8 years is called on to provide new writing strategies.

Richardson concludes with five consequences to herself of the experience of producing and disseminating the story of "Louisa May." We hear about changed relations with children; spirituality; Richardson's integration of "the suppressed 'poet' and the overactive 'sociologist'" (p. 135), including her return of the advance from the book contract because she is no longer able to write conventional sociology; her increased attunement to differences in others and herself, including more caution "about what 'doing research' means" (p. 135); and, finally, some disillusionment at "the hold of positivism on even those I consider my allies" as she has presented this work (p. 135). "I experience isolation, alienation, and freedom, exhilaration. I want to record what they are saying; I want to do fieldwork on them. Science them" (p. 136). Her "feminist mission . . . intensified," she positions herself as "a sociological revolutionist in community with others who are questioning how and for whom we write sociology" (p. 136).

I deliberately use this most scandalous exemplar first. Presenting the interview data from one single mother as a poem, Richardson blurs the lines between the genres of poetry and social science reporting. As theories out of autobiography, her practice collapses the private/public distinction. Richardson is mother, wife, scholar, and poet in her desire to move toward some way of doing science more in keeping with her feminist poststructuralism. Bringing ethics and epistemology together, Richardson's authority comes from engagement and reflexivity rather than some canonical "objectivity." Her practices of textual representation, by hegemonic standards, "go too far" with the politics of uncertainty, self-conscious partiality, and embodied knowing.

A second example of feminist poststructural work is a recent dissertation on African-American women and leadership positions in higher education (Woodbrooks, 1991). Woodbrooks's study was "designed to generate more interactive and contextual ways of knowing" (p. 93), with a particular focus on openness to counter-interpretations: "The overarching goal of the methodology is to present a series of fruitful interruptions that demonstrate the multiplicity of meaning-making and interpretation" (p. 94).

In analyzing interview data, Woodbrooks made extensive use of two familiar qualitative practices of validity: member checks and peer debriefing (Lincoln & Guba, 1985). Using both to purposefully locate herself in the contradictory borderland between feminist emancipatory and poststructural positions, she attempted to interrupt her role as the Great Interpreter, "to shake, disrupt, and shift" her feminist critical investments (Woodbrooks, 1991, p. 103). Peer debriefing and member checks were used to critique her initial analysis of the data, her "perceptions of some broadly defined themes that emerged as I coded the transcripts" (Woodbrooks, 1991, p. 132). After reanalyzing the data and her original analysis, Woodbrooks sent a second draft out to participants and phoned for responses. This resulted in a textual strategy that juxtaposed the voices of the white female researcher with those of the African-American female participants.

In her textual strategy, Woodbrooks first tells "a realist tale" (Van Maanen, 1988) that backgrounds the researcher's shaping influence and foregrounds participant voices. Here the voices of the women she interviewed are presented, organized around the emergent themes of assertiveness, cultural diversity, identity construction, and the double jeopardy for women of color. Each "realist tale" is interrupted with "a critical tale" that reads the data according to Woodbrooks' theoretical investments. Here Woodbrooks uses feminist and critical theory to "say what things mean" as she theorizes out of the words of the African-American women research participants presented in the realist tale. Finally, in a third-person voice, she tells "a deconstructive tale" that draws on participant reactions to the critical tale. Here, she probes her own desire, "suspicious of . . . the hegemony [of] feminism" (p. 140) in her analysis. Her feminist analysis marginalized both African-American identity as a source of pride and strength (ascribing it totally to gender) and participant concerns with male/female relations. "This strategy [of feminist consciousness-raising] perpetuates feminism as a white middle class project and trivializes the deep emotional ties that black women share with black men" (p. 200). In sum, holding up to scrutiny her own complicity, Woodbrooks creates a research design that moves her toward unlearning her own privilege and decentering the researcher as the master of truth and justice via her expanded use of the familiar techniques of member checks and peer debriefing.

A third example of feminist poststructural work is that of an Australian dissertation student, Erica Lenore McWilliam. In a study of how students talk about their needs in preservice teacher education, McWilliam (1992a, 1992b) developed a research design that elaborated three research moments. First, researcher preconceptions were put under scrutiny by analyzing survey data from 314 preservice teachers that examined their attitudes toward New Right discourse and conducting a discourse analysis of avant-garde literature in teacher education. This initial reflexive phase was designed to allow contradictory evidence to inform the researcher's growing complexity of thought about the issues at hand, particularly to challenge her own preconceptions about the researcher's role as "transformative intellectual" come to "save" the oppressed that is too typical of critical, emancipatory research (Lather, 1991).

Second, a qualitative phase was designed that proceeded "from a new set of social relations in which the dominance of the researcher's 'versions' of student needs is already challenged" (McWilliam, 1992a, p. 11). This phase studied preservice teacher understandings of theory and practice over time by using interactive, dialogic interviews that situated preservice talk about needs "as fluid social phenomena . . . open to change over the duration of the pre-service course" (1992a, p. 12). A third and final reciprocal phase was designed as reflection in action. Moving toward practices of cotheorizing that created conditions for both researcher and researched to rethink their attitudes and practices, McWilliam performed multiple readings of the Phase 2 data in order to fragment researcher authority over data analysis. Of note is McWilliam's learning that research practices that interrupt researcher privilege must construct "an interrogative researcher text . . . a questioning text" that overtly "signals tentativeness and partiality" (1992b, p. 271).

Each stage paid particular attention to discrepant data, the facts unfit to fit tidy categorical schemes. Ranging across rather standard attitudinal surveys, dialogic, reciprocally self-disclosive interviews, and sustained interaction, McWilliam works to decenter both her own expertise and the participants' common sense about teaching practices. Her "double-edged analysis" (1992b, p. 30) uses feminist, critical, and poststructural theories to problematize one another. Remarking on the "untidiness" of "this straddling of agendas" (1992b, p. 91), she delineates the "state of tension" (1992b, p. 257) that exists between feminism and unproblematic siding with or against Enlightenment projects of social transformation via consciousness raising. As such, her work enacts what it means to let contradictions remain in tension, to unsettle from within and to position "facts" as a "discourse of the real." Dissolving interpretations by marking them as temporary, partial, and invested, she continues her paradoxical continuing investment in transformative praxis.

Like Woodbrooks, McWilliam is particularly noteworthy for attending to the creation of interactive social relations in which both researcher and researched can rethink their attitudes and practices, rather than focusing exclusively on textual strategies. In exclusively textual strategies, questions such as "Who is speaking to/for/with whom, for what reasons and with what resources?" are displaced by "What is the object of my analysis? How have I constructed it? What are the conventions of disciplinary practice that I seek to put under erasure?" As Whitford (1991) notes in her book on Irigaray, "Playing with a text . . . is a rather solipsistic activity; it is not a dialogue with the other which includes process and the possibility of change" (p. 48). It is one thing to ask whether new voices are being heard and quite another to ask whether voices are hearing themselves and one another fruitfully.

My final exemplar of feminist critical work that gestures toward the problematics of representation is my beginning study of women living with HIV/AIDS (Lather, 1992). A Lyotardian (Lyotard, 1984) "small narrative," the following questions based on the early phases of my inquiry offer a specific pragmatic context for fashioning a field of possibilities for practices toward a *reflexive* science.

Following Foucault, I ask myself: Am I telling stories that are not mine? Do research participants become narrators of their own stories? On the other hand, if I as the researcher tell the stories, do I work to not see so easily in telling the stories that belong to others? Do I try hard to understand less, to be nudged out of positions customarily occupied when viewing "the Other" (Brown, 1992)?

In terms of researcher/researched relations, who are my "others"? What dualisms structure my arguments? What hierarchies are at play? How can I use Irigaray's concept of the "We-you/I" to disrupt such oppositions, to create a constantly moving speaking position that fixes neither subject nor object, that disrupts the set boundaries between subjects (Game, 1991, p. 88)?

What does all of this have to do with we/they positionings? For example, what does my getting tested for HIV mean within this context? I am considering when to do this: now? at the end? midway through writing? There is a methodological interest here. Is this instrumental? exploitative? What does it mean to position these women and this project as a Gramscian (Gramsci, 1971) historical laboratory in which to explore a science marked by practices of productive ambiguity that cultivate a taste for complexity?

In terms of the role of the researcher: how do I struggle with the task of an I becoming an *eye* without the anxiety of voyeurism that entangles the researcher in an ever more detailed self-analysis (Quinby, 1991)? What are my practices of self-reflexivity? Do I as researcher address the inadequacies of language, or do I position myself as telling a "real" story with a "final" say? Do I use disruptive devices in the text to unsettle conventional notions of the real?

What is my goal as a researcher: empathy? emancipation? advocacy? learning from/working with? What is the romance of the desire for research as political intervention? What would it mean to "come clean" about my methodology? How is this work tied into what Van Maanen (1988) refers to as the by no means trivial "demands of contemporary academic careers" and disciplinary logics (p. 53)? What is this fierce interest in proving the relevance of intellectual work? To what extent is my work tied to "the pretensions of sociology toward politics" (Riley, 1988, p. 54)?

Situated so as to give testimony and witness to what is happening to these women with HIV/AIDS, I have the methodological desire to probe the instructive complications of this study. As I learn how these women make sense of their experiences, my hope is to generate a theory of situated methodology that will lead me to a place where I do *not* conclude that "I will never do research this way again."[6]

Offered as more problem than solution, the exemplars I have recruited as provocateurs of critical inquiry after poststructuralism are performances that work from spaces already in the making. Situated in the crisis of authority that has occurred across knowledge systems, I face the challenge of making productive use of the dilemma of being left to work from traditions of research that appear no longer adequate to the task. Between the no-longer and the not-yet lies the possibility of what was impossible under traditional regimes of truth in the social sciences: the "micro-becomings" of a science defined by a dispersal, circulation, and proliferation of becomings (Deleuze & Guattari, 1983, p. 70). My intent has been not to make a general recipe but to forge from a scattered testimony a methodology that is not so much prescription as "curves of visibility and enunciation" (Deleuze, 1992, p. 160). An experiment "that baffle[s] expectations, trace[s] active lines of flight, seek[s] out lines that are bunching, accelerating or decreasing in speed" (Deleuze & Guattari, 1983, p. 111), it evokes the "horizons toward which experiments work" (Ormiston, 1990, p. 239) as we try to understand what is at play in our practices of constructing a science "after truth."

CONCLUSIONS

> Post-modernism involves the development of new rhetorics of science, new stories of knowledge "after truth." . . . The postmodern world is without guarantees, without "method.". . . All we can do is invent. We must construct and exemplify the rhetorics of the future . . . through . . . endless stories. Like this one. (Tomlinson, 1990, pp. 44, 57)

In this chapter I have probed the challenges of "the postmodern moment" to explore how critical and feminist research is reinscribing qualitative inquiry. The role of feminist critical work in reinventing the social sciences is both cause and effect of the larger crisis of authority in late 20th-century thought. Awareness of the complexity, contingency, and fragility of the practices we invent to discover the truth about ourselves can be paralyzing. Taking into account Martin Luther King's caution regarding paralysis of analysis, reflexively getting on with doing such work may be the most fruitful action we can take.

NOTES

1. I put "paradigm" in scare quotes because of the deconstructive argument that we are in a "postparadigmatic" era (Caputo, 1987).

2. Although I am suspicious of the desire for definitions that analytically "fix" complex, contradictory, and relational constructs, I generally use the term *postmodern* to mean the shift in material conditions of late 20th-century monopoly capitalism brought on by the micro-electronic revolution in information technology, the fissures of a global, multinational hypercapitalism, and the global uprising of the marginalized. This conjunction includes movements in art, architecture, and the practices of everyday life (e.g., MTV). The code name for the crisis of confidence in Western conceptual systems, postmodernism is born out of our sense of the limits of Enlightenment rationality. All of this creates a conjunction that shifts our sense of who we are and what is possible in the name of science (Lather, 1991, 1993; Rosenau, 1992).

I generally use *poststructural* to mean the working out of academic theory within the culture of postmodernism, but I also sometimes use the terms interchangeably. Structuralism is premised on efforts to scientize language, to posit it as systematizable. Poststructuralism's focus is on the remainder, all that is left over after the systematic categorizations have been made (Lecercle, 1990). For such French poststructuralists as Barthes, Derrida, Foucault, and Lacan, structuralism's basic thesis of the universal and unconscious laws of human society and of the human mind was part of the bureaucratic and technocratic systems that they opposed. Their interest was in the "gaps, discontinuities and suspensions of dictated meanings in which difference, plurality, multiplicity and the coexistence of opposites are allowed free play" (Bannet, 1989, p. 5).

The goal of *deconstruction* is to keep things in process, to disrupt, to keep the system in play, to set up procedures to continuously demystify "the real," to fight the tendency for categories to congeal. Deconstruction foregrounds the lack of innocence in any discourse by looking at the textual staging of knowledge, the constitutive effects of the use of language. Though impossible to freeze conceptually, deconstruction can be broken down into three steps: (a) identify the binaries, the oppositions that structure an argument; (b) reverse/displace the dependent term from its negative position to a place that locates it as the very condition of the positive term; and (c) create a more fluid and less coercive conceptual organization of terms that transcends a binary logic by simultaneously being both and neither of the binary terms (Grosz, 1989, p. xv). This somewhat linear definition is deliberately placed in the endnotes in order to displace the desire to domesticate deconstruction as it moves across the many sites of its occurrence, such as the academy, architecture, and the arts.

3. Habermas would not approve of my addition of the column of "deconstruct," given his worries about postmodernity. In essence, Habermas identifies postmodernism with neoconservativism and argues that the Enlightenment project is not failed, only unfinished. His polemical defense of universalism and rationality is positioned explicitly against what he sees as the "nihilism" of Foucault and Derrida and, implicitly, against Lyotard's challenge to the "great ideological fairy tales" that fuel Habermas' praxis of universal values and rational consensus (Calinescu, 1987, p. 274). For his own statements, see Habermas (1987).

4. I use the term *exemplar* to mean not a cookbook recipe to follow or an instance of "the best of," but as a concrete illustration of a number of abstract qualities. Exemplars are not used in the Kuhnian sense of paradigmatic cases that dominate a research community's sense of both normal and revolutionary science. To the contrary, my exemplars are a quite idiosyncratic selection from the not-yet-published work of friends and dissertation students with which I happen to be familiar. Like Mishler (1990), I offer them as resources, "springboards" (p. 422).

5. Kroker and Cook state: "*Feminism is the quantum physics of postmodernism* " (1986, p. 22, original emphasis). Quantum physics opened up a world otherwise than Newtonian linearity, subject-object duality, and universal covering laws. Hence I read Kroker and Cook as situating late 20th-century feminism as the paradigmatic political discourse of postmodernism. For more on this, see Lather (1991, chap. 2).

6. This sentiment comes directly out of my experience of presenting a talk on my research project to a small gathering of women at the research conference of our dreams in Wisconsin, August 7-8, 1992. It is also spurred by Paul Marienthal's (1992) dissertation experience with "participatory research," from which he concluded that "I will never do research this way again" when his use of "member checks" blew up in his face, causing great consternation on the part of everyone involved in the inquiry.

II

Staking out the Territory: Perspectives on Provider Behavior Research

Many different disciplinary perspectives define any research problem area. Research in any one discipline or subdiscipline is often conducted independently of others working in the same problem area. These are what we call the conversations behind the many walls. To take advantage of these many conversations, it is necessary to create a space for a larger integrated conversation.

The first step in opening the space for this larger conversation is to identify the many voices that should be participating. A major component of identification is a comprehensive literature search that includes both the scholarly literature and the public media. One of the traps of doing such a search is the feeling of security one gets from relying on computerized searches; these are only as comprehensive as the databases they search and can easily miss important areas. For example, those working in medical settings often fail to adequately search the social science databases (and literature), a major problem for some important topics such as access to care, health-seeking behaviors, and so forth. In addition, books such as this would not appear in a Medline search.

In deciding who to invite to the conference, we began with a summary article by Schwartz and Cohen (1990) that overviewed the current approaches to changing provider behavior in primary health care. From this summary it was immediately apparent that an *economic perspective* was extremely important

(Eisenberg, 1986; Hillman, Pauly, & Kerstein, 1989). Schwartz and Cohen also identified the work of Greenfield, Kaplan, and others on empowering patients or *patient perspective* (Greenfield, Kaplan, & Ware, 1985b; Greenfield et al., 1988; Kaplan & Ware, 1989). Schwartz also made it apparent that the federal government and funding agencies had an acute interest in research on this area, indicating that we needed a *federal government perspective*. The direct concern of the federal government is also illustrated by the tremendous efforts that the Agency for Health Care Policy and Research has put into guidelines research (Clinton, 1990; Gray, 1992).

We were also aware of the work of Richard Frankel (Beckman, Frankel, & Darnly, 1985; Frankel & Beckman, 1989), who, along with others (e.g., Inui & Carter, 1988; Roter, 1977; Steele, Jackson, & Guttman, 1990), had been investigating the *clinical process* using audio and video tapes of clinical encounters. We were also aware of the work of Jeffrey Borkan (Borkan, Quirk, & Sullivan, 1991), who had been investigating specific health problems (e.g., lower back pain, hip fractures) using a more anthropological approach in what could be referred to as a *health problem perspective*. Finally, to balance the patient perspective, and because the focus was on providers, a sixth area was included, the *provider perspective*.

These six perspectives were represented at the conference by important leaders in the field: Louis Rossiter (economics); Sherrie Kaplan (patient); Carolyn Clancy (federal government); Richard Frankel (clinical process); Jeffrey Borkan (health problem); and Robert Pantell (provider). Because of the overlap in the content of the patient perspective and the health problem perspective, these two areas were combined in this volume into a single chapter that overviews both.

Representation of the public was also felt to be a critical perspective not included in any of the above. To this end, Kate Brown organized our "public voice discussion group" at the conference and wrote a chapter on the issues engendered by including public representation in research endeavors.

The six chapters in Part II represent areas or perspectives that the editors thought essential in thinking of cross-disciplinary research on "provider behavior." Even though some of the chapters cover common ground, we found additional questions worthy of consideration arose from each.

As we review the complexities of the *problem voice* (Chapter 11) and the ambiguity of primary care concerns, it seems that more effort on better understanding the context of different problems would be helpful. In addition, what influences does the power differential between patient and professional cultures have on how problems are defined? Do the distinctions between and among sickness, illness, and disease have part of this voice? How are these related to the International Classification of Primary Care (ICPC)?

The *physician voice* (Chapter 12) is only one of many provider voices. What about other providers? Physicians are said to be unhappy with their role: what does that mean? Much of primary care practice requires a local perspective; private practice is in fact a cottage industry. There are key questions regarding provider behavior change that remain. Is office flow disrupted? We might look to the disciplines of organizational development, management, or nursing to address this question. Is the patient satisfied with the care and the provider? Here we might look to clinical psychology. Is income maintained or increased? Here finance or management might be helpful areas.

With the *encounter voice* (Chapter 13), questions such as "What are different diagnostic strategies?" and "What are different encounter models?" still seem to be ripe for clarification. Although there has been little work in this area from the physician perspective, nursing research has focused considerable effort on different models of care that could be represented.

The *health economy voice* (Chapter 14) has been widely heard in "changing provider behavior" research; however, is there a need for new theory integrating macro/micro perspectives?

The *government policy voice* (Chapter 15) is central in funding provider behavior research. This voice is an amalgamation of many voices. Has the government policy voice sufficiently checked its own assumptions about what research questions and approaches are relevant? What about participatory research approaches (i.e., Balint seminars, action research, critical research)?

Finally, the *public voice* (Chapter 16) in research is reviewed. The public is critical for the ultimate success or failure of change in public health and provides the ultimate measure of the success or failure of primary care research.

As cross-disciplinary research develops, a large number of questions remain that will ultimately affect the success of research. The chapters in Part II summarize how researchers have conceptualized many of these questions and provide provocative insights into what questions they see as remaining unresolved. These chapters also afford an opportunity to see how collaborative research might offer new insights.

11

CHANGING HEALTH PROVIDER BEHAVIOR

Jeffrey Borkan

> With the biomedical model successfully bolstered by the dualism of Descartes, the reductionism of Newton and the automotive culture of General Motors, change is held to be unnecessary by most and impossible by a few. (White, 1988, p. 50)

This chapter provides an overview of changing provider behavior, giving particular attention to patient issues and health-related problems. Information was collected through literature review, research, and interviews with "key informants," authorities with special knowledge of the field. *Provider* connotes a health care practitioner involved in the direct delivery of health services, including both diagnostic and treatment modalities, particularly the legal right to prescribe drugs and materials. Currently in the United States this includes physicians, osteopaths, podiatrists, and, in some states, nurse practitioners and chiropractors. Much of the discussion here focuses on physicians, however, because of the weighting of research and publication toward this group and the authors' greater familiarity with this literature. Limited extrapolation can be made to other providers because, for instance, the office-based care that nurse practitioners provide has been shown to be indistinguishable from physician care (Sox, 1979).

CHANGING PROVIDER BEHAVIOR: AN OVERVIEW

Provider behavior affects the lives, health, and well-being of the world's population. Gaining insight into this phenomenon is important because physician decisions are responsible for over 80% of medical care costs (Harris,

1990), with other health care providers accounting for additional expenditures. Practitioners' conduct in the realm of healing is determined by a myriad of interconnected micro and macro factors. The understanding of provider actions draws on multiple disciplines with an extensive body of research, from psychology and medical decision making to management and economics, sociology, anthropology, nursing, and public health.

By all accounts, changing provider behavior is not a simple task (Harris, 1990; Schwartz & Cohen, 1990; White, 1988). In the recent past, priority has been focused on improving provider, particularly physician, decision making (Schwartz & Cohen, 1990). This emphasis places physicians at the locus of the behavioral equation and accentuates the importance of rationality and cognitive factors such as knowledge, information, and judgment. Interventions are naturally weighted toward education, as well as improving motivation. Such approaches have been shown to be insufficient for achieving change, however (Eisenberg, 1985, 1986; Schwartz & Cohen, 1990; Soumerai & Avorn, 1990). Protocols, guidelines, and consensus panel reports do not alter practices, whether in the treatment of breast cancer or cesarean section (Kosecoff et al., 1987). Even where there is relatively uniform dissemination of medical information, as between European countries and between counties in a single American state, dramatic variations in diagnostic categories and practice patterns exist (Chassin et al., 1986; Payer, 1988; Wennberg & Gittelson, 1973). Low blood pressure is a treated ailment in West Germany but a health advantage in the United States (Payer, 1988). Tonsillectomies vary between regions in Vermont, with a probability that a child will have his or her tonsils removed by age 20 ranging from 16 to 66% depending on the area (Wennberg & Gittelson, 1973).

What influences the ease or difficulty of changing providers' actions? Does the choice of medical treatments depend more on folklore and habit than on scientific evidence? To change behavior, one must take into account both cognitive factors and motivations and aspects of physicians' culture that serve as deterrents to change. One of the few anthropological studies of physician decision making (Katz, 1985) showed that real world choices have as much or more to do with professional "turf," passing responsibility, and money as they do with biomedical theory. One must also understand that provider behavior is not monolithic and that different factors may operate in different cases.

Unfortunately, few consistently effective strategies other than economic incentives have been identified to change physician practice (Lomas et al., 1991). Creative combinations of methods may be needed to induce change, including education, administrative changes, incentives (both rewards and penalties), feedback, and physician participation (Eisenberg, 1986; Eisenberg

& Williams, 1981; Schwartz & Cohen, 1990; Soumerai & Avorn, 1990). Methods may vary, from continuing medical education to financial bonuses, but continuous quality improvement (Kritchevsky & Simmons, 1991) is a goal toward which to aspire.

Additional difficulties exist when trying to formulate plans for behavior change in primary care. Chief among these are problems with the sources of the data: medical research and education often take place in tertiary care sites dominated by subspecialists. In such settings, not only are the questions and the populations different, but the actual diseases may be dissimilar, whether back pain or depression. In addition, there may be deficits in the language used for discussing the problems, with diagnostic bracketing that "lumps and sorts" in ways that do not reflect lived experience (for instance, using "acute" and "chronic" pain labels for all pain experiences). Categorization may be incomplete and differentiating syndromes difficult. Information about practice patterns, practitioners, and their motivations may be lacking.

A PRACTICE ECOLOGY METAPHOR
FOR CHANGING PROVIDER BEHAVIOR

An alternative model for changing provider behavior has arisen that is based on a *practice ecology metaphor* (Schwartz & Cohen, 1990). This is a contextual framework that highlights the micro and macro administrative and organizational levels at which the provider operates. Bias can be introduced from any of the multiple elements: from *society*, the *health care industry*, the *medical profession*, and from the *provider* to the *patient* and the *medical problem*. Each needs to be examined, from the influence of financial remuneration to the influence of patients' expectations and professional etiquette. Naturally there is an assumption of a dynamic interaction between determinants, as well as a realization that other issues may play a role. Chapter 12 will cover provider behavior more fully from the physician perspective, Chapter 13 will focus on the clinical process, and Chapters 14 and 15 will look at the effects of the health economy, political forces, and health care industry. After a brief overview of these perspectives, the remainder of this chapter will focus on the patient and problem perspectives.

Community and Society

The community and society in which the patient and provider coexist are the arbitrators of behavior change because health and illness are ultimately "socially constructed." The community and the society contribute to defining everything from disease categories and the manner and method of diagnosis and treatment to who will be healer and who will be patient. Changes in the health care profession generally follow shifts in the larger society. For instance, homosexuality became a Western disease classification in line with church doctrine, only to be excluded in the 1970s and 1980s from the psychiatric diagnostic domain by social pressure. The growth of medical specialties in the 1950s and 1960s corresponded with the post-Sputnik emphasis on technology, and the inclusion of women in non-nursing medical roles was furthered by the feminist movement of the 1970s and 1980s. Birthing centers arose during the same period as an answer to women's dissatisfaction with traditional labor wards.

Society has broad regulatory and licensing functions and can dramatically influence behavior with the stroke of a pen. Such was the case with the so-called Gag Laws of the Bush era, which altered physician-patient discussions of abortion, only to be reversed by another signature in 1993. Similarly, the Clinton health reforms are expected to introduce dramatic changes in the practice patterns of the 1990s.

The Health Care Industry and the Medical Profession

The next ecological level, that of the health care industry and the medical profession, includes everything from the individual provider practices and professional organizations to the "medical-industrial complex," the amalgamation of health-care-related industries and institutions such as pharmaceutical companies and research centers.

On the American scene, several factors interact to favor innovations that increase utilization, particularly those involving new drugs and procedures. These include an aggressive medical culture focused on a narrow technological and biomedical concept of medical science (Eisenberg et al., 1990), physicians' intolerance of uncertainty, and a fee-for-service system that encourages the growth of reimbursable services (Epstein, Begg, & McNeil, 1986; Franks, Clancy, & Nutting, 1992). For instance, the disproportionate rewards that medical procedures receive compared to cognitive skills (Hsiao et al., 1988) have encouraged medical graduates to enter procedurally based specialties and health care providers to introduce reimbursable procedures into their practices whenever possible. Ownership of facilities has also been shown to play a role in medical decision making. Patients referred to for-profit facilities were more likely to be dialyzed than their counterparts at nonprofit or public institutions (Schlesinger, Cleary, & Blumenthal, 1989). Higher rates of referral have been found to occur if the physician has an economic stake in the referral institution (Mitchell & Sunshine, 1992; Swedlow, Johnson, Smithline,

& Milstein, 1992). The few studies looking at the impact of economic *dis*incentives on physician behavior seem to agree that such actions have little effect. For example, the quality or quantity of care is not influenced by the risk of withholding physician remuneration when the physician is the gate-keeper (Franks et al., 1992; Hillman, Pauly, & Kerstein, 1989).

Drug companies have worked to perfect their ability to influence provider behavior in connection with medication choices. Their methods range from direct advertising to "detail men" and postmarketing clinical trials (Phase 4 studies) that promote the introduction of new drugs in exchange for complimentary fees. All of these can lead to inappropriate prescribing behavior (Soumerai, McLaughlin, & Avorn, 1989).

The medical profession actively encourages behavior change through such functions as regulation, certification, guideline formation, and education. Though not always successful, these efforts can make a difference. For instance, the use of sodium bicarbonate decreased rapidly in cardiopulmonary resuscitation after Advanced Cardiac Life Support recertification was required every 2 years. Active antismoking campaigns by groups from the American Cancer Association and the American Association of Family Practice have induced physicians to stop smoking and to include antismoking education and interventions in their practices.

Physicians, osteopaths, podiatrists, and chiropractors have patterns of organization that vary from small cottage industries, such as solo or small group practices, to corporate-style health maintenance organizations (HMOs). Nurse practitioners, often labeled "ancillary medical personnel," may themselves be organized into independent practices or operate as solo practitioners. Little is known, however, about how these environments affect behavior change.

The Provider

Provider factors influence behavior change, from personality issues to those of education and professionalization. Practitioner competence, knowledge, and experience with a particular disease state or diagnostic procedure can lead to higher rates of referral and test utilization. Just supplying guidelines or information is not enough, however. Certain aspects of providers' culture act as deterrents to changing behavior, whether in response to new insights from clinical trials or scientific breakthroughs. These include the following.

General Acceptance of Standards of Care

Although practices may not be based on more than empiricism or tradition, they can become incorporated into "standards of care" and resist change.

Factors such as "professional turf" can exacerbate these tendencies, and new technologies or insights may not be accepted if they require shifting patients to other types of specialists or practitioners. Examples of such conflicts include coronary artery bypass surgery versus angioplasty, gallstone lithotripsy as opposed to cholecystectomy, and orthopedic care versus chiropractic manipulation.

Reverence for tradition and autonomy rather than science may deter behavior change. Physicians and other health care providers often listen to their colleagues about the use of a drug or procedure, following the local medical gospel or the "teaching of the elders" rather than searching the scientific literature (Spodick, 1982). Part of this originates in the social organization of medicine, whereby experience, tradition, and the opinion of one's peers are highly valued. Responsibility also lies with medical providers' perception of themselves as a "free profession," as independent actors, the small businessmen of the medical marketplace, and their consequent wariness about relinquishing their mandate to new findings, guidelines, or outside authority (Epstein, 1990; Feinstein, 1985).

Professional Ideology: Bias Toward Action

Among providers there is a bias toward action that has been demonstrated in regard to tympanotomy tube placement and the ordering of radiographic studies in pediatric ambulatory practice (Ayanian & Berwick, 1991). This inclination is reflected in the surgeons' beliefs that "A chance to cut is a chance to cure" and gynecologists' inclination to intervene in labor and deliveries that do not meet their narrow definitions of "normalcy."

The Provider-Patient Relationship

New scientific breakthroughs may not be incorporated due to providers' wishes to "protect" their patients from the possible side effects of new drugs or treatments. Similarly, protocols and algorithms may not be utilized because practitioners fear that they lack individualization, dehumanize medical care, and may get between the patient and the provider.

Fear and the Chagrin Factor

A "chagrin factor" (Feinstein, 1985) influences providers to make decisions that will minimize personal exposure. The chagrin factor operates, for instance, in ordering chest x-rays for nonmedical reasons, such as to avoid regret over a mistake, please patients, or avoid malpractice suits (Epstein, 1990; Heckerling, Tape, & Wigton, 1992). Issues regarding the attribution of responsibility and the anticipation of chagrin or regret may be more important than straight questions of medical utility or effectiveness (Elstein et al., 1986).

THE PATIENT AND CHANGING PROVIDER BEHAVIOR

The patient has a crucial part in changing provider behavior. He or she is the consumer and the ultimate bill payer, as well as a member of the society— the final arbitrator of health care. There are four clearly separable roles for patients: (a) as sociocultural beings with distinct demographic characteristics; (b) as holders of expectations; (c) as evaluators of care and health status; and (d) as participants in care.

Patients' first role in changing provider behavior arises from their *sociocultural* characteristics. Several sociocultural variables have been said to affect medical decision making, including the patient's sex, class, income, ethnic background, physical appearance, "social worth," and family (Eisenberg, 1979). For example, lower class patients are less often referred for psychiatric care and psychotherapy. When treated, they receive briefer and less intensive care and are prescribed more organic interventions, such as medications and electroshock (Hollingshead & Redligh, 1958). Critically ill alcoholics, drug addicts, the aged, and those considered more deviant by society get fewer heroic or life-prolonging measures than others who are thought to contribute more to society (Crane, 1975; Sudanow, 1967). Even physical appearance may play a role in the type of care one receives (Duff & Hollingshead, 1968; Eisenberg, 1979).

Second, patients' *expectations* influence practitioner behavior. Good, Good, and Cleary (1987) found that patients' attitudes about the appropriateness of physicians' treatment of psychosocial problems are significantly related to physician recognition of psychiatric symptoms and family difficulties. Similarly, patients' requests for particular services, such as alternative techniques, seem to be related to providers instituting those healing modalities or referring to others who do (Borkan, Neher, Anson, & Smoker, 1993). If patients want lifestyle counseling or better cancer treatment facilities, they eventually get them either within or outside of conventional medicine.

A third role for patients is as *evaluators of care*, supplying information to be used by others in appraising the care they receive—ultimately inducing change. Every state medical board has a consumer complaint department that can censure practitioners or revoke their licenses. In Israel, a "Black List" of gynecologists considered inhumane or callous is maintained and disseminated by women's groups. When patients are dissatisfied, they can respond by shopping for a new provider, changing health plans, suing, or not adhering to prescribed therapy (see Kaplan & Ware, 1989, Table 4).

A fourth role for the patient is as a *participant in care*, shaping the nature of care and influencing the provider-patient relationship itself (Kaplan & Ware, 1989). The former has to do with the self-reporting of health status and behavior that makes the patient a key source of medical information. The latter addresses the issues of how much and in what ways meaningful systematic participation in medical decision making can be made in everyday reality.

There is considerable evidence suggesting that patients in the United States want more say in their medical care. Furthermore, expanding the role of patients has now been shown to affect both the medical care process and medical care outcomes (Kaplan, Greenfield, & Ware, 1989a, 1989b). Interventions have been designed to include patients in decision making by training them to obtain information and negotiate effectively on their own behalf. These modified behaviors have been shown to positively influence patient health (Greenfield, Kaplan, & Ware, 1985a, 1985b; Greenfield et al., 1988). The method for expanding patients' participation in care includes informed consent, incorporating patients' values into decisions for cost-effective analysis, and increasing patients' involvement during office visits.

The primary care office visit represents the most favorable context in which to expect change and enhance the patient's role in medical decision making, especially over the long run. Primary care visits provide a sensitive moment during which early decisions are made—before the cascade of referral or hospitalization.

The effects of increasing patient participation have been tested in randomized trials across a series of diseases including peptic ulcer, hypertension, diabetes, rheumatoid arthritis, and breast cancer (Greenfield et al., 1985a, 1985b, 1988). Doctor-patient conversations were measured using audiotapes, follow-up health questionnaires, patient reports, and physiologic measures before and after interventions over a period ranging from 6 to 18 months. The intervention was to get patients to be more active using patient training. This included meeting with them for 20 minutes just before the physician visit. During this meeting, the patients reviewed their medical records with the intervenors, who used a branching logic format guide to assist them in interpreting information. Patients were also coached to ask questions and to return to issues that had not been satisfactorily dealt with. This included rehearsing questions and demands when possible.

The experimental group using these interventions was compared to a control group that received education only rather than coaching. Relatively consistent relationships were found in this and similar studies between the various conversational behaviors and functional status at follow-up (Greenfield et al., 1985a, 1985b, 1988; Rost, Flavin, Cole, & McGill, 1991). Patients who were more controlling were also more effective in eliciting information from the doctor, showed more emotion during the baseline visit, and reported fewer functional limitations at follow-up.

Although the patients' role is critical in changing provider behavior, it is tempered by at least three factors. (a) Obscuring of medical knowledge is a common medical strategy that makes the simple seem complex and the complex simple (Katz, 1985). For instance, "knee cap pain" becomes "chondromalacia patella," and "dry skin" becomes "xerosis." (b) Differences in quality are not always apparent to the patient (Palmer et al., 1985). (c) Provider culture determines part of its own behavior. Providers have cultures of their own, with language, rituals, symbols, and initiatives. Occasionally these ambitions are at odds with the needs of their patients—such as turning out subspecialists when society demands more generalists or attempting to maintain a fee-for-service environment when 35 million Americans remain uninsured.

THE PROBLEM AND CHANGING PROVIDER BEHAVIOR

How does the *problem* influence providers' behavior? Are there some problems for which it is easier to change practitioners' decision making and actions and others for which this is difficult? By *problem* we are referring to a disease or illness state identified by the provider and/or the patient as a diagnosis, issue, condition, malady, complaint, or ailment—whether acute appendicitis, sore throat, depression, or family dysfunction. It may vary from the stated chief complaint to the unstated reason for seeking care.

Surprisingly, in reviews and research studies, the effect of the problem on physician behavior change is rarely considered, and its importance remains unexplored. The literature on guideline formation and therapeutic trials transects the issue in several ways, however. These efforts focus on a specific illness or disease state, with the ultimate goal of changing physician behavior.

Not all problems receive equal priority: significant efforts go into creating protocols and guidelines in only a limited number of areas. There is a bias in therapeutic trials leading to rigorous scrutiny for drugs, whereas surgical procedures and psychotherapies are allowed "General Acceptance" (Spodick, 1982). Thus there are extensive guidelines regarding oncologic treatments and pediatric immunizations but scant interest in protocols for psychiatric care or surgical consultations. "Nonpharmacologic" algorithms include cardiopulmonary resuscitation, laboratory testing (Davidoff, Goodspeed, & Clive, 1989), and common problems in pediatrics, family practice, and gynecology.

How can this selectivity be explained? Guidelines, protocols, or algorithms are generally constructed only when the problem examined fulfills one or more of the following (see also Gottlieb, Margolis, & Schoenbaum, 1990).

**The problem is identified, unambiguously defined,
and fully incorporated into the biomedical model.**

Problems must clearly be detectable and categorizable, be part of the biomedical domain with distinct, unambiguous boundaries, and have both "disease" (physiological) and "illness" (psychological or subjective) components before they become the focus of behavior change. As in all investigations, the eyes of medical practice are limited in "seeing" by what they look for. Life forces, spirit worlds, and ailments that cannot be detected by the senses or available technologies do not "exist." For instance, how does one construct an algorithm regarding spirit possession, chronic candidiasis, or chronic fatigue if the characteristics of the syndromes remain in question?

Schwartz and Cohen (1990) conclude that problems that lie within the classical medical model will be more amenable to change with education alone, whereas those outside (prevention, cost, cost effectiveness) are more resistant. Problems not completely contained within the biomedical domain, such as homelessness or malnutrition, might demand interventions that would clearly not be followed by providers, such as "change the family system" or "increase social safety net." Few practitioners would be willing to take the radical step of writing prescriptions for "food" or "housing."

The problem is very common.

It is more likely that guidelines will be requested and written for common rather than esoteric problems. In a list of primary care physicians' most frequently requested algorithms, routine clinical conditions predominate (Gottlieb et al., 1990). Algorithms for rare problems are not useful because the practitioners' unfamiliarity will probably convince them that the condition is outside of their "turf" and should be referred to the appropriate specialist.

On the other hand, guidelines for common problems may not be utilized. In one study of algorithm usage, physicians resisted protocol implementation for common, everyday problems when these were felt to be more of a nuisance than an aid (Margolis et al., 1992). Doctors contended that they knew how to diagnose and treat the common ailments and that the algorithms introduced time-consuming steps without clear benefit.

Protocols may be more useful and have greater potential for changing behavior in the group of primary care diseases that are common but not seen on a daily basis. Conditions such as thyroid nodules, mental health problems, and temporal arteritis are among primary care physicians' most requested algorithms (Gottlieb et al., 1990). These conditions are part of primary care physicians' domain, but because they do not see several cases per day, they may not have a "reflex" approach and may be amenable to referring to a text or guideline. Protocols can thus assist in directing work-ups and treatment.

The problem is costly.

If the problem is costly, in terms of either money or risk, there will be more interest in changing behavior regarding it. Thus there will be more interest in changing behavior around the ordering of MRI (magnetic resonance imaging) scans than around the ordering of CBCs (complete blood counts), and more in changing behavior around life support codes than around removing fingernails. This may be particularly true if there are constraints on resources (Gottlieb et al., 1990). If the problem has apparent medicolegal ramifications, then the development of protocols is favored because these provide a "standard of care" for risk management.

**The management of the problem is controversial,
but there are effective, clear-cut, and accepted
diagnostic and management choices.**

For instance, if there is only one approach and little variation between providers, as with abscess formation or hip fracture, there will be little need for changing behavior or making algorithms. Practice guidelines are more likely to be effective where there is "substantial consensus and limited uncertainty regarding appropriate practices, but where there remain large deviations from these well accepted norms" (Schwartz & Cohen, 1990, p. 49). Protocols may also be useful when the practitioner has the freedom to choose between reasonable diagnostic or treatment options, as with post-myocardial-infarction care.

Ambiguity about effectiveness may impede provider change. For example, the construction and use of algorithms for such problems as URIs (upper respiratory infections) are hampered by practitioners' lack of belief in the effectiveness of any of the possible interventions, from antihistamines to amantadine. The attitude of "everything works, nothing works" makes the process of carefully weighing choices seem irrelevant. This is similar to the case of lower back pain (LBP); here the current medical model is dominated by a "black box" approach stating that outcomes are influenced neither by specification of the exact pathoanatomical diagnoses nor by treatment regimens (Deyo, Loeser, & Bigos, 1990; Reis, Borkan, & Hermoni, 1992; Waddell, 1987). Radiological findings are weakly correlated to symptoms (Modic & Ross, 1991), and only 10 to 20% of LBP sufferers can be assigned a precise pathoanatomical diagnosis (Frymoyer & Cats-Baril, 1991). These factors create a situation for the practitioner wherein the choices for diagnosis and treatment appear arbitrary even with the most thoughtful practice guidelines.

The problem is associated with the introduction
of new technology, diagnostic tests, procedures, or medications.

As mentioned above, multiple factors encourage the introduction of new drugs or procedures. The author found that introducing on-site "Rapid Strep" testing for pharyngitis into six rural family medicine clinics where he practices encouraged more change in behavior patterns among the nurse practitioners than countless lectures and admonitions (see also Gottlieb et al., 1990; Spodick, 1975).

The problem is not taboo.

If a problem is considered forbidden or taboo in medicine, then discussion, forming guidelines, and changing physician behavior will be impeded. Taboos vary by society and are based on cultural and ethnic beliefs and practices. Current American examples include the use of oral abortifacient drugs (such as RU 486), laboratory tests on fetal material, and lobotomy.

Another way to explore the effect of the problem on changing physician behavior is to examine efforts to simultaneously alter conduct for numerous laboratory tests, diagnostic studies, or medical conditions. Most research that has attempted to change multiple behaviors simultaneously has been conducted with ancillary medical services, such as ordering laboratory tests or X-rays. Overall, providers' behavior is easier to change for admission screening when the disease or illness state is still poorly defined (Everett, deBlois, Chang, & Holets, 1983) or in multitest chemistry and complete blood count panels (Davidoff et al., 1989; Schroeder et al., 1984), where practitioners "fish" for unexpected abnormalities. Similarly, physicians can be convinced to decrease their requests for "unnecessary" tests such as electrocardiograms, chest x-rays, and clotting times because these screen for disease states of low probability (Davidoff et al., 1989). However, once providers are focusing on particular diagnoses, monitoring the progress of a hospitalized patient, or requesting a less common test, they are reluctant to alter their usual test ordering patterns, irrespective of the educational intervention (Everett et al., 1983; McPhee, Bird, Jenkins, & Fordham, 1989; Novich, Gillis, & Tauber, 1985). Presumably, test ordering in these latter situations is more immune to change because it has already undergone a level of scrutiny and justification as "medically necessary," unlike "knee-jerk" screening.

One of the few studies that has examined changing provider behavior around multiple medical problems showed that there was greater improvement following a quality assurance intervention for actions that were thought to have less impact on patients' health (Palmer, Strain, Maurer, Rothrock, & Thompson, 1984). After the intervention, physicians were more prone to perform cancer screening or otitis media follow-ups. Less improvement was seen for actions that physicians believed had greater importance to health, such as monitoring diabetes mellitus or digoxin levels. Presumably, in these cases, physicians already maintained high baseline monitoring quality due to the severity of the disease state, leaving limited room for progress. In another study of provider compliance with guideline recommendations for cancer screening, practices with ovarian cancer were found to be particularly resistant to an educational intervention (Grilli et al., 1991). This may be due to the lack of practitioner belief in the value of screening for this particularly aggressive and often treatment-resistant cancer. Providers may ask, "Why change behavior if the outcome will be the same?"

SUMMARY

In summary, changing provider behavior is not a simple matter. Priority has been focused on improving provider, particularly physician, decision making. This approach has been shown to be insufficient for achieving change, however. Protocols, guidelines, and consensus panel reports do not alter practices. The practice ecology metaphor is an alternative model for changing provider behavior. This is a contextual framework that highlights the micro and macro administrative and organizational levels at which the provider operates, from society, the health care industry, the medical profession, and the provider to the patient and the medical problem. Each needs to be examined both separately and in terms of its dynamic interaction with the other levels.

The importance of the patient cannot be overestimated. Patients have a complex impact on changing provider behavior. This impact is influenced by patients' sociodemographic status, expectations, evaluations of care, self-assessment of health status, and degree of participation in their care. The empowered patient is one of the more recent and exciting developments in this field.

The impact of the *problem*, the actual disease or illness state, on provider behavior change has been insufficiently considered in the past. Further exploration of this link to decision making and action may prove valuable. At this point, it is possible to conclude that changing provider behavior may be easier for diseases or illness states with the following characteristics:

- The problem is detectable and categorizable, is part of the biomedical domain, and has distinct, unambiguous boundaries, with both "disease" and "illness" components.
- The problem is common but not "routine."
- Society recognizes and regulates the problem, and patients are concerned about it.
- Providers receive education for it.
- Providers can "do something" for the problem, in terms of effective options for both diagnosis and treatment (drugs, procedures, etc.).
- Diagnosis and treatment of the problem are associated with high levels of remuneration.
- The problem is new, without set guidelines or practice standards.
- Individuation of treatment is possible.
- Practitioner "chagrin" can be avoided.
- Quality of treatment is apparent to patients.

In the future, creative combinations of methods may be needed to induce change. These include patient and health care provider participation and cooperation, as well as ongoing evaluation, education, administrative changes, incentives, and feedback.

Acknowledgments

The author wishes to acknowledge the valuable contribution of Sherrie Kaplan, Ph.D. of the New England Medical Center Hospital to the literature in this area and the thoughtful comments of Professors Carmi Margolis, Joseph Herman, and Avi Porat of Ben Gurion University, Beer Sheva, Israel, who helped to guide this endeavor.

12

PHYSICIAN BEHAVIOR
CHILDREN'S ISSUES AND
ANOTHER PERSPECTIVE ON CHANGE

Jane Bernzweig
Robert H. Pantell
David A. Bergman

It has been a quarter of a century since Barbara Korsch's pioneering work on communication between physicians and parents (Francis, Korsch, & Morris, 1969). Since then researchers have documented the importance of improving communication for children and adults (Kaplan, Greenfield, & Ware, 1989a; Pantell & Lewis, 1986).

The chapter by Borkan in this book provides an overview of issues in changing physician behavior in patient-physician interaction. In this chapter, we will discuss additional elements of patient-physician interactions as well as barriers to changing physician behavior and health outcomes. Our conceptualization of the forces involved in a medical interview are detailed below and discussed in depth elsewhere (Pantell, Lewis, & Sharp, 1989).

The focus of our work has been the pediatric medical interview. Pediatric visits are unique because there are at least three participants: the physician, the patient, and the parent. Communication difficulty during these visits can arise from several sources. First, both parents and children may not express major worries and concerns to physicians (Francis et al., 1969; Korsch, Gozzi, & Francis, 1968; Pantell & Goodman, 1983). Second, the dominant communication model during pediatric visits is one that includes children in information gathering but excludes them from management and diagnostic information

(Pantell, Stewart, Dias, Wells, & Ross, 1982). This model may give a message to children that they are competent to give but not receive health-related information. This passive role for children undermines efforts to promote knowledge, healthy habits, and a sense of control over health that are essential to controlling health (Atkins et al., 1987; DiGuiseppi, Rivara, Koepsel, & Polisar, 1989; Lewis, Racheleefsky, Lewis, de la Sota, & Kaplan, 1984).

A third source of communication difficulty arises from misunderstanding children's cognitive level of development. Children's concepts of health, illness, and bodily functioning change with age (Bibace & Walsh, 1980; Perrin & Gerrity, 1983), and physicians may have difficulty judging what can be understood by children of different ages (Perrin & Perrin, 1983). Further difficulties arise from the provider's limitations: failure to uncover or address important problems can be potentially explained by insufficient time scheduled, unwillingness to spend additional time, lack of knowledge or skills to address problems, lack of interest or enthusiasm for discussing certain issues, other agenda items in a visit, failure to recognize the significance of the problem for the parent and child, or impatience with the parent, child, or visit (Sharp, Pantell, Murphy, & Lewis, 1992).

Several interesting lines of research to address these communication difficulties have emerged. Rather than focusing exclusively on changing physician behavior, this research has focused on parents and children as well. First, experimental studies of hospitalized children have demonstrated that preoperative communication can reduce surgical morbidity and improve physiological and behavioral outcomes. The presumed mechanism for the improved outcomes is that providers, by allowing parents to ask questions, can reduce parents' anxiety and enhance their ability to be supportive of their children. Opportunities for children to actively play and talk through fears are the basis for many hospital-based child life programs. Older children are principally concerned with immediate events, such as procedures. However, they also are quite interested in prognosis and even concerned about the cost of their illness to their family (Lewis et al., 1988).

Second, a variety of health education programs targeting children and their families, instead of providers, have been effective in improving child health outcomes and consequently reducing utilization of medical services. Most of these programs are conducted in groups, including school settings. In randomized controlled trials, Charles and Mary Ann Lewis showed that school programs designed to increase children's personal competence and decision-making and self-management skills led to fewer emergency room visits and fewer days of hospitalization. Children also developed an improved sense of social competence (Lewis et al., 1990).

Finally, considerable work is emerging that is trying to fix the numerous problems of medical encounters. Although the traditional model for changing the process of the medical visit focuses almost all attention on the physician, growing research (see below) suggests that a better way to change physician and patient behavior is within the context of "patient activation." The traditional model for changing physician behavior assumes that when information is disseminated to providers they accept the communication and integrate it into their normal practice. It is our experience that physician behavior change can occur through a process of actively involving patients in the interview.

SHARED DECISION MAKING MODEL

The *shared decision making model* focuses on the interaction between the doctor and patient as an arena for improving communication that will lead to better patient health behaviors and health outcomes. Educational interventions have shown that effective communication between the physician and patient can be learned, and that shared decision making between the physician and the patient is a model of preferred interaction (Kaplan et al., 1989a). Improved interaction between the doctor and the patient also has a positive effect on better health outcomes for adults (Kaplan et al., 1989a). Physician-patient communication can promote prevention-oriented behaviors among patients.

Participants in the process of communication bring sets of demographic features, psychological traits, and medical experiences to the interview. At the same time, the physician's conceptualization of the patient is also important. Demographic characteristics of the physician, personality traits, training, experience, understanding, and expectations all influence the process of communication during the medical visit. The situation and setting in which the visit occurs will also affect the process of communication.

Demographic Characteristics

Certain demographic characteristics of patients, such as social class and gender, influence the interaction process. The way in which doctors interact with children is determined in part by the demographic features of the child (Pantell & Lewis, 1986). For example, physicians interact more extensively with older children and tend to give more information about the nature of an illness and its management to boys than to girls (Pantell et al., 1982).

Demographic features of physicians have also been studied. Male and female physicians exhibit gender-linked differences in interviewing styles. Most recently there is strong evidence that female patients of female physicians are more likely to receive major diagnostic and therapeutic interventions than female patients of male physicians (Franks & Clancy, 1993).

Physician Conceptualizations of the Patient

A physician's level of training, experience, and understanding of patients is important for communicating with patients and developing rapport. For instance, Perrin has shown that in pediatric settings physicians are poor judges of the level of conceptual information that can be understood by children of different ages (Perrin & Gerrity, 1981). Physicians tend to overestimate what young children can understand and underestimate what older children can understand. Physicians need to be particularly careful with the vocabulary they use and how they explain procedures to children so that a child with diabetes, for example, doesn't leave the office feeling that she is going to "die of betes."

Providers' familiarity and knowledge in particular areas of interest to patients will affect the content and process of communication. In one study, less than half of the pediatricians responded to parents' psychosocial concerns (e.g., behavior problems, insecurity, learning difficulties) with information, referral, reassurance, or guidance (Sharp et al., 1992).

Patients' previous experience with illness, their emotional status, their expectations about what will occur at the visit, and their beliefs about the seriousness of their illness affect the amount and type of information they provide for the physician and the way in which it will be presented. Each of these patient factors will potentially influence the ways in which physicians think about and interact with their patients.

Situation and Setting

In order to understand the communication process, it is important to be aware and sensitive to the overall context in which the visit occurs. Patients present themselves differently for health supervision visits than they do for acute illness visits. In a health supervision visit, parents, children, and adult patients tend to be more relaxed and better able to talk with the provider. For acute care visits, the raised level of emotion experienced by parents and children may not be conducive to discussions about behavior change since injury prevention is salient, but discussion may occur when the crisis dissipates. A clinician must judge whether injury prevention information is best given at the time of visit or at a follow-up appointment. In first-time interactions between physician and family, the process of communication will be different than if there is already an ongoing relationship between the family and the physician. Both treatment in the hospital and what may have recently occurred in the waiting room have the potential to influence communication between the physician and the patient.

The Outcomes of Shared Decision Making

Despite difficulties in overcoming barriers to effective doctor-patient communication, a number of programs targeting physicians, children, and their families have had demonstrated efficacy. As noted previously, experimental studies of hospitalized children have demonstrated that special opportunities for preoperative communication with a health care provider reduce surgical morbidity and improve physiological and behavioral outcomes. Allowing parents opportunities to ask questions reduces their anxiety. Their ability to be supportive of their children is the presumed mechanism for the improved outcomes (Pantell & Lewis, 1992). School programs designed to increase asthmatic children's personal competence and decision-making and self-management skills led to fewer emergency room visits and fewer days of hospitalization (Lewis et al., 1990).

The work of Kaplan, Greenfield, Ware, and colleagues has shown that "active" patients have improved functional and physiologic status, and that passivity during medical visits presents a "hazard to health" (Borkan, this volume; Greenfield et al., 1988; Kaplan et al., 1989a; Pantell et al., 1982). We have shown that a brief (8-minute) videotape shown to children, parents, and physicians can improve the process and outcome of medical care. Following exposure to a brief videotape intervention modeling assertive behavior and active discussion with their physician, children took a more active role in the office. Asthmatic children (ages 5 to 14) felt better about dealing with their disease, knew more about their medications, missed fewer days of school, and scored better on modified versions of two functional status measures (Lewis, Pantell, & Sharp, 1991).

Although videotapes are useful in modeling active, assertive interactions, it is clear that physicians can incorporate this approach in their interactions with children. Physicians continue to control the flow of communication in medical visits. By addressing children directly and encouraging their participation, they can improve children's health behaviors and competence. As discussed elsewhere, adults who learned to become more actively involved in their medical care improved their blood pressure (hypertension), glycosylated hemogloblin (diabetes), and functional status.

The shared decision making model points to the significant influence that patients and parents have in shaping the process and outcome of medical visits for major improvements in health status. Taking the total context of communication into account, researchers have begun to show the interplay between what patients, parents, and physicians bring to the visit and the process of communication and health outcomes. In the next section, we present an overview and a discussion of some of these attempts to change physician behavior, but caution the reader to take the total context and physician, patient, and parent contributions into account when thinking about changing the process of the medical interview.

DIFFUSION MODEL

Although the shared decision making model for changing both physician and patient behavior is the foundation of much recent work, a great deal of effort has also been focused on changing physician behavior using a *diffusion model.* The most effective interventions also involve taking into account physician demographics, attitudes, personalities, and peer acceptance and the setting in which change is to occur.

Guidelines now exist for physician screening and communication about preventive practices such as the early detection of cancer (American Cancer Society), HIV prevention (American Medical Association, U.S. Public Health Service [*Healthy People 2000*], Surgeon General), Smoking Cessation (U.S. Department of Health and Human Services), cholesterol education and the prevention of coronary heart disease (National Heart, Lung and Blood Institute), the use of bicycle safety helmets, and child abuse prevention. The rate of successful implementation of clinical practice guidelines has been disappointingly low. The mere development and dissemination of guidelines rarely leads directly to changes in medical practice. For example, even though guidelines exist for counseling all new patients about reducing the risk of contracting AIDS, only about 28% of physicians in one recent national survey said they "always" or "usually" counsel new patients, and 48% of those who did counsel remarked that they did so because the patient brought up the discussion (Gemson et al., 1991). Lomas et al. (1989) studied the impact of a widely disseminated and nationally endorsed consensus statement recommending decreased use of cesarean sections. They found that most obstetricians were aware of the guidelines and that over 80% agreed with them. When asked if the guidelines changed their practice patterns, one third of the hospitals and obstetricians reported that a significant reduction in cesarean section rates had occurred after dissemination of the guidelines. However, when obstetricians were questioned concerning the content of the guidelines, knowledge of the guidelines was poor. When actual data from hospital discharge summaries were examined, it was apparent that there had been no significant change in cesarean section rates. Modifying physicians' behavior to conform more closely to recommended practice guidelines has proved to be a difficult task (Mittman, Tonesk, & Jacobson, 1992).

Barriers to physician acceptance of guidelines include lack of physician training on, knowledge of, and experience with a specific problem, as well as incomplete information concerning the value of guidelines. Guidelines are seen by some as a threat to physician autonomy and patient choice or as an unnecessary and/or inappropriate substitute for clinical judgment. Other possible barriers to guideline use include custom and habit, malpractice concerns, organizational structures, and reimbursement rates. In terms of specific guideline recommendations to communicate about psychosocial issues, some physicians believe they may offend their patients by raising sensitive topics, some believe their patients will be unable to change, and some believe that it is not their role to bring up these topics with patients. For these reasons, practice guidelines are unlikely to be universally accepted or automatically implemented without specific efforts and interventions (Mittman et al., 1992).

The key assumption in the diffusion model is that exposure to new clinical information is sufficient to bring about changes in clinicians' practice patterns; clinicians are consumers of information who want to keep abreast of new medical developments and have the wherewithal to do so. Therefore when the clinician encounters information that recommends a change in practice patterns, that clinician will be most willing to change. Attitude, personality traits, and the differences between "early" versus "late" adopters have been given as reasons that some adopt new practices and others do not.

Faced with a profusion of frequently conflicting medical studies, the clinician may retreat to a reliance on personal experience, take solace in the safety of numbers, and do what his or her colleagues do. David Eddy (1984) has described several tried-and-true heuristics that are used in the face of such confusion: "If there is any chance of the disease, the procedure should be performed"; "If one patient is saved, the effort is worthwhile"; and "Costs should not be considered in decisions about individual patients." Physicians usually do not have the time to sort out complex problems; they know they are less likely to be punished for doing too much than for doing too little.

The Nature of the Information Provided to Clinicians

For clinician practice patterns to change, information must be provided in a way that is easily comprehensible and utilizable in the context of everyday practice. Currently the clinician is confronted with a mixture of randomized clinical trials, prospective cohort studies, and clinical studies that often present conflicting evidence. Review of these studies frequently leads to more confusion than clarity. To remedy this situation, efforts have been made to bring together content experts during consensus conferences with a goal of distilling the medical literature and their clinical judgment into a set of recommended treatment alternatives. Recent studies evaluating the impact of these conferences have demonstrated that dissemination of these recommendations is not sufficient to change clinician practice patterns.

For dissemination to be more effective, breaking the clinical process into a series of discrete steps makes it possible to classify decision steps according to the quality of the evidence available. Some steps can be classified as essential in that the medical evidence supporting the recommendation is incontrovertible. Some steps can be classified as controversial in that the evidence is less clear and there is more room for clinician variability. It is also possible to define decision steps in which the choice of action by the physician is dictated by patient preferences. This way of employing practice guidelines represents a step forward in helping the clinician to effectively use the results of outcomes research in clinical practice. This type of guideline provides information in an action-oriented format that allows for flexibility in a decision making process that depends on the quality of the evidence and the impact of patient preferences on treatment choice.

So that guidelines are not placed on the bookshelf and forgotten, a means must be found to integrate this knowledge into the activities of the clinician during the medical encounter. One possible mechanism to accomplish this goal was evaluated by Duggan, Starfield, and DeAngelis (1990), who examined the likelihood of successfully implementing health supervision guidelines during a pediatric office visit. A group of pediatric residents was divided into two groups; one group was given the health supervision guidelines to read and the other group was given the guidelines and structured data forms, including a checklist for important information to be collected during the encounter. The researchers found a much higher adherence to the guidelines in the group that utilized the structured data forms and the health supervision guidelines than in the group that received only the guidelines. The coupling of clinical guidelines with structured data forms that prompt the clinician to collect critical information and order appropriate tests at key clinical junctures can provide a useful mechanism of integrating the medical information in practice guidelines with the activities of everyday practice.

Other easily administered interventions targeted at changing physician practice behavior, such as manual and computerized reminders that provide notices and feedback to physicians about specific clinical events or guidelines, have also been very useful (Murrey, Gottlieb, & Schoenbaum, 1992). For example, reminders have been used to increase utilization of services and counseling (Cheney & Ramsdell, 1987; Turner, Day, & Borenstein, 1989). Other programs have supplemented the use of medical record reminders with patient self-help booklets (Cummings, Coates, et al., 1989) and brief seminars in which physicians can role play and discuss patient counseling practices

(Cummings, Richard, et al., 1989). These reminders have provided medical information in an action-oriented format that suggests to the clinician the appropriate therapeutic and diagnostic choices at key clinical junctures.

The Setting in Which Changes Are to Be Made

The effective implementation of the results of outcomes studies is directly dependent on the setting or clinical context in which changes are to be made. This is best illustrated in a study by Myers and Gleicher (1991) that evaluated the impact of a program to lower the cesarean section rate in their hospital. Their program was based on the findings of a 1981 National Institutes of Health (NIH) Task Force that concluded that 75% of the rise in cesarean section rates could be attributed to three diagnostic indications: previous cesarean sections, dystocia, and breech presentations of the fetus. Even though many of the routine indications for cesarean section that had been disseminated to obstetricians were known to be no longer valid, cesarean section rates showed little change. The authors reviewed the literature and concluded that a large majority of these infants could have been delivered vaginally. They designed a program that consisted of (a) voluntary participation by the physicians, (b) a mandatory second opinion by colleagues, (c) local generation of the most common indications for cesarean section, and (d) distribution of a detailed peer review of all cesarean sections and of individual physicians' rates of performing them. The intervention was able to decrease the cesarean section rate from 17.5% to 11.5% of all deliveries without adversely influencing fetal or maternal outcome. This was accomplished during a period of time when the national cesarean section rate remained unchanged.

The interventions recommended by Myers and Gleicher most likely contributed to the decreased rate of cesarean sections because (a) the problem was defined at the local level in such a way that it reflected the shared values of the obstetrical staff, (b) the medical knowledge and national recommendations were reviewed and formulated into a set of "home-grown" guidelines for the common indications for cesarean section, (c) physician performance was constantly monitored, and (d) a comprehensive program of peer review was initiated to ensure adherence to the guidelines.

This study has several important implications. First, successful utilization of medical knowledge requires a recognition that there is a problem at the local level. Second, solutions (in this case guidelines for cesarean section) have to be created by the participating clinicians and customized to meet site-specific needs. Third, once initiated, the program needs to continuously monitor physician adherence to the guidelines. Fourth, physician performance needs to be monitored through peer review feedback to ensure adherence to the guidelines. It is evident from this study and the experience of others that the battle to change clinician behavior in light of new information has to be fought in the office, clinic, or hospital, not in the halls of NIH or the medical subspecialty society.

The Process for Implementing, Monitoring, and Maintaining Change

Creating an environment where new information can translate into changes in clinician practice patterns can be a daunting task for any health care group or institution. Recently several major health care institutions have begun to adapt industrial quality management methods to health care. These methods provide an operational philosophy that lends itself to the implementation, monitoring, and maintenance of practice guidelines. Industrial quality management ascribes to the theory that success is achieved by focusing on the complex processes and procedures that determine the quality of health care. It has as its goal the design and implementation of processes that are efficacious, appropriate, and consistent. To achieve this goal, these processes must be well understood and constantly monitored. Any improvement in a health care process must involve all the individuals who are critical to its success. Solutions to identified problems must address the needs of all those who are integral to the success of the process as well as those who depend on it for their well-being.

Many of the methods of industrial quality management are the same as the success factors Myers and Gleicher used in their intervention program to lower cesarean section rates. Their formula included the local production of a set of clinical guidelines along with monitoring unnecessary variability in the utilization of health care resources and in the measurement of medical outcomes.

What Motivates the Clinician to Change?

What motivates clinicians to integrate new medical information into their practice and change their practice patterns? Most clinicians want to stay abreast of current knowledge and practice high quality medicine. Only about 5% to 6% of clinicians clearly provide substandard care. Yet many clinicians are resistant to change. Part of this resistance stems from the uncertainty of interpreting studies in the context of the individual patient. This uncertainty engenders a desire to stay with the status quo and practice in a manner indistinguishable from that of colleagues. This resistance is also rooted in a desire not to be an outlier in clinical practice patterns. Current quality assurance activities seek to establish minimal levels of care and relentlessly search out those that do not meet these standards. This leads to a climate in which conformity to established standards of practice can be the safest course of action.

In order to motivate clinicians to incorporate new knowledge into their practice, several objectives must be met. Decisions to change practice patterns should be made in conjunction with peers. By moving a group of clinicians toward optimal care, the security provided by "safety in numbers" can be maintained. New medical knowledge must be interpreted in light of specific organizational needs. This ensures "buy-in" by clinicians at the local level. National practice guidelines then become clinicians' own guidelines. Once new practice guidelines are established, the performance of the participating clinicians must be monitored and the results discussed among peers. Peer review feedback must be done in a climate that seeks to move all clinicians toward an optimal level of care.

SUMMARY

The *shared decision making model* of communication between doctors and patients has demonstrated improved patient outcomes in recent studies. For behavior change to occur, the *diffusion model,* although focused exclusively on changing physician behavior, takes into account the context in which the physician practices. Interest in physician attitudes, personality, peer relationships, and "local" needs has recently become part of intervention efforts aimed at changing physician behavior. Future interventions that are designed to change physician and peer group acceptance of practice guidelines, while simultaneously incorporating active patient involvement with appropriate shared decision making, should have the effect of changing patient and provider behaviors and patient outcomes.

13

THE CLINICAL INTERVIEW PROCESS

Richard M. Frankel

In my view, the interview is the most powerful, encompassing, sensitive, and versatile instrument available to the physician. (Engel, 1988, p. 115)

The idea that the interview is the core clinical tool of medical practice is a provocative one. For one thing, it challenges the widely held notion that power in medicine lies in technological or biomedical domains alone. For another, it suggests that the clinical process is a fundamental feature of doctoring, not merely a matter of having a "good bedside manner." This means that effectively communicating information is as important as arriving at a correct diagnosis or treatment plan.

Provocative or not, evidence in support of Dr. Engel's assertion continues to accumulate. Despite rapid and striking advances in the area of life support, for example, important and nagging questions about end-of-life decision making, comfort care measures, and the definitions of life and death persist. Poor communication between clinicians and patients is frequently cited as a factor in patients' decisions to sue for malpractice (Volk, 1992). Other studies show that most patient dissatisfaction can be tied to communication problems that arose during the clinical encounter (Goleman, 1991). Finally, studies of nonadherence consistently show that anywhere between 40% and 90% of patients who seek advice from medical professionals do not follow the recommendations they are given.

This chapter will focus on the recent history of the clinical interview process as an area of scholarly interest and review the current status of the field, with particular attention to the methods, assumptions, and outcomes used by researchers in this area.

HISTORY

Although the importance of the clinical interview process has been recognized for millennia, serious scientific inquiry into the subject is of relatively recent origin. Students of the medical interview, such as Stoeckle and Billings (1987), mark the beginning of contemporary research on the clinical communication process in the late 1930s. It was during that period that William F. Murphy and Felix Deutch began recording encounters between psychiatric residents and their patients. Before recordings of actual interviews were available, research on clinical communication was limited to anecdotal experience and case reports, neither of which contained accounts of the actual dialogue that transpired between physician and patient (Deutch & Murphy, 1954). The advent of audio and video technology made possible a view of the clinical process that could be reliably reproduced and described in greater or lesser detail.

In much the same way that the invention of the microscope permitted a basic science of biology to be elaborated through careful observation, visual representation, and classification, audiovisual records of the clinical process have permitted both qualitative and quantitative researchers to begin to develop a basic science of human social interaction and its application to the clinical interview in medicine. Although there are many different, and in my view legitimate, ways of studying the clinical communication process, audiovisual recordings provide an independent means for documenting and reproducing the actual moment-by-moment flow of interactional events. In contrast with other field methods that rely upon a reconstruction of interaction as experienced in real time, audiovisual records can be inspected by observers and/or participants an unlimited number of times for a variety of purposes. As a methodological approach, the use of audiovisual records as a primary data source appears to be a distinguishing feature of a range of studies across medical specialties, content areas, and disciplinary boundaries. In this respect, I agree with Erickson (1982) and others who consider such records to constitute a distinctive approach to investigation and analysis.

In addition to the contributions of technology to research, World War II provided an opportunity to study the clinical process as it related to disabling emotional conditions such as "shell shock" and "battle fatigue." Both the number of cases and involvement from both general practitioners and psychiatrists led early researchers to focus intensively and descriptively on the clinical process and its importance as a social relationship.

In the modern era, research on clinical communication process has grown dramatically. Currently, there are some 7,500 articles on the topic listed in *Index Medicus* and the *Social Science Citation Index* combined. Inui and

Carter (1985, 1988) have recently reviewed the spectrum of research designs used to investigate the clinical communication process. In addition to increased methodological sophistication, they also note that the field is maturing scientifically, as evidenced by the movement of research methodologies over the past 30 years from developmental-descriptive to subexperimental-etiologic and, most recently, to interventional.

Similarly, in terms of an overall approach, Inui and Carter (1985) note that although the field has developed rapidly it has been without a great deal of theoretical or conceptual integration. More recent efforts have focused on defining the interview in terms of three major functions and the requisite skills to achieve them (Bird & Cohen-Cole, 1990; Cohen-Cole, 1991; Lazare, 1989; Lipkin, 1987). There is now general agreement that the three functions of the medical encounter are to (a) elicit a complete understanding of the reason or reasons a person seeks care, (b) provide empathy and support in relating to patients, and (c) deliver diagnostic information and develop appropriate treatment plans. I will review some of the generalized findings relating clinical communication process to outcome. I will then review three studies that establish such linkages using qualitative research methods.

Recent Developments in Research
on the Clinical Communication Process

A number of recent studies point to the relationship of clinical communication process to outcomes of care. Inui and Carter (1988) investigated the characteristics of humane care (defined by the American Board of Internal Medicine [1982] as empathy, compassion, and respect) and identified a number of barriers to the effective delivery of care. These included lack of courtesy, failure to discuss patient problems thoroughly, failure to assess functional impact of disease or illness, and failure to give clear and complete explanations. In a related study of the decision to obtain a flu vaccination, Carter, Beach, and Inui (1986) found that they could increase acceptance rates by over 30% above baseline by assessing communication barriers and adjusting standards of practice to better meet the needs of their target population. These studies suggest that it is both possible and desirable to describe the standards of clinical communication practice as a step toward changing outcomes in the direction desired.

In several related studies, investigators have focused on specific behaviors associated with poor outcomes and dissatisfaction. In an early study, Roter (1977) investigated the effect of patient question asking on satisfaction and outcome. Roter demonstrated that patients coached to ask more questions had better functional outcomes than patients in a control group. In a sophisticated intervention study, Greenfield, Kaplan, and Ware (1985b) taught patients in a 20-minute coaching session to be more assertive in the medical encounter (*assertiveness* was defined in terms of the number of questions patients initiated). Although patients in the experimental group asked no more than those in the control group, there was a significant positive effect on functional status for patients in the experimental group at 3-month follow-up. Studies of specific communication behaviors such as question asking are useful in understanding the extent to which patients have been given an opportunity to express *all* their concerns and the extent to which the absence of opportunities to ask questions affects outcomes such as satisfaction and functional status.

In addition to the effect of question asking on outcome, a number of other investigators have identified clinical communication process dimensions that are related to outcomes of care. The Headache Study Group of the University of Western Ontario (1986) reported in their collaborative study of chronic headache that patients' perception of having been fully listened to and appreciated by their doctor correlated most highly with the resolution of symptoms. This study suggests that specific types or sequences of questions are differentially valued by patients, and that this difference may in turn be reflected in terms of health care outcomes. Additional behaviors that have been related to dissatisfaction and poor outcome are shame and humiliation in the encounter (Lazare, 1987), lack of empathy and caring (Cohen-Cole & Bird, 1985), and being insulted or ignored (Beckman, Markakis, Suchman, & Frankel, in press; Frankel & Beckman, 1989a). A final dimension that has been positively related to outcomes of care is agreement. Starfield (Starfield et al., 1979, 1981), in a series of studies in pediatric populations, found that agreement between the provider and patient on the nature of the problem and the proposed solution was positively associated with the outcomes of care.

RESEARCH ON CLINICAL COMMUNICATION PROCESS UTILIZING QUALITATIVE METHODS

In a recent review of research on the doctor-patient relationship, Inui and Carter (1985) suggest that the development of an integrated theory about the medical encounter has been hampered by the relative lack of attention to the sequencing and social context of medical discourse. The authors suggest that the most commonly used strategy of analyzing the presence or absence of communication behaviors does not capture either the richness or the meaning of the events being communicated about. "This approach is analogous to describing 'Hamlet' as a play with 21 principal characters, a ghost, a group of players, and various lords, ladies, officers, soldiers, sailors, messengers, and attendants, one of whom dies by drowning, one by poisoned drink, two by poisoned sword and drink!" (Inui & Carter, 1985). Since their paper was published, several qualitative studies that address these concerns have appeared. I will review three in some detail to illustrate the kinds of questions they address and how these in turn relate to traditional quantitative concerns.

Determining the Nature of the Problem

In a study designed to address the issue of how successful patients are at expressing the full range of their concerns at the beginning of routine ambulatory visits, Beckman and Frankel (1984) found that, on average, patients were interrupted after 18 seconds, with 54% of the interruptions occurring after the first stated concern (Table 13.1). In addition, they found that once interrupted, patients were highly unlikely to express additional concerns for consideration early in the visit. When all the concerns, whether interrupted or not, were abstracted and given to a group of blinded internists to rank in terms of clinical importance, it was found that there was no relationship between the serial ordering of concerns and clinical importance. The second, third, or fourth stated concern was as likely to be clinically important as the first. The cost of interruption to the decision making based on premature focus is an incomplete database.

The authors concluded that the opening moments of the visit are critical in establishing the agenda from the patient's point of view and are one source of dissatisfaction with the care provided. In a follow-up study, Beckman, Frankel, and Darnley (1985) found that early interruption was significantly correlated with so-called hidden agendas raised by patients at the end of the visit. In another related investigation, Rost and Frankel (1993) studied elderly diabetics' perceptions of the relative importance of items they wished to discuss with their physicians. They found that patients identified their third concern as most important from their perspective. Frankel and Beckman (1989b) have also related interruption to other aspects of care such as compliance. Not surprisingly, Frankel and Beckman suggest that early interruption may lead to an inadequate understanding of a patient's needs and concerns, which in turn may act as a disincentive to follow physician recommendations (Frankel & Beckman, 1989b).

Delivering Diagnostic Information

Early work by Lipton and Svarstad (Lipton & Svarstad, 1977; Svarstad, 1974; Svarstad & Lipton, 1977) on the delivery of information to parents

TABLE 13.1 Relationship Between Interruption and Elapsed Time for the 52 Interrupted Opening Statements

Number of Concerns Expressed Before Interruption	Number of Encounters	Mean Elapsed Time to Point of Interruption (in Seconds)
0	6	6.83
1	28	16.48
2	8	25.00
3	7	37.50
4	3	37.00

SOURCE: Beckman & Frankel (1984), pp. 692-696.

about mental retardation points to the importance of diagnostic news delivery style as an influence on outcome. Unfortunately, the studies on which this assertion were based were coded, rather primitively, for the presence or absence of the clinicians' mentioning the child's IQ or diagnosis. Such category codes do not allow an assessment of effects or style on interaction dynamics to be made and thus have been of limited value in studying stylistic effects.

More recently, Maynard (1989, 1991, in press) has taken up the question of diagnostic news delivery in the context of developmental disabilities by specifically comparing and contrasting sequences of discourse containing diagnostic information. Maynard identified two distinct styles by which news is delivered. The first style, which might best be termed "noninteractionalized," involves the delivery of diagnostic information without respect to the point of view or perspective of the recipient. A segment of transcript from Maynard (1989, p. 56) illustrates this style.

Dr. D: I think—you know I'm sure you're anxious about today and I know this has been a really hard year for you. And I think you've really done an extraordinary job in dealing with something that's very hard for any human being or any parent—and you know Mrs. Roberts that I can talk as parents as well as—

Ms. R: True.

Dr. D: Uh my being a professional. It's *hard* when there's something not all right with a child, very hard. And I admire both of you really and, and as hard as it is seeing that there *is* something that *is* the matter with Donald, he's *not* like other kids, he *is* slow, he is retarded.

Ms. R: HE IS NOT RETARDED!

Mr. R: Ellen—

Ms. R: HE IS NOT RETARDED!

Mr. R: Ellen. Uh please—

Ms. R: NO!

Mr. R: May—look—it's their way of—I don't know—

Ms. R: HE IS NOT RETARDED! (sobbing)

Maynard notes that although the pediatrician who delivers the news is very complimentary toward the parents, she has not solicited their view of their child's problem. In interactional terms, the news is not well designed for its recipients (Sacks, 1972) and leads to a series of strong rejections on the mother's part. Such rejections are difficult to handle, interactionally, when they occur and may ultimately damage or destroy trust and compassion in the relationship. Similarly, being given undesirable news without sensitivity to the states of knowledge of its recipients may induce parents to seek additional assessments/opinions out of a sense of frustration or anger at the style in which the news was delivered.

Maynard contrasts the "noninteractionalized" style of news delivery with one in which some effort at interactional alignment precedes the actual news delivery. A portion of Maynard's (1989, p. 59) transcript appears below.

Dr. R: Have you noticed any improvement since I saw him last? . . . [author's ellipses]

Mr. H: . . . You know I think basically the problem is as I also said to Ellen that uh when you reach the age of about four or four and a half you more or less stop maturing right there.

Dr. R: Okay. Well that kind of leads into what we found uh, essentially what we have found in David is that at a certain point his development *has* stopped.

Mr. H: Right.

Dr. R: And um, when tested he then tends to look to us like a kid with retarded development.

Ms. H: Mm hmm.

Mr. H: Mmm.

Dr. R: This is a kid who's reached a certain point and then he stopped.

Mr. H: Right.

Maynard notes about this sequence that the physician has preceded his delivery of diagnostic information with a question designed to assess the parents' knowledge and perspective on their child's problem. Once having elicited their perspective, the physician frames the diagnostic news delivery, first using terms that the parents have offered and then transforming those terms into a more technical vocabulary, "a kid with retarded development." Maynard notes further that the physician's attempt to first assess and then align herself with the parents' state of knowledge results in an informing that is both more interactionally and in general more acceptable to the parents.

Adherence/Compliance

One criticism of statistical approaches to analyzing clinical communication offered recently by Stiles (1989) is that they assume that all patients have equal needs and that in the aggregate all exchanges have the same value and/or impact. Much the same might be said about the unreflective use of communicator profiles based on the presence or absence of particular behaviors.

Both common sense and evidence from sequence analysis point to the fact that some questions are more important than others and that some types of information have more impact than others. This is true from a patient perspective for receiving diagnostic information; it is also true from a physician perspective in terms of gathering information about patient compliance.

Traditional studies of compliance point out that anywhere from 20% to 80% of patients who seek the professional advice of a physician do not follow the advice they are given. Many reasons for these disappointing results have been posited, including differences in education, status, ethnicity, clarity of instructions, and so forth. Until recently, little attention has been paid to the actual discourse context in which providers ask and patients answer questions about compliance. In a study of compliance monitoring discourse, Steele, Jackson, and Guttman (1990) studied 75 encounters between hypertensive patients and their primary care providers in a university clinic. In reviewing the tapes, the researchers identified two distinct styles in which information about compliance was elicited. One style, which they termed *information intensive*, was used by providers who requested specific information about medication names, dosages, and the number of noncompliant episodes between visits. A second style, which they labeled as *indirect*, was used by physicians who were often vague and unclear about compliance information sought. An example of an *indirect* compliance monitoring sequence from Steele et al.'s (1990, p. 296) data is reproduced below.

D: Okay, good. The last time I saw you was when we started you on your blood pressure medication.

P: Yeah, uh huh.

D: Alright? Okay. Have you noticed any changes since you've started taking that medication?

P: Well, I go to the bathroom quite often.

D: Alright. That's—that's fairly a normal effect of the medication.

P: (laughs)

D: It's a water pill, a diuretic, and it takes some of the extra fluid out of your body. . . .

Steele et al. (1990) note about this sequence that the question

"Have you noticed any changes since you started taking the medication?" . . . displays an apparent presupposition on the part of the clinician that the patient is indeed taking the prescribed medication. She does not ask the patient if she is taking her medications but rather to report on "changes" coincident with the presumed taking of those medications. The patient obliges by stating, "well, I go to the bathroom quite often." This in turn prompts the doctor to normalize the "change" described by the patient and to briefly explain the relationship between fluid balance in the body and blood pressure control. Immediately following this discussion the clinician . . . congratulated [the patient] on her good work. (p. 296)

In contrast with the "indirect" style, Steele and his colleagues identified a style that they termed "information intensive." The "information-intensive" style of compliance monitoring differs from the "indirect" style by virtue of the specificity of questions and the types of assumptions that are inherent in the questions used. The following segment of transcript from Steele et al.'s (1990, p. 297) study illustrates the "information-intensive" style.

D: Okay. What um, medications are you takin' now?

P: Propanolol and hydrochlorothiazide.

D: Mmkay. An' ya takin' those how? How often do you take 'em?

P: I take the Propranolol, I think it's eighty grams. . . .

D: Umm hmm.

(several utterances deleted)

D: Okay. Have you noticed any side-effects from the medication at all? Have you—

P: Well I, ah as far as the n-n-not really. Just ah—I have to u-use the bathroom a little more that's about it. Yeah.

D: From the hydrochlorothiazide. Yeah. Okay. You haven't noticed anything like nausea and vomiting? Headaches or any— . . .

P: No.

D: . . . anything unusual from them? Okay. Good. . . . (Topic shift)

According to Steele et al. (1990), "the clinician initiated her inquiry in such a way as to give the patient an opportunity to display her knowledge of the regimen, and through the use of more specific problems, to report on how it had been implemented" (p. 297).

In order to assess the effects of each style on accuracy of knowledge, each clinician in the study was asked on the basis of the information he or she had collected to predict the compliance status of his or her patients. When the sample was analyzed, the investigators found that 80% of the physicians studied used the indirect style in monitoring for compliance. In terms of predicting actual compliance (which was assessed independently by in-depth interviews), it was found that the physicians who used the indirect style had no better than chance probability of correctly predicting the compliance status of their patients. By contrast, the 20% of physicians who used the information-intensive style were 80% successful in predicting the compliance status of their patients. From these data Steele et al. conclude that a component of noncompliance may be related to the communication process.

In addition, as is evident from reviewing the description of the indirect compliance monitoring approach, it is possible that practitioners might actually *reinforce* noncompliance by using forms of praise to conclude compliance monitoring sequences. Steele's approach very clearly demonstrates the value of focusing on a particular type of sequence or exchange in the medical encounter. It also stands as a striking example of the effect of participation structure on communication process and outcome. In this case, clinicians' assumptions about compliance may be at fault for maintaining and even encouraging some patients' noncompliance.

Combining Approaches: Dream, Dogma, or Desiderata

Three decades ago, the cultural anthropologist Thomas Gladwin (1964) wrote a paper entitled "Culture and Logical Process," in which he examined two methods for navigating on the open seas. One system of navigation, represented by European cultural tradition, is distinguished by the fact that its users typically begin a journey according to a preestablished "plan." The European navigator, according to certain logical principles, first develops a diagram or chart of the course he or she will follow during a journey. Once underway, the navigator uses such a chart as an instrument by reference to which all decisions regarding location will be made. The major operating principle of the system is to provide an assured final outcome; the major motivation for a user, therefore, is to maintain the strictest attention possible to remaining "on course."

> Western navigators plan their entire voyage in advance. A course is plotted on a chart and this in turn provides the criteria for decision. Progress is assessed at any given moment relative to a position along course, he does not carry in his mind a physical sense of where he is going. In his mind is an overall plan, and an estimate of the amount of this plan which has thus far been accomplished. He can always draw a line on the chart between his on-course position and his destination, thus determining where he is relative to his goal, but unless someone inquires he need never be aware, as he stands by the helm, just where over the horizon his destination lies. (Gladwin, 1964, p. 172)

In another context, the Islanders of Truk also face the problem of managing long distances over uncertain conditions. The Trukese navigator, however, embarks upon his task far differently from his European counterpart. There is no preestablished plan of any kind; not even the simplest of navigational tools, such as a compass, is used. Experience from previous voyages plus the available information at hand during a current sailing trip account completely for Trukese navigational expertise. Under these conditions, distances of 100 miles or more are navigated successfully according to "dead reckoning" and correction procedures consisting primarily of responses to conditions as they arise during the unfolding course of the journey. The Trukese navigator must continually be aware of his objective and interpret from the information at hand whatever adjustments will have to be made in order to ensure its success. As a basis for making decisions, it is of great importance for a Trukese to pay the strictest attention possible to his current circumstances and the practical consequences they may have for his eventual goal of reaching his destination.

> His [a Trukese's] information consists of a large number of discrete observations, a combination of motions, sounds, feel of the wind, wave patterns, star relationships, etc. Each is a concrete, largely unequivocal factual observation. Either the boat is heading toward the correct star or it is not. The wind is from a certain direction and of a certain velocity; although it takes practice to observe this accurately, the fact is unambiguous. . . . The navigator's mental image is analogous to a radar screen on which a moving spot of light shows his position relative to other objects at any moment. His navigational decisions are then made on an "ad hoc" basis to assure continued progress toward his goal. The operational judgements regarding changes in sailing directions would actually be arrived at in exactly the same way as if he were constantly in sight of land; the difference lies not in how the boat is handled but in being able to "know" where the landmarks are without being able to see [or verbalize] them. (Gladwin, 1964, p. 172)

I want to suggest a certain parallel between the systems of navigation described by Gladwin and the debate among researchers of the medical encounter over qualitative and quantitative methods. Much of the debate in medical interaction research has focused on comparing methods independent of particular contexts, questions, or outcomes. Although it is quite clear that the methods used by Gladwin's navigators differ in both type and degree, it is also the case that they both solve the same practical problem successfully. The value of Gladwin's analysis is that it includes both context and outcome as determinants of methodological practices. The presence or absence of map-making skills is essentially irrelevant to the Trukese navigator, as is the ability or inability of European navigators to read local wave patterns.

Roter and Frankel (1992) have recently proposed that methods of research, like those of navigation, are open to description in their own terms and should be judged on the extent to which they succeed in answering the questions that they raise in the context in which they were raised. They encourage combining methods where feasible and applicable. Crabtree and Miller (1992) have also advocated the use of a multimethod approach in primary care research. Finally, granting agencies such as the Agency for Health Care Policy and Research (AHCPR) are beginning to endorse the concept of multimethod research, as evidenced by a multiyear award to Levinson, Roter, and Frankel in 1992 to combine qualitative and quantitative approaches in studying communication aspects of medical malpractice.

CONCLUSION

I began this chapter by citing George Engel's idea that the clinical interview represents a powerful tool available to the physician. I then argued that there is increasing research evidence of a link between specific elements of the clinical interview process and both biomedical and functional outcomes of care. Although it is probably too early to test Dr. Engel's assertion in any meaningful way, the evidence regarding the importance of the interview is incontrovertible.

As research has progressed in scope and sophistication, so too has the potential for linking various conceptual, methodological, and philosophical domains. As we approach the 21st century, we may well find that we are at the beginning of the next great advance in medicine: developing a true understanding of how biological, psychological, and social forces influence health, illness, and disease. Although it is impossible at this point to know the shape or substance of that advance, it is not hard to predict that research on the clinical interview process will be at the heart of the effort.

14

THE HEALTH ECONOMY AND POLITICAL FORCES ON PROVIDER BEHAVIOR

Louis F. Rossiter

Long ago dubbed "the dismal science," economics began to apply its particular view on health care in earnest in the United States about the time the federal government became involved. The federal government needed answers to how it should spend its new commitment to purchase health care. The field of health economics rose up to provide those answers—or at least provide people who pretended to give answers for a fee.

This chapter is an introduction to health economics with a policy focus. That is, it covers several basic tools and concepts from the field of economics and applies them to health care with an eye toward the policy implications of such an exercise. Policy issues regarding primary care are emphasized, but not without recognizing the interaction between primary care and other types of health care.

The chapter is intended to inform the reader uninitiated into the ways of economists and the economists' cheerless view of things as they are or even as they ought to be. Economists' tools should provide a reasonable approach to many problems in primary care research (e.g., see Folland, Goodman, & Stano, 1993). Those working in interdisciplinary teams to answer basically clinical questions with economic overtones should gain tolerance and understanding by an exposure to the economists' tools.

WHAT IS HEALTH ECONOMICS AND POLICY?

Health economics is the application of economic methods of analysis to an understanding of the health care industry in any economy (e.g., see Fuchs,

1986). The tools of the economist include (a) a clear statement of assumptions, (b) marginal analysis, and (c) the use of theoretical and statistical models to describe and make predictions. Health care is defined broadly and can include questions about:

- The contribution of health care services to the overall economy
- The measurement of health status and the impact on health status of spending on health resources
- The ways in which participants (consumers—that is, patients, physicians, hospitals, and other participants) in the health care sector act
- The impact of government policy on the performance of the health care industry

This list is just a partial description of the types of questions that have been addressed.

THE ECONOMIST'S APPROACH TO PROBLEM SOLVING

Economists have a unique way of approaching problems. Highly mathematical, they have a way of thinking that relies upon abstractions and theories that on the surface appear irrelevant. In actuality, these abstractions can be quite illuminating because the economist uses several tools to approach problems.

One important tool is the assumption of rationality. In order to sort out the various reasons for human actions, economists routinely assume that people are rational and will always behave in perfectly rational ways. This assumption is accompanied by a heavy reliance, some say overreliance, on economic rationality. Thus consumers are driven by a need to maximize satisfaction— greed, in a sense. Even beneficent actions are viewed as merely means to an end. The end is viewed as self-satisfaction and satisfaction maximization related to good works. Organizations, or firms in economic parlance, are motivated by profits—nothing more, nothing less. In one classic view from health economics, even the not-for-profit hospital operates not for the good of the community but to maximize the incomes of the affiliated physicians. Adopting this view, economics can strip away the other possibly important determinants of behavior and focus on one or a few key ones. The approach is not to say that other factors are not important, just that they are not important for the moment. This can be a useful tool at times, but noneconomists can find it a myopic view.

Another important tool is the use of abstraction, usually in the form of graphs and charts. Some of the more common graphs that are the tools of economists are included in this chapter. Such charts help one to think in two-dimensional space, or in terms of cause and effect. They also help one to think strategically in a way that projects proposed changes and their impact. This type of thinking can be useful in planning for change and providing leadership.

Finally, economists use models as metaphors. The models can be theoretical or empirical. Health economics is especially reliant upon empirical models because it tends to be more applied and data driven than other areas of economics. The models sometimes add an unrealistic air. But they help to carefully lay out the problem or the hypothesized behavior in a way that can be understood clearly.

What Economics and Policy Determine

Turning now to the question of provider behavior specifically, there are a number of large or macro questions that economics purports to study and understand. These are discussed very briefly here.

What Type of Health Care Services Exist in Society

One estimate of the role of the physician in the delivery of health care suggests that physicians are the largest single determinant of the amount and types of health care produced. Although spending on physicians accounts for less than 30% of total spending on health care, physicians actually control, through admissions to hospitals or prescriptions for services or pharmaceuticals, about 80% of all health care spending. This basic fact is a major rationale for researching physician behavior, given the major concern about rising health care spending.

On the whole, the U.S. economy and that of most other industrialized countries are remarkably similar in their health care spending, which is about 14% of total spending in the economy. If we will soon be spending nearly $900 billion in the near future on health care, that means about $720 billion will be controlled by physicians' decisions about their patients.

The trend has been toward more costly and catastrophic care. If the 80% figure is correct, that trend is largely influenced by physicians and the desires of society.

In an earlier study, Berk and Monheit (1992) traced trends in health spending from 1928 to 1980 and found health expenditures concentrated among the top 1% of those spending money for health care. In an update to that study, the authors found that the trend toward concentration had increased. In 1987 the top 1% of spenders accounted for 30% of health spending, up from 26% in 1970 and 29% in 1980. If physicians are largely responsible for these decisions, what is going on here?

Talk of rationing, caps on spending, redesigned insurance benefits, and controls on technology is obviously driven by these spending trends. But a better understanding of the nature of medicine, training in medicine, and patterns of care in practice should be addressed to explain the phenomenon.

Who Will Receive Services and on What Basis

Economics concerns itself with the distribution of income and wealth in society. In health care, the concern is with who gets what type of care.

Social insurance has increasingly played an important role in answering this question. Compulsory national health insurance had its start in Germany at the turn of the last century. More than 100 years later, it appears that the United States may also pass compulsory national coverage of some kind.

Of major concern in such programs for economics is how the payments are made to providers under the social insurance program. In the United States, the two major social insurance programs, Medicare for the elderly and Medicaid for the poor, have relatively huge budgets for studying the economic impacts of changes in payment policy. These also have a direct bearing on who will receive what services and on what basis.

Who Will Deliver Services

Manpower issues also concern the economists' policy perspective. Numerous economic studies exist on the number and types of physicians and other health care personnel. Economists with special training in labor economics concern themselves with such issues. Regulations are thought to play a very important role. And again the dismal aspect of the economists' views rises to the surface. Most regulations in the professions, especially the health professions, are viewed not as protection for the patient or the consumer but as protection for the profession. Regulations limit who will deliver services, reduce competition, and are economically motivated.

How the Burden of Financing Services Will Be Distributed

A well-worn economic saying is that "there is no such thing as a free lunch." That is to say, in keeping with the first law of thermodynamics, you cannot squeeze blood out of a turnip. The second law of thermodynamics says that if you could squeeze blood out of a turnip it would not be much. A similar concept is important for understanding how we pay for health care.

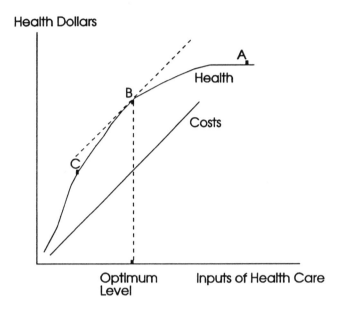

Figure 14.1. Relationship of Resources to Produce Health Care and Health Care Dollars

The diagram in Figure 14.1 illustrates the point. Here, dollars are measured on the vertical axis. Resources used to produce health care are on the horizontal axis. Two basic curves are shown in this graph. One curve is a cost curve. It tells us that as more resources in health care are used, more dollars are required to purchase them. This is shown as a straight-line relationship. It could be shown in other ways, but this is the simplest way to show it. It just means that unit increases in health resources used in an economy (number of physicians, hospital beds, expensive equipment) require unit increases in dollars to purchase those resources.

The other curve is more complicated. It is a curve of the level of health that comes from using more resources. The curved nature of the "health" line is significant. It tells us that as more resources are used for health care in an economy, the level of health of the population will increase, perhaps very sharply at first. But as more and more resources are used, the added amount of health in the population does not increase at the same rate. It increases at a decreasing rate and eventually levels off. There comes a point, in other words, where more spending does not increase the level of health.

Two points need to be made about this construction. First, the point labeled A is what some have called the point at which "flat of the curve medicine" is practiced. This is where, arguably, most doctors practice. They use services, require pharmaceuticals, and order tests and procedures until the work done adds nothing else to the care of the patient except that it does no harm.

Second, the optimal level of the use of resources is at Point B. This is where the difference between the benefit obtained (health) is greatest compared to the cost of resources. We worry a great deal about how much of the Gross Domestic Product is devoted to health care. It is increasing in almost every country. It is largest in the United States. An economist would say that the amount devoted to the GDP is not at issue as much as how far beyond the optimal Point B we are. The United States is far beyond this point. Many physicians are far beyond this point with their patients, often because the patient wants them to be.

JUST TWO LITTLE WORDS: SUPPLY AND DEMAND

The contribution of health care to health, in summary, is highly questionable. There are clear relationships between poverty, or the lack thereof, and good health. The contribution of the formal medical care market is much less clear and undocumented, despite all that we spend on it.

Why is so much spent? One thought is that we spend so much on physicians because we want to. We demand what physicians have to sell. Some of what physicians sell is caring and attention, even if it does not always do all that much good. And people want that. We call this phenomenon the demand for health and medical care. As a concept, it represents the willingness of people to purchase various amounts of physician services at varying prices. When these services are mixed in with the supply of health and medical services, one has a market for such services and prices for transactions.

In terms of physician behavior, what is quite clear is that physicians certainly initiate demand for services because after all that is why patients pay physicians. Patients want physicians to tell them what to do to restore good health. If we ask whether a portion of the services they initiate is induced demand, that is, above and beyond the level demanded by a fully informed consumer, the answer is also affirmative. The sources of induced demand are not one-dimensional (Rossiter & Wilensky, 1987). Demand may be induced by physicians because insurance encourages it. Particular physician characteristics may be associated with physician-induced demand, and patient characteristics, particularly health status, may determine the level of physician influence on demand. The supply of physicians could influence physician-induced demand and would be considered self-interested, physician-induced demand. But estimates suggest that this type of supply-induced demand is rather limited. Practice style variation and the tendency for patients in physician-rich areas to have multiple physicians are also newly recognized and important factors.

One of the major policy questions surrounding the whole debate about physician behavior is the answer to the question of whether enrollment in U.S. medical schools is too high, too low, or just about right. Today, we seem to be saying it is the right number but not the right mix of generalists and specialists. With the largest supply of physicians ever in existence in the United States, fee discounts are commonplace, utilization review has flowered as a newly discovered form of business management, and the medical profession is visibly shaken. This hardly describes a field that, when faced with more numbers of its own kind, simply generates demand sufficient to meet income or other objectives. Few would argue that the excessive supply of physicians has not been an important enabling factor in the United States for the reforms in the system, especially managed care. Such structural reform may give us better policy tools to bring the optimal quantity of resources devoted to health, along with more useful contexts for applying our growing understanding of physician behavior.

15

PROVIDER BEHAVIOR
A RESEARCH PERSPECTIVE

Carolyn Clancy

> Interventions . . . are available. The challenge is how best to implement them, maintaining positive changes over time while continuing to advance our knowledge of risk-reducing strategies through research. (Lee, 1985, p. 783)

The Agency for Health Care Policy and Research (AHCPR) was established in December 1989 with a mission directed toward several broad goals: (a) promoting improvements in clinical practice and patient outcomes through more appropriate and effective health care services; (b) promoting improvements in the financing, organization, and delivery of health care services; and (c) increasing access to quality care (Clinton, 1990). The creation of the AHCPR represented a shift in priorities toward outcomes and effectiveness research in medical practice and made explicit the federal government's role in developing practice guidelines (Gray, 1992). This chapter reviews the relationship between provider behavior and the major objectives of the AHCPR.

Research in practice variations, including the work of Wennberg (Wennberg & Gittelson, 1982), Chassin (Chassin et al., 1979), and others, has demonstrated that substantial variations in medical practice exist that cannot be explained by observed differences in patient disease severity or access to care. These observations corroborate work done as early as 1938 by Glover, who reported a tenfold difference in rates of tonsillectomy among different areas

The author gratefully acknowledges the thoughtful comments of Drs. Howard Brody, Norman Weissman, and Eric Wall. The views expressed in this chapter do not represent the official views of the U.S. Public Health Service or the Department of Health and Human Services.

in England (Glover, 1938). The interest of policymakers was provoked by these findings, particularly in view of failures to contain costs in the 1980s.

The etiology of practice variations has been the subject of extensive debate. Practice variations can reflect variations in access to care, unmeasured variations in severity of illness, professional uncertainty, or providers' practice style. In addition, variations are not evenly distributed across conditions: for example, there is far less variation observed in hospital admission rates for acute myocardial infarction or hip fractures than in rates for hysterectomies or prostatectomies. These observations suggest that a significant proportion of practice variations is due to professional uncertainty or lack of consensus on the best course of action (Wennberg, 1984).

AHCPR was established to achieve the following objectives: (a) to increase the knowledge base concerning the effectiveness of different interventions; (b) to use the information developed from this research to improve decision making by physicians and patients; (c) to develop and disseminate guidelines that will help physicians provide appropriate, cost-effective care; and (d) to evaluate the effects of practice guidelines on the processes and outcomes of patient care.

The ultimate test of both research in medical effectiveness and the development of practice guidelines is the effect on patient outcomes. To the extent that practice variations reflect an inadequate knowledge base, additional research can assist providers and patients in making better decisions, which may result in improved outcomes. The AHCPR believes that clinical practice guidelines can enhance the efforts of both providers and patients to make the best decisions possible about medical interventions. Providers will make practice decisions that rely more on scientific-based knowledge and respected professional judgment than is currently the case, and patients will become better informed health care consumers and participate more fully in the clinical decisions that affect them. The emphasis on outcomes of significance to the patient underscores the hope that these efforts will also lead to improved quality of care and possibly increased value for health expenditures.

Efforts to translate the results of clinical research or guidelines into improvements in clinical practice are not new. Providers have adopted some innovations rapidly, such as laparoscopic cholecystectomy, but at other times have failed to change their behavior even when randomized controlled trials have demonstrated the efficacy of a new treatment (Greco & Eisenberg, 1993). A growing recognition of the gap between the *efficacy* of an intervention—the demonstrated potential under ideal conditions for a narrowly defined patient group, often in a tertiary care setting—and the *effectiveness* of the same intervention—the observed effect when applied to the average patient in a variety of settings—has also been a driving force behind the recognition of the importance of medical effectiveness research.

For example, the Lipids Research Clinics (LRC) Trial was intended to establish whether lowering serum cholesterol could prevent coronary artery disease (Lipid Research Clinics Program, 1984) and has become widely used as a basis for preventing coronary artery disease. The study showed decisively that lowering serum cholesterol prevented heart attacks. However, LRC enrolled fewer than one in 100 eligible people and restricted participants to well-educated men between ages 35 and 69 with unusually high cholesterol levels that did not respond to diet and without other major diseases or long-term medications. An expensive drug with unpleasant side effects was used. The researchers made unusual efforts to ensure that the patients took their medications. The main outcome of the study, reduction in the incidence of coronary disease and death, was only a partial triumph because the overall death rates were not changed. The generalizability of these results to less compliant or less well-educated patients, women, or those with major comorbidities is not well established.

Providers must rely on clinical judgment to decide whether to translate the results of this study to the care of their patients who are not represented in the study population. Several studies have in fact documented that providers do not apply the National Cholesterol Education Program guidelines (based on the LRC) to all of their patients. It is less clear whether this failure to do so represents lack of awareness of the study, the failure of providers to incorporate these recommendations into their daily routines, patient noncompliance, an informed decision by patient and provider not to act on an elevated cholesterol, or some other explanation. Much of the previous research in improving provider behavior has been directed toward improving providers' decision making. This approach focuses on the individual provider's knowledge, information processing, judgment, and motivation. Eisenberg (1986) has proposed six major ways of changing physicians' practice patterns: education, feedback, participation, administrative rules, incentives, and penalties. Education of practitioners and feedback have produced marginal improvements, but changes in financial incentives have decreased the utilization of ineffective practices in some instances. Other studies have noted that the development and dissemination of consensus recommendations have had little apparent effect on medical practice (Lomas, 1991). Multiple studies of practitioner attitudes and behavior have demonstrated that (a) practitioners frequently overestimate their compliance with recommended practices, and (b) sustained behavior change requires a commitment of the practitioners to the guidelines and their implementation.

Other research suggests that additional perspectives are required to improve provider behavior. For example, although most physicians recognize the importance of examining the feet of diabetic patients, they often fail to do so.

Cohen has shown that merely having the patient remove his or her socks and shoes when placed in the exam room substantially increases the likelihood that the feet will be examined (Cohen, 1983). This finding suggests that organizational changes can enhance and reinforce the behavior of knowledgeable, motivated providers.

In addition to increasing providers' knowledge and addressing practice barriers, the effectiveness of interventions in changing providers' behavior is influenced by communication, the messenger, and the setting. Theories of adult learning tell us that active participation is an essential component of acquiring and using new knowledge. Interventions are more likely to be successful when there is interactive communication with learner involvement. Also, people become committed to an intervention when they are involved in its development (Donaldson & Povar, 1985).

The messenger used to implement the intervention is also important to its success. The success of investigators who have borrowed so-called "academic detailing" from successful pharmaceutical companies offers evidence that behavior change is facilitated by respected peers and opinion leaders (Soumerai & Avorn, 1990). Finally, the success of an intervention will be enhanced or diminished by the setting. Interventions are best implemented at the local level by well-known change agents (Schwartz & Cohen, 1990).

Interventions that do not consider the daily realities of busy clinicians in practice are unlikely to succeed. The most cogent guideline is of little value if the information is not accessible when the relevant clinical situation occurs, or if the intervention cannot be easily incorporated into a particular practice site.

RESEARCH ISSUES

The effectiveness of implementing clinical practice guidelines—or other attempts to change provider behavior—is dependent upon (a) the extent to which the guidelines provide useful information on the detection, evaluation, and management of specific diseases and conditions, and (b) the degree to which practitioners alter practice behavior to incorporate the guidelines. Although multiple guidelines have been developed by professional organizations, insurers, utilization review panels, and others, the optimal method of implementing guidelines to effect sustained change in behavior has remained elusive. Previous research has shown that even when practitioners view guidelines favorably, they are slow to change their practices (Lomas et al., 1989). A recent survey of practice guidelines done for the Institute of Medicine found that implementation and evaluation have received secondary emphasis relative to development and promotion (Audet & Greenfield, 1989).

The limited successes of many previous efforts to change provider behavior are a reminder that significant challenges remain in translating the findings of effectiveness research and dissemination of clinical practice guidelines into improved quality of care. The principles of continuous quality improvement (CQI) incorporate many of the previously noted conditions for success. This model engages the support and participation of all members of the health care team in an effort to achieve continuous improvement in quality, defined to include the needs and preferences of the patient (Kritchevsky & Simmons, 1991). A fundamental precept of this method is the recognition that medical care is not delivered by a physician working in isolation but rather requires the smooth functioning of a team of workers and a commitment of all members of a health care organization to the underlying philosophy of CQI. The AHCPR is currently funding a cooperative agreement in which the investigators are using CQI to evaluate strategies for implementation of clinical practice guidelines (for hypertension and depression) and to improve understanding of the process and effects of incorporating guidelines into practice. We believe that these studies will provide important insights regarding the implementation of practice guidelines. The broad outlines of CQI would appear to satisfy many of the hypothesized requirements for effective interventions to change provider behavior. This approach has not yet been validated, however. In addition, there is an inherent tension between CQI, by definition a local process, and implementation of guidelines developed by a national organization. Further, CQI in its purest form implies that providers select the topics or interventions, suggesting an inherent tension between guidelines and CQI that requires further exploration. Finally, CQI is based on a systems approach to reducing unnecessary variation in practice. Most of the previous research on practice variation, however, has focused on the physician as the principal actor/decision maker. Perhaps this framework should be modified to examine the health care team or organization as the locus of accountability for clinical practice. In short, it is quite likely that these studies will raise as many issues as they resolve.

As we look to the future to determine whether effectiveness research and practice guidelines have resulted in improved patient outcomes, there are many issues that will be critical to the success of AHCPR's efforts. Some important topics that will engage health services researchers in the future include (a) the effect of practice guidelines on practitioners' knowledge and behavior, (b) the effect of guidelines on practice, and (c) the impact on patient behavior and, ultimately, patient outcomes.

The Effect of Practice Guidelines
on Practitioners' Knowledge and Behavior

A central issue is how practitioners will adopt new recommendations and adapt them to their practices. Methods from the fields of education, psychology, decision making, marketing, sociology, and social learning theory, to name a few, can be applied to this area. Efforts to link changes in knowledge with changes in practice must continue, particularly those that help inform the translation of guidelines developed at the national level to changes in behavior at the level of the provider-patient encounter. Additional research that clarifies the most effective incentives for changing provider behavior is also needed, particularly in an environment in which there is tremendous enthusiasm for economic incentives that are based more on theory than on empirical findings.

The Effect of Guidelines on Practice

Ultimately, efforts to change provider behavior, whether in the form of practice guidelines or other intervention, will succeed only if they enhance rather than disrupt the provider-patient relationship. Primary care providers and patients frequently negotiate among multiple concerns to select the most important issue(s) to address in a single encounter. There is very little research that describes how providers select among multiple guidelines that are relevant to an individual patient, and how these are incorporated in the ongoing care of a patient. The relative cost effectiveness of strategies to change providers' behavior and the study of barriers to delivery of recommended services in daily practice have also received little attention. Of special relevance to primary care providers is the effect of practice guidelines on referral to specialists.

One key difference between guidelines facilitated by AHCPR and those developed by other organizations is the incorporation of the consumer perspective. Each guideline panel includes one consumer representative, and each guideline also includes a consumer version. Many thousands of people have obtained copies of the consumer guidelines for the first three guidelines, and the effect of this information on patients, providers, or the process and outcome of care has not been studied.

The Impact on Patient Behavior, and Ultimately on Patient Outcomes

Persuading patients to modify "unhealthy" behaviors has long been a challenge to primary care providers, and additional research that helps primary care providers target specific behavioral strategies to individual patients is critical. An important issue that has received little scrutiny concerns the relationship between practice guidelines and patient satisfaction, particularly when a guideline recommends doing less rather than more. Existing research has emphasized adding recommended practices and has attempted to assess why this doesn't happen. There is far less known about how providers and patients abandon practices that are no longer considered effective.

Finally, the work of AHCPR in effectiveness research and clinical practice guidelines has just begun. A great deal of work remains to determine the best methods of assessing the impact of practice guidelines and new knowledge. The establishment of the AHCPR was founded on studies of conditions for which claims data (e.g., procedures) were particularly useful, but many conditions in primary care are not easily captured by such data. Innovative approaches to capturing the content of primary care encounters are clearly required.

At the Third Primary Care Research Conference in Atlanta (January 1993), George Lundberg, M.D., said that his personal choice for the name of the *Journal of the American Medical Association (JAMA)* would be *JPBC (Journal of Physician Behavior Change)* because the ultimate value of the journal should be assessed in terms of its effects on physician behavior to improve patient care. It is clear that these issues will offer ample opportunities for researchers in the foreseeable future.

16

THE PUBLIC VOICE IN RESEARCH

Kate Brown

Benjamin F. Crabtree

Who is the public? Is it ever possible to know, let alone tap, the public's reality? Do special interest associations and organizations speak for the public? How can researchers best call forth, understand, and then convey the public's needs, opinions, or behaviors? Is it hubris to try? Are the endless tabulations of random polls the voice of the public? Or is the voice of the public better carried through the stories told in detailed ethnographies of neighborhoods and villages around the world? Can one person's story speak for many? Whose voices have gone unheard or even silenced when researchers have presumed to report the public's voice?

These days answers to such questions swirl in a heady mix of theory and praxis at professional meetings and in social science literature. The issues have particular relevance for applied researchers concerned with providing humane health care that more closely matches the unmet needs of patients. Always an issue in a democracy, public constituencies are legitimately demanding a voice alongside the "experts" in crafting health care reimbursement policies and health research priorities and funding decisions. This chapter examines some of these questions: Can the "public" be defined adequately to have its "voice" represented? And if so, how can researchers best understand and communicate the content and meaning of this voice? These questions will be examined in light of previous research eliciting public responses to health-related issues.

METHODOLOGICAL QUESTIONS

Social scientists have always made it their business to be the translators of others' voices. In contrast with analytic philosophy, social science methodology has the implicit goal of reaching into the heads and lives of actual people as the source of our knowledge and commentary. But in the spirit of postmodern reflexivity, researchers are raising critical, self-conscious questions about claims to speak on another's behalf. Specifically, this reflection pivots on important questions about who speaks in the name of the public, what is heard, and how that information is interpreted.

There is growing concern about whose voice is represented in the research record. Research findings are influenced by whom we ask for information, whose reasoning we investigate, and whose expression of need we elicit. Given constraints of money, time, and method, empirical researchers will always be compelled to limit the number of voices heard, the depth of voices heard, or both. Anthropologists have traditionally advised fieldworkers to develop rapport with one or two "key informants" who can help make sense of what is being said and done in the group. However, fieldworkers are simultaneously cautioned not to rely too heavily on the words of their informants, who are predictably known to be the "deviants and stranger-handlers" (Agar, 1980, p. 120) of the group (for more on informant issues, see Johnson, 1990; Poggie, 1972; Romney, Weller, & Batchelder, 1988). Researchers also need to attend to the one whose voice appears loudest and why.

Systems of random selection are recommended by quantitative researchers to correct for such potential biases. But no matter how careful and complete the randomization, the problem of bias in initial selection of the universe of respondents remains (also see Newman and Stanfield, this volume). Conscious efforts must be made to counter historical patterns of sample selection that have systematically excluded the voices of women, ethnic and racial minorities, stigmatized groups, and people without money or homes (Harding 1991; Lather, this volume; Stanfield & Katerndahl, this volume).

We must similarly be aware that the methods we choose provide different types of information about the public, inevitably muting some aspects of voice and amplifying others. The forced-choice questions of a survey provide one type of information, and more open-ended interview and observational techniques provide another. Instead of arguing which data are more "true" to the public's view, those with a multimethod perspective would try to develop an interactive, self-correcting dialogue between data sources created through different methods (Denzin, 1989; Janesick, this volume).

"Truthful" representation also varies according to the eye of the beholder. As ethnographers well know, researchers are always confronted with conflicting, irreconcilable accounts of the same events (Heider, 1988; Trend, 1979). Furthermore, information can be encoded and framed in multiple ways in the analysis, and theorists such as Clifford Geertz caution researchers about the "illusion of swimming in the stream of their [another's] experience" (Geertz, 1983, p. 257). More accurately, we may be telling our own stories, masking our subjective renditions of reality through the phrases of others that we are translating (Rabinow, 1977). For these reasons, the authority of an outsider speaking unreflexively on behalf of insiders' worldview and interpretations is no longer credible. Instead, researchers such as James Clifford suggest another type of "dialogic" methodology that builds on triangulation of methods by allowing both subject and researcher to coconstruct and thus share authority for the eventual account or cultural representation (Clifford, 1983, p. 147).

THE PUBLIC VOICE IN HEALTH CARE RESEARCH

Despite these methodological hazards—or perhaps because of them—researchers should insist on the value of including the "public voice" in health services and policy research. The importance of eliciting participatory input in public health research (Paul, 1955) and in medical anthropology and sociology has long been recognized. Much of the approach of current international public health programs harkens back to the International Conference on Primary Health Care held in Alma-Ata in the USSR in 1978 (World Health Organization, 1978). Key provisions in the Alma-Ata Declaration are *community participation*—"Community participation is the process by which individuals and families assume responsibility for their own health and welfare and for those of the community, and develop the capacity to contribute to their and the community's development" (World Health Organization, 1978, p. 50)—and *community diagnosis*—"There are many ways in which the community can participate in every stage of primary health care. It must first be involved in assessment of the situation, the definition of problems and the setting of priorities" (World Health Organization, 1978, p. 51). These same ideals expressed at the Alma-Ata conference have also been developed in the Community Oriented Primary Care (COPC) model described by Nutting (Nutting, 1990; Nutting & Connor, 1986) and Starfield (1992). The COPC model seeks to better integrate primary care clinical practice into the needs of the community. A key concept of the model is for primary care practice to identify community health problems based on the subjective impressions of the practitioner and/or consumer groups (Nutting & Connor, 1986, p. 143).

Various methodologies can be useful in providing access to patients' and caregivers' understandings of how to make medical care more responsive to their needs. For instance, ethnographies by qualitative researchers such as Anselm Strauss have provided windows into the daily existential and inter-actional encounters of people living with disease (Strauss, 1975). The auto-biographical literature and data collection of patients, relatives of patients, and providers can also be an important source of firsthand information about the health care system (Moustakas, 1990). Focus group methodologies have been used productively by several analysts to elicit the variety of opinions about complex policy questions (see Morgan, 1993). For example, Cheri Pies consciously structured her policy recommendations concerning the ethical use of Norplant on the basis of input from many diverse "stakeholders" in the debate (Pies, 1993). Bell, Gimarc, and Brown (1993) at the Department of Health in South Carolina have used focus groups made up of community members in different locations around the state to inform and mobilize public participation in health care reform legislation.

Given the previous discussion, it would be naive to assume that neutrality reigns automatically when researchers select who will speak for the interests of the community, patients, or providers. Even when researchers strive for a cross-section of experience and opinion, bias can prevail. The research agenda is often determined in the first place by those who articulate their needs and perspectives. Thus those who speak through the research channel can often be successful in lobbying for attention to their constituencies' needs. Being able to effectively speak through the research channel is thus also a question inseparable from considerations of power and influence (see Lather, this volume; Stanfield and Katerndahl, this volume). There are considerable fruits to be won as a result of what is placed on the agenda. Not only will needs presumably be met, but money will flow in the direction of those concerned about meeting these needs. It is not surprising that significant effort is made by interest groups lobbying for attention to their constituents' needs.

Representatives of such organizations as the AARP (American Association of Retired Persons) and disease-related voluntary associations such as the American Lung Association have long known the effectiveness of using political influence to ensure attention for their research needs. After years of neglecting women's health, in 1990 the National Institutes of Health were moved by advocacy and legislative forces to establish research guidelines and funding for including women in research protocols and focusing on conditions specific to women in the Women's Health Equality Act. Grassroots AIDS activists such as the National Gay and Lesbian Task Force and ACT UP (AIDS Coalition to Unleash Power) have had to use political organizing and media attention to counter prejudice and denial to stimulate funding for AIDS and HIV research. These activists are credited with accelerating the protocol used by the FDA to approve experimental medical treatments for AIDS

(Misztal & Moss, 1990). An innovative primary health care model has been proposed by Seifert and colleagues (Early & Seifert, 1981; Seifert, 1982a, 1982b, 1987, this volume), who create a "patient advisory board" to participate in both clinical and research decisions.

The process of how research agendas are set would itself be an interesting field of inquiry and deserves study, especially in light of the need to ensure the inclusion of those who are without the political clout to be heard.

CONCLUSION

The public can serve an important role in health care research. We suggest the metaphor of "dialogue" for guiding how to maximize the usefulness and validity of research into the experience, opinions, and attitudes of patients, families, providers, and community members. First, there needs to be dialogue between researcher and subject. Researchers must consciously seek input from the users and providers of health care in ways that respect their expertise and advice (see Borkan, this volume; Miller, this volume). This can occur at all stages of the research, from conceptualizing the research question and collecting the data to the analysis and dissemination of the results. Lay advisers can help to define relevant areas for research, identify problems and suggest solutions in the proposed methodologies, and hold researchers accountable for the reliability and impact of their analyses. This description includes many of the strategies of action research (Reason, 1994; Schensul & Schensul, 1982; Tax, 1958; Whyte, 1991), in which members of the community are trained as collaborators (see Borrero, Schensul, & Garcia, 1982).

This dialogue would enhance the other dialogues suggested in this volume for the development of collaborative research. Just as researchers need to create opportunities for dialogue between the findings from different methods, both quantitative and qualitative, they need to create dialogues between researcher and researched, and between public and policy makers. Both the comparison of methods and the comparison of voices can lead to a richer, more complete understanding of the depth and range of such complex issues as patients' satisfaction and providers' decision-making strategies. It will be important for researchers to learn a common language in order to accomplish this difficult but important interchange.

In the spirit of these suggestions, the conference planners decided that some inclusion of the public voice was important to the content and process of the overall conference that inspired this book. Milton Seifert, Jr., one of the conference observers, had observed a lack of representation by patients and the public in the original conference agenda. The conference planners had two objectives for adding this public forum: (a) the group, relatively untainted by current intellectual trends and disciplinary debates, would provide fresh perspectives about primary care research priorities; and (b) the planners wanted to emphasize the impact of listening to the patients themselves for AHCPR, research and funding policymakers, and the broader primary care research community.

Using a small group of informants as spokespersons for the public voice can be a valuable but provocative model of process for research and group dynamics. The planners hoped the format would elicit useful information to direct research priorities and also demonstrate the value of such a method while raising some sticky methodological questions of validity, generalizability, and subjectivity for general discussion. In so doing, the conference planners hoped to encourage an actual exercise in multilevel dialogue including members of the public and researchers from diverse disciplinary backgrounds. The challenge is for researchers in primary care to move beyond current models that rely heavily on having research questions defined in academic centers and begin to solicit more active participation of the public voice in research.

III

The Search for
Multimethod Research

Attempts to integrate different disciplinary perspectives and methodologies into a research team have achieved variable success. One suspects that many more efforts fail than succeed as planned. The Conference on Multimethods Research in Primary Care was planned so that participants of different backgrounds, different beliefs, and different preferred ways of solving problems could meet, agree on a few important questions, and design multimethod studies to address these questions.

In many ways, the conference was an effort to model a community of inquiry that rarely occurs in the academic environments with which we are familiar. Peck (1987, chap. 5) describes four stages of community development and characteristics of each stage:

1. "Pseudocommunity," during which there is conflict avoidance. This stage is characterized by:
   - Polite rules of discourse
   - The minimization of differences
   - Limited expressions of feelings
2. "Chaos," in which there is open conflict. Now one finds:
   - Openly recognized differences
   - A desire to convert

- An urge to resolve chaos and conflict by (a) escaping into organization (return to pseudocommunity), or (b) moving to emptiness

3. "Emptiness," where participants empty themselves of communication barriers. They let go of:
   - Expectations/preconceptions
   - Ideology
   - Prejudices
   - Need to control/fix/solve

4. "Community," characterized by:
   - Inclusivity, commitment, consensus
   - Shared leadership
   - Graceful fighting
   - Emotional realism
   - A safe place
   - Community spirit

The chapters in this section examine how the participants at the conference followed these stages of development. They tell the story of the five people who planned the "multimethods" conference and the 20 who joined with them in Omaha to share knowledge and perspectives and work on strategies to solve important problems. The process story is told in Chapter 17. In this chapter, the editors share their reflections about what was intended for this conference and what they learned from the experience. The process story is complemented by Chapter 22. In this chapter, the four invited observers provide an interpretation and critique of the conference from the perspectives of researcher, practitioner, and funding agency.

The introduction in Chapter 17 describes the events that led up to the conference, including the rationale for the structure and anticipated outcomes. This is followed by an in-depth description of the broader community development at the conference, including the process used by four small groups who were assigned to design a study around a particular question or content area.

Chapters 18 through 21 describe the work of the four small groups. Each is a reflective case report of the process of constructing cross-disciplinary research communities. Each of the four case reports readily accepts the need for multimethod research utilizing methodology appropriate to the research question at hand. The importance of triangulation or "converging operations" (see McCall, Chapter 22) was also central to operationalizing multimethod research.

As participants began to explore their assigned areas, the importance of linking the research to the clinical context became apparent. Central to this linking was including the role of public voice in addition to the clinical voice. Another feature that was deemed essential was the balance between local knowledge (and context) and generalizable knowledge.

In both the larger conference (Chapter 17) and the case reports (Chapters 18-21), there were several recurrent conversations at the wall. Quantitative experts had a need to talk only about methods/tools, qualitative experts were compelled to talk about paradigms and ending the dominance of logical positivism, and critical theorists kept focusing on power. Academicians had difficulty in not defending the value of their disciplinary turf, and clinicians had a need to keep the focus on outcomes. Remarkably, communication did occur, and a great deal was learned by all the participants.

The conference covered many ways to combine numbers and words in a cross-disciplinary fashion. These included combining statistical approaches and conceptual analysis (also see Mitchell, 1986); combining methods as a way to corroborate (provide convergence of findings), to elaborate (provide richness), and to initiate (offer new interpretations) (also see Rossman & Wilson, 1985); quantifying descriptive reports; presenting quantitative outcomes narratively; and allying statistical and descriptive evidence while maintaining the integrity of each (also see Light & Pillemer, 1982).

The six chapters in Part III provide important and helpful insights about some of the key issues in creating collaborative research and multimethod designs. These insights, along with a review of past proposals such as those of Morse (1991), Steckler, McLeroy, Goodman, Bird, and McCormick (1992), Miller and Crabtree (1992, 1994), and DePoy and Gitlin (1993), hold promise for the development of true collaborative transdisciplinary research. Specific suggestions from an analysis of these data are presented in Part IV.

17

THE CONFERENCE AS
COMMUNITY DEVELOPMENT

Anton J. Kuzel
Valerie J. Gilchrist
Richard B. Addison
Kate Brown
Benjamin F. Crabtree
William L. Miller

In May 1993, with the sponsorship of the Agency for Health Care Policy and Research (AHCPR), the editors brought together researchers with expertise in qualitative and quantitative methods and researchers with expertise in primary care provider behavior to discuss applying multimethod approaches to difficult primary care questions. We did so because we had concerns that the people doing and reporting primary care research were not imagining all the possible problems or the means to approach those problems. We hoped that bringing knowledgeable and open-minded people together from many disciplines would allow for sharing and creating new problem-solving approaches. Two assumptions underpinned this hope: (a) multimethod approaches would be an improvement over using individual isolated methods, and (b) reasonable people would be able to incorporate different perspectives and methods.

Conference objectives included the group's sharing their knowledge of primary care behavior (theory) and their expertise with many different research approaches (methods), identifying important unanswered questions about provider behavior research, and determining suitable multimethod approaches for investigating these questions. In the process we hoped to expand the imagination of the research community, to create a common language for cross-disciplinary communication, and to model a workable process for multimethod research.

The concept for the conference took root during a preconference on qualitative methods held immediately prior to the 19th Annual North American Primary Care Research Group Meeting in Quebec City on May 22, 1991. The level of interest for this preconference was overwhelming. Participants were strongly in favor of efforts to add qualitative approaches to the research agenda in primary care. However, we still struggled with the problem of how to proceed. Paul Nutting, then Director of the Division of Primary Care at AHCPR, suggested we consider a conference that would focus on a primary care research priority area as defined by the funding agency and by acknowledged experts in the field. In this way the research "establishment" would clearly "own the problem."

A key underlying assumption in the development of the conference was that questions should define methods, and not vice versa; thus the goal was to examine how both quantitative and qualitative models of inquiry could be applied to important questions in primary care research. The area of primary care provider behavior change was selected because it was a content area of interest and importance to the "audience" for the conference—fellow researchers and practitioners, funding agencies, and policymakers (e.g., see Schwartz & Cohen, 1990).

WHO TO INVITE?

Representatives from both quantitative and qualitative traditions were considered, especially people who were methods experts and who could articulate the essence of their method clearly and simply. Ideally, they would be able to apply their method to the arena of health care research. The quantitative methods we thought to represent were econometrics, randomized controlled trials, surveys, psychometrics, and statistical analysis (including meta-analysis). Qualitative methods on our list were observation, interviewing, document/artifact analysis, interpretive analysis, and critical analysis. We also wanted people who knew the field of changing provider behavior from multiple theoretical perspectives. These would be people who were not wedded to any one method but who understood and could describe the way they made sense of the topic and what was problematic about the topic. After discussions among ourselves and consultation with staff at AHCPR, we invited individuals from family medicine, internal medicine, pediatrics, anthropology, biostatistics, educational research, epidemiology, health policy and economics, psychology, and sociology to attend.

CONFERENCE FORMAT

In the fall of 1992 after AHCPR decided to fund the conference, the five coeditors gathered to discuss, debate, and plan the details of the conference. At this time, we articulated how we hoped to structure the conference so that it would model an invitational, transformational, and empowering discourse process in which (a) the role of power would be kept explicit; (b) our planning process would be shared with all participants; (c) the public would be given voice at the conference, especially informing question development; (d) the powers and principalities affecting the process would be acknowledged; and (e) diversity of gender, ethnicity, discipline, tradition, and perspective would be sought.

PRECONFERENCE SUMMARIES

The conference was organized as a working conference. To start a conversation across disciplines, each method and content expert was asked to prepare a 10-page summary that would introduce his or her perspective to a reader with no familiarity with that perspective. These summaries were sent to the editors, who distributed them to another participant, who we thought would have little or no familiarity with the topic. The reader was then asked to interview the author of the summary to confirm his or her understanding and fill in any gaps. Each participant was thus to learn from a "key informant" and then, in turn, to act as a key informant for someone else. We hoped this process would assist each participant in considering his or her assumptions and language.

Although all the participants were able to complete preliminary summaries, a significant number of the writer/reader dyads did not have the fullness of communication prior to the conference that we had intended. This limited the learners' ways of gaining understanding, at least prior to the conference.

PRESENTATION OF SUMMARIES

During the first half-day of the conference, each of the content area experts and methods experts was asked to present his or her *new* area. The participants were intentionally asked to present a perspective other than their own so that they could begin the process of thinking of other perspectives in a language conducive to communication.

Each of the content-area papers was presented in a 10-minute overview with 5 minutes for discussion. In general, this format was followed, although the discussions often exceeded the 5 minutes allotted.

The next two methods sessions (qualitative and quantitative) took place at the end of the morning and into the afternoon. A qualitative method was presented by someone with expertise in quantitative methods, and vice versa. During these presentations, some presented the broad overview and the basic assumptions as we had hoped; however, several presenters could not resist discussing their difficulties with the principles of the method, luckily with some humor:

> A clear advantage of the interview as a technique is that it permits the interviewer to dig in when necessary and advisable, justifying the cliche of the "in-depth interview." I keep looking for the people who are going to do shallow superficial interviewing in their projects, but . . .

> As you might well imagine, I am giving you the very basics of a controlled comparison, randomized control comparison. There are multiple variations on this main form; I think they came about with the advent of promotion and tenure at American universities and colleges.

Both initially and recurring throughout the conference, disciplinary critiques emerged. Although each participant spoke from, and at times defended, his or her own discipline, there was a tendency for

- the quantitative methodologists to focus on which method was best: "Well, I would like to go over it once again. In defense of some of the quantitative methodologies, many of the problems, many of the objections that are raised would run afoul of my dictum that you don't have to do stupid things. . . . I'll forgo the opportunity to get to the stupid use of the qualitative methods, but I can refer you to any number of mindless examples where qualitative researchers have gone wrong. . . ."
- the qualitative methodologists to focus on taken for granted assumptions: "I think we throw too many eggs at each other, between qualitative and quantitative, without looking at the more pervasive issue, and that is, how do you define what science is?"
- the clinicians to focus on "What difference does it make?": "For those of us who are clinicians, what are the implications about the therapeutics of this method? What is the therapeutic value or effect or not?"

By the end of these presentations of content and methods, the group evidenced much frustration. They were being asked to absorb a lot of information outside their area of expertise. The presentations were seen as superficial and not presented by the expert, and participants had little chance to respond and discuss areas of controversy. We saw bruised egos, staunchly defended disciplinary boundaries, and an effort to convert. Feelings of frustration and distance were articulated. The participants were fatigued, both mentally and physically.

GROUP PROCESS AT IDENTIFYING QUESTIONS

In the afternoon of the first day, a series of "discussion group" sessions were organized in an "inner circle/outer circle" format in which participants rotated in and out of a loosely moderated inner circle while the outer circle observed. The purpose of this process was to identify key questions that would be explored in detail by small groups the following day. The original plan was to have four discussion sessions of approximately 45 minutes each. The first group was composed of persons selected from the Omaha area to represent a nonacademic, public perspective. The six content area experts were to form the second inner circle and discuss their initial impressions of the current research issues. They would be followed by the 10 methods consultants, who would then discuss the methodological issues that might be used for different questions. Finally, the six content area consultants would enter the inner circle for a second time to make preliminary identification of four questions for the small groups the following day.

The Public Group

The initial inner circle consisted of persons identified to represent the public's perspective on provider behavior. We selected people from diverse backgrounds who could clearly articulate about their experiences with health care and were available on a weekday afternoon for the conference. There was no pretense of randomness, but we did strive for some diversity of experience within these stated constraints.

Five people joined us for the discussions. *Dorothy* was 76, a minister and community activist; after a lifetime of robust health she had recently experienced some health problems, including the sequelae from a serious automobile accident a year earlier. *Mike*, a lawyer for a corporate bank and a recovering alcoholic, was 40 years old and married with two young children. *Carol,* the only person of color in the group, was a 34-year-old African American living with diabetes; she had a degree in gerontology and two young children. *Chris* also had two children, one born with short bowel syndrome requiring skilled nursing care and parenteral nutrition; at 45 she was a professor of public policy and administrative law. *Julie* was a social worker whose clients were low-income women, many of whom had Medicaid coverage; she was 37 years old and married.

Before beginning, Kate explained to the public voice participants that the morning had been pretty intellectual, a review of different research methods, and that she, for one, welcomed their input from the "real world." Finally, she reviewed the staging for the conversation and said she would begin by asking the questions they had received in the invitational letter: "Tell about your best or worst experiences with health care services, or tell what you would change about the way health care providers behave towards patients."

Julie started off with a story about throwing "a fit" in order to persuade a physician to let a woman on Medicaid remain an additional day in the hospital following hernia surgery. She summed up this story, and stories of other clients she had consulted in preparation for the conference, with the following:

> The consistent thing is that health care providers do not listen to the patients, and I've heard that from older women, I've heard that from men, I've heard that from just everyone. . . . If they could just get their practitioners to listen to them and not just look at their watch and say, "Oh, this is okay, since the throat is sore, then we will do the strep culture and that is all we do."

Julie's words about the importance of "listening" were echoed in the stories and opinions provided by the entire group. Group members identified their perceptions of listening behavior: For instance, when clarifying questions were asked, eye contact was made, a handshake was offered in greeting, names and titles were respected, and adequate time was available with the clinician. The sense of being heard by a considerate listener was one aspect of feeling "treated like a real person," as Chris articulated it. This quality of relationship with the provider was, in essence, what all of the group participants desired from their caregivers. However, their stories generally illustrated a lack of feeling listened to by providers. Cooperative listening was desired, not only from the physician and "the receptionist, on down the line" but, as Dorothy's story illustrates, between staff themselves on behalf of the patient's needs.

A positive version of this attribute of provider behavior was illustrated by Dorothy's remarkable tale of her car accident and subsequent care in the emergency room. She described what most impressed her about her care in the emergency room: "Immediately the doctors came and listened to the intern, and listened to the nurses, and everybody shared, and they listened to the ambulance drivers and everybody shared with everybody, and it was a wonderful sense of cooperation I had never experienced before."

In addition to "listening" behavior, the group members prioritized another related theme for future research on provider behavior that contributed to their sense of not being treated as they would have wished. This theme pertained to their observation that providers often made inappropriate assumptions. Too often these assumptions, based on racist, ageist, or sexist stereotypes, obscured providers' capacity for understanding individual health care needs. Carol was the first to raise this issue. Her experience is illustrated in the following quote:

> A lot of them assume that you don't know anything, and they kind of talk to you like you are a 2-year-old, . . . assume that I wouldn't understand . . . so they never really discuss what is wrong with you and how you can be a part of your own health care plan. . . . And that really makes me angry at times when I don't feel like I am getting all the information that would benefit me.

As Will Miller summarized at the end of the discussion, Carol's experience cautioned against "making assumptions about others and stereotyping, which is linked in with racism, sexism, or ageism." Chris also spoke to this theme when describing her young son's treatment by providers who were, as he calls it, "fake friendly." Even as a 7-year-old her son preferred a straightforward approach from his providers, including information about procedures and potential pain. As Chris said, "You know being treated like you're not capable of understanding what is happening to you, and even for a 7-year-old child that can be a very deep experience." Mike added some levity to the issue in objecting to the standard hypocrisy used when injections are given: "One thing I would like to see—if anybody in the medical profession has a needle in their hand, they have to quit telling me that 'this won't hurt a bit.' They don't believe it, I don't believe it. . . . Why is it even said?"

The fourth identified theme for research suggested investigating the advantages and disadvantages of providers attending to the context or lifestyle of patients, not just their immediate disease problems. Two stories were told that illustrated problematic medical consequences when the big picture of patients' lives was overlooked. Mike's story was concerned with his undetected alcoholism:

> I've never had a doctor ask me if I was alcoholic, and I think that is extremely important. I mean, if a doctor ever asked me about my lifestyle when I was younger, he would have had to been an absolute idiot not to surmise that I had a drinking problem.

Dorothy told an excruciating story involving a series of painful diagnostic tests that could well have been avoided if she had been asked early on about her recent travel to the Colorado mountains, where she had picked up bacteria in the drinking water. Julie cautioned that inattention to context of patients' lives when scheduling appointments and prescribing remedies could cause problems. She attempts to be sensitive to her clients' difficulties with following medical advice due to transportation, poverty, and limited insurance coverage.

Drawing on her own experience with her son, Chris moved from the general observation that "they ought to be a little more aware of the context in which this person is coming to them, and what they have been through to get there. . . . They should be aware too of what they are sending the person home to," to the more specific experience in her own life, reminding us of the overarching concern for each of the group members that he or she be treated as a "real person" in the context of a medical relationship. She said:

> We have a nurse who is on Life Line and she will tell [my son's] subspecialist to "get a life" when the specialist recommends something that we should be doing for [him] that is just totally out of the realm of reality for real people living in a real home with real children.

Several consistent themes emerged from the discussion. When the participants were asked to establish priorities from all the various issues discussed, the following emerged as key: empathy; active listening; a sharing and team approach; issues of ageism, racism, and sexism; and the necessity of knowing the person's needs and values in order to empathize with him or her.

The Content Expert Group

The inner group consisting of the content experts began on schedule with an agenda of a preliminary identification of research questions. Their discussion identified areas such as "What is behavior change?" "Is it desirable?" and "Who defines it?" They also identified both doctors' and patients' feelings of victimization, their sense that medical care was somehow controlled by external forces. The issue of "patienthood" was identified. Much discussion centered on "dealing with the person in a contextual way." Issues of differences in gender and race were identified, as well as the issue of "appropriateness of care, the appropriateness of response, the appropriateness of listening," which varies from person to person. The relationship between the training of physicians and their expectations was probed: "You can't ask a physician to deliver high-quality, person-centered care if they're a product of a non-high-quality, non-person-centered form of education." As the context of the patient was acknowledged, the lack of control of the physician over disease in practice situations was recognized.

After a slight breakdown, there was an attempt to refocus the group on the question of "What is the relationship going to be between patients and physicians?" Several areas of content were then discussed, such as the economic constraints, the role of other caregivers and support personnel, and the role of technology. There were more frequent bursts of large group conversation rather than just the inner group discussion as planned. Although different ideas and questions emerged, the group was unable to arrive at any concrete suggestions for questions. Differences were clearly articulated between qualitative and quantitative perspectives and discussion was moving into more open conflict when time constraints prevailed. Despite the time constraints, the discussion involving numerous individuals and open conflict continued until the group took a break.

A Change of Plan

After the break, the group was to reconvene, with the methods experts forming the inner circle. At that time, the moderator interpreted the groups' process:

> Two observations—one is a sense of fatigue and tiredness and some frustration, another is a sense of wanting to participate and some frustration with the inner/outer format. Is the tiredness and frustration a reflection of physical fatigue or . . . a reflection of the fact that there are some big issues and questions that we are still not identifying?

The process of moving through frustration was identified as important and articulated by one member of the group: "What was more important is sort of the process you go through to deal with the question. It's not the question per se that necessarily is important, process is more important." It was then decided to continue with a large group discussion rather than continue with an inner/outer circle. *At this point, the group process was consciously articulated as data, important data, for understanding multimethod/ cross-disciplinary research process.*

The conflicts nevertheless continued as the methods people had a first opportunity in the large group discussion: "I want to say that I think we really do not know what the problem is at all, and we do not know what the magnitude of the problem is. We have heard a lot of anecdotes." As the speaker continued to question the assumptions about the previous discussions, someone responded: "You're fighting anecdote with anecdote." Although considerable and often insightful discussion continued for nearly an hour, most of it reflected one individual participant's perspective. The group found it difficult to agree on questions, or even an agenda. Just before the group ended, one participant identified what he believed to be the underlying emotional tension:

> This conversation is taking place which isn't the most respectful, certainly not the most compassionate, and I hope that we can address that because it feels like we

are skipping back and forth between speaking professionally, but behind that professionalism is also some very deeply held, personal values and personal ways of thinking and being.

This final articulation began to move the group into a mutual recognition of the need to be open to new ideas. Thus, during the afternoon, the conference community had begun to recognize the need to work together to accomplish the larger goals.

That night the moderators met to reassess the progress of the conference. Rather than an orderly progression of disparate groups integrating, there was now frustration and chaos. Emptiness prevailed at the end of the day. In order to facilitate a healthier dialogue, we realized that we needed to give all the members a chance to interact, question, and articulate their thoughts in small group sessions. Thus, rather than continuing with large group sessions (after the observers' reflections) in the morning as planned, we would go immediately to small group sessions, with each small group working in a problem area rather than on a specific question. After the small group sessions, we would then have break time for people to reflect.

OBSERVER FEEDBACK

Four "process observers" were asked to observe the discussions throughout the conference and provide feedback to the participants. They also were asked to keep a written log of their observations and give summary comments to open the sessions on the second and third days of the conference. These individuals were selected to maintain cogency from a federal perspective (Morgan Jackson), from the "real world" perspective of the primary care physician (Milton Seifert), from a qualitative researcher's perspective (Valerie Janesick), and from a quantitative researcher's perspective (Robert McCall).

These auditors were specifically asked to (a) identify unanswered issues as they emerged during the conference, (b) redirect the agenda when necessary, and (c) identify biases as they emerged. It was anticipated that they would help participants identify their own expectations and preconceptions and overcome communication barriers.

When the conference resumed on the second day, the initial observer's comments, however, further fueled the participants' frustration when she described the previous day's discussions: "I didn't see any moment where you actually communicated," followed by "But whatever method you do choose, you'd better know it. I mean, if you're going to do qualitative stuff, you have to be rigorous about it."

Rather than being moved to open discussion about the issues, many of the participants felt misunderstood: "Now wait a minute, wait a minute. Your perception is that I needed to have control over the group [the public voice]. As a good ethnographer, you should use me as a key informant and to find out whether that is true or not." The other observers articulated different aspects of their reflection on the group process and the progression of the meeting and helped to refocus the group. Individuals then retreated into their small groups.

SMALL WORKING GROUPS

Participants were divided into four small groups that were composed of a content area expert, a qualitative research expert, and a quantitative research expert. The moderator was responsible for keeping the discussions on track, taking notes, and keeping a running summary of the proceedings of each group. Each group was given the assignment to work on exploring questions and designs within one of the four research areas identified by the participants and the moderators during the first afternoon's discussions. These were patient issues, physician caring issues, practice organization, and dissemination. Each group met twice and developed its own style.

The *patient group* opened with personal introductions and began to explore issues in a very collaborative and open manner. None of the members of this group had previously been particularly vocal. Their openness at this time may have reflected their readiness to discuss issues in a small group rather than within the polarity of some of the discussions in the large group.

The *physician caring group* had many members who had been involved in strongly worded dialogue in the large group setting. This dialogue continued in their small group. This inhibited further discussion and the sharing of ideas during that session.

The *practice organization group* used, rather than escaped, the large group's discussion to continue those themes but in a much more open dialogue. They had a chance for discussing, listening, and developing appreciation of one another's perspective.

The *dissemination group* also began a very fruitful dialogue. Rather than articulate and fully discuss the issues from the large group, individuals in this group tended to avoid some of these issues and spoke from their own particular perspective.

After the initial small group sessions, the anxiety and tension level of the conference decreased. Although there was still some frustration, people were beginning to feel that there was progress. The participants also had some unscheduled time to withdraw and reflect.

The moderating group met again on the second night to evaluate the sessions. Feeling some pressure to accelerate the small group process, the moderators established a specific question for each of the small groups. The next morning each of the groups began to devise a research design for its question.

The *patient group* felt frustration at the imposed question, and although there was continued sharing of ideas, the task orientation resulted in a less integrated, more traditional research design investigating "why doctors don't listen."

The *caring group* moderator imposed strong format and helped this group focus on the particular question of "what does it mean to be a caring physician?" This allowed the group to leave the fractious discussion of the previous day and focus on the task at hand. Again, the research design was much more traditional and less integrated.

The *practice organization group* used a framework to develop some content applied to the question "How does practice organization influence physician provider behavior?" This framework allowed for a more integrated approach, but one less developed than those of the preceding two groups.

The group dealing with *dissemination* of information continued some of the discussion from the previous day. This allowed them to articulate and then resolve some of their disagreements such that they began to appreciate one another's perspective. The resultant research design showed much richness.

In each one of these small groups, the pressure to produce a research design within a certain amount of time did not facilitate further integration and appreciation of the diverse perspectives within each group. No new conceptual frameworks evolved, although in three out of the four groups there were beginnings.

DISCUSSION

We began this project believing that primary care research needed to be opened up methodologically. To answer some of the thornier and more complex questions, especially around the problems concerning provider behavior, we sought to employ an approach that combined quantitative and qualitative methods. When we envisioned the conference out of which this book evolved, we imagined seasoned and experienced primary care researchers, each expert in a method or content area, getting together to learn from each other's expertise and then collaboratively planning important multimethod research projects around the practices of the health care provider.

The conference did not proceed in such a straightforward fashion. It raised more questions than we could have imagined and left us struggling to understand what had happened, what it meant, and where to go from here. The researchers were offended that their expertise was not accepted without question by a diverse group of experts. Most of these researchers were academics trained to be critical and to speak from a particular paradigmatic, disciplinary, or methodological stance. Careers had also been built on staking a distinctive claim within a discipline. All of this contributed to arguments in defense of ego and territory throughout the conference. The more quantitative methodologists seemed to envision a clash of methods, whereas the more qualitative methodologists seemed to perceive a clash of paradigms.

The dominant theme from the public focus group was how physicians did not listen well enough for the patient to feel understood and cared for. A parallel process occurred at the conference: just as physicians had difficulty listening, expert researchers were unable to broaden their perspectives or communicate this to each other. In reflection, none of this should have been any surprise.

Our hope was to overcome these entrenched and disparate encampments in small facilitated groups whose charge was to explore a research question and if possible design a research project. Some small groups began with members unable to let go of their "disciplinary preferences." Some groups were able to overcome this to experience some of the processes Miller talks about in the summary chapter in this volume: accepting and validating each other, sharing expectations, declaring group process, moving toward an action consensus, opening up a shared common space, and proceeding with sustaining activity. Some groups were able to collaborate enough to arrive at a study design to address their assigned question. Some of these designs may even receive funding and be carried out.

After the conference, we pursued some of the questions the observers had posed: Can researchers move beyond "disciplinary prejudices" and "methodo-logical preferences" to build research projects that embody such primary care principles as "availability, comprehensiveness, continuity, coordination, ac-countability, [and] collaboration"? Will researchers be "more open to the variety of techniques that can be used to undertake research and to get questions answered"? Will researchers work with other researchers "who represent the range of disciplines"? Will such collaborative research or publications be undertaken? Will such research have any effect on policy, physician/provider behavior, or better outcomes for patients?

As we pored over the chapter drafts, the transcripts from the conference and our reflections, a few understandings became clearer: our original objective, to facilitate multimethod research, was not the answer. Combining methods in an additive fashion was not a satisfactory way of approaching the complex and difficult problems in primary care research. What is needed is a dialogue among a diverse group of researchers who embody divergent interests and practices. Such a dialogue would aim at opening a clearing for conceptualizing how health care practices came to be problematic, how they continue to be problematic, and whether collaborative ways of investigating those problems can be arrived at.

Such a dialogue would optimally include those people most concerned with the problems at hand: patients; physicians; other providers; clinics; and agencies and legislative bodies that set and carry out policies on treatment, funding, and reimbursement on local, regional, and national levels. Health care delivery systems are complex and complicated.

If we are to better understand and improve such problematic issues in health care as the doctor-patient relationship, organization of practice, and dissemination of knowledge into practice, this dialogue must go forward. Though painful and frustrating, the conference pushed the dialogue forward. We envision this book as the next step in the ongoing dialogue. As this book goes to press, our dialogue continues.

18

RESEARCHING PATIENT ISSUES IN PRIMARY HEALTH CARE

Valerie J. Gilchrist

> The point of doing this is to draw into view unarticulated assumptions and expectations that operate silently within one's theories. Knowing how theories of change understand the world helps one to understand how these theories can act in the world, what they may accomplish, what their unintended consequences might be, and what possibilities might lie unexamined within the terrains they inhabit. (Ferguson, 1993, p. ix)

On May 15 and 16, 1993, five people convened to discuss the "patient issues" in changing provider behavior. These members were participants in a conference on "Multimethods Research in Primary Care." This group was one of four designated to explore how interested individuals from disparate disciplines bring different perspectives to bear on any particular problem. Each small group contained a range of "experts," but individual assignments were arbitrary. None of the participants knew one another. Each moderator chose one of the four previously designated topic areas for his or her group. Our small group consisted of a pediatrician epidemiologist (our quantitative methodologist), a sociologist with an interest in interaction (our qualitative methodologist), a family physician interested in medical education and an economist (our content experts), and another family physician (myself) interested in multimethods primary care research, who acted as the moderator.

These small groups were designed to illustrate how one's personal and professional background frames one's question about any particular topic. In planning the conference, we had hoped this eclectic mix of individuals would generate new approaches to a particular research question. Not only would each individual bring a disciplinary perspective, but, from the discussion, new ideas irrespective of an individual's discipline would emerge. The degree of success of these groups in the small amount of allotted time was remarkable.

This chapter will describe both the content of the discussion concerning "patient issues" and the process of formulating and refining research questions. For those involved in research, the formulation of a "researchable question" will be recognizable. It consisted of a great diversity of discussion around related topics and then the development of a more focused area. The difference in this group was the struggle to articulate our own questions to others outside of our own discipline. It also required considerable effort to listen respectfully and incorporate other members' perspectives. Each of us looked at the "patient issues" from a different perspective.

The first session of the small group lasted two and a half hours. This was both the most difficult and most stimulating. The struggle to define the presuppositions that in turn dictated each individual's perspective and the resultant methodology took place in the first session. By the second session on the next day, when the question had narrowed, it became easier to offer methods. However, the group lost much of the earlier rich discussion and challenging of assumptions when we had a defined research question. I will outline the content of the sessions roughly chronologically and will use exemplary quotes to illustrate either a particular perspective or the tensions that existed within the group.

HOW TO APPROACH THE TOPIC—UNDERLYING VALUES

Aside from the individual disciplinary differences in approaching the question of "patient issues," there were two recurring tensions within this small group. These evolved not only from a disciplinary background but also, I suspect, from a personal perspective about the value of knowledge. By this I mean that the "usefulness" of any particular information derived was the most important element to some group members. Others felt it was essential to understand more completely any particular issue before consideration could be given to "using" that knowledge. These two perspectives are not diametrically opposed. They represent ends of a continuum. The other tension existed between those who wanted to focus on individual patients and interactions and those who wanted to focus on the larger picture or "systems" perspective. Although nobody wanted to focus on one level of analysis exclusively, group members disagreed in their opinions as to which had priority.

The sociologist articulated the value of understanding and exploring issues before offering interventions during his discussion of nursing home residents:

> It's not clear what resident satisfaction is. They don't know what satisfaction is. . . . Sometimes you ask them these kinds of questions [satisfaction surveys] and they're not quite sure what you're asking. What they're satisfied with. They can give you a response but they don't know what they're saying yes or no to. That's the issue.

The epidemiologist expressed the pragmatic view that the research needed to take current information and apply it:

> I'm saying that actually knowing what patients mean by listening . . . may be less important because I kind of feel we already know what that is. . . . It's not that subtle, and I'm eager to get more to the point, can we improve the doctor relationship with some intervention that could then be disseminated widely, and if we do, what will happen.

Although most of the discussion focused on the individual provider-patient relationship and individual patients, the economist kept articulating for our group the importance of looking beyond the individual interaction. "I think there are situations where what we call the patient-physician relationship becomes the patient-plan relationship." He continually refocused the group on the societal needs of an "efficient health care system," "issues of access," and "issues of racism." "The patient-physician relationship, whatever that is. These nice, warm, middle-class, probably white concepts that really come out of our own experiences shouldn't be funded because the government has a larger responsibility to the people who don't have coverage at all."

There were also disciplinary perspectives that became evident during the discussion. Physicians tend to be very much the pragmatists and want to "do something." Statements such as "You're in there to treat the patient, so you don't want to get too informal" reveal the training in medical school to maintain an emotional distance between physician and patient. The economist's perspective was evident as "Well, it all comes back to payment again." In a discussion of the doctor-patient relationship, parallels were evident to the sociologist between the provider-patient relationship and the teacher-student relationship. "We talk about the question of how students evaluate the professors—the analogy is with how patients might evaluate their physicians." The epidemiologist's perspective was evident in his proposal of a randomized control trial, "meaning not only is it [listening] related to outcome, but can we change it." Although group members clearly articulated their disciplinary perspectives, this did not seem to inhibit discussion. Challenges from the group members furthered the richness and complexity of discussion. Frequent use of humor facilitated these exchanges. "Am I being too economically imperialistic?"

Finally, this group of academics also recognized that a traditional academic or discipline-based approach to these issues might miss important information. Another means suggested to understand the issues in the doctor-patient relationship was to describe what was innovative and currently happening in some practices. The example was the management of Dr. Milton Seifert's practice by a patient advisory board:

> People who are so good as academics identifying problems, and then we just assert that we don't know enough about that or this, when actually there are people who have thought about it for years. It's just hard to understand and we don't quite know what to do with it.

BRAINSTORMING

This section began with my introduction and the statement, "Our task is to go where we go with these ideas." The following question was "What's our time frame on this?" (The pragmatists begin to assert themselves!)

Power

The first issue articulated by our group was the need for patient empowerment. "I would say one big issue would be patient empowerment or the very asymmetric nature of the relationship." All of the group members recognized this as part of the provider-patient relationship. Group members mentioned access to information and the legal structure that allows only physicians to write prescriptions as everyday examples of this asymmetry of power.

Throughout our discussion of patient issues, a recurring focus was that of the patient group that we'd heard the previous day. Six individuals were invited to discuss, in a modified focus group type of format, the relationships they had with the medical care system. Clearly the message was that we wanted to improve this relationship. All of the patients spoke about their dissatisfactions with their physicians—about "not listening," "being disrespectful," and "not really communicating to the patient." One group member remarked that when asked, none of those patients had confronted their physician about their dissatisfaction. This reinforced a research direction of "We should think about how we can empower patients or how can we teach patients to help physicians do that [listen]" and "Can we get accountability and feedback into a system?" This led to a discussion of mechanisms by which patients could exercise control at the level of the individual interaction. We discussed prior research, such as that done by Robert Pantell teaching asthmatics to ask their physicians specific questions, and by Sherrie Kaplan and others preparing questions with patients for their physician encounter. This focus was individual and within the provider-patient relationship. "If power is experienced at all, it's experienced in these local kinds of areas."

"Whereas the doctor was supposed to be the agent for the patient, now employers and insurance companies are becoming agents for the patients." This quotation illustrates a focus on the larger health care system. Traditionally, patients express dissatisfaction by switching health care providers. The group members all recognized, however, that patients' ability to switch providers was constrained and limited by employers' decisions to fund health care only in certain ways, and by the limited number of providers in certain areas. Within this type of system, patients might exercise their control through representative patient advisory boards. We also realized that the impact of payment systems on the individual provider-patient relationship was very poorly understood and only recently considered in research. "I think your point is definitely something we need to research, which is how third-party payers interact in the physician-patient relationship."

In discussing how to empower patients, one suggestion was to provide them with information that would allow them to make decisions. "The patient-physician relationship and the concerns we've heard should be reflected more in the data that's fed back to the consumer." One could give patients information to facilitate resource allocation decisions in a cooperative health plan or to choose individual providers in an open plan. Ideally, the patient should decide "who they want to hire to provide these services, and decide what data they will collect to decide who does it better."

Trade-offs

As the discussion then focused on an "efficient health care system," the underlying question articulated by one member of the group was "What is cost-effective care?" and "Is it your impression that cost effectiveness is always sort of diametrically opposed to humanistic care?" The answer by one member was as follows:

> Is there a trade-off between humanistic provision of care and the need for efficiency, and when doesn't more humanistic provision of care cost more? Can we afford it? Maybe we shouldn't be looking at that. Maybe we should be looking at balancing the need for efficiently moving the patients through the system and providing technical care the way the auto mechanic might and getting the right kind of managed care.

Whereas one person talked about the physician-patient relationship as dead— "We can't afford it anymore"—the response from another in the group was

"It's not clear that it would cost more, it depends a lot on who the physician is and what variances there are." This framing of the question led to the question of "Where do patients need to trade off? I think that's something we know nothing about."

Complexity

Everyone recognized that we could not generalize and that any discussion of "patient needs" was complex. As the group discussed the provider-patient relationship, the complexity of it became more apparent. "We've identified different kinds of patient styles, different kinds of demands, needs, and so forth, and we've identified different kinds of physician styles." "The art of medicine is, in part, finding . . . that common ground quickly—common ground, meaning the different kind of patients, different kind of physicians, and different needs, at that particular interaction." Another participant stated:

> It's just a constant fluidity, that relationship from the moment you walk in as a physician or provider. It's this constant interchange which shapes it all along so that your preconception of [what] coming into the doctor was all about, or many of the other subconscious things you may not even be aware of, are going to then be shaped and further transformed in this relationship that you can pursue for 2 minutes or 2 hours, depending on what the case may be.

This group had, in a very short amount of time, recognized the difference between the health care provider, the patient, and the relationship. They were also acknowledging how the immediate context would influence all three of those factors and how the larger systems context, such as payment, would also influence this interaction. Thus the richness of this discussion had increased much more than I had expected.

Typology and Taxonomy

Again turning to individual interaction, the group was asked, "Do we have a taxonomy on empowerment?" Those who wanted to understand and focus on interaction saw the recognition of the fluidity or ever-changing nature of the provider-patient relationship and the resultant complexity as the very reason to develop a typology. "So if there's no closure on this, that we can't develop some type of order or typology or what have you, then it seems to me that we're stuck in not knowing how the patient-physician relationship can develop."

Although we realized that we needed to look at the provider and patient and the relationship and develop a typology, another member suggested,

Maybe there's a different way of looking at this. Maybe the medical interview is more a series of critical incidents. "We need to be looking at ways to identify those critical incidents at a point in time. And then for most people, maybe most encounters, there are no critical incidents.

The need to develop a taxonomy or typology of patients, physicians and other health care providers, practices, and empowerment was discussed. "There are types of 'patienthood' we need to identify." "Do we have a taxonomy of being able to classify practices?" "How do we define *physician-hood*?" One group member, while feeling that Sherrie Kaplan's use of the word *patienthood* was very helpful, noted that

> the idea of patienthood, it seems to me, is separated from the different kinds of perspectives that are brought to bear on what the patient is. It's a dangerous one because it tends to define them . . . in terms of someone's perspective. If you were to list what good patienthood is, and if you took all the perspectives into account, it would be a contradictory list. Is patienthood a significant portion of most peoples' lives? Are there types of patienthood that we might need to identify?

Others felt that this black box of the provider-patient relationship was a given and that trying to discern the complexities of it was less important than moving on. "Listening is sort of an intermediate variable that we presume changes in some intervention aimed at doctor/patient communication." The important questions were stated as "one is, can you increase it, and then if the answer is yes and it relates to outcome, then the next group of questions is, how can we disseminate it, and how can people do it?"

Training

One provider issue raised was whether the physician-patient relationship was different from the provider-patient relationship.

> The relationship, or whatever we want to call it, is it different among physicians, nurse practitioners, PAs and other providers? And if there were similar system constraints, would the relationship qualitatively or quantitatively be different? Is there something about the training of those providers, the socialization of those providers, or the context in which the care is provided?

Another aspect of training discussed was the conflict between the physicians' teaching and the realities of practice in meeting the needs of patients. The medical student who recorded our meeting described his conflict between what he was taught at medical school and what his patients wanted. "I'm having a little trouble with what we're taught and reality." Another conflict recognized by the three physicians present was that of trying to balance patient requests with the need to control costs. "You have this conflict between your role as gatekeeper, watching out for the finances of the organization, and your role as patient advocate trying to have a satisfied patient." We recognized the need to investigate the way in which these conflicts affect the provider-patient relationship.

Guidelines

As discussion repeatedly centered on the provider-patient relationship and its influential factors, the group returned on many occasions to the discussion of guidelines. Guidelines are distributed to patients and thus potentially empower patients; yet one physician outlined three critiques of guidelines.

> What we know about guidelines is very little, and it is hardly translated into actual practice. Secondly, we don't know anything about how to disseminate those guidelines or whether they change behavior, either of patients, providers, or systems, and thirdly, it is unclear what we really want to accomplish, i.e., what do patients really want, and will guidelines function to establish medical-legal limits or as an effort to increase provider conformity or to improve patient care.

All the participants were aware of these limits: "My sense of this whole guideline process and movement is . . . as another case of the emperor not having very many clothes."

One participant said that even if the guidelines were well developed, he would have some concerns about the influence on practice because of the nature of the provider-patient relationship. "If we are to conceive of the relationship between patients and physicians as in many ways, let's say, a nonpredictable one, then it raises very serious questions about what the nature of guidelines can be." "If they're too concrete and too directive, then they can't somehow address the fluidity of the doctor/patient relationship." One needs "the flexibility of any clinical guideline to have the ability to match its recommendations to a particular patient to a given patient population to the practice setting."

Dissemination

The need to study dissemination of information was another recurrent theme. "In those rare instances where we have knowledge, package it, we haven't a clue about how to disseminate that effectively or change behaviors of patients, providers, systems, or whatever perspective we want to take." This topic was discussed extensively by another small group (see Chapter 21).

Context

We recognized that exploring "patient issues" by looking at only the patient or provider was ignoring the importance of context. The issue of context was perhaps the most recurrent theme of our discussions. This ranged from such comments as "I think there are probably big differences between different kinds of patients and different providers" to reflections on health care in the United States: "And what is it about this society that makes this system of care built on the generalist provider versus the specialty provider?" The multitude of contexts that might influence the provider-patient relationship are outlined in the next section describing the development of the research questions.

Current Research

We often reflected that there is need for much more research in this area. "I mean, what we know is precious little, and it hardly translates to actual practice, ecological validity." "What do patients really want?" "How can we accurately identify patients' information needs and communicate needs accurately?"

THE QUESTION

At the beginning of the second session, I, as group facilitator, introduced to the group our task for the session—to define a "researchable" question and to refine it as much as was possible in the hour and a half available to us. I suggested to the group that they consider the refrain from the patient group that we had witnessed on the opening day—"Doctors don't listen!" I hoped that as a clearly articulated patient issue, it would give the group a flexible focus for discussion. The response was "Get a life!" With much humor and discussion, again different disciplinary perspectives asserted themselves. "So the question isn't really that so much as how do you get doctors to listen. How do you change this relationship so that it's more satisfactory, and if you do that, what difference does it make?" "Is listening cost-effective, and what is cost-effective listening?" "But my problem is, it doesn't seem to me that any of these things tells us what this means. What do you mean by listening? So what I'm saying is perhaps what we might want to do in a research design is to decompose this, you know, listening business into different kinds of meanings."

Nonetheless, each member of the group did contribute to the following research approach to the investigation of "listening." Our outline of the resultant questions follows. All of the group members recognized that these questions needed a blended approach of methods and recognized and incorporated each other's suggestions.

1. What is it that patients perceive as listening?

This was the perspective articulated by our sociologist as "describe, not measure." This consists of an effort to "decompose the meaning of listening" to both patient and provider. Listening may mean very different things from one person to another. The understanding of listening as a perceptual variable was key. "Perception, that is the significant variable. Perception of satisfaction, perception of congruence, negotiation, and of health that in fact determines various outcomes."

Questions considered included the following:

- What is it that is perceived as listening?
- How much is verbal behavior?
- How much is nonverbal behavior?
- What behavior results in satisfaction—for both the patient and provider? Is it the same behavior that is perceived as listening? Is this behavior consistently related to satisfaction with the same individuals, or does it change?
- What are patients willing to trade off? For example would patients be willing to pay more for "listening behavior" by their health care provider? If so, in which circumstances and with which patients?
- What is the relationship between "listening" and a sense of negotiation or power sharing by the patient?
- Is "listening" related to health and if so how?

These questions, searching for understanding, can be best studied using such methods as focus groups of both doctors and patients and narrative inquiries of the worst and best examples of "listening" from patients, physicians, and other ancillary medical personnel. Participant observation and interviews would be informative. Time studies, path analysis, and correlational statistics also might be helpful.

2. How is listening influenced by, or how does it vary with, characteristics of the patient, the health care provider, their relationship, and the practice context?

All of the group members quickly realized that the complexity of studying "listening" reflects the differences among patients, health care providers, their relationship, and the context of that interaction. As one group member challenged, "What patient, what doctor?" We summarized some variables as follows:

- patient variables—age, culture and ethnicity, family dynamics, gender, socioeconomic status, race, disease (diagnosis, acute or chronic, life threatening or benign), problem presentation (urgent or nonurgent), expectations of that particular physician and of medicine in general

- physician variables—age, culture and ethnicity, gender, race, training, anxiety or comfort with this patient or disease, experience
- provider-patient relationship variables—the match of demographics between patient and health care provider, length of that provider-patient relationship, the history of that provider-patient relationship
- system variables—medical care system (private practice, group practice, HMO, clinic), practice site (rural, urban, suburban)
- contextual variables—waiting time for that visit, interaction with ancillary personnel at that visit (for both the provider and patient), do either provider or patient have other concerns that might distract them, pressures or time constraints at the time of the visit
- other variables such as geography—"Just as prostatectomy rates vary, does the type or rate of listening vary across the country?" "Being a patient in suburban Omaha is different from downtown Washington."

3. Can this behavior, "listening," whatever it is, be changed?

This and the next question were basic for the more pragmatic members of the group. This statement articulated as "But let's suppose we answered all those questions [describing listening]. Picture that they were answered. Tell me how we would be better off, and what we would do next, different from what we're doing now."

We discussed what interventions could influence the provider-patient relationship. These suggestions focused on both the individual relationship and larger systems issues. Some interventions focused on the individuals included

- having another staff member review or even just remind patients of any questions they might have for the physician prior to that visit
- coaching doctors to ask for listening behavior: "Did I answer all your questions? Did I listen to you?"
- using videotapes to educate patients about their illness and how to ask their health care providers questions, as in Pantell's work with asthma
- having the patients review their charts before their physician visit

Interventions on a larger scale concerned giving patients information— such as operative rates or other patients' satisfaction ratings—that might help them decide when and where to seek health care and, most importantly, having patients determine "what data they will collect to decide who does it better."

Finally, we suggested that a focus group with both patients and providers could be both an intervention and a means to study the pertinent issues of "listening."

4. If listening is changed in any way, will this result in improved outcomes?

This question led us also to examine our outcomes. "What is cost-effective? Is listening cost-effective and what is cost-effective listening?" Again, we realized that our definitions of cost effectiveness might not be consistent with the patient's definition. "Talking about cost effectiveness, most of it is technical, physician based and not patient based."

Some of the outcomes that we considered are listed below:

- satisfaction—one might use a survey or interviews focusing on how to improve the provider-patient relationship. If patients are simply asked about satisfaction with the individual relationship, they often state satisfaction, but when they are asked what could be done to improve the provider-patient relationship, more discriminating information becomes available.
- compliance with medication or recommendations
- whether the patient stays in the particular health care system or with a particular provider
- disease-specific health outcomes, such as blood pressure, weight, hemoglobin A1C
- functional abilities
- global measures of health or well-being as evaluated by the patient
- cost measures, such as the visit time, number of visits, and types of visits (outpatient, emergency room, hospitalization), number of tests or consultations

5. Finally, if listening can be changed and outcome is improved, can that intervention be disseminated and applied in different settings?

The group did not answer this question although they recognized it as an important question. One participant described how Pantell's work with videotapes, though clearly effective, is not used consistently within the institution in which it was developed.

RESEARCH DESIGN

With the questions outlined above, our group imagined a research design that might answer some of these questions. This design is summarized in Figure 18.1. The basic design involves two aspects: the exploration and description of "listening" and the manipulation of behaviors in an attempt to influence the perception of "listening." The provider-patient relationship

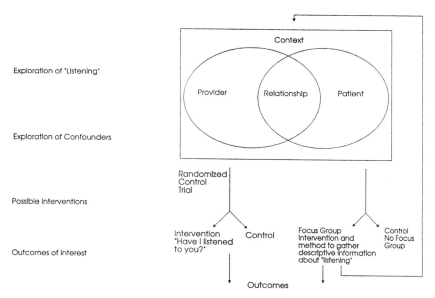

Exploration of "Listening"

Exploration of Confounders

Possible Interventions

Outcomes of Interest

Figure 18.1. Research Design Conceptualized by the Patient Issue Group

would be observed and patients and providers interviewed both individually and as part of a focus group to try to decompose and understand the meaning of "listening" for these individuals. Concurrently some practitioners and providers would participate in a trial of an intervention such as having the provider ask, "Have I listened to you?" The provider then would take whatever time was necessary to answer these concerns or would reschedule a visit. All the outcomes previously noted in Question 4 might be examined. All of the variables in Question 2 might also be examined. As one began to explore issues with a group of providers in a focus group, the effect of this focus group would change these providers such that the focus group itself would become an intervention.

This very simple research would yield much information about "listening" within the provider-patient relationship. A challenge would be to focus the study. Our group, for example, wanted to focus the description or decomposition of "listening" to explore what patients might be willing to trade off for either more or less of this behavior on the part of their provider. The confounding variable of interest was that of health care practice organization, that is, HMO or private practice. The outcomes of interest were the office visit time, patient satisfaction, and subsequent utilization throughout the health care system.

Conclusions

The quotation opening this chapter describes why we would plan to bring together these diverse individuals to discuss a topic such as "What are the patient issues important to consider in researching health care provider behavior?" None of us was an expert in this area. This chapter illustrates what may result from individuals with methodologic and related areas of expertise exploring a particular area in which they were not expert.

In retrospect, there were elements in our group's research questions that illustrated each individual's framing of these questions from his or her own disciplinary perspective. For example, the epidemiologist outlined a randomized control trial, whereas the sociologist expressed interest in gathering information on the meaning of the patient or provider's understanding of "listening." There was, however, evidence in the final design and list of questions of each participant's input to the question of "listening." Each participant added suggestions that increased our understanding of this issue. An example is how the proposed focus group of health care providers also might become the intervention in a randomized trial. Finally, there were glimpses of truly new conceptual frameworks concerning the area of "listening" in the provider-patient relationship. One example of this includes the conceptualization of the provider-patient relationship as fluid or constantly changing. This has great implications for measurement, both quantitative and qualitative. It also has policy implications for such things as trying to establish guidelines. The need to look beyond correlations to potential typologies or taxonomies will be necessary with this conceptualization. The second conceptualization that provoked much discussion and seemed to prod all the group members to examine their suppositions was the conceptualization of "cost-effective listening." This not only prompted consideration of what is a cost and what is "listening" but also raised the questions of cost to whom and who defines that cost. This prompted the discussion of when and where patients might see "trade-offs." This in turn led to a discussion of how patients might be involved in any research to define costs. The involvement of patients as active partners in the research is an example of participatory research.

Reflections

Why is it that this group of individuals could in only a brief time articulate many sophisticated research questions in this area? Does this exemplify the typical outcome of mixing people of different disciplinary perspectives or was it idiosyncratic to these individuals? I think it is a little of both. All the members of this group expressed interest in health care reform. Although none were experts in this content area, all were knowledgeable. Perhaps because we were not intimately acquainted with the framework of, and difficulties with, previous research, we were able to pose relatively new questions. No one had turf or ego to defend. Each group member also spoke of the need for change in this country's health care system. The individuals also all said they enjoyed challenge and that is one reason why they came to the conference. "I know I have biases, and I enjoy having them challenged because it reinforces my biases." As the last quotation indicates, this group of individuals often also used humor. Finally, I think initial individual introductions and personal stories established a relationship between these relative strangers that permitted subsequent open dialogue.

At some time during the discussion every individual used narratives to articulate and give an example of a point he or she was making. Each individual told a story of which he or she was personally aware. Some of these stories also led to the individual's understanding of issues. One clinician related feeling vulnerable about living at a distance from his father-in-law when his father-in-law was ill. "It was a new experience for me to feel this way and really kind of scary to be so dependent on this physician." One individual described a patient at an ethics committee meeting who was pregnant and had metastatic breast cancer. Another described his work with nursing home residents. Our medical student reporter became involved at one time and described an interaction he had with a clinician with whom he was working. All these examples reinforced to me the importance of stories as a way in which we understand our world that transcends any discipline (Hired, 1991; Witherell & Noddings, 1991).

In 1989 Conrad Lewis, giving the William Pickles lecture, challenged British general practitioners to use the disciplines of epidemiology, anthropology, psychology, and sociology (cited in Harris, 1989). He described the current practice of medicine as "seeing only what we expect to see and defending ourselves in the name of common sense." However, as he articulated the value of working with other disciplines, he also stated, "There is a dilemma: if we stay within our existing frameworks, we learn nothing new. If we go outside them, we run the risk of becoming butterfly collectors." It is this tension between being butterfly collectors and trying to apply new perspectives to our research that this exercise in multimethods and cross-disciplinary research addresses. It is an exciting and essential step in the evolution of primary care research.

19

Researching the Nature of Caring in Health Care Settings

Anton J. Kuzel

Difficult Beginnings

As moderator, I began the group process by suggesting we each express our ideas about how we would work together to define important research questions and approaches to the general topic of provider relations, particularly physician-patient relations. It became quickly apparent that many members of the group were not clear enough about the overall conference agenda to be comfortable in answering this question.

> I haven't the foggiest notion of what it is we're doing. The conference was billed as a conference on methodology and on the qualitative versus quantitative methodologies and so forth, but these issues have gotten tied up with a lot of other issues having to do with political agendas. . . . This group is not duly constituted to set political agendas for changing patient and provider relationships, for talking about [how to] organize practices and so forth.

> Yes, I think I share these concerns in that I get the feeling the outcome that we're hoping for is a set of research questions or a set of directions that we're supposed to be going. Even though I heard some opinions to the opposite yesterday, I'm a firm believer that our choice of methods for approaching a problem is dependent on what the research question is.

> I never understood it to be just a methodology conference because once the word *primary care* was attached to the end of methodology, it opened up far more than just methodology once the issue of provider behavior was introduced. I don't think

methodology is apolitical. I sure don't think primary care is apolitical, and I don't think behavior is apolitical. So I think that the fact that politics has become involved in this is to me just inevitable, no matter what cut you take on it.

There was also discussion of who should be coming up with the questions:

> There's a handful of people here, six people, that are content people, and they're in a position much better than I to say what we know and what we don't know around the provider-patient relationship. I'm not in a position to say that, and I think that's what's come out here is that we need to go from not knowing what we don't know to knowing what we don't know; and I am not in a position to take that step. I think Richard is, but I'm not, and so I'm not sure how I can contribute at this stage.

> If we keep the three identified methodologists in this room out of the process of question formulation, it makes me feel anxious about the kind of question that we come up with. My sense is, the more the merrier.

This issue was not fully resolved when we agreed to step back from discussing our task and share autobiographical information with one another. Our stories focused mainly on professional background and research experience and perspectives, but included family information as well. The earlier tension seemed to abate.

We returned to the question of what we hoped would happen in our group. One member stated, "Well, I guess my goal is to reach some level of respectful dialogue and consensus, even if the consensus has disagreement in it or dissenting views." He and others in the small group expressed concern about some of the feedback they had gotten from the "conference observers." They indicated that their personal experience did not fit well with the experience described within some of the observer comments.

We also spent some time debating who should get to say what the really important questions were, and where the public voice was in the process. "If we don't have any representation from the people who ultimately we're attempting to serve, it seems to me that we're in grave danger of duplicating the problem that people are complaining about." "What does the public have to do with the question, how is medicine being practiced and what is known about it?"

This sort of discussion led some members to feel anxious about the group's authority to set research agendas. "My feeling is that we don't have that mandate. I hope that AHCPR would listen to what comes out of this group, but I don't think we should conceive of ourselves as an agenda-setting body." "I personally had that same sense yesterday, and I articulated it as an arrogant stance for us to decide that we know or we can come up with questions." Yet we were brought to a sense of responsibility for a product:

> One of the things that the agency is on the line for is justifying these grant funds, and so I think it would be most unfortunate if all that came out of the grant funding in 2½ days was that people had a lot of nice conversations and agreed that they didn't have the authority to ask any questions. . . . Where the rubber hits the road is that questions will be asked, and as long as questions are going to be asked, it's useful for them to be more informed as opposed to less informed questions; and as long as they are going to be more informed questions, we might as well put our hats in the ring and see if the ones we put forth have some validity.

WHAT ARE THE QUESTIONS?

> What is the nature of caring, and does it make a difference? That's what I propose is a question worth researching.

> I'm very glad to hear you say that because I hear a lot of people say it's so important for us to be caring, and yet my impression has been, we haven't actually demonstrated that it is important in terms of outcomes.

Over the next hour, the group generated a list of questions that two members grouped into three categories:

1. Culture and Caring
   - What is the nature of caring, and does it make a difference?
   - How is caring culturally defined?
   - What is cultural competency?
   - What needs to be changed in order for physicians to be culturally competent?
   - What are the effects of cultural incompetence?
2. Relationships and Expectations
   - What do providers expect from patients?
   - What are the effects of congruence or lack thereof on the doctor-patient interaction?
   - Why do doctors and patients perceive the interaction differently?
   - What occurs in the provider-patient relationship?
   - What do patients want from primary care providers?
3. Systems Issues
   - What are the incentives/rewards of practice?
   - What are the constraints of practice, and how does that affect how physicians provide service?

- What are the effects of health care reform on doctor-patient relationships?
- Is there such a thing as an effective health care team? What is it?

These questions were generated in a process of "brainstorming," in which one member's question prompted comments or new questions from another member. This continued until the group began reflecting on its own process:

> There's been a lot of exchange. Some of it's been sharp. Some of it's been collaborative.

> I think it would be impossible to address something like this, as we all come from different perspectives, without there being real responses to it, because these are not purely academic issues. They are issues that have effects on all of us. We all see doctors.

> I think about research and how people come up with questions. What is it that you're personally passionate about? That's what we're being public with one another about, and it's inevitable that it's going to be a personalized statement.

In selecting *the* question on which to focus in order to develop a multimethod research design, the group seemed to be guided by a respect for pragmatism and a desire to uncover the assumptions behind the "conventional wisdom."

> If something is not practical, from my standpoint, it has no benefit.

> How about challenge to the myth of caring? I think if you did ethnographic work, you would come up with some more challenges to traditional notions of caring.

These themes of uncovering assumptions and looking for practical consequences are expressed in one of the questions that the group concurred was the most important for them to address: "What is the nature of caring, and does it make a difference?" There was general agreement that the other questions were related but secondary to this question. The members also felt that the question was best examined from multiple perspectives (e.g., the physician's, the patient's) and in multiple contexts (i.e., not just in middle-class white practices).

A PROGRAM OF STUDY

When the group reconvened the following day, their task was to describe how one might best try to answer the question. One member expressed concern that the question might be too big in its present form:

I'm concerned that this is not a good question to get into, although it is at the beginning of it, but the problem is that it's so complicated, and it involves a variety of regressives that are pretty deep. What caring is, and what the differences are in different groups, and specialties, and so forth. It isn't the sort of thing that lends itself to a particular design. If you ask, "What is the nature of caring," it sounds to me like a program of study, and you might have a team working on this for several years without exhausting the problem.

After considering an alternative goal—to narrow the question and more completely specify a research design—the members decided that they preferred to outline a program of study. This would specify stages of research as well as the participants, contexts, methods, and theories that might be particularly useful or important. The group would also speculate about the potential outcomes for each stage of the study.

Stage I

1. "Focused" question: What does "caring" consist of in many contexts?
2. Potential relationships to look at:
   - Doctor-patient
   - Nurse-patient
   - Clergy-faithful
   - Family
   - Teacher-student
   - Psychotherapist-client
   - "Nontraditional caregiver"
   - Other customer servers
3. Background concepts and theories that apply:
   - Healing versus curing
   - Communications (at multiple levels)
   - Sociology of relationships (including power)
4. Potential methods:
   - Literature review
   - Describing critical incidents via focus groups, key informant interviews, or ethnography (participant observation)
   - Meta-analysis—quantitative or qualitative
5. Potential participants:
   - Those who are "naive" about the doctor-patient relationship
   - Critical theorist

- Providers
- "Customers" of physicians
6. Potential outcomes:
   - Measures of caring (guard against risk of "settling in" on particular measure)
   - Differences between establishing and maintaining relationships
   - Typology of caring—variables that matter
   - Barriers to caring; incentives for caring
   - Exemplars
   - Definitions (e.g., for *empathy, support, reassurance, caring, relationship*)
   - Challenge to the "myths" about caring (for example, is caring a skill?)
   - Validation of measures (requires quantitative and qualitative methods)
   - Understanding relationship between caring and disease

This stage of the program of study is concerned with developing an understanding of "caring" and related concepts that goes beyond the confines of a limited group of individuals looking at a limited context. Because it is exploratory research, it relies heavily on qualitative methods: document analysis (literature review), key informant depth interviews, focus groups, and participant observation. The sampling of documents, informants, and contexts is purposefully varied: it is maximum variation sampling. One of the preferred strategies in qualitative inquiry (Guba & Lincoln, 1989), maximum variation sampling helps investigators to obtain the broadest range of information and perspectives on the subject of study. This may suggest new ways of "framing" issues or problems, which may in turn suggest new solutions. Within a given context (e.g., the nurse-patient relationship as viewed by patients receiving home health care), the emphasis is on describing and understanding critical incidents—those interactions which the participants believe are particularly significant or meaningful. These cases are likely to be especially rich in information and enlightening (Kuzel, 1992; Patton, 1990).

The variety of constructs, or ways of making sense of caring, is implied in the list of "background concepts and theories that apply." Clearly, these are just examples of the many ways one can think about "what caring consists of." It is also the place where personal perspective becomes most evident, and where vignettes and metaphors are frequently used to illustrate one's point of view:

> You've seen Star Trek. You know Bones, when he does primary care, the patient really doesn't need to say anything. You just lie down. He has this thing that looks like a cellular phone and he passes it over you.

I think your example of Bones is a marvelous one for looking at caring as a setting that includes a set of expectations and not necessarily a particular action or skill at all. I mean, most of the people who go into Bones seem to already know what's going to happen, so there is some shared set [of expectations].

I was just thinking yesterday about the fact that I can call up my travel agent and the travel agent knows, for example, whether I like an aisle seat or a window seat. The travel agent knows kind of when I like to fly. The travel agent knows special meal preferences. The travel agent knows a whole lot about me. And I can go into the physician, and the physician can scarcely remember my name. Now, why is that?

The "theories of communication" and "sociology of relationships" are abstractions of everyday experiences that each member of the group finds significant and meaningful. This process of sharing the interesting and important stories with one another serves two functions. First, it is a means whereby members use metaphor or analogy as part of their rhetorical argument for their position. Second, by making their point, they make their point of view apparent. If one thinks of the group's dialogue as a part of interpretive research on provider behavior, then the sharing of stories can be seen as making one's prior understandings and assumptions explicit. Addison (1989) emphasizes the importance of this process:

Heidegger argues that in order to know anything at all, we must have some pre-understanding of what is knowable. This pre-understanding, or fore-structure, remains largely in the background as taken for granted. However, when the object of investigation is human activity, it is important to recognize the influence of our fore-structure in order to arrive at a more explicit interpretation or account. (p. 52)

Having begun an exploration of the nature of caring, the group turned its attention to the question "So what difference does caring make?" Members suggested the following framework for approaching it.

Stage II

1. "Focused" question: Difference in what? (Variables affected could include persistence, ethical presence, cost, tolerance for range of behavior, satisfaction, return to clinic, continuity of provider, adherence, or lifestyle change.)
2. As judged by whom? (Those judging could include providers; patients, especially those with limited access, or "difficult patients"; families; and communities.)

It is at this stage that the context of inquiry is narrowed to places where people experience health care, with particular emphasis on interactions with physicians. The types of differences or desirable outcomes that the group discussed included aspects of the relationship, such as persistence, satisfaction, or mutual tolerance; aspects of patient behavior, such as adherence or lifestyle change; and aspects of the health care system, such as continuity of provider or cost.

Which of these differences and outcomes will receive attention depends on who is asking the question. Providers may be concerned with patient adherence, lifestyle change, or mutual tolerance. Patients may have the same interests or may be more intrigued by satisfaction or costs of care. Communities will certainly be interested in differences in cost and may also want to look at measures of community health, such as rates of preventable diseases.

Defining "stakeholder" groups and the values they bring to this phase of the study could be done by surveys and/or ethnographic studies. Once these were identified, the inquiry could focus on the questions they want answered. For example, an outcome of Stage I might be a measure of caring defined in behavioral terms. These behaviors, in turn, could be taught to providers. In Stage II, a community might want to know, "If we teach physicians to exhibit these behaviors, will it make a difference in patient participation in prevention activities?"

One way of approaching this question would use analog studies. Individuals would participate in "laboratory" scenarios in which caring behaviors would or would not be exhibited. The task in the scenario would be an analog of the task in the natural setting: in this example, it might be deciding whether to purchase a life insurance policy. In the intervention group, the caring behaviors (as defined in Stage I, and using measures developed and validated in Stage I) would be part of the process by which the participants would make the decision about the life insurance. In the control group, the caring behaviors would not be present. If a significant difference was found in a positive direction, one might consider a design that would test whether these same behaviors would have an analogous positive influence on patient participation in prevention activities (e.g., blood pressure screening, mammography).

This part of Stage II could involve a randomized control trial, employing the same strategy as in the analog study, but applied in actual clinical settings. Representative physicians, settings, and interactions would be randomized to control or intervention groups, and the outcome—for example, patient participation in mammography or blood pressure screening—would be measured.

These strategies—analog studies and randomized control trials—are particularly useful for testing hypotheses. If one found that some definable caring behavior on the part of physicians was associated with significantly greater patient participation in screening activities, one might be interested in seeking confirmation or elaboration of the hypothesis using qualitative studies. For example, let's say that one has found that physicians who exhibit a lot of eye

TABLE 19.1   The Relation of Eye Contact by Physicians to Patient Adherence to
             Mammography Recommendations

| | Eye Contact by Physicians | |
Patient Adherence	High	Low
High	A	B
Low	C	D

contact have patients who are more likely to follow advice to have mammograms. One could consider a qualitative design built around the 2 × 2 table
shown in Table 19.1.

If resources were limited, one might choose to look at doctor-patient
interactions in those cells that represented surprises. Cell B, for example,
represents physicians who show very little eye contact with their patients, yet
those same patients are very mindful of the doctor's recommendation to get
a mammogram. Conversely, Cell C represents physicians who show a great
deal of eye contact, yet whose patients don't follow recommendations for
mammography. One might choose to videotape some of those interactions,
or perhaps to interview some of those patients and doctors (individually or in
focus groups), or all of the above. Here the intriguing question is, "Because
we know from previous studies that eye contact is normally associated with
patient adherence to screening recommendations, what is going on with these
doctors and these patients that is making eye contact irrelevant?"

A more extensive qualitative study would also learn from doctors and
patients represented by Cells A and D. Here, patients might be asked, "How
did you decide to have (or not have) a mammogram this year?" Physicians
might be asked, "What did you do (while interacting with your patient) to
help them decide to follow your advice to get a mammogram?" In this way,
one is looking at the meaning of the statistically significant association
between eye contact and adherence to screening recommendations. Taken
together, these two qualitative approaches challenge and further develop
theory relating caring behaviors and patient participation in prevention.

Stage III

Stage III of the inquiry would include continuing work on areas of particular interest. For example, if one were particularly interested in the notion of
training for caring, one could consider ethnographies of socialization toward
caring. These might be similar to the studies of socialization of family
physicians by Addison (1989) and Bogdewic (1987). Continuing in the

manner suggested for Stage II, one could construct experimental designs that looked at different ways of training for caring. These approaches would be complementary, for the qualitative studies of socialization would probably yield principles and perspectives that would support the development of caring physicians. The experimental approaches would produce training techniques and programs that could be particularly effective in teaching knowledge and skills of caring that have practical significance.

THE RESEARCH TEAM

As we indicated for Stage I, this program of study requires a team with expertise in many different types of research methods and traditions. This fits with the many types of questions that can flow from the question "What is the nature of caring, and what difference does it make?" One can imagine team members from the disciplines of sociology, anthropology, education, psychology, public health, nursing, and medicine. These individuals would bring their preferred styles to the task of inquiry, including field, survey, document-historical, philosophical, and experimental research (Miller & Crabtree, 1992). To be most effective as a team, they would have to understand and respect one another's beliefs and traditions and stand on the common ground of questions and problems they agreed needed answers and solutions.

As indicated at the beginning of this chapter, our small group took some time to explore whether it could work as a team and, if so, how it would do that. We had to begin by stating our positions and our beliefs: the different professional traditions in which we were raised. The discussions were reminiscent of the "paradigm dialogue" between Phillips (postpositivism), Lincoln (constructivism), and Popkewitz (critical science) (Guba, 1990a). And some common ground was achieved:

> Steve and I have agreed on something by this discussion. We've agreed that we both favor and accept the necessity for, the desirability of multiple methods for triangulating on some truths, and this suggests we're both realists. You know, that we accept that there is something out there that at least makes it worthwhile to pretend that it's real for the time being. And that's a remarkable advance. . . .

The unanimity was even clearer when the group came to consensus on what the really important questions were. What was started off by one member was finished by another when he said: "It seems to me that the bottom of all this, the rock bottom question or the top question or whatever, is that question, 'What is the nature of caring, and does it make a difference?'"

The conversation was easier when the group stopped talking about beliefs and preferred styles of research and focused more on what was interesting about provider behavior and what some of their questions on the topic were. As different members offered ideas and suggestions, others would remark, "Now that's an interesting question" or "That's well put." Members often reflected on presentations that had been made to the large group. "The focus group of the public seemed to emphasize . . ." or "I'd like to bring up something Milt Seifert said." New perspectives led to new ways of thinking about provider behavior and new questions. The dialogue was also fluid when the task was "How can we approach this question?" By now there was more of a sense of ease with one another, and the job at hand was a matter of fitting the best strategies and methods to the types of questions that we were asking. A developing sense of humor helped the work, as illustrated by this exchange:

We need to simply answer the question "What do you want to do with the rest of the afternoon?"

"Simply answer the question?" My feeling after a day and a half is that nothing is simple in this group!

NEXT STEPS

Creating a Team

The challenges of many disciplines working together highlight the importance of selecting members who (a) own the research problem, (b) are flexible and open to personal change in how they conceptualize and solve problems, and (c) are available for frequent discussions with other members of the team. These features feel more important than even *what* disciplines are represented on the team, for assumptions about this are inevitably based upon conventional wisdom. The ownership of the research problem by team members may be for very different reasons, but it seems necessary that each have a personal passion for the problem to sustain them through the sometimes difficult process of cross-disciplinary work. In Chapter 23 Will Miller addresses these concerns in some detail and outlines what is required for sustainable cross-disciplinary research.

Refining the Program of Study—Fleshing Out the Design

Although it is not possible, much less appropriate, to specify the qualitative portions of the program of study in advance, some features seem likely to be incorporated. Stage I, which explores the nature of caring in multiple contexts, is clearly a multisite case study design that could involve, for example, three to five research teams (each involving multiple disciplines). One or more members of each team would be responsible for sharing information and analysis as it was developed with the other teams. It might be useful to have periodic meetings of these coordinators at key phases of the concurrent, multisite study. These same teams could reiterate their efforts at additional sites that would be selected to expand upon, confirm, and/or challenge the findings from the initial three to five sites.

Stage II and Stage III designs are discussed earlier in this chapter, but I want to add a suggestion: The same teams involved in producing the concepts of the Stage I multisite study—even those with more traditional quantitative designs—should be involved, at least as consultants. This continuity will help ensure theoretical connection and coherence between the development and application phases of the program of study. It will also make the work and the findings of Stage II and Stage III investigations more accessible and more relevant to Stage I participants—providers and patients.

Identifying Funding Support

Funding support will flow from those who have a stake in solving the research problem. As medical research is becoming more outcome oriented, the second question, "What difference does caring make?" may prove to be especially appealing. Any approach to this question assumes some type of operational definition of caring, so a proposal would need to include Stage I work. Recent experience also suggests that a proposal that highlights the quantitative (traditional) arm of the program is more likely to be funded, with qualitative pieces serving supporting roles. This can be thought of as a qualitative/quantitative sandwich (or Oreo cookie), in which a qualitative beginning defines key characteristics and develops hypotheses, a quantitative middle tests the hypotheses, and a qualitative ending explores the meaning of the quantitatively derived findings. Experience in nonmedical fields also suggests that, at least initially, private foundations may be more amenable to nontraditional research designs than the federal grant programs that support biomedical research.

Practical Obstacles to Implementation

Two major problems are inherent in this program of study. The first is the difficulty in identifying and bringing together a multidisciplinary team of investigators. Although once in vogue in academe, these types of working groups and centers are rapidly disappearing. The second is perhaps a major cause of the first—scarce funds for nontraditional research designs.

Suggestions for Overcoming Barriers

Rather than providers trying to bridge both disciplinary and geographic boundaries, I favor using teams of people who all live in the same place. Given the difficulty in creating and sustaining a multidisciplinary research group, it seems prudent to look first for those few places where these collections already exist.

The strategy of engaging multiple individuals from the same community is consistent with Miller's call for developing local knowledge (Chapter 23). These people will all be drawn to the same vexing, local problem, and the problem will be the shared space where they will begin their work of creating a community of investigators. Attention to local solutions to local problems implies seeking support from sources inclined to care about more narrowly defined concerns. Private foundations, therefore, seem more likely to consider funding for Stage I studies. If Stage I is a success, however, the applied studies of Stages II and III might attract federal support.

20

RESEARCHING PRIMARY CARE
PRACTICE ORGANIZATION

William L. Miller

The organization, delivery, and financing of health care are the focus of intense national debate, and primary care is at the center of most discussions (White House Domestic Policy Council, 1993). Unfortunately, the practice organization of primary health care is a research black box. There are known wide variations in practice patterns both between and within regions, but it is currently not possible to separate organizational effects from payment system effects (Luft, 1986). There is research examining the impact of new organizational formats such as health maintenance organizations and preferred provider organizations on cost, access, and quality, but there is little research exploring the effect of practice organization on changing primary health care provider behavior (Starfield, 1992, pp. 108-131). In response to this paucity of data, an Agency for Health Care Policy and Research (AHCPR) national conference report recommends the need for more understanding of what goes on in primary care practices and how organizational structures and processes relate to practice activities and outcomes (Nutting, 1991). This brings us to a small gathering in Omaha.

GATHERING

How practice organization relates to an understanding of changing primary care provider behavior was the topic given seven researchers who met for two half-days in May 1993. These seven were a diverse group consisting of two family physicians also trained as medical anthropologists, a third family physician whose practice is comanaged by his patients, a multimethod family nurse researcher with special expertise in randomized controlled trials, a qualitative research methodologist from the discipline of education, a general internist and administrator from AHCPR, and a sociologist with proficiency in document analysis.

This group was charged with collaboratively probing the topic of practice organization. Their goals were to identify the critical and salient questions, to suggest approaches to their study, and, if possible, to design a study demonstrating the use of mixed methods. This case report describes the content of the group's discussions and sketches the group's collaborative process.

GETTING STARTED: IDENTITY, LANGUAGE, AND AGENDA

Before exploring any questions, the group first wanted to know who each other was and how each was feeling. The discussion opened where many such mixed disciplinary conversations begin: "I felt like . . . the whole overriding question [was] who's legitimate." Once each person had an opportunity to mark his or her disciplinary territory, express fears and frustrations about being together, and receive acknowledgment of his or her *identity* from the others, participants felt less vulnerable and more willing to listen to each other. What they heard was a confusion of language—different words representing similar meanings and the same words representing different meanings.

A rhetoric of justification was slowly replaced by collaborative discourse as the group defined a *common language*. Earlier in the day, the larger conference of which this group was a part identified the following five themes related to the organization of practice: systems, diversity, interactions, incentives, and teamwork. Each of these terms was challenged by someone in the small group and alternative language collectively named.

Creating this common language began with the term *systems*. Many in the group believed *systems* implied a sense of functionalism and order that they thought did not acknowledge the immense complexity and pluralism of society. More acceptable to the group was the concept of micro and macro *organizational levels*. The micro level consists of the many smaller organizations and practices that make up a particular local world. These are placed within a macro context that includes the political and economic environments.

Diversity was originally intended to capture issues of power and marginality, including concerns about sexism, ageism, racism, and professionalism. The group quickly recognized two very different aspects of diversity. The first, *cultural pluralism*, refers to the many different cultural backgrounds of the people providing and receiving primary health care. The other aspect of diversity refers to the *patterns of dominance and subordination* between and among cultural groups and social institutions. Further discussion of power dynamics revealed the need to pay attention to the many *linkages* between different micro sectors and between micro and macro levels of organization.

Interactions was changed to *relationships* because the latter word seemed to embrace both a behavioral and a moral sense of connection. Concern about the behavioristic bias connoted by *interactions* was more forcefully addressed when discussion turned to incentives. The theme of incentives came from comments by economists at the conference. The utility of economic and behavioral incentives was recognized by all but feared by some. Dialogue continued until all finally agreed that incentives and disincentives were one of several types of *enabling factors* and *barriers to outcomes.*

Everyone thought *teamwork* was an unsatisfactory term. For some of the group, *team* was a sexual metaphor that represented a pattern of domination. For others, it implied more cohesiveness within health care practice than really exists. Once again, the challenge was to identify language that was both more inclusive and still meaningful. *Work patterns* was the final selection because it invited many different descriptors, such as *hierarchical, adversarial, interdisciplinary, collaborative, and interdependent.*

Changing the language made it easier for the group to challenge itself and its hidden assumptions. Several group participants originally assumed the organization of health practice referred to office or hospital-based medical care organizations. For example, one of the physician participants identified four elements—a theoretical knowledge base, a set of techniques, an expert practitioner, and a patient—as necessary for something to be labeled a health practice. One of the social scientists immediately challenged, "Now I'm hearing history. Why must there be an expert practitioner?" The group was reminded that health practices occur in a plethora of settings involving numerous types of people and activities, many of which are outside the traditional spheres of medical power and influence. Participants shared many examples, including stories about other ethnic health care arrangements, self-care, nurse-managed care, and public health programs. At this time, the group tentatively reached a reluctant consensus on four features common to any health practice. Health practice is always *relational*, involves the use of several *types of knowledge*, is always *situated* in time and place, and produces *outcomes.*

The group was finally ready to *set an agenda* and identify some important questions. What emerged from the ensuing free flow of critical commentary were three sets of questions thought to be foundational for any understanding of the influence of practice organization on changing provider behavior. One set of questions reflected issues of structure and substance; a second set of questions explored the processes of health practice. The third set of questions examined outcomes. If only it were this simple.

DISCOVERY: WHAT ARE THE QUESTIONS?

The group continued with what they thought they knew only to discover what they did not know. What is health practice? Everyone had a different notion. Two distinct senses of practice emerged. The first refers to an activity through which social relationships are organized to produce something—health care as a product. The second refers to the process of constituting a particular profession or identity. Nearly all the questions developed by the group had reference to both senses of practice.

Substantive Questions

What is health practice? Substantive and structural questions about health practice comprise the who, what, and where. *Who does health practice?* The *who* includes patients doing their own self-care, nurses, indigenous healers, special books, physicians, or neighbors with specially recognized skills. *What are the structural features of health practice?* The *what* refers not only to the different organizational types of health practice, such as solo, same provider-type group, and multiprovider group, but also to the method of reimbursement, such as fee for service, fee for time, salary, and capitation. It also refers to the ways in which these two structural features are combined, as in HMOs or PPOs. *Where is health practice?* Locations can consist of a single site or a connected network of sites that situate the health care for a particular episode of illness. Thus health practice occurs at the individual, group, or community level.

Who are the stakeholders in health practice? This question seeks to know who benefits and who and/or what suffers as the result of particular health practices. It opens inquiry into the patterns of domination and subordination and raises questions about the processes of health practice.

Process Questions

How is health practiced? Process questions began with questions about access. *Why do patients attend or not attend particular health practices?* At the micro level this question probes for the actual reason patients choose to go to a particular health practice at a specific time and then how the practice recognizes or fails to recognize the reason. At the macro level this question explores the historical, social, and political influences on how people are or are not able to get into health practices. These concerns introduced the role of insurance carriers, attorneys, and pharmaceutical representatives who are also regular participants in health practice. *How do third parties influence the daily activity of health practice?*

Once providers, patients, and third parties are in a practice, attention shifts to the internal workings of a health practice. *Who's doing what within a health practice?* Who makes up the practice, and how do those persons relate? This includes the receptionists, billing clerks, and phlebotomists, not just the providers and recipients of health care. How do macro-level processes influence what goes on inside the practice? *What information/knowledge is being created and maintained?* Practices create and maintain multiple types of data, including billing information and patient chart notes. What are the intents of the different data sets, how do they compare, and why are certain ones kept and others not? In other words, *who wants to know what?*

Finally, *how does health practice work?* This question refers to the everyday activities within each practice and among the many micro/micro and micro/macro linkages. *How are needs matched with skills?* Needs are assessed at either the individual or the community level. Patients and practitioners usually make these decisions, but managed care systems are now beginning to limit choice. Community-oriented primary care offers one approach to such community-level assessment (Nutting & Connor, 1986).

Outcomes Questions

What constitutes the value of health practice? This question bridges structure and process and seeks to identify those essential features and activities that give value to health practice. Essentially, this is a question about outcomes. *What works in health practice?* The group defined outcomes in terms of the triad of efficiency, effectiveness, and satisfaction. When discussing outcomes, it becomes important to specify which possible stakeholders benefit from particular outcomes and to include the different stakeholders in decisions about which outcomes matter.

ADVENTURE: RESEARCH APPROACHES

Start with definitions. "When you say, 'What is health practice?' we say, 'What is practice?' and 'What is health?' We're looking for the outcomes, and the outcomes, of course, are dependent on who's talking about it . . . a lot of very embedded terms." The group never agreed on definitions of health, practice, or outcome. This was not surprising because there is no existing database describing what actually happens in health practices. The group also insisted that the complexity and context of health practice be captured by any proposed research. The opening study in a planned research program about practice organization apparently needs to minimize assumptions, be open to changing meanings, and capture the interpreted, lived, and measured worlds of health practice. The group decided to start at the community level using descriptive methodologies.

Two communities, demographically and geographically similar but with widely divergent levels of morbidity and mortality, would be selected. A comparative case study using both traditional epidemiological survey methodology and ethnography would be designed to answer two broad questions, "What is health within each community?" and "What are the practices related to health in formal systems of care as well as informal systems of care?" A challenge is to make the communities comparable so as to "be more persuasive in the construction of your setting." The group went on to debate assumptions about "What is a healthy community?" These discussions noted the difference between quality of life and longevity of life and pointed out the common assumption within the medical community that health is equivalent to avoiding illness.

This large comparative case study design provides exploratory answers to substantive questions such as "What is health?" "Who does health practice?" "Where is health practice?" and "Who are the stakeholders?" The comparative case study also provides a framework or context for the process question, "How is health practiced?" as well as guiding the refining of future research questions.

The next phase of research could entail a series of intensive, mostly ethnographic, case studies addressing all the process questions noted above with a special emphasis on the four features of health practice—relations, types of knowledge, location, and outcomes—and on the two senses of health practice—what it does and how it is constituted. In each case, the investigator would specifically record the organizational levels and their linkages, patterns of domination and subordination, issues related to cultural pluralism, enabling factors and barriers to different outcomes, and work patterns. These five themes would serve as the filters through which the researcher would look and listen. The group assumed the above studies were completed prior to designing the illustrative multimethod study discussed in the next section.

TREASURE: AN ILLUSTRATIVE MULTIMETHOD DESIGN

The discovery process of refining questions centered on language and assumptions. The adventure of creating a multimethod research design was,

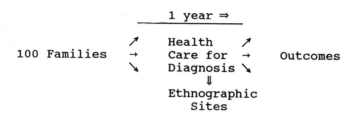

Figure 20.1. Research Design With Community as Focus

for this small group, an iterative process centered on the question. One starts with the question, which then triggers a design idea. This idea is elaborated until several problems and conflicts begin to emerge, at which point one revisits the question. This leads to new design ideas, and so the spiral continues until consensus is reached such that the design adequately answers the question from the group's multiple perspectives. Thus a key to the treasure of good multimethod research design is the persistent reasking, "What do we want to know?"

In this case, the group wanted to know, *"How do different practices work, and do the differences affect outcome?"* The group went through three design iterations. In each cycle the unit of analysis changed. *How do different practices work and do the differences affect outcome?* "We could focus on HIV care." Immediate controversy followed. "By focusing on a particular condition, you have stripped primary care of one of its main functions in medicine . . . that is, what the patient walks in with." "Comprehensiveness." "By focusing on conditions, we tend to get compared to specialists." This discussion quickly moved the focus from the health practice to the patient in the community. Someone suggested starting in the community and following people into practices in order to get a sense of how the practices work in transit.

Someone else pointed out that patients often choose many different health practices for different purposes such that they create unique patterns of care. This raised the question of how disease outcomes reflect patterns of care. Figure 20.1 illustrates the design that emerged from this discussion. This design suggests randomly selecting 100 families and following them for one year while concurrently conducting ethnographies at the health practices attended by the patients. At the end of the year, specific disease outcomes would be measured and the results compared to the patterns of care and practice organizations. This design quickly raised serious objections, including the impracticality of doing ethnographies at all the health practice sites in

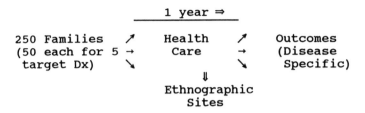

Figure 20.2. Research Design With Health Problem as Focus

a community. Finally, the group was reminded that the research question wasn't about the community. We returned to the question.

How do different practices work and do the differences affect outcome? The second design iteration returned to health problems as the unit of attention. The discussion focused on which problems. One suggestion was to address the five most common problems. Another idea was to use some typology of problems, such as infectious, acute, and chronic. Figure 20.2 illustrates the rudimentary design that resulted. The design was similar to the first except that five target diseases were chosen and then 50 people with each disease were randomly selected. The same objections were raised, so again the group returned to the original question.

How do different practices work and do the differences affect outcome? "So, sample the practices!" The third design discussion finally focused on health practices. The group began with sampling issues. Qualitative methodologists continued to argue for the ethnographic case study while the quantitative methodologists recommended a sampling approach based on outcome measures. The different types of practitioners in the group, however, were concerned that choosing sites on the basis of outcomes might be too exclusive. For example, would a nurse-managed site be included?

The discussion shifted back to the variety of health practices but then returned to sampling concerns. The group got stuck on trying to decide whether the practice sites or the patients were the unit of analysis. The impasse was broken by one of the participants asking, "What are we trying to know here?" Another quickly answered, "To know what is going on in those [health practice] sites." A third person jumped in, "Maybe focusing on ideal types!" The concept of "ideal types" helped frame comfortable territory for everyone. There were now three sections to the emerging design. One part of the design focused on using ethnography to describe selected health practice sites representing the best and the worst. Another part of the design involved targeted outcomes needing accurate measurement. Finally, there were micro/macro

6 Ideal Cases

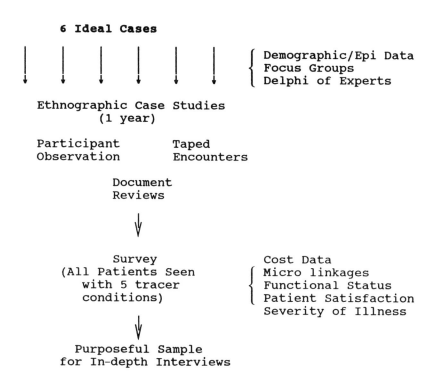

Figure 20.3. Research Design With Practice as Focus

linkages to be explored. Everyone in the group now had a place in the design. It was time for specifics.

The remainder of the discussion concerned details about practice site "case mix," identification and selection of ideal types, outcomes, and what "tracer conditions" to track. Figure 20.3 illustrates the combination multimethod research design developed by the group. The design sequences a concurrent study using three qualitative methods followed by a nested design using depth interviews within a survey design. Six "ideal cases" are selected from a common community in order to ensure a shared macro environment. The six cases represent the "best" and "worst" of a family nurse practitioner (FNP) small (3-5) group model, a family physician (FP) small group model, and a collaborative FNP/FP small group model. These cases are selected on the basis of the following: (a) how the practice reflects the demography and epidemiology of the community—determined using community and practice surveys and record reviews; (b) how the practices are perceived by patients, providers, and payors within the community—discovered using focus group data; and (c) how "experts" and/or power brokers in the community perceive the practices—derived from data based on use of a Delphi technique.

Over the next year, ethnographic case studies using a combination of participant observation, document review, and videotaping of practitioner-patient encounters take place at the six sites. At the end of the study year, a record review identifies all the patients with one of five tracer conditions seen that year in each practice. These patients are then surveyed using measures of functional status, patient satisfaction, and severity of illness. Those patients with the highest and lowest measures for each are also interviewed in depth to help explain the discrepancies. Data are also collected on cost to both patients and the practice for each illness episode. Finally, the numbers of referrals or linkages to other micro-level organizations are counted as an additional possible influence on both cost and quality.

REFLECTIONS: COLLABORATIVE PROCESS

"I thought people were meeting, but the meeting points were randomly distributed around the universe. . . . I'm feeling not quite as the whipped child, but feeling a little bit like I'm not sure . . . of where I'm going, what the expectations are." This is how it felt in the collaborative, cross-disciplinary sweat lodge. It also felt exhilarating. A four-step process kept recurring in this small collaborative group that made the joy worth the sweat.

The first step was *acceptance and validation*. Both small group sessions began with everyone wearing his or her respective disciplinary and methodological robes. Each person had to present his or her personal historical stance and have others validate it before he or she was willing to risk moving outside it. For example, in the opening discussions on research design, it now seems obvious that health practices should have been the focus of attention in order to answer the research question. It isn't so obvious, however, when each person reads the question from a different perspective. Sociologists start in the community; it's how they see and talk. Health policymakers start with outcomes; it's how they see and talk. These perspectives had to be voiced, acknowledged, and, later, incorporated into the groupthink before we moved iteratively toward a shared perceptual space.

The second step involved reaching agreement on *shared expectations*. Once everyone felt validated and willing to listen to others, everyone needed to agree on a common set of expectations about the purpose of meeting and the rules of discourse. In both the question and design meetings of the small group, this agreement came about only after initial sparring over small, often tangential issues. The point is that seemingly trivial diversions off the main topic are probably an essential part of moving toward common ground. The persistent healthy tension between the pragmatists seeking a plan and the contemplatives seeking complex insight kept the group open to diversions but conscious of time and goals.

The third step involved *revealing assumptions* and *creating a common language*. This process was most clearly illustrated by the lengthy debates over the meaning of words during the discussions about the research questions but occurred again in the design conversations. It was only after each person felt validated, agreed on expectations, and shared a common language that the fourth step, *group action*, was successfully initiated.

For every issue that arose, from refining research questions to research design to research results, the diverse mix of the group resulted in a more complex and more complete sense of knowing. It was quite a journey from gathering a group of cross-disciplinary strangers, to getting started, and then discovering many adventures along the road to the treasure. In the end this knowledge gathered felt more robust because one person *knew the numbers*, another *knew the words or meanings*, another *knew where the power was*, and yet another alerted us to *knowing the what else*. The advantages for doing collaborative, multimethod research seemed clear to this group. Their hope is that similar groups get funded and start doing the research.

21

RESEARCHING DISSEMINATION OF INFORMATION INTO PRACTICE

Richard B. Addison

As other chapters in this volume have argued, the dissemination of research is a problematic endeavor. In discussing the topic of dissemination, our small group of primary care researchers (Crabtree, Lather, McCall, Mueller, Pantell, and Addison) spent much time exploring the area, trying to unearth and sift through salient and relevant issues about dissemination, its domain, content, process, goals, context, complexity, barriers, and background conditions.

Our group was charged with exploring the topic of dissemination, eliciting the important questions, developing approaches to research, and, if possible, putting forth a research design to investigate some aspect about dissemination. In this chapter, I will try to convey the issues and flavor of the discussions, outline the approach to investigating dissemination that evolved, describe the specific study we arrived at, and point briefly toward the future.

EXPLORING THE AREA—WHAT ARE THE QUESTIONS?

What About Dissemination Should Be Researched?

To begin looking at dissemination, our small group of researchers grappled with some basic questions. One member asked "What is it that needs to be changed out there, and how can dissemination of information help that?" Did we want to study the content of dissemination, the process of dissemination, or both?

In terms of content, we talked about *what* should be disseminated: research findings in total, a simplified version of those findings, or recommendations only? Should this be in the form of guidelines, advertisements, regulations, or some combination of the above?

In terms of the process of dissemination, the group considered *how* knowledge and practices were disseminated: direct mailings, professional journals, newspapers, magazines, TV advertisements, national guidelines, local guideline development, or patient-viewed videotapes. One of the innovative examples of dissemination offered that of patients shown videotapes of simulated patients talking about their satisfaction or dissatisfaction with having or not having undergone prostate surgery, seemed to be quite effective in helping patients with prostate cancer decide whether to undergo surgery.

We discussed *whom* we should study: physicians (all physicians or primary care physicians), other health care workers (other types of providers, office managers, receptionists, nurses), patients, or all of the above. Should research on dissemination target a random, stratified, targeted, or comprehensive sample of the population?

We recognized that the specific study undertaken would dictate the answers to these and other questions. But no matter what study would be undertaken and what methods used, we wanted to take all these questions into account.

Why Study Dissemination?

We also asked questions about the larger purpose of studying dissemination: Why study dissemination? What are the goals and possible benefits of doing research on dissemination? The group questioned the connection between dissemination and health outcomes: "*Does* dissemination have an impact on health outcomes?" The hopeful argument is that dissemination has the potential to institute standards of practice, change provider behavior, and improve overall health care. If dissemination were more effective, the potential would exist for less utilization of (and less money spent on) unnecessary and inappropriate health care services and greater satisfaction for both patient and provider.

The group also asked how to agree on what makes for a desirable outcome and how the success of dissemination should be measured. We struggled against the prevailing notion and current dominant perception that dissemination means dissemination of guidelines. Embracing recommended guidelines may or may not be the best measure of success in regard to dissemination.

What are the real outcomes? [In] the old model, . . . the outcome would have been that this guideline is implemented. The new outcomes are more functional status

measurement of kids. . . . Do the kids feel better? Do they have more energy? Do
they have better self-esteem? Do they miss fewer days of school?

Deciding on a desired outcome is undeniably related to the agendas of the
researchers and has political, economic, and ideological ramifications.

Is Research a Neutral Activity?

The group quickly moved to the notion of a research agenda as a motivated
activity. Was research a neutral topic? This was a rhetorical question for our
group:

[Researchers] have got this agenda they're wanting to foster. It's not just a neutral
study of what's going on out there.

Nobody has neutral studies anymore. . . . Everybody has an agenda of some sort.

Some are more overt than others.

As researchers, you're actually part of the process. You have an agenda.

Group members identified their various agendas, which ranged from helping
patients to shifting the center of the dissemination process to completely
changing a health care system whose priorities are askew.

What Are the Background Economic Issues?

Just as researchers have a stake in their research projects, so do the
stakeholders in the arena of changing physician behavior. Members of the
group were especially energetic in exploring the economic background of
research on dissemination. Cost containment was identified as a driving force
behind efforts to change physician behavior and make physicians more
efficient and cost effective. And, in large part, the dissemination of guidelines
for appropriate treatment grew out of a need to control medical costs by
showing physicians how not to overutilize health services. The assumption
behind this line of thinking was that all physicians would immediately
recognize their inefficient practices and adopt the recommendations of the
guidelines. This was not the case, and in fact utilization increased. To slow
down increases in health care costs, authorities instituted a revised reimbursement schedule: the Resource Based Relative Value Scale (RBRVS). However, one of the responses physicians had to the enactment of RBRVS was

to upcode, to provide more services, to unbundle things that they ordinarily provide in a bundled way. . . . When they set prices, physicians change behavior by doing more services, volume changes when price caps are applied. . . . One of the ways you contain quantity is to get physicians who are providing inappropriate services to provide appropriate services. Well, what is appropriate? Well, that's how they drifted into this area of guidelines.

The group explored the likelihood that the bottom line of changing physician behavior may not be *effectiveness*, that is, how many people change, but rather *efficiency*: "how many people changed at what cost." Given the emphasis on cost control, the next question becomes, "Does an infusion of dollars into the dissemination of recommendations pay off, in terms of the economy of changed practices or health outcomes?"

The group was also concerned about the expense of funding both research on provider change and dissemination of recommendations from such research. (It was not surprising that a group of researchers would be attuned to issues of funding.) One member talked about funding for the research on developing asthma guidelines and the subsequent publication and dissemination of that research. He marvelled that

this is the first time in history that not only have they put probably millions of dollars into developing guidelines, they have mailed packets and executive summaries to virtually every physician in the country. . . . There's hundreds of billions of dollars and you put it 2 inches from the patients and providers, and you get nothing.

He was doubtful about the benefit of pouring more money into comprehensive guideline dissemination to change physician behavior.

How Is Dissemination Affected by Power Issues?

Economic issues often go hand in hand with power issues. The group conceptualized power issues in terms of both research and dissemination. For example, does the legitimation of recommended practices affect the dissemination effort? That is, if the practices to be disseminated are backed by some person or organization that is well respected ("to sort of buy in participation"), will providers be more likely to embrace those practices? And how does the locus of dissemination affect dissemination? For example, if recommendations originate at a national level (the center), are the recommendations more or less likely to be taken up than if they are generated and disseminated at a local level (the periphery)?

The group discussed the differences in effectiveness of dissemination by designated experts (at both local and national levels); by respected organizations (such as AAFP or SGIM) in attempts to buy physicians' compliance; by power relationships in a local setting (physicians versus other providers), and by larger market forces (do physicians have any alternative, given the transition to managed care and capitation?). Different political climates are likely to heighten or dull the effects of different forms of dissemination.

How to Capture the Complexity of Research in Context

The group was staunch in insisting that the complexity of the problem be honored in any research design. In any study involving human interaction, enormous complexity exists. The group felt that research designs that are simple, straightforward, and elegant often miss critical and significant aspects of a problem: "I'm recoiling from the 'Let's look at the dissemination of this month's magic bullet.' It used to be penicillin. Now it's a guideline, and it's still very reductionistic and linear." The group saw a need to look at how health care practices get negotiated in the context of the office setting: "They forgot office practice. They forgot what 90% of it is all about."

The group criticized simplistic research designs that did take into account the larger context of interaction. One of the group members talked about a study of whether physicians complied with guidelines to offer female patients mammograms. The results of the study were boiled down to whether the physician proposed a mammogram during the visit. The study did not take into account whether other, perhaps more important issues (such as situations of spousal abuse or domestic violence) were instead discussed during the visit. If a mammogram was not discussed, the visit was classified as not complying with the guideline to offer patients mammograms.

> Whatever dissemination studies there have been, they have reduced the complexities. They've been reductionist in the very way they've been set up. There haven't been dissemination studies that have tried to access the complexity of what's going on. . . . Unless you start looking at the context of what's going on, you start . . . making all sorts of false interpretations of "the doctor's doing a bad job; they didn't follow the guidelines" when in fact what they're doing is . . . talking about domestic violence, which may have a lot greater immediate impact and consequences on a person's health. . . . One of the troubles is the guideline model assumes one patient, one problem, one time.

The group also emphasized that one implication of not settling for simplistic designs was being open to and looking for unanticipated outcomes: "We'd do dissemination of complex processes. We're looking at a wide array of outcomes, and we need to be open to the unanticipated outcomes." "How do we capture the unanticipated? I think I'm the most excited about that."

For the most part, the group was in agreement on how complex any thorough investigation of dissemination would have to be. The members also wanted to know whether the simplicity or complexity of the disseminated information or practice would affect the success of dissemination. Intuitively, simple information or practices should be more easily disseminated than complex information or practices. One member told a story of a 3 × 5 index card with a simple dosage recommendation that mysteriously appeared on a bulletin board. The 3 × 5 card proved more effective in changing physician behavior than a whole set of complex guidelines posted for patients and physicians to read.

The group also asked about the practicality of utilizing guidelines: given that health care visits have grown shorter, is it practical or reasonable to assume that even if guidelines are disseminated and agreed upon, health care providers will have the time to implement the guidelines? And how can this best be measured, especially if it may take multiple visits to implement the guidelines?

The group also wondered if legal changes would affect the success of dissemination efforts. That is, if recommendations or guidelines become law, do dissemination efforts improve greatly?

The members discussed the relationship between the creation of knowledge and dissemination of that knowledge. They also wanted to look at barriers to the dissemination of information and practices. The question selected for investigation (described below) deals directly with this question by looking closely at how current methods of dissemination succeed or fail in particular contexts and how information and practices get negotiated within these contexts.

In trying to come up with a specific research project, the group would struggle greatly with complexity and context: how comprehensive a study could be undertaken with hope for funding and completion? And how generalizable would any contextual study be?

DEVELOPING AN APPROACH FOR INVESTIGATION

After allowing ourselves to explore some of the above questions about dissemination and research on dissemination, we set about to choose a researchable question. Before doing this, we laid out the larger assumptive framework of what we were looking at. Without disregarding the research on dissemination in other fields (especially education, psychology, and advertising) or exemplary applications of that research (such as the practices of drug company representatives), we wanted to focus on learning more about how new information and practices do and do not get negotiated in everyday settings. We felt if we learned more about the *process* of dissemination, the study would be more valuable.

What would be the best way to study dissemination? A first step would be to identify our assumptions and presuppositions as researchers about both the substantive issue of dissemination and the process of research. For example, as researchers we might have prejudices against the effectiveness of dissemination via federal guidelines. If so, and if we identified this as a prejudice, we would have to be careful to solicit researchers for our team who were open to exploring such prejudices. Also, in a multimethod design, both quantitative and qualitative researchers would need to be open to examining their prejudices.

We decided that our next step in designing such a study would be to look at previous models of how information gets negotiated in a setting. The communication model crafted by Pantell and Lewis (1986) was proposed as a possible starting framework (see Figure 21.1). Familiarity with such a model of provider-patient intervention-outcome-situation seemed helpful for attending to the complexity of the context of dissemination. This model encompassed descriptions of the setting, the situation, verbal and nonverbal dimensions, interventions aimed at providers and interventions aimed at patients, and outcomes for each. Relevant provider outcomes might include receipt of information, increase in knowledge, change in practices, change in satisfaction, and the degree of each of the above over the short and long term. Relevant patient outcome measures might include satisfaction, compliance, functional status, and health care utilization over the short and long term.

We then decided to boil down the object of inquiry by focusing on specific dissemination cases. We first looked at a four-square model (Table 21.1). We wanted to contrast simple and complex interventions such as guidelines for immunization and guidelines for the treatment of asthma. We wanted to look at these cases in contrasting situations of effective and ineffective dissemination and implementation.

An earlier discussion in the conference was raised again at this point. Should the object of study include other providers in addition to physicians? Our group clearly felt that the problem lay not with providers such as nurses and nurse practitioners, but with physicians. The practices of physicians are the ones that are difficult to change; physicians tend to hold on to their habitual ways of treating patients even in the light of contrary research. Also, physicians tend not to refer out when they are not competent. And physicians

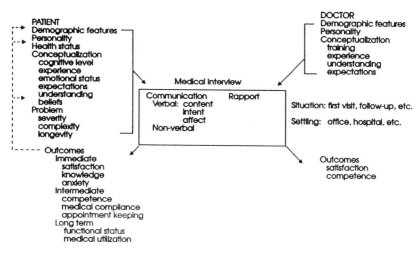

Figure 21.1. Communication Model of Pantell and Lewis (1986)

TABLE 21.1 Four-Square Table for Selecting Case Studies

	Simple	Complex
Successful		
Unsuccessful		

control 80% of health care costs. We therefore chose to focus on the knowledge and practices of physicians. Overwhelmed by sampling possibilities, we decided we would include only primary care physicians: family physicians, pediatricians, and primary care internists.

To be as comprehensive as possible, we wanted to look at both traditional (e.g., guidelines) and nontraditional (e.g., computer-driven interviews) methods of dissemination. To see how the dissemination efforts affected behavior and outcomes in the local setting, we also wanted to already be in the field, observing when the guidelines arrived or another method of dissemination was enacted.

At this stage we were overwhelmed with the enormous complexity of the project we had begun to outline. We began in earnest to design a researchable study.

THE STUDY

With the clock ticking, we set about to design a specific researchable study on dissemination. We decided somewhat arbitrarily to study the dissemination of current guidelines on asthma that were distributed to all physicians (National Asthma Education Program Office, 1991). We were interested in looking at how the dissemination of the asthma guidelines was negotiated in practice settings. We wanted to look at successful dissemination situations and barriers to successful dissemination. We recognized that it was important how we defined successful dissemination: a simple definition would not suffice for our purpose of investigating the negotiation of the guidelines in the local setting. The definition of successful dissemination had to include the physician receiving the guidelines and implementing them with patients, as well as successful health outcomes for patients. In order to be thorough and comprehensive and not to cost a fortune, even in its scaled-down form (focusing just on the dissemination of asthma guidelines, not contrasting it with dissemination of the less complicated immunization guidelines as we had originally intended), this study would be a complex one.

Our next step would be to conduct a review of the literature on dissemination practices, both in and out of medicine. We thought that other disciplines would have a great deal to offer on dissemination of knowledge and practices.

After completing the literature review, we would conduct a group interview (or mini-focus group) with physicians from various settings and in various specialties. Out of this focus group, we hoped to construct a questionnaire on providers' knowledge and practices of treating asthma. This survey would then be sent to a stratified random sample of providers to determine providers' practices and justification for practice in the treatment of asthma. We would be trying to ascertain a measure of the effectiveness of implementing the asthma guidelines.

We would need to define our sample, send out the questionnaire (probably more than one or two mailings would be required), and collect and analyze data from the questionnaire. To arrive at a greater understanding of how guidelines are effectively disseminated in an everyday setting, several sites would be chosen from the questionnaire results for further investigation. These sites would be selected for maximum variation in terms of impact: that is, sites where we might predict that the dissemination of the asthma guidelines would have the greatest effect, or sites that have changed dramatically, perhaps because of the guidelines. We would use the survey to identify these cases of maximum variation.

Depending on the level of funding, time, and other resources, we would then begin intensive observational case studies to understand how information does and does not get disseminated at those sites. Each case study would involve observation, interviewing, and chart reviews. We would proceed according to the method of grounded interpretive research (Addison, 1989, 1992; Glaser & Strauss, 1967; Strauss, 1987), concurrently gathering, sorting, and analyzing data to generate a model of how information and practices recommended by the asthma guidelines do and do not get negotiated at each of the chosen sites.

After a provisional model had been generated, we would read the model back to the research participants (providers) at each site for their reactions, comments, questions, criticisms, and concerns. We would refine the model and then show it to other providers for their questions and criticisms. After further refining the model, we would show it to research colleagues, especially critical ones.

We would then construct a second survey from the model incorporating the significant, interesting, and anomalous findings of our initial survey and case studies. We would send this survey to a sample of physicians who treat asthma patients. The purpose of this survey would be to ascertain whether respondents agreed with findings from the initial survey and case studies: whether what we would have come to understand as significant or important in the dissemination of the asthma guidelines was also what the providers believe to be important. We would try to construct this survey to be as sensitive to contextual elements as possible, taking into account different settings, different types of providers, and different patient populations. We would publish process and outcome results in journals.

NEXT STEPS

The group struggled greatly with the complexity of designing a study from scratch, of narrowing the focus of the topic enough to do so, of agreeing on a substantive issue of common interest, and of defining a comprehensive enough approach to encompass some of the enormously complex aspects of dissemination. The group was always clear that dissemination consisted of more than merely handing down guidelines from above: that negotiating these guidelines in the local setting was a critical part of dissemination.

The statement that probably best captured the future direction of the group's work was offered by one of the members: "If we could come out energized or produce something that would help energize people, that would lead to some good work." It is the hope of our group that our work will energize some of us, other researchers, or funding agencies to further the efforts begun at this conference.

22

PERSPECTIVES ON CONFERENCE PROCESS

Morgan Jackson
Milton Seifert, Jr.
Valerie Janesick
Robert McCall

Four "process observers" were asked to observe the discussions at the conference, to provide feedback to the participants during the conference (see Chapter 17), and to provide written summary comments. These individuals were selected to give insights from the perspectives of the federal system (Morgan Jackson), from the "real world" of primary care practice (Milton Seifert), from qualitative research (Valerie Janesick), and from quantitative research (Robert McCall). These individuals were specifically asked to (a) identify unanswered issues as they emerged during the conference; (b) redirect the agenda when necessary; and (c) identify biases as they emerged. It was anticipated that they would help participants to identify their own expectations and preconceptions and help participants to overcome communication barriers.

In this chapter, these four individuals reflect back on their experience and provide extremely valuable insights in the process of developing collaborative research. Their comments also highlight the need for the role of the observer/ auditor in collaborative research where it is essential to have ongoing evaluation, to keep the process honest, and to have ethics overseers.

CREATING SPACE FOR COLLABORATIVE RESEARCH—
MORGAN JACKSON

Personal Perspectives

In reflecting on the conference and the implications for primary care research, I want to share some thoughts from a personal perspective first and then from the perspective of the AHCPR. In personalizing my experience, one of the things that comes to mind is a story from the Japanese culture regarding a very, very famous general who at the end of a long career decided that the one thing he needed to do to complete his life was to learn to meditate. He went to a Zen master and presented himself. After the appropriate formalities, the Master invited him to have tea. The general sat down, and according to the ritual, the Master started pouring the tea. As the Master was pouring the general's tea, the cup naturally began filling up, but as it became increasingly full, the Master kept pouring. As I'm sure you know, the codes for rituals in Japan are very, very rigid, so the general really didn't want to say anything—but the tea was getting closer to the top of the cup and the general was concerned that it would spill if the Master continued pouring. The Zen master kept pouring and all of a sudden, the tea was overflowing the cup. The general again didn't want to say anything because of his position, but finally, after the tea was spilling on the table and the floor, he said, "Please, Master, stop pouring the tea. The cup is full, and it's spilling out of the cup." The Master very calmly put the pot down and said, "Your mind is like the teacup, there is no room for more information so long as it is full. You first must empty your mind in order to receive these teachings."

I see a parallel in the experience that the participants had at the conference. We came with full cups—I'll personalize it: I came with a full cup, with my biases and perspectives that made it difficult for me to hear some of the things that were said early in the conference. Since then I have taken the opportunity to relax the assumptions that I use to operate in the world and to try to see things from other perspectives. This has given me an opportunity to create space in my experience for the other ways that the world might be perceived or the other ways that people might do things. I have benefited personally from this, and I invite others to do the same.

In observing the conference, I was reminded of the delusion of objectivity: a concept to which I was introduced through the study of Eastern philosophies and cultures. It makes me appreciate a remark made at the conference that "anybody who is breathing has a bias." It's probably useful for all of us to recognize, if not admit, this. I'd like to talk about us as a group (avoiding the us/them dichotomy) that is trying to accomplish a result, and I have a problem with us, including me, sharing information and not acknowledging the assumptions from which we might be speaking—assumptions that might influence those perceptions.

The duality evidenced at the conference was interesting. It was articulated on one level as qualitative versus quantitative; the challenge might be to transcend both. It is hoped that primary care research can work to find middle ground.

We also need to be aware that the map is not the territory. One misperception that I continuously find throughout my entire life, in addition to my medical career, is that of people assuming that the models we create are the subject reality. That models are representational is forgotten; they take on lives of their own and after a while become accepted as realities. In no time, we're relating to the models and not the realities. All of us do this.

The term *reductionism* was referenced by one of the participants, and I think that it is one of the critical areas we need to confront. For example, at the conference we were often talking about the "doctor-patient relationship," and I prefer this distinction to "provider-patient" because I think that doctors embody more of the problems in this context than do other types of providers. If nurses and other providers want to take on the baggage that the medical profession has spent years accumulating, they are welcome to do so. I would assert that, in general, nurses are much better at communicating with and relating to patients than are physicians. (Even the term *patient* has a certain value or "spin" that I'm not sure I like.) Although there are perspectives from which it's useful to lump all providers, in this particular case (identifying questions for the conference), we should probably recognize that nurses, in general, do these things a lot better than physicians and that we get into other problems when we lump all providers. That's another duality—lumping versus splitting.

We need to recognize that the so-called "doctor-patient relationship" has a historical definition. There are certain assumptions that I make: (a) that patients have access; (b) that patients have options; and (c) that patients can exercise choice regarding their options. Those are amazingly important assumptions! One conference participant made reference to the fact that many of the people who have grown up in this country have not been in circumstances in which they were allowed to exercise choices about their preferences. I would assert that the doctor-patient relationship is in fact a power relationship where historically one of the critical components was the relationship between one individual (who took on a certain mantle when using the label *patient*) who would go to another individual (who took on a certain mantle when using the term *doctor*) in order to have a certain activity and result accomplished. I think we should explore the dynamics of human relationships that result when somebody who has a specific body of information uses that information to influence the relationship with another individual who does not have that information. In these and similar circumstances, that information and those methods can be used as tools, and they also can be used as weapons. We will get a lot more accomplished if we use them as tools rather than as weapons.

The conference experience reminds me of the Hindu religion, in which Brahma (the creator), Vishnu (the preserver), and Shiva (the destroyer) are the three aspects of the Divine. The first day at the conference was a Shiva experience. We knocked our heads against the proverbial wall where we could not agree on the agenda because of our conceptual blinders. In order to survive we needed to put aside the conceptual blinders within which we all operate in general and, I would say, within which we have to operate in order to get our agendas accomplished in society. By putting these blinders aside for a short period of time, we were able to have meaningful communication instead of miscommunication and create a Brahma experience.

Part of the problem is the rigidity of the roles that researchers have. A message that came up frequently during the conference had to do with change, but we need to look at the distinction between imposing change and inviting change. I would assert that none of us is willing to be changed by somebody telling us we have to, but if the right incentives are incorporated under realistic circumstances, it may be possible to create mechanisms that invite or induce change.

It was very gratifying to hear so much attention placed on the importance of listening during the conference. It takes me back to an instruction that I received from my grandfather, who was a country doctor. My mother reported that he always said, "As long as you listen, the patient will tell you what's wrong." Listening is not just the capacity to have the ears open and to register signals in the brain. Listening is an activity that is very similar to the "observer" role I had at the meeting. It requires the suspension of the critical mind as a judge in order to allow the impulses of experience to register in the brain before they are judged by the mind.

We must remember that communication is what is heard, not what was said or what was intended. We can benefit from this realization. I'll never forget the counsel of one of my instructors during my residency. I was sharing my frustrations about a patient who had major life problems and was crying a lot. My instructor said, "You know, sometimes all a patient wants is for you to be there, and you don't always have to do anything. Sometimes you don't even have to say anything. You only need to listen." That was a critical lesson in communication that even goes beyond realizing the difference between what is heard as opposed to what is said.

In terms of outcomes, there's the short run, there's the medium run and, as John Maynard Keynes said, "In the long run, everybody's dead." The short-run perspective looks at the conference in terms of what happened over one weekend. I feel good about what we accomplished and invite all the other participants to feel good about it as well. Nevertheless, there are other levels on which change might occur in other time frames. In the intermediate run, on a perceptual level, it's possible that we might now be more open to the variety of techniques that can be used to undertake research and to answer important questions. At still another level, it's possible that we might even think about working with people or even interacting with people who represent the range of disciplines that can make contributions to a product. Finally, research could be undertaken collaboratively and/or publications might be generated that represent greater collaboration than currently exists.

Institutional Perspectives

In terms of whether AHCPR benefited from the conference, there is a certain reality test that's called the world beyond the front door. That world will or will not be able to register changes occurring as a result of the conference. One of the things we can do is to be willing to embrace diversity in a variety of ways, not only intellectually but also regarding disciplines and individuals, and in other ways as well. I'm not referring to merely tolerating differences; I know that we all have had the experience of trying to put up with very well-meaning people whom we'd like to invite out of our experience. I assert that in addition to being concerned about the audience that might be receiving the tome that will be developed from this conference, it's very important for us to think about the beneficiaries. The purpose of our endeavors in primary care health services research is to improve the circumstances for people as patients. Our role is to do what work we can to improve health care, by informing health care providers and the health sector regarding operations, so that ultimately people in the role of patient can benefit.

POSSIBILITIES FOR CONSENSUS AND COLLABORATION:
OBSERVATIONS OF A PRACTITIONER—MILTON SEIFERT, JR.

As each of us prepared for our part in the conference, we no doubt hoped that we would contribute to the formation of a consensus that would lead to one or a number of collaborative efforts. We all knew we had biases, and we also knew we had to communicate with and accommodate to one another in order for the process and the outcome to be successful. This chapter will record the observations of a practitioner, will offer some consensus strategies, and will argue for the importance of experience-near knowledge.

Observations

At the outset, it was clear how differently we all had been socialized. It was greater than one expected. Everyone spoke in a different language. Participants appeared independent, competitive, and distant, and time appeared to be an enemy. One wondered if the diversity of the participants would lead to collaboration and creation or only to more diversity. Perhaps, at first, we didn't know what we didn't know; but to a large extent, with the help of one another, we were able to learn what we didn't know. For example, we learned that we didn't know what practice is, what patients want, how to change clinician behavior, when there is congruence between practitioner services and patient needs, whether satisfied patients are healthier, what happened to people who provided pro bono services, how you negotiate new information with patients in a practice setting, what the values and mindset of a practitioner are, how patients learn that they are full participants and share the power equally, what the nature of caring is, and what the intricacies of the practitioner-patient relationship are. Some of us were misinformed about the nature of primary care, especially in the setting of an ordinary medical practice. Others did not understand how a true professional could legitimately refuse or limit Medicaid patients. These could be characterized as deficiencies in cultural awareness.

We learned that our main bias should be in favor of the patient and in understanding patient needs. Many times we learned about the value of qualitative research in understanding these needs. Similarly, we learned that we needed a grounded interpretive approach to understand how practice is organized, and that focus groups, the personal narrative, the Delphi process, and qualitative methods would be the most helpful in achieving these understandings.

In the sociological sense, we learned that we needed data from the practice setting to understand the social relationships within this organization and then to understand what these relationships produce. It is hoped that this would lead to restoration of an appropriate autonomy to practitioners and patients— that is, autonomy for the practitioner and the patient that would enhance their ability to negotiate good health practices.

We were instructed that we could be in control only by not being in control. In other words, don't plan to produce research results to change public health policy; instead, try first to produce a program of care along with a professional research method that accurately describes the value of this program. This would require much trust in the process.

It was suggested that we love what we do and that we be passionate in the process. Also, a commitment over time would lead to better candor between the participants, and this, in turn, would lead to better collaboration.

In the end, our heterogeneous group demonstrated a greater capacity to listen and care. We were able to focus our talent in a more coordinated way and with mutual respect. There was evidence of some cohesion, and some thought that this group was capable of coordinated collaboration. Perhaps what was most important is that we learned we could and should think in new ways about empathy, caring, and satisfaction.

Strategies to Aid the Consensus Process

If it was our consensus intent to improve health care, it was our consensus belief that it is patient needs we are trying to satisfy. Yet, given our great deficiency in experience-near knowledge, one wonders where to start. Some organizing strategies are offered.

Option 1: A Major Federal Investment

Begin with a 1-billion-dollar, 5-year study of patient needs. If the results were valid and reliable, the investment would be worthwhile. This would provide a firm baseline for the construction of a demonstration model, and multiple secondary and tertiary studies would be naturally spawned by the initial process. It would be expected that the spinoff studies would employ multiple methods both qualitative and quantitative. A multidisciplinary group would be required and would contain all of the stakeholders as well as an agency of government to whom this group would be accountable.

Option 2: The Biopsychosocial Model

This model has been developed and studied rather extensively from a conceptual point of view but has not been widely implemented in the community and then studied for its health care outcomes (Brody, 1990; Engel, 1977, 1992). It would be a good time to seriously consider widespread implementation and study. A multidisciplinary group containing all stakeholders would be required, but funding could be much more modest and could begin with demonstration projects and a number of researchers are already active in the research of this concept.

Option 3: The Deming Approach

This approach would construct a prototype medical practice model using known principles from the literature. For example, one could start with the 1978 study by the Institute of Medicine (1978) of all of the current models of primary care practice. This study is nicely complemented by the earlier book *Ferment in Medicine* by Richard Magraw (1966). Both of these references suggest that the basic organizing principles be accessibility, continuity, comprehensiveness, coordination, accountability, and appropriate autonomy for practitioner and patient within their relationship so that it might be truly a therapeutic alliance. Principles from community-oriented primary care (COPC) would also be used in constructing a prototype (Connor & Mullan, 1982; Nutting, 1987; Seifert, 1982a, 1987). These conference reports from 1982 and 1987 contribute principles that help in understanding the needs of a population in order to design better programs to deal with specific health problems of individuals (see Eisler, 1987; Makiya, 1993).

The dominant form of quality assurance in our country today is that of inspection. In contrast to this, Dr. Deming teaches that quality can be designed into a product or a service (Deming, 1986; Dobyns, 1990). Once the prototype is adequately developed for the needs of patients in a medical setting, then an outcomes research can be developed in a scientific manner. These data can inform the continuing development process and further refinement of the prototype can continue. The final steps in the process of designing a prototype medical practice would be the inclusion of a values framework (Priester, 1992) and incorporation of information on prevention effectiveness. Similarly, one would incorporate current knowledge on the care of health along with care of disease (Antonovsky, 1987).

This approach would also require a multidisciplinary research team. All stakeholders would be represented, but this time some would have priority status in the design process. Those with priority status would include the practitioner, the patient, and the purchaser. This is because these three have the greatest interest in a good outcome and therefore should have the greatest voice in the design process. Eventually, all stakeholders would have an appropriate degree of participation. The work could begin with modest funding, could be combined with efforts to test the Biopsychosocial Model, and has the advantage of focusing primarily on experience-near knowledge.

Another advantage to the Deming approach is its ability to lead to a more rational governance system. Our current inspectional system has grown increasingly inhibitory through the growth of regulations, conflicting directives, expensive administration, and the promise of punishment. All of this has greatly exceeded the growth of incentives, methods, and principles that promote positive action along correct lines. The Deming approach would promote the latter and make the former unnecessary.

The principal participants would be easier to choose because they already exist in the real world. They would participate in the choice of professional researchers and other resource people. We are still left with the problem of identifying to whom the project would be accountable. However, this approach does suggest that it be a population-based group.

Experience-Near Knowledge

Although we may believe in experience-near knowledge, there is little evidence that it is a widely held belief. A Society of Teachers of Family Medicine (STFM) unpublished (1985) survey of research activity in 54 community programs and 16 universities showed little or no interest in community-based practices. Similarly, an unpublished 1988 study of the American Academy of Family Physicians (AAFP) research database showed a 10% interest in psychosocial issues, a 10% interest in disease prevention and health promotion, and an 80% interest in projects that were biomedical, nonqualitative, and not family medicine. If one were to visit the annual meeting of the North American Primary Care Research Group, one would find 6 to 10 practitioners among the 200 presentations. This is a major concern when the discipline still lacks an adequate database for its existence.

Acquisition of experience-near knowledge would require a laboratory practice. This would consist of practitioners who thought of themselves as researchers, their patients as coresearchers, and their offices as human services research laboratories. The task would be to integrate the medical services and research activities so that it would all be a part of a single, efficient health care process. Even in its rudimentary form, some striking results have been achieved by focus groups in this setting (Seifert, 1992). When the research-based practices are conducted in collaboration with a university setting, the availability of research professionals and research resources promotes more effective collaboration and the use of better research methods.

The Eagle Medical model is an example of a group that has attempted to build a prototype practice model using the Deming approach. It is characterized by health educators' teaching of life management skills, which usually results in adoption of greater individual responsibility and healthier personal behavior. This model also has a system of outcomes measurement that continues to evolve and a Patient Advisory Council that affords patient participation in practice management. Together, these innovations actualize the organizing principles described by the Institute of Medicine and the proponents of Community Oriented Primary Care. The Patient Advisory

Council provides a population-based group to which the medical practice can be accountable (Early & Seifert, 1981).

Finally, experience-near knowledge would make sense to practitioners and patients alike. The development of such knowledge would most certainly describe patient needs. It would also be accommodating to cultural diversity. Anything that makes sense to both practitioners and patients is likely to be sustained over time and will have much to do with the promotion of appropriate clinician behavior.

But perhaps the most exciting possibility is the view of Mary-Jo Delvecchio-Good that this type of knowledge has a potential for revolution (Delvecchio-Good, 1992). She points out that it promotes a bottom-up type of approach to the redesign of the health care system. This, like the Deming approach, would foster accountability and make regulation unnecessary. In the final analysis, practitioners and patients would be able to achieve an appropriate and legitimate degree of autonomy.

UNCOMMON SENSES: THE QUALITATIVE RESEARCHER AND MULTIMETHODS RESEARCH—VALERIE J. JANESICK

The role of the qualitative researcher in multimethods research projects is often determined by the researcher's stance and intent, much like the role of a historian. In addition, the researcher's role is one in which all senses are used to understand the context of the phenomenon under study, the people who are participants in the study, and their beliefs and behaviors, and of course, to understand the researcher's own orientation and purposes. Still further, it is like the ending in an O. Henry story. In other words, it is complicated, is filled with surprises, is open to serendipity, and often leads to something unanticipated in the original design of the research project. At the same time, the researcher works within the frame of a disciplined plan of inquiry, adhering to the high standards of qualitative inquiry, and looks for ways to complement and extend the description and explanation of the project through multiple methods of research, providing that this is done for a specific reason and makes sense. Qualitative researchers do not accept the misconception that more methods mean a better or richer analysis. If multiple methods are used, they are used with a purpose in mind, not to match up with another set of assumptions from the quantitative paradigm.

Meaning is constructed in the social relationship between the researcher and the participants in the study. It is no longer an option to research and run. The researcher is connected to the participants in a most profound way, and that is how trust is established, which in turn allows for greater access to sources and which ensures an involvement on the part of participants that enables them to tell their respective stories (see Guba, 1990b; Roman & Apple, 1990). Those of us who have conducted long-term qualitative studies know that participants in the study want their voices to be heard and do not want to be abandoned after the research project.

In my field, education, there is a long history of researchers who come into a school, collect data, and flee. Thankfully this is changing in terms of researchers' sensitivity to maintaining contact and a relationship with participants in the study, in order to maintain that sense of community that is part of any qualitative research component in a multimethod study. For those researchers who are planning to include a qualitative component in the multimethod project, it is important to realize that once the researcher establishes a relationship with participants, that relationship is not easily dissolved or ignored. It remains as part of the research context throughout a significant period of time well beyond the end of data collection.

I think that multimethods research projects rely on intuition as much as on a strictly qualitative or strictly quantitative project. Researchers ought to have the opportunity in their training and in practice to sharpen their intuitive skills, which often open up avenues of data previously unknown or hidden. In exercises I give my students to become better listeners and better observers, I often see prospective researchers refine some of those intuitive skills so needed in research and life.

Metaphorically speaking, I like to think of the O. Henry twist on life as a virus that each of us as qualitative researchers carries within us, a virus that in the proper setting and context becomes full blown. For those who have not delighted in O. Henry's work,[1] a great deal can be learned from this superb writer, a master of description and one of the great observers of the human condition in all its frailty and silliness. All of O. Henry's stories describe people, places, and events from everyday life and celebrate the ironies, contradictions, and twists of fate that circumscribe anyone's life. I think of O. Henry as the quintessential model for the qualitative researcher because his endings are filled with surprises and make perfect sense, given the story. So too, the qualitative researcher often stumbles onto something in the course of a research project that leads to a rich course of inquiry and that was unplanned in the original multimethod design of the study. If there is an advantage to multimethod research projects, this is it. In other words, by including various methods and techniques in the research plan, one builds in a type of latent flexibility that enables one to find, through serendipity, a tremendous amount of meaningful data for a fuller picture of the study.

To use just one example, in a recently completed 8-year study of successful deaf adults, I interviewed one of my sign language tutors, who was from

Canada. In a chance moment, she mentioned that she was going to meet some other international students and asked me to come along. By doing so, I met three more individuals who wanted to take part in the study and who in their respective interviews opened up new facets of deaf culture to me. One of the deaf students was friends with her interpreter, who was a child of deaf adults. This then opened up to me that part of the deaf community is made up of CODA members, Children of Deaf Adults. By meeting and interviewing these participants, I came to a fuller and more meaningful understanding of what it means to be deaf with a capital "D," deaf of deaf parents versus deaf of hearing parents. For the full-blown ironies and twists of fate that emerged from this study, the reader will have to read the report, which will be published elsewhere.[2]

The role of the qualitative researcher in multimethod research projects can be determined by the researcher's intent and stance, similar to the role of a historian who relies on primary sources and other sources for data. In addition, the qualitative researcher is in touch with all of his or her senses, including the intuitive sense, or informed hunches based on key incidents and data from the research project. Furthermore, the qualitative researcher may expect the unexpected—surprises much like those demonstrated by the writer O. Henry in his short stories. Such serendipitous discoveries are like a virus that qualitative researchers carry and that becomes full blown under a particular set of circumstances in a given social setting, with key participants who allow for amazing twists and turns in everyday life. The role of the qualitative researcher in multimethod research is expanded in that the number of options for coming upon new data is enlarged—for one can always count on serendipity, contradictions, and surprises in everyday life, the true domain of the qualitative researcher.

QUANTITATIVE METHODS, QUALITATIVE METHODS, AND VALUE-BASED CRITICAL INQUIRY—ROBERT B. MCCALL

Methods in health care and in a variety of other research fields (e.g., program evaluation, education) recently have been dichotomized into *quantitative* and *qualitative* approaches. After reading the accusations of some of the protagonists in this discussion (e.g., Lincoln, 1991; Sechrest, 1992), one could only conclude that an academic war is being waged. Mixed into the debate, but potentially independent, are the propositions that science is not innocent of values, that this lack of objectivity should be recognized and admitted, and that research and advocacy should consequently be blended for the express purpose of interrupting power imbalances and making transformations in society (e.g., Lather, this volume). The latter approach is called *value-based critical inquiry*.

These issues would seem to challenge some of the fundamental assumptions of scholarly inquiry, and therefore they cannot be ignored. On the other hand, I will argue that at least the quantitative versus qualitative dispute is largely artificial and rests more on methodological chauvinism than on fundamental distinctions. Value-based critical inquiry, however, is a different matter in my view, in that it does threaten the very basis of scholarship.

The Qualitative/Quantitative Debate

The debate often consists of each side criticizing the limitations of the other (e.g., Lincoln, 1991; Sechrest, 1992). The "qualitative people" often complain that *an unfounded and unreasonable prejudice against qualitative approaches exists*, even when they are used and interpreted appropriately. Quantitative methods unreasonably dominate the journals, grant review sections, and tenure review boards to the exclusion of qualitative methods. It might even be observed that analogous prejudices exist within the quantitative domain: that is, experimental manipulation is vastly preferred over observational methodology (e.g., McCall, 1977). Quantitative methods, it is further alleged, *do not help much to understand a phenomenon*, often *lack applied relevance or ecological validity*, and *force measurements when measurements are not always appropriate*.

On the other hand, qualitative approaches *refuse to objectively measure variables of interest*. Although some qualitative proponents argue that the essence of what they describe and interpret cannot be quantified, Sechrest and Sidani (this volume) point out that if a concept can be defined and specified so that it can be determined to exist or not exist in a particular context and at a particular time, then a simple (1,0) metric may be assigned to its existence/nonexistence, thereby constituting measurement of the concept. It follows, therefore, that any specifiable concept can be measured, albeit perhaps crudely, and if a concept can be measured, then *issues of reliability, validity, and comprehensiveness should be examined*. Qualitative methods also are frequently criticized for *disregarding issues of generality* and *ignoring cause and effect validity*.

Research Methods as Tools

Essentially all research methods were initially developed for a specific purpose, to answer a specific type of question in a specific research context. All techniques have limitations, even when the method is used and interpreted in the context for which it was designed. Methodologies and statistical techniques are tools, not ends in themselves. As a result, a method is not intrinsically valid or good; instead, it is more or less valid or useful for a specific purpose, to answer a specific question in a specific research context.

The Real Problem

In any dispute of this sort, it is easy and common to criticize a poor or unusual example of a category and generalize the liability to the entire category. A survey, for example, might simply ask physicians if they are dissatisfied with the state of primary care practice without asking the nature of that dissatisfaction or why respondents feel the way they do. This failure is not a limitation of the survey method per se but a shortcoming of this particular exemplar of it (assuming that physician satisfaction/dissatisfaction with primary care practice was a major purpose of the survey). If one is going to attack a method, one needs to attack the *best exemplars* of that method.

Bearing this caveat in mind, I argue that one or a set of these approaches is not better intrinsically than the other. They have different purposes and are ideally suited for addressing different questions in different contexts. The current furor over these methods occurs when a protagonist extends a particular method or its interpretation beyond its appropriate context. Then it is a case of methodological chauvinism, and the perspective that methodologies are tools is replaced by methodology for its own sake.

Even when each approach is used appropriately and optimally, one is not necessarily preferred over another because the two approaches may address different questions. Ethnographic description may be needed to capture the events and emotion of a cultural ritual, whereas systemic measurement may be more suitable to quantify the intelligence of different American children.

But suggesting one use a method only when it is optimal and appropriate for the question to be studied would be a tidy solution if all problems could be addressed in this way. Alas, they cannot. We are not able to randomly assign individuals to many treatment conditions, for example, yet this is required for a clinical trial. In such cases, which occur in all disciplines, less than ideal methodology must be employed, but this is no excuse for glib, improper interpretations or assertions that one approach is necessarily superior to another in all contexts.

What is required in science is to obtain the best available data about a phenomenon, interpret it in the context of the limitations of its methodological categories, and converge operations across methodological categories. Converging operations refers to the convergence on a single conclusion, often a cause-and-effect conclusion, of the results of different methodologies, each of which has marked limitations if viewed separately but all of which collectively constitute substantial indirect or circumstantial evidence for the causal proposition.

One can imagine, then, an important role for each of the methodologies presented in this volume to play in the study of many major issues confronting us. Instead of fighting with each other, we should be collaborating, bringing our different methodological expertise to bear on the same problem in complementary ways. For example, many experimentalists make what appears to be a blind run into a massive forest of issues to study a single tree in a highly experimental manner without sufficient description of the phenomenon, investigation of relevant independent and dependent variables, and reasonable hypotheses about parameters and cause-and-effect relations (McCall, 1977; Wohlwill, 1973). Substantial time, effort, and money could be saved if systematic observations of a qualitative sort (e.g., interviews, participant and nonparticipant observations, interpretative interactionism, historical documents) were used initially to scout the conceptual and methodological territory. Similarly, quantitative researchers would do well to "debrief" their subjects through systematic or dynamic interviewing to ensure that subjects interpreted the experimental situations in a uniform and accurate manner and that the thoughts of subjects on why they behaved as they did and how they felt about it are included in interpretation of results.

Critical Inquiry

My ecumenicism, however, stops short of the door to value-based critical inquiry, the purpose of which is to blend science and advocacy to adjust power relations in society and produce transformation and change in systems and societies (Lather, this volume). I agree with many premises of this argument, but I object to the conclusion and feel it does not follow from the premises.

Premises

I believe some research should be directly useful to practitioners and society, and most, if not all, should have this potential. Gone are the days in which anything that is studied in a scientifically respected manner will be funded and published regardless of whether anyone wants to know the information the research produces. We can no longer, if we ever could, afford that luxury.

I also agree with the propositions that research is not "innocent," that is, it is not without its biases, values, and prejudices, and I believe that when such values influence scholarship they should be acknowledged.

Conclusion

But to recognize that we are not *valueless* is not a reason to make science *value laden*. Because laws are broken in society does not mean we should encourage lawlessness. Because we are not perfect does not mean we should give up and strive to be imperfect.

I believe the value of scholarship to society is that it provides a system of rules of evidence and procedures for describing nature, including society, and that it offers information and a variety of alternatives that could be used for social good (one hopes). But the entire system is based upon trust—trust that the data are accurate, unbiased, faithfully reported, and so on.

Were we to jump whole hog into blending science with advocacy for the purpose of social change (for example), I would lose substantial trust in researchers. I can conceive of science as an advocacy system, similar to the law, and some would say the current system is close to that. But I would prefer an open system of inquiry that does its best to adhere to the values of honesty, balance, and objectivity even though it may be flawed in its pursuit of them. Although we are not perfect in achieving this role, I would argue that we are *relatively unbought*, at least more so than most other institutions.

Yes, science should be used for the public good, including adjusting power imbalances and making transformations in society. But I believe society is best served by keeping science and advocacy separate and labeling each appropriately. The great imponderables of balancing apples and oranges in society should be decided by politicians and called "advocacy," "politics," or "government." One hopes that such decisions will take into account objective, unbiased observations called "science."

NOTES

1. O. Henry is the pen name of William Sydney Porter, one of the key writers of the early part of this century. His work is marked by razor-sharp description as well as by his authenticity in capturing the human condition. He is an exemplar of thick description, irony, and literary excellence.

2. I have prepared a manuscript entitled "Proud to Be Deaf: An Ethnographic Study of Deaf Culture," which is at the time of this writing out for review to the *International Journal of Qualitative Studies in Education.* This manuscript is based on my 4 years of data collection living in the deaf community in Washington, D.C., and 4 years of analysis removed from the field with intermittent member checks over the entire 8-year period.

IV

Creating a Space for
Transdisciplinary Research

This project began with the belief that primary care research needed to be opened up methodologically. We began with the idea that an interdisciplinary approach was desirable (see Figure I.1b); however, insights provided by the conference led to our conceptualization of the need for transdisciplinary research (see Figure I.1c).

The four case reports gave insights into many of the issues of collaborative research community development. We saw in Chapter 18 how the "patient" group entered quickly into "emptiness" (Peck, 1987, chap. 5; also refer back to the introduction to Part III) through their sharing of experience and touching on "community" by end of their first session. Questions asked were inclusive and expansive, thus mapping new territory and involving all participants in a collaborative way and reflecting a transdisciplinary process. However, due to time constraints participants were unable to sustain this community, and no clear design emerged as the group reverted to its disciplinary turf (multidisciplinary process).

The "caring" group (Chapter 19) became stuck in "chaos" (Peck, 1987, chap. 5) in the first session, and many wanted to abandon ship. The list of questions generated was a "free listing" and was organized only after the fact by the moderator. The design created was an example of a traditional staged, multidisciplinary research program (Figure I.1a), starting with descriptive and critical studies and progressing to correlational and outcome-based designs. The group stayed within a clear framework and kept away from collaborative design issues.

The "practice" group (Chapter 20) entered "emptiness" (Peck, 1987, chap. 5) by reaching consensus on a common language and touched on becoming a collaborative community by the end of the first session. Questions were inclusive and expansive, as in the "patient" group, and reflected a transdisciplinary process. The final design was collaborative and integrated but did not chart new conceptual ground. It allowed for a distinct place for each expert and might best be characterized as interdisciplinary.

The "dissemination" group (Chapter 21) moved back and forth between "chaos" and "pseudocommunity" (Peck, 1987, chap. 5) in their first session and made a late breakthrough into "emptiness." The question list reflected a systematic brainstorming of each person's expertise with little integration (multidisciplinary process). Although the design started out looking like a traditional program of study, it unfolded into a more interdisciplinary project.

In Chapter 22, the four observers each asked us to act on one or more of the essentials for collaborative research. Valerie Janesick insisted we move to "knowing what you don't know" (transdisciplinary); Milton Seifert said we should seek "experience-near local knowledge" and "collaboration"; Robert McCall reminded us to seek "the best available strategy" (appropriate methodology); and Morgan Jackson entreated us to stay with and "define the question" (problem focus). Each of these points is central to the argument in Chapter 23.

POLICY IMPLICATIONS

The conference process and subsequent reflections on this process have made profound changes in our thinking about how to facilitate multimethod research in primary care. The conference highlighted at least four issues relevant to how researchers and policymakers may think about future research.

1. Multimethod research in primary care is a conceptual reality.

It was clear that multimethod research was a conceptual reality in the minds of all those attending the conference, regardless of disciplinary background. Participants readily identified many questions of importance to primary care clinicians and policymakers that were not easily addressed with widely used epidemiological or survey methods. In working toward approaches to address these questions, all participants readily agreed that it would be necessary to integrate both qualitative and quantitative research methods to address the diversity of relevant and important research questions in primary care.

2. Multimethod research in primary care is not yet a practical reality.

Despite agreement that primary care research issues should be addressed with multimethod approaches, it was equally clear that a lack of training and a lack of acceptance of how and when to include qualitative methods creates an environment in which multimethod research is not yet a practical reality within primary care. A major reason for this appears to be a lack of training opportunities for primary care clinicians and academic researchers to learn qualitative research methods and a lack of models for effective integration of methods. There is also a perception that qualitative research is not fundable within the federal grant review system that funds primary care research.

3. Many important primary care research questions are not being asked or addressed or are being examined in ways that limit their scope and impact.

Both large group and small group discussions provided compelling and lucid demonstrations that many important primary care research questions are not being asked or addressed or are being examined in ways that limit their scope and impact. Each of the four small working groups focused on a problem area of a larger research agenda around issues in changing primary care provider behavior and easily identified many compelling research questions. Many of these questions require the use of research methods or disciplinary perspectives that have not been used extensively in primary care research. To illustrate, the following are some examples of questions that emerged through the small group process.

- *Patient Issues Group:* What is it that patients perceive as listening? What behavior results in satisfaction for patient and provider? How is listening influenced by, or how does it vary with, characteristics of the patient and health care provider? Can this behavior of "listening" be changed? If changed, will it make a difference in outcomes?
- *Nature of Caring Group:* What is the nature of caring, and does it make a difference? What do providers expect from patients? What are the incentives/rewards of practice? What does "caring" consist of in many contexts?
- *Practice Organization Group:* How do different clinical practices work, and do the differences affect outcomes? What constitutes health practice? How is it that patients come or don't come to particular health practices?
- *Dissemination Group:* What are the goals of dissemination? Why are current dissemination efforts ineffective at changing provider behavior? What are the

practicalities of utilizing guidelines in practice environments? How do new health care practices get negotiated in practice settings?

4. Primary care research needs to move beyond being multimethod and into being collaborative and cross-disciplinary.

The conference process and key findings provide clear evidence that primary care researchers and policymakers need to move beyond thinking of just multimethod approaches. Researchers need to (a) create opportunities for broader perspectives in primary care research and (b) begin thinking in terms of cross-disciplinary research. Although methodological diversity is important, the tendency to maintain disciplinary boundaries limits the ways questions are conceptualized so that many important primary care questions are simply not asked.

A review of the transcripts from the conference and the literature about collaborative research makes it apparent that our original objective to facilitate multimethod research was insufficient. Just combining methods in an additive fashion was not a satisfactory way of approaching the complex and difficult problems in primary care research. What is needed is a sustained dialogue among a diverse group of researchers who embody divergent interests and practices. Such a sustained dialogue would aim at creating a space for conceptualizing how health care practices came to be problematic, how they continue to be problematic, and whether collaborative ways of investigating those problems can be created.

The critical issues in creating such a dialogue are presented in Chapter 23.

23

COMMON SPACE
CREATING A COLLABORATIVE
RESEARCH CONVERSATION

William L. Miller

Abundance appears when scarcity is shared. This is the hope of immigrants seeking a home. It is also the hope of collaborative research. Are we, as primary care researchers, ready to create common space with strangers? Like immigrants, we arrive with past belongings and initially maintain protective walls and distinctive languages. But shared hurt and hope foster courage to risk humiliation, to seek conversation with strangers, and to cocreate new visions, new situated knowledge (Haraway, 1991). Changing provider behavior has been this book's vehicle for exploring the horizons and quagmires of the landscape of collaborative research. This chapter reflects on the journey and suggests the abundant possibilities when conversations are risked outside the walls.

Specifically reflecting on existing literature about multimethod and cross-disciplinary research and on the process and content of the four case reports in this book, we propose a six-stage process for creating collaborative research relationships and six essential ingredients for its success, including the methodological standards of critical multiplism and the notion of a generalist researcher or conductor for the collaborative orchestra. The chapter concludes with an overview of seven barriers to collaborative primary care research followed by recommendations for overcoming them and creating a space that funds future imagination.

COLLABORATIVE RESEARCH RELATIONSHIPS

Doing collaboration across disciplines is both exhilarating and exhausting. The process of bringing together people with different languages, different assumptions about ways of knowing, different conceptual frameworks, different values, and different bases for their career success in order to engage an identified problem seems intimidating. It is, but if approached with patience and forethought, it becomes a transforming adventure. Knowing how strangers can form community is essential. We identified and will describe six stages of collaborative relationship: acceptance/validation, shared expectations, declaring group process, action consensus, common space, and sustained common action. These stages are developmental; each builds on the preceding one and involves more intense group commitment. These levels of collaborative relationship help define the three types of cross-disciplinary research (see Figure 23.1) and mirror the stages of community development.

Collaboration starts with affirmative listening. There is no meaningful conversation without *acceptance/validation*. A belief in the supernatural power of rationality can lull one into believing that accurate knowledge, good intentions, and the rules of polite academic discourse will automatically result in "progress." Knowledge, good will, and civility are necessary but not sufficient for successful collaboration. Knowledge is never accurate enough, intentions are never clear enough, and civility is not safe enough for people to risk being vulnerable and bold. We each need to feel stroked, listened to, and affirmed by another; without these we cling to safety and control and retreat into our disciplinary shells. The collaborative relationship stage of acceptance/validation is reached when each person reveals his or her disciplinary expertise and status and senses acknowledgment and appreciation by others.

Once a group of researchers experience acceptance and validation, they go in pursuit of *shared expectations*. This usually begins with each person sharing his or her specific agenda for the problem at hand. Once agendas are understood and accommodated within a group-defined common task, the second level of collaborative relationship is reached. We see groups functioning at this level as doing *multidisciplinary research*. Each person comfortably remains within a disciplinary tradition and independently focuses his or her expertise on the group-defined common task. Very little direct group communication takes place. This is the most common sphere of collaborative research and avoids the complexities of moving the group relationships into another, more intense stage (see Figure 23.1). The group is enjoying "pseudocommunity" similar to the experience of dating.

Staying together, as in marriage, is a different matter, and relationships get messier. The group enters the chaos stage of community development. Despite

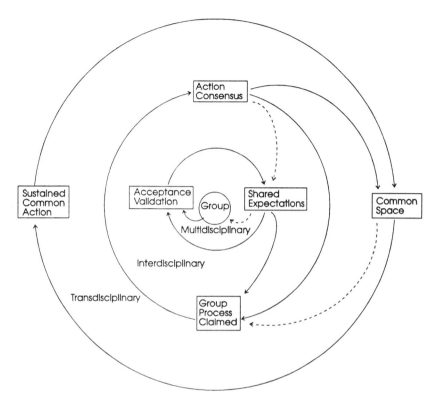

Figure 23.1. Levels of Collaborative Relationship and Types of Cross-Disciplinary Research

reaching acceptance and shared expectations, most collaborative research groups, if they pursue more intense group interaction, struggle toward accomplishing their task. Bion describes three characteristic patterns of such task avoidance: flight or fight, pairing, and dependence (Rioch, 1970). All were exhibited in the four cases described in this book (Chapters 18-21). Some members "disappear," either by physically leaving or by remaining silent. Other members keep creating arguments about off-task issues, and still others pair off and have their own private dialogue. Finally, some members passively wait for the group leader to impose an agenda. Underlying most of these task avoidance behaviors are unexpressed differences and fears of misunderstanding. One's disciplinary expertise may be acknowledged and one's agenda accommodated, but this does not necessarily mean one's language, paradigmatic assumptions, and values are understood. The physician's assumption that medical services are inherently valuable is confusing to some social scientists, who may assume medical services are a location for social control and potential adverse outcome (Stein & Jessop, 1988). One person's everyday language is another's jargon. Unspoken assumptions and differences frequently result in misunderstandings that lead to one person's trying to convert another. When a group begins working effectively and behaving as if they have named the task avoidance issues, openly acknowledged their differences, and confessed the desire to convert, then a third stage of collaborative relationship is reached, *declaring group process.*

Once group process is manifest, the research group moves toward an *action consensus.* One action path is to agree on an organizational framework for maintaining group work and staying on task. Examples of such frameworks include conceptual models developed by the group leader or from a "dominant" discipline and traditional multimethod design strategies. The latter usually consists of having qualitative researchers do exploratory field work followed by epidemiologists and psychometricians designing survey instruments used in observational epidemiology studies in preparation for the development of randomized controlled trials (see Chapters 19 and 21). We interpret selecting an organizational framework at this stage of collaborative relationship as working within the sphere of *interdisciplinary research* (see Figure 23.1) and as a return to pseudocommunity.

Another action path is to remain with the group tensions and to continue unpacking or emptying communication barriers (Peck, 1987). These barriers include prejudices, hidden expectations and preconceptions, and the need for some, especially clinicians trained in the biomedical model, to fix, solve, and control. Living with tension, disagreement, and public self-revelation is difficult and painful (see Chapter 17), but it is a way toward *shared common space.* This common space is reached when a group defines a shared language and creates a shared conceptual framework that evolves out of the unpacking process (see Chapter 20).

If a collaborative research group remains in shared common space, it reaches the collaborative relationship stage of *sustained common action* and is now practicing within the sphere of *transdisciplinary research.* It has created true community. The difficulty in doing this, however, is evidenced by how rarely it occurs.

Who speaks what language is an accurate guide to which sphere of collaborative research is operative at any particular moment. When each person consistently speaks in the language of her or his home discipline, then multidisciplinary research is occurring. If members of the group begin using the language of other disciplines, then the group has moved into the sphere of interdisciplinary research. When the group repeatedly uses a newly agreed-upon language, it is engaged in transdisciplinary research.

Barriers to Collaborative Process

Collaborative group process can be blocked at any stage. We identified four dams to the flow of group communication: "rhetorical stones," the power of hegemony, and the tensions between pragmatism and reflection and between an individual focus and a systems focus. *Rhetorical stones* refers to forms of speech that, often unintentionally, build a protective wall around or elevate the speaker while simultaneously wounding and diminishing others. Three such stones include power heaping, shaming, and jargon hurling. *Power heaping* occurs when a speaker uses special expertise, past successes, or prestige claims to take over a conversation or win a point: "This is old stuff. I published several definitive works resolving this debate 10 years ago." *Shaming* refers to comments that question the knowledge, intentions, or status of others in the group: "I'm shocked! No one uses the word *system* anymore." *Jargon hurling* is the use of discipline-specific jargon or abbreviations as if the terms were part of common, everyday language: "That's not so. We know that cost centers for HMOs differentially affect provider productivity compared to those in IPAs or PPOs." Armor and delicate dexterity are required for a group to keep ducking the stones, getting hit, picking them up, and going on. The best defense is recognizing that rhetorical stones usually indicate the thrower's perceived need for protection.

Within the Western world of primary health care, physicians and rationality wield a *powerful hegemony.* The dominance of these cultural forces must be acknowledged by collaborative groups. The power of hegemony was amply demonstrated by all four groups described in the case reports. For example, members of each group kept using the word *physicians* and kept referring to health care concerns using the language of allopathic physicians despite persistent reminders about alternative primary health care providers. Participants were apologetic, but the cultural hegemony of physicians proved more persuasive than good intentions.

The groups were also pervaded by a more powerful and potentially more dangerous belief in rationality as a sole truth-defining force. Whenever tensions surfaced, someone usually requested more facts or asserted the need to "stay objective." Emotional needs, concerns about the power of bureaucracies and the influence of money, issues about personal security, the biases of gender difference, and insinuations of racism were usually overwhelmed by the powerful hegemony of rationality. The importance of wonder, confession, petition, gratitude, and receptivity to gift and mystery is undermined.

What never gets challenged is rationality's role in authorizing existing modes of power. Who is it that seeks to overcome wonder and why? Awe is potentially threatening to those wanting order, prediction, and control, but it is important to recognize these as the needs of managers and not of collaborative researchers. Otherwise, a group's imagination remains trapped by powerful vested interests, deep fears, and unresolved hurts (Brueggemann, 1993). The effect is to undermine the legitimacy of other modes of knowledge and power and to prevent a group's move into creative emptiness. Shifting from hegemony to perspectivism opens the space for imagination (Bruner, 1990).

A third stumbling block is the dynamic *tension between pragmatism and reflection.* Clinicians, policymakers, and applied researchers usually strive for the practical implications of knowledge and research and often get annoyed with long, reflective discussions about nuances of meaning and epistemological concerns. On the other hand, academic basic science and humanities researchers care deeply about reflective discourse concerning issues of definition and core assumptions that get at the heart of disciplinary identity and purpose. The tension between pragmatism and reflection is further complicated by conflict over the role of values in research (see Chapter 10). The quest for objectivity and certainty often generates a fear of joining "science" with advocacy. This fear frequently sustains a reluctance to even acknowledge values in "scientific" discourse.

The *tension between an individual focus and a systems focus* is a fourth stumbling block. Sociologists, anthropologists, and policymakers frequently focus on group structure and process, whereas psychologists and clinicians are more likely to focus on the individual as primary causative agent. In the realm of research, this tension manifests as confusion and conflict over the appropriate unit of analysis.

Clearing the Flow

There are at least four tactics for clearing the flow of collaborative group process: brainstorming, humor, storytelling, and silence. *Brainstorming* involves the temporary suspension of any debate and asks the group to spontaneously contribute ideas related to some agreed-upon problem. This technique works particularly well when a group is starting or generating ideas.

Humor, especially in the form of wit, repartee, and irony, is helpful at soothing and lightening moments of tension and conflict. Frequent doses of gentle, clever humor help everyone maintain better spirits and enthusiasm. Humor promotes collaborative relationship when the comedy is not at the expense of a group participant; thus satire and sarcasm are best avoided.

Storytelling is a powerful tool for helping the diverse participants in collaborative research groups step off their disciplinary turf. Narrative stands on the ground of life experience and comfortably includes emotions, values, and other subjectivities excluded by the powerful hegemony of rationality. It is easier to risk personal vulnerability when you hear others do so within the relative safety of sharing stories (see Chapter 18). The judicious use of narrative and anecdote is particularly helpful when trying to declare group process, when unpacking communication barriers on the way toward action consensus, and when the group is highly conflicted. People rarely change on account of cognitive or moral appeal; rather, they change because they are part of a group experiencing the possibilities inherent in a new story. Shared stories help make a home, a new community (Wilder, 1983).

Silence or time out for play is a useful tactic when the group is stuck. Being quiet can still the mental roar and enhance intuitive receptivity to patterns not noticeable when listening to linear discourse. The joy and spontaneity of play can also serve a similar purpose while boosting fatigued and frustrated spirits.

The reality of collaborative relationships is not as neat and straightforward as the above descriptions suggest. Complexity is the norm. Collaborative working groups move back and forth among the different stages and, at any given time, may demonstrate a blurring and blending of levels. In addition, different group members are likely to perceive that the group is at different stages at any given time. The dash lines in Figure 23.1 illustrate that groups can return to prior stages of relationship. Time pressure is a frequent group destabilizer. The four case reports reveal this dynamic complexity of collaborative relationships. Flexibility, tact, patience, and persistence are all necessary in the face of such complexity.

Dangers of Collaborative Research Relationships

Collaborative research, especially transdisciplinary, may also harbor potential dangers. The dominance of a few group members can lead to others neglecting the critical thinking learned in past disciplinary training. Sloppiness resulting from this *training down* is accentuated by a loss of accountability to disciplinary peers. Three additional dangers relate to downsides of being in community. *Suppression of individuality* is a primary motivating force for leaving community. What starts as a group with exciting diversity can, over time, become oppressive and defensive of its newly claimed territory. As roles become blurred and disciplines become interchangeable, the group may lose perspective and become less tolerant of subtle differences. An eloquent study by McClelland and Sands (1993) about the "missing voice" on a collaborative evaluation team sounds a warning: "Even a team working together over a long period of time may be unaware of the observational categories of its disciplines" (p. 88). Open community can also convert to *cultism* and a new hegemony. A more positive twist on this process is the creation of a new discipline. Finally, communities are slow, inefficient, messy, and *political.* This is the key to both their enduring value and to people's reluctance to work in them (Bellah, Madsen, Sullivan, Swidler, & Tipton, 1985). If a transdisciplinary group remains open and self-reflective, all of these dangers can be minimized, but substantial energy is required.

Knowing when to expend this energy and conduct transdisciplinary research depends on the answer to three questions: for what? how long? what's the future? When the problem area is complex, contextual, resistant to prior interdisciplinary efforts, and a regional, national, or international priority, transdisciplinary research should be considered. In addition, there must be sufficient funding and time (at least 5 to 10 years) to support a successful transdisciplinary research effort. Finally, transdisciplinary research is more helpful during a period of shifting paradigms. Although we believe such a paradigm shift is underway, we still think there need to be more efforts at effective interdisciplinary research before an investment in transdisciplinary research is justified. What we recommend as key ingredients in future collaborative research is discussed next after a brief historical review.

COLLABORATIVE RESEARCH ESSENTIALS

A diverse and colorful history of collaborative research includes the fields of international primary health care (Nichter & Kendall, 1991), agriculture (DeWalt, 1985), biology (Soule, 1985), education (Salomon, 1991), psychology (Sewell, 1989), applied anthropology (Pelto & Pelto, 1992), family systems medicine (Ramsey, 1989), health policy (Higginbotham, 1992), nursing care (Dzurec, 1989), and evaluation (Rossman & Wilson, 1985). The efforts in education and social psychology are generally presented as evidence that the cost of collaborative research exceeds the benefits. Examining these perceived failures and the relative success of collaborative agricultural research provides lessons for the future.

In the 1970s four large, national, multimethod, multisite education studies were funded. The Rural Experimental Schools Study evaluated the efficacy of local school control in rural areas (Herriott, 1982). The Study of Parental Involvement examined the role of parents in schools (Smith & Robbins, 1982). Two other studies investigated dissemination efforts in schools (Huberman & Crandall, 1982; Louis, 1982b). Although all four studies resulted in multiple publications and the investigators agreed on several findings, none of the studies had significant impact on either educational theory or policy. What went wrong? At least four major problem areas were identified by the primary investigators.

Data management problems are a major source of frustration. There was inadequate preparation for dealing with discrepancies in data sets, especially those between qualitative and quantitative data. Miles (1982) notes the need to focus "steady and recurrent attention to the real consequences of different data sets" (p. 123). Another data management problem involves balancing the need for structured data so cross-site data are comparable and the need for flexibility in data collection so as to preserve site uniqueness. A second problem area related to the first is *quality control problems.* Louis (1982a) stresses the need for explicitness concerning all data manipulation from data collection and database formulation through data analysis. Smith and Robbins (1982) emphasize the need for careful selection and training of local field researchers. *Budget disputes* are a third problem area resulting from internal squabbles over which department gets which funds. Herriott (1982) notes the need for an interdisciplinary group of outside experts to help arbitrate the intersubsidy budget decisions. A fourth problem area is *low credibility/utility.* The study results challenged several cherished beliefs about education. The academic community responded by criticizing the many data management and quality control problems. The policymakers responded by acknowledging these critiques. The forest was lost for the trees. Herriott (1982) now suggests that future policy research work more closely with both scientific and political constituencies throughout the research process.

Similar problems were noted during the "golden age" of interdisciplinary social psychology from 1945 to 1955. Sewell (1989), in recent reflections about this time, identifies four additional factors leading to the failure of the programs: (a) their threat to traditional departmental structure, (b) lack of adequate funding, (c) lack of major theoretical breakthroughs, and (d) only modest research gains. He also reminds readers of many important methodological contributions coming from these efforts. Easton and Schilling (1991) discuss three similar efforts in the context of trying to overcome the deficiencies of specialization. Citing the experiences of management, policy analysis, and area studies, they note that interdisciplinary training fails because the pieces of knowledge, like Humpty Dumpty, don't fit together. Teamwork flounders because there are no generalists or translators for the many different languages and assumptions. Finally, there is no general theory agreeable to everyone that can serve as an organizing framework.

The success of collaborative agricultural research suggests ways to overcome the many obstacles just reviewed. The International Potato Center in Lima, Peru, uses an interdisciplinary team consisting of local farmers, anthropologists, and agricultural technologists to solve local farming problems identified by the farmers. Some very successful innovations have resulted (Rhoades & Booth, 1982). The critical ingredients appear to be the creation of linkages at a local level with a specific problem focus and the underlying philosophy "that successful agricultural research and development must begin and end with the farmer" (Rhoades & Booth, 1982, p. 132). A similar program is thriving in Iowa and directed by local farmers and the Leopold Center for Sustainable Agriculture at Iowa State University in Ames (McDermott, 1990). This same strategy of local linkages between funding sources, providers, and scientists around a problem focus is now being recommended by clinical anthropologists for health care research (Baer, 1993).

Ingredients for Successful Collaborations

After reviewing these past and present efforts and our own experiences with collaborative research, we recommend six essential ingredients for future collaborations. We suggest that key linkages be formed within a local context where a complex, prioritized problem is named and addressed using appropriate methodology within a framework of critical multiplism and coordinated by a generalist researcher. Each of these factors is now examined in more detail.

A *linkages perspective,* developed in the Netherlands for designing research on problems of international development (Van der Geest, Speckmann, & Streefland, 1990), views the focus of research as linked to higher and lower levels of social organization, also designated as micro and macro levels (DeWalt & Pelto, 1985). These levels refer to international, national, regional, and local forms of social and cultural organization. What is linked is any form of information, such as political power, cultural values, research results, and history (see Chapter 20). There are vertical, horizontal, and time linkages. *Vertical linkages* specifically correspond to connections between different levels, such as the linkage between a national insurance corporation and a local primary care practice, whereas *horizontal linkages* concern informational flow and exchange between sectors within the same level of social organization, such as the relationships between different practice organizations within the same community or between practices and local schools. *Time linkages* refer to how the same behavior, institution, commodity, or word within a particular sector and level changes meaning and connections over time, such as the changing referral patterns of a particular practice over a 20-year period. A research focus serves as a vehicle by which linkages are explored. This multilevel, multisectoral linkage perspective transcends traditional disciplinary divisions of reality into economic, social, cultural, educational, political, religious, medical, historical, and psychological fields and facilitates a collaborative research process.

Linkages from academe to the public, practitioners, and policymakers are also important for the linkages perspective to succeed. Ideally these linkages take the form of including representatives from clinics, policy agencies, and affected public constituencies on the research team. None of these linkages is a new idea. Efforts to link the applied and basic science subdisciplines within a common field have a long history and yet still flounder (Zemke, 1989). What we recommend is linking both applied and basic science researchers, including laboratory researchers (Topf, 1990), with clinicians around topics of common interest such as changing primary health care provider behavior. The recent development of practice-based research is an example of such linkage (Christoffel et al., 1988). The linkages between academics and policymakers can include not only funding agency representatives but also legislators and pertinent corporate and labor leadership. Recent calls for participatory and action research are exciting first steps toward involving the public in collaborative research (Reason, 1988; Whyte, 1991). More connections between the public, the scientific community, clinicians, and policymakers are necessary if future research is to have genuine utility. We recommend that future collaborative research pay close attention to these multiple vertical, horizontal, time, and academic linkages.

Collaborative research relationships and linkages are facilitated by *local* action, by the multiple personal contacts between collaborators that are made easier by a shared geographical region. For example, many existing practice-based research networks are regional. *Local* defines a particular place and public for creating and informing research questions. It is a scale in which collaboration works, the concrete experience of a problem energizes the collaborative effort, and the problem's contextual complexity is preserved (Lynch, 1976; Turner, 1932). Collaborative research, as noted earlier, also demands intense commitment from the researchers toward the group and the project. This, too, is more forthcoming if members are already part of a community and if the project focus is of personal and local relevance. The example of changing primary health care provider behavior discussed in this book illustrates this well. The existing research demonstrates that providers will change inappropriate behavior if they feel ownership of the problem and the solution. This is local knowledge; this is knowledge at the scale of human experience and motivation. We suggest that linkages created and investigated by collaborative researchers begin locally with a focus on local knowledge (Geertz, 1983).

Local knowledge refers to how researchers entertain and form ideas about their own research interests from local contexts and concerns and then include local ways of knowing, perceiving, and understanding in their data collection and analysis (Good, 1992). Geertz contrasts local knowledge with universal forms of knowledge. This contrast is helpful insofar as conventional science often perseverates on universalistic knowledge claims, but the contrast is overdone. The construct of local knowledge is not intended to restrict the scope of research; multisite studies are encouraged. Each site's collaborative research team, however, needs to be locally grounded and its findings adequately contextualized. Theory development and generalizable knowledge come from the comparison and convergence of multiple local knowledges over time. The best randomized controlled trial (see Chapter 4) is generalizable only to local populations with the same inclusion criteria.

What constitutes "local" is more complex. Anthropologists, for instance, see it as a culturally bounded unit, whereas ecologists see it as a biotic community, defined as that area in which particular species of plants and animals predominate. A bioregional perspective offers one exciting way of combining the many conceptualizations of local within a common framework and still preserving flexibility (Sale, 1991). *Bioregion* is a term coined to link cultural and biotic understandings of region (Van Newkirk, 1975). A bioregion is defined on the basis of biotic communities, watersheds, cultural distinctiveness, and a "sense-of-place" (Devall, 1988). This is consistent with the cultural and natural connections of the clinical parish or traditional practice communities of primary care providers based on shared watersheds, topography, local economies, and history (Spitzer, 1977). Many of the historical leaders in primary care research conducted their investigations bioregionally: Curtis Hames in Evans County, Georgia, Will Pickles in Wensleydale, England, and Paul Frame in the tri-county area surrounding Cohocton, New York.

A bioregional perspective also introduces ecological thinking into collaborative research. Researchers have traditionally acted as if research were independent of ecological limits. This is especially true in health research, in which the search for cures and the delivery of care proceed without regard for or even debate about carrying capacity, environmental degradation, and limited resources. We doubt that this can or will continue. We suggest that *sustainable research*, in the form of research that returns as much or more to living systems as it removes, become a new norm. Research grounded in local ecology is more likely to meet this norm of sustainability (Berry, 1972). Collaborative research, with its diversity of "voices," is in an opportune position to explore the possibilities of a sustainable research. As local family practitioner Milton Seifert, Jr., commented, it can seek "experience-near, local knowledge" (see Chapter 22). We recommend that collaborative researchers think locally, act locally, and then think globally.

Linkages and local knowledge point directly toward the importance of knowing what the questions are (Gorenberg, 1983). Just as the care of a particular patient links many disparate caregivers in a common local endeavor, the research problem area can do the same for collaborative researchers. We suggest that collaborative research be *problem focused*. Research groups can organize locally around a problem of local consequence much as community-oriented primary care does (Nutting & Connor, 1986). From a collaborative perspective, there are many different questions related to a particular problem. The differing perspectives, values, and motives of "structure seekers" and "meaning seekers" (Pearlin, 1992), policymakers, clinicians, and consumers spawn a plethora of related questions. The research questions generated from local experience and context pose vexing challenges to research design. That is the point. Multiple methods are necessary. The research designs are driven by focusing on how the many research questions derived from the problem focus are best answered.

Which methods are used depends on what is appropriate for answering the multiple questions. Collaborative research is thus concerned about *appropriate methodology* (McKinlay, 1993), or what McCall refers to as "the best available strategy" (see Chapter 22). The conventional approach is to refine and narrow the question until it fits available methods. Appropriate methodology means the reverse. The original questions, derived from local experience, are preserved, their underlying assumptions explored, and their perspectives expanded. Methods are then refined or created to fit the many different questions. The appropriateness of any research design is thus a function of the particular phenomenon under study; the setting; the current state of theory and knowledge; available collection, measurement, and analysis tools; proposed uses for any derived information; and the intended audience for the research. Because most experience-based questions are complex, an abundance of creativity is needed as well as multimethod designs of the type described in this book. Thus we recommend that collaborative research groups include a diverse mix of methodological expertise. In order to maintain rigor while using diverse methods, we recommend *critical multiplism* (Cook, 1985).

CRITICAL MULTIPLISM: RIGOR IN COLLABORATIVE RESEARCH

The concepts of linkages, local knowledge, and problem-focused, appropriate methodology are comfortably subsumed within a research strategy called critical multiplism. Developed within social psychology (Houts, Cook, & Shadish, 1986) and borrowed by nursing (Coward, 1990), critical multiplism assumes that multiple ways of knowing are necessary for scientific inquiry (Dzurec, 1989) and that the many possible options that result require critical thought and choice. *Multiplism* refers to multiple perspectives and methods, and *critical* refers to the critical selection of the multiple options (Coward, 1990). The use of the word *critical* also implies a place for critical theory (see Chapter 10).

Critical multiplism seeks to capture complexity and contextuality while maintaining validity; thus it incorporates *multiple triangulation* (Campbell & Fiske, 1959; Denzin, 1970; Fielding & Fielding, 1986; Mitchell, 1986; Webb, Campbell, Schwartz, & Sechrest, 1966). Mitchell describes four types of triangulation (1986) designed to enhance some aspect of validity. Data triangulation includes multiple sources of data within the same study, whereas theoretical triangulation occurs when several alternative explanations or multiple working hypotheses are evaluated within the same study. The latter requires a cross-disciplinary literature review (Cooper, 1987). Investigator triangulation takes place when multiple data collectors, coders, and/or analysts are involved with the same data. Methodological triangulation refers to mixing methods within the same study. Multiple triangulation occurs when two or more types of triangulation exist within the same study.

Another option in the critical multiplism strategy includes the use of *multiple stakeholders* for developing questions and influencing design and analysis. The impact of the public voice in research (Chapter 16) and at the conference reported in this book (Chapter 17) illustrates the importance of this option. Control over the questions means control over the agenda of discussion; therefore, it is important that everyone be invited. The goal is not to eliminate objectivity but to open the space for new questions. *Multiple studies* is a third multiplist option. It includes conducting multiple, interconnected studies within a common research program and synthesizing multiple studies on a common problem, all variations on the replicative case study design (Yin, 1989) but each done in different contexts using different data collection tools. Once all the possible options for a particular research program are identified, the challenge is to choose among them.

Choose your multiplist package *critically.* Traits that foster creativity include a preference for complexity, tolerance of ambiguity, and independence of judgment (Burke, 1978). Multiplism embraces the first two of these. Critical thought refers to the third and involves two types of decisions. The first is to decide how the different options methodologically complement each other, on the basis of their strengths and weaknesses and their relevance to the questions and goals of the research. The second is to pay attention to pertinent local history and the role of power and patterns of domination and to choose options accordingly.

Several traps lie in wait for the unwary critical multiplist or any other researcher seeking to combine methods, paradigms, or people. For example, it is easy to forget the assumptions supporting particular methods and strategies. Data triangulators may forget that different data sources must focus upon a common phenomenon and that each data source must meet the necessary criteria for the analysis method anticipated. Theoretical triangulators must remember to develop their competing hypotheses a priori and to test them within the same data set. Those using multiple investigators as collectors, coders, or analysts must remember to select them for clear reasons and then have them work on the same data. Methodological triangulation refers to combining the results, not the data, derived from different methods (Morse, 1991) in order to get more of the whole story—to understand a particular phenomenon from more than one perspective.

Several principles help to avoid danger when applying critical multiplism. The first principle is to *know why you choose to do something.* Convenience and curiosity are rarely sufficient reasons for methodological decision making. Think critically about each choice. What is the paradigm supporting the question? Is the method appropriate for the question? What are the consequences of using it? Who benefits? What will and what will not be known? What are the contingencies for using this method? Are there alternatives, and if so, why are they not as appropriate? Have you asked others their opinion, especially those who may not agree? The remaining five principles follow from the first.

The second principle is to *preserve method and paradigm integrity.* The debates between qualitative and quantitative researchers are not without some justification. Their respective methods are designed to answer different questions, have different sources of bias and error, are often derived from different paradigms, and require different sampling strategies and designs (Duffy, 1987). Fielding and Fielding warn researchers not to leap into linking multiple methods without simultaneously accounting for each method's foundational assumptions and bias-checking procedures (1986).

The third principle asks that investigators *pay attention to units of analysis.* Different methods within the same study may well use different units of analysis. This can make comparison of results both more difficult and more rewarding. Simultaneously exploring illness behavior from the perspective of family patterns, practice organizational patterns, historical national patterns, and individual patterns using different methods enhances understanding of the phenomenon. Blurring the micro/macro boundaries and uncritically comparing the different units of analysis, however, will lead to inappropriate conclusions.

The fourth principle is to *remember the research questions* that bound each particular study. As noted throughout this chapter, the questions direct decision making. Which design, which methods, and which unit of analysis are all dependent on what one wants to know. We recommend prominently posting the original questions as a constant reminder of why everyone has gathered. In a multimethod design in which several questions or perspectives related to a particular problem focus are being explored, the different questions need to be kept separate until after analysis so as to preserve the integrity of the methods. This is particularly true if the questions relate to different paradigms. A question presents through the lens of a particular paradigm at the time the question is asked. What matters is to identify the paradigm from which the question arose so that appropriate design and methods are selected.

The fifth principle requires that *the strengths and weaknesses of each selected option should complement each other.* How they complement depends on the research problem and purpose of the study. If the research goal is to better understand how nurse practitioners' perceptions of malpractice influence their practice behavior, then combining retrospective self-report methods with prospective observational ones is complementary. The respondent biases of the one become a strength when counteracted by the other. Combining focus groups and depth interviews is not complementary because both share similar respondent biases.

The sixth principle reminds us to *continually evaluate methodology throughout the study.* The momentum and excitement of research and the tensions and complications of collaborative research, in particular, often overwhelm critical thought. It is essential to maintain the discipline of periodically reevaluating the study through the eyes of the previous five principles.

Who conducts this collaborative research orchestra? Having a research conversation by creating linkages, learning local knowledge, discovering a shared research problem, and using appropriate methodology—all within the framework of critical multiplism—requires investigative leadership with an unusually broad theoretical perspective and knowledge of research methodology and proficiency in multiple disciplinary languages. We suggest the use of *generalist researchers, the sixth ingredient in successful collaborative research.*

THE GENERALIST RESEARCHER:
INTERPRETER OF COLLABORATIVE RESEARCH

Why create a new type of researcher? A similar question, "Why create a new type of doctor?" was raised in the late 1960s. The discipline of family medicine was formalized as a response to excessive medical subspecialization and to a shortage of primary care providers. Three decades later, generalist practitioners are considered the foundation upon which a national health care plan is being structured. The parallels between generalist clinicians and generalist researchers are illuminating.

Medical specialists fix their gaze on the presence or absence of particular diseases. The clinical generalist focuses on the patient as a person within a family, community, and health context. The clinical generalist uses whatever knowledge, special expertise (including consultation with specialists), or tools are necessary to help a person toward health throughout his or her lifetime, providing comprehensive, continuous, preventive care. The generalist practitioner is trained in the art of listening and in the core essentials and language of the different specialties, possesses global perspective of the health care system, and serves as translator and negotiator for patients (Spitzer, 1977).

These same characteristics pertain to our proposed generalist researcher, who focuses on a local research problem and views it within its systemic context, not just from a specialized disciplinary perspective. The generalist researcher uses whatever knowledge, special expertise, or methods are necessary to better understand and address the problem and its associated questions and ensures that vertical, horizontal, time, and academic linkages are not neglected. It is the generalist researcher who is trained in the core essentials and languages of the various disciplines and research methods and serves as translator and negotiator within a collaborative group.

The call for generalism is now being heard in many disciplines and echoes many of the themes discussed thus far. The fragmenting effects of specialization are raising concerns in nursing, sociology, molecular biology, and anthropology. The case of family medicine, a generalist discipline, illustrates this trend. The American Board of Family Practice has recently turned down the path of subspecialization, with separate certifications now required for sports medicine and geriatrics and additional subspecialties being considered. Alarms are sounding. Stephens (1989) warns academic family physicians not to worship rationality and power but to stay connected to the needs of patients. Baughan (1987) reviews recent theories in physics concerning the multiplicity of truth, the limits of reductionism, and the importance of patterns and relationships, and suggests the need for family medicine to embrace these and move outside disciplinary boundaries. Rodnick (1987) echoes this plea, and that of Goodale (1984) for more joint research, and calls on family medicine researchers to be a counterpoint to biomedical tradition and to initiate community-based, interspecialty, cooperative research. More recently, Culpepper (1991) stressed the need to answer questions rooted in practice; to pay attention to linkages between individuals and context and between doctors, families, and communities; to learn multimethod skills; and to create a primary care research community. A 1980 conference entitled "Research in Family Practice" listed seven categories of consensus recommendations including one stressing the importance of collaboration. This group noted that

(a) viable outcomes need collaboration, (b) mutual respect between collaborators is key, (c) the amount of collaboration must be individualized for each project, and (d) strategies must be developed to ensure that strong leadership and respectful collaboration are mutually supportive concepts (Seifert, 1982b). We suggest the generalist researcher as one such strategy.

Disciplinary generalists, including primary care and nurse researchers and applied social scientists, are ideal candidates for becoming generalist researchers. They are often trained in multiple methods, in working within different paradigms, and in collaborating with community groups. The difference is that the generalist researcher is problem focused, not discipline focused. We identify six core characteristics for the proposed generalist researcher: he or she must be (a) a theoretical pluralist, (b) a methodological pluralist, (c) practice based, (d) community oriented, (e) a translator, and (f) a negotiator.

The generalist researcher requires basic knowledge of the language, assumptions, theoretical perspectives, and history of the different liberal arts disciplines. This *theoretical pluralism* is horizontal and refers to familiarity in breadth, not vertical expertise in depth. Like the orchestra conductor who is familiar with multiple musical theories and all the instruments and free of obvious preferences for any particular section, the generalist researcher must be free of paradigm preferences and familiar enough with all the instruments of knowledge to perform a problem-focused symphony. This is similar to the defined knowledge base of primary care providers with respect to the different specialties.

Methodological pluralism refers to a working familiarity with multiple research methods. This knowledge must span the qualitative-quantitative continuum and include skill with mixed method designs (DePoy & Gitlin, 1993). The pluralism in both concepts refers to knowledge and perspective, not to belief. It trivializes the complexities and differences in theories, paradigms, and methods to assume that one person could simultaneously believe in all of them (Nagle & Mitchell, 1991). An important task of the generalist researcher as methodological pluralist in a collaborative research group is to prevent premature closure on methods options for investigating a particular problem. Two other tasks are to oversee the complexities of quality control and data management when working with multiple, different data sets.

The generalist researcher, in our opinion, needs to maintain an active relationship with one or more clinical *practice bases*. The clinical practice is a local centering post, the social focus for engaging the problems of interest, and the fount of research questions, public linkage, and policy action. The practice base provides both a source of credibility and an ongoing means of accountability for the generalist researcher coordinating a collaborative research group. The clinical practice also provides a point of entry for enacting a *community orientation*. *Community oriented* refers not only to local knowledge and linkages but also to knowing how to develop and sustain community. This requires understanding group process issues and learning how to identify and access the plurality of public voices.

Standing in the nexus where the languages of multiple disciplines, methods, clinical worlds, community groups, bureaucracies, and public voices meet requires patience, a love of noise, and cultivated skills at *translation* and *negotiation*. Otherwise, a tower of babble is rebuilt (Miller & Crabtree, 1994). From a policy perspective, these may be the most critical skills of the generalist researcher (Aiken & Mechanic, 1986; May, 1975). One mammoth stumbling block to having research inform policy decisions is the absence of an independent researcher committed to synthesizing the many research perspectives on a particular problem. The problem of cross-disciplinary budget disputes will also test the negotiating skills of the generalist researcher.

Donald Campbell (1969) appears to see collaborative research differently: "Too often in discussions of interdisciplinary training one hears calls for breadth, for comprehensiveness. Too often we attempt the production of multidisciplinary scholars" (p. 329). Campbell's solution to overcoming what he calls the "ethnocentrism of disciplines" is not to train broad multispecialists but to encourage more narrow specialization in interdisciplinary areas, thus creating enough overlapping fish scales of knowledge to cover the body of omniscience. He fears that breadth translates into lowest common denominator shallowness and reminds us that the locus of scientific knowledge is social—"chains of over-lapping neighborhoods" (Polanyi, 1966, p. 72)—and not within any one individual. He proposes creating multidisciplinary combinations of faculty at smaller colleges and forming local interdisciplinary interest groups with a problem focus. He sees these becoming the nidus for the emergence of new interdisciplinary specialties (Campbell, 1969). We agree; this is an echo of our call for problem focused research linkages at the local level. The apparent disagreement is in our understanding of generalism. The generalist is *not* a multispecialist, a reincarnation of Leonardo da Vinci; no one can know it all in the 21st century. The generalist is facilitator, seed planter, coordinator, conductor, mediator, and organizer. The generalist researcher makes Campbell's dream, and ours, possible. This becomes clearer as we discuss the training of generalist researchers.

The six core characteristics of the generalist researcher are the pillars of any training program, but certain skills need emphasis. These include grass-roots organizing skills such as the ability to work with and process lots of information, problem-solving skills, and the ability to engage in cooperative decision making (Montuori & Conti, 1993). It also includes sensitization training directed toward differences of gender, ethnicity, race, social class, sexual orientation, and professional cultures and toward learning the art and science of listening. The generalist researcher must also know how to facilitate a group working through the stages of collaborative relationship. This process requires consensus-building skills, keeping a problem focus, maintaining a creative tension between outcomes and process, and staying flexible to group needs.

We foresee numerous opportunities for someone trained as a generalist researcher. A job description would include the following options: (a) principal investigator of collaborative research grants, (b) head of a major policy or guideline consensus panel, (c) director of a bioregional practice-based research network, (d) major adviser for graduate students doing collaborative dissertation research or pursuing interdisciplinary degrees, and (e) "gatekeeper" for funding agencies. The combined trends toward dwindling resources and privatization may lead to a system of competitive managed research similar to the emerging system of competitive managed health care. If this happens, the role of gatekeeper will become more important. We have articulated our vision for collaborative research and outlined the status of a generalist researcher. The challenge is making it happen.

WHAT NEXT: MOVING TOWARD COMMUNITY

The hopes for collaborative research are high, but history has forewarned us of hazards. The barriers to interdisciplinary and transdisciplinary research remain impressive. These barriers include methodological limitations, lack of funding, few generalist researchers, academic and organizational constraints, limited publishing opportunities, past perceived failures, and human tribalism. Each of these is briefly reviewed.

Several *methodological limitations* were noted in the earlier review of multisite, multimethod education research. The cost of maintaining quality control across multiple sites and managing multiple data sets with different types of data and units of analysis is distressingly high, and the strategies for doing so are still early in development and problematic (Louis, 1982a). Despite more than two decades of experience, the research literature is still vague about what to do when quantitative and qualitative findings don't converge (Chesla, 1992; Sieber, 1973; Trend, 1978). The problem is worse when not anticipated. Fortunately, innovative approaches to linking the two in a planned manner are starting to appear (Carey, 1993; Dzurec & Abraham, 1993; Goodwin & Goodwin, 1984; Stange & Zyzanski, 1989) and include ways of counting narrative data (Weller & Romney, 1990). Another problem has been communicating qualitative data in a manner consistent with the needs of administrators. Huberman and Crandall recommend that qualitative researchers consider operationalizing a set of predictions based on their data, which are then evaluated 1 year later (1982). All of these methodological problems need more research and thus more funding.

There is funding available for problem-specific research, and more funding committees are now both multidisciplinary and multimethod. There is a *lack of funding* for long-term (10-year) projects and methods research and for training generalist researchers. Collaborative research groups need time to be together and to learn together in their local areas. In addition, collaborative projects usually involve sequential studies as part of a comprehensive program of research.

Correcting the present *lack of generalist researchers* will also require the allocation of more funds for training. Another factor preventing the establishment of generalist researcher training programs is *academic and organizational barriers*. These are fiercely resistant to change. The powerful departmental structure in universities is a major obstacle to cross-disciplinary efforts (Rosenfield, 1992). Because of this segregated and rigidly guarded organization with control of budgets and promotions, there is limited access to others' knowledge, little career reward for collaborative work, and a perceived threat from interdisciplinary efforts (Sewell, 1989). Graduate school emphasis on the solo researcher also poses an impediment to teamwork (Steckler, McLeroy, Goodman, Bird, & McCormick, 1992). *Limited publishing venues* are another type of academic barrier in that most scholarly publications are discipline based. There are too few interdisciplinary journals, too few journals for communicating ideas as opposed to research results, too few methods journals, and too few opportunities for publishing research problems and "failures." The hegemony of rationality surfaces again. Editors conventionally look for articles that represent substantive universals or theoretical breakthroughs (Easton & Schilling, 1991). Collaborative research results are more likely to represent contextual, dynamic local knowledge. How is this communicated?

Another barrier to collaborative research, discussed earlier, is the *perceived failure of past efforts*. The model of collaborative research presented here has not failed and has demonstrated early success in agriculture and international public health (Commission on Health Research for Development, 1990). Of the six essential ingredients proposed for collaborative research, only appropriate methodology was part of the interdisciplinary programs of social psychology. Lacking was a linkages perspective, especially with regards to practitioners and the public, a local knowledge emphasis, a problem focus, the framework of critical multiplism, and the presence of generalist researchers. We agree that bringing bright people and good methods together is not enough.

Collaborative research is a human endeavor and thus affected by the human penchant for *tribalism* (Schmookler, 1984). For better or worse, we witness to our lives as members of tribes. We are inescapably challenged by the pronouns *us* and *them*. Some degree of daily conflict is unavoidable, and rational thought alone will not resolve it or make it go away. For this book's readers, tribal memberships probably include academic disciplines, work institutions, families, ethnic groups, colleges, religious organizations, and nation-states. Each of these holds us to a set of beliefs and standards, pulls for our commitments, and questions our worth when we fail. It is often difficult to remember the "I" within the "we." This aspect of tribalism represents a frightening barrier to collaborative research. Campbell (1969) recognizes that the ethnocentrism of disciplines represents "the symptoms of tribalism . . . in the internal and external relations of university departments, national scientific organizations, and academic disciplines" (p. 328). Courage and risk taking are necessary if we are to collaborate and seek intimacy in the midst of "them."

Tribalism also offers hope. Within healthy tribes we can discover intimacy, develop identities strong enough to risk their loss, experience the consequences of accountability, and learn responsibility. As we approach the 21st century, there is much tribal unrest. Belief systems and institutions are not making sense to many (Bellah, Madsen, Sullivan, Swidler, & Tipton, 1991). Collaborative research is one response to this perceived need for change and offers the possibility of a counterimagination and hope for tribal health. The move toward community begins with our proposal for funding imagination (Brueggemann, 1993).

CONCLUSION: FUNDING IMAGINATION

In this chapter we propose a framework for future collaborative research. In the book we focus on the problem of changing primary care health care provider behavior and suggest multiple questions and research strategies. We present multiple linkages and the local knowledge of an AHCPR conference. We overview multiple methods and their appropriate use and utilize a critical multiplist framework. We try to demonstrate the characteristics of the generalist researcher by modeling theoretical pluralism, methodological pluralism, a clinical and community orientation, and translation. The editors have moved toward community and are continuing their collaborative research journey. Do clinical and academic departments have the courage to make time and space available and risk supporting and rewarding such collaborative research efforts and training programs? Do governments and funding agencies have the courage to risk funding collaborative centers of excellence, long-term block grants, and training opportunities? In our opinion, funding future imagination will require training more generalist researchers and creating a space for collaborative research by providing adequate funding and protected institutional space.

There are at least three avenues for training the generalist researcher. One is to fund Generalist Researcher Faculty Development Programs at several bioregional centers of excellence in collaborative research. These programs could offer eight week-long workshops over a 4-year period covering core content. Another strategy is to create 1- or 2-year fellowships at these same centers of excellence. A third strategy was developed at the University of Medicine and Dentistry of New Jersey-Robert Wood Johnson Medical School and Rutgers University. Students with diverse health degrees enroll in the Family Health Track, shaped around the interdisciplinary subject matter of family health science, and earn a master's degree in Public Health (MPH). The goal of the program "is to equip students with the knowledge, skills, and attitudes needed to become action-oriented health professionals capable of working at the interface between clinical practice, public health, and health care policy" (Like, Breckenridge, Swee, & Lieberman, 1993, p. 152). Emerging from the ideas of Kerr White (1991), the training is experiential, multimethod, and multidisciplinary. Their emphasis is producing generalist practitioners, but a similar track emphasizing research is certainly possible. Graduates of training programs need a space for their newly acquired skills.

Creating space begins with safe funding space. We recommend establishing several bioregional centers of excellence in collaborative primary care research. Strategically, these are probably best administered out of community hospitals with multiple primary care, community group, and college linkages; this avoids having to directly challenge the departmental structures of university medical centers. Once established, these centers could receive large 10-year block grants for innovative problem-based research projects. Part of the funds for these projects should be earmarked for investigating the methods used. In addition, we recommend continued funding of primary care research networks, with priority given to those involving generalist researchers. Finally, we propose funding small, marginal, highly innovative, local, practice-based collaborative research projects as seeds of creativity.

Once collaborative research is funded, the challenge switches to preserving it. Institutional space must be created. Establishing bioregional centers of excellence is a strong start. Opening publication and communication space is also necessary. Journals such as *Family Systems Medicine* and *Culture, Medicine, and Psychiatry* are exemplars, but paper journals may be too expensive as future vehicles for collaborative research communication. We encourage the development of alternative information exchange systems using computer and telecommunications technology. This will benefit collaborative research, however, only if there is departmental space created in academic centers.

Department chairs must provide sufficient time and opportunity for cross-disciplinary activity (Sherif & Sherif, 1969). This can take the form of supporting more cross-disciplinary conference attendance, interdisciplinary graduate degrees, collaborative dissertation research, and new tenure tracks based on collaborative research productivity. All of these are short-term innovations. We believe it is time to reexamine the organizational structures of academics and policymaking. Frenk (1992) has written one of the few articles directly articulating these concerns. He suggests the need for a new "organizational design that brings together the advantages of proximity to decision making [policy] and the structures, procedures and incentives developed by universities to ensure academic quality" (p. 1400).

Collaborative research imagines local spaces where open, nonhierarchical institutions based on partnership and shared power begin moving toward a reinvigorated research community of trust and support. The primary effects are personal, local, and institutional and have more to do with building community than building theory. If we nurture our roots behind the wall, acknowledge our weaknesses (Schmookler, 1988), and step outside our walls with prophetic imagination, the human tribe can discover that being together in our differences is better than proving we are ahead.

Is the vision possible? Hall (1991) warns that in order to prevent more bureaucratic control and a new paternalism of society toward the medical profession, there must be "a willingness to share . . . in a transdisciplinary manner" (p. 340). The shifting winds are in our favor. Mauksch and Leahy (1993) describe how the Group Health Cooperative of Puget Sound has, over the past four decades, slowly dissolved barriers to communication, following processes and constructs similar to those discussed in this chapter. They are moving toward community and better health care. The vision is not only possible but happening. It is time for partnership and collaboration. Abundance appears when scarcity is shared.

REFERENCES

Abel, E. (1991). *Who cares for the elderly?* Philadelphia: Temple University Press.

Addison, R. B. (1989). Grounded interpretive research: An investigation of physician socialization. In M. Packer & R. Addison (Eds.), *Entering the circle: Hermeneutic investigation in psychology* (pp. 39-58). Albany, NY: State University of New York Press.

Addison, R. B. (1992). Grounded hermeneutic research. In B. F. Crabtree & W. L. Miller (Eds.), *Doing qualitative research* (pp. 110-124). Newbury Park, CA: Sage.

Agar, M. (1980). *The professional stranger.* Orlando, FL: Academic Press.

Aiken, L. H., & Mechanic, D. (Eds.). (1986). *Applications of social science to clinical medicine and health policy.* New Brunswick, NJ: Rutgers University Press.

Aldrich, J. H., & Nelson, F. D. (1984). *Linear probability, logit, and probit models.* Beverly Hills, CA: Sage.

American Board of Internal Medicine. (1982). Subcommittee on evaluation of humanistic qualities of the internist. *Annals of Internal Medicine, 99,* 720-724.

Anderson, G. (1989). Critical ethnography in education: Origins, current status, and new directions. *Review of Educational Research, 59*(3), 249-270.

Antonovsky, A. (1987). *Unraveling the mystery of health.* San Francisco: Jossey-Bass.

Atkins, C. J., Patterson, T. L., Roppe, B. E., et al. (1987). Recruitment issues, health habits, and the decision to participate in a health promotion program. *American Journal of Preventive Medicine, 3,* 87-94.

Audet, A., & Greenfield, S. (1989, November). *A survey of current activities in practice guideline development.* Paper prepared for an IOM Meeting on Medical Practice Guidelines: Looking Ahead, Washington, DC.

Auster, R. D., & Oaxaca, R. L. (1981, Summer). Identification of supplier induced demand in the health care sector. *Journal of Human Resources, 16,* 327-342.

Ayanian, J. Z., & Berwick, D. M. (1991). Do physicians have a bias toward action? *Medical Decision Making, 11,* 154-158.

Baer, H. A. (1993). How critical can clinical anthropology be? *Medical Anthropology, 15,* 299-317.

Bannet, E. T. (1989). *Structuralism and the logic of dissent: Barthes, Derrida, Foucault, Lacan.* Urbana: University of Illinois Press.

Baughan, D. M. (1987). Contemporary scientific principles and family medicine. *Family Medicine, 19*(1), 41-45.

Becker, H. S. (1967). Introduction. In H. S. Becker (Ed.), *Social problems: A modern approach* (pp. 1-31). New York: John Wiley.

Becker, H. S. (l986). *Doing things together.* Evanston, IL: Northwestern University Press.

Becker, H. S., & Horowitz, I. L. (l986). Radical politics and sociological observation: Observations on methodology and ideology. In H. S. Becker (Ed.), *Doing things together: Selected papers* (pp. 83-102). Evanston, IL: Northwestern University Press.

Becker, P. (1993). Common pitfalls in published grounded theory research. *Qualitative Health Research, 34*(2), 254-260.

Beckman, H. B., & Frankel, R. M. (1984). The effect of physician behavior on the collection of data. *Annals of Internal Medicine, 101,* 692-696.

Beckman, H. B., Frankel, R. M., & Darnly, J. (1985). Soliciting the patient's complete agenda: A relationship to the distribution of concerns. *Clinical Research, 33,* 714A.

Beckman, H. B., Markakis, K., Suchman, A., & Frankel, R. (in press). The doctor plaintiff relationship: Lessons from plaintiff depositions. *Archives of Internal Medicine.*

Bell, N., Gimarc, J. D., & Brown, T. (1993). *Using the grassroots to set health policy: Establishing moral consensus for health care reform.* Paper presented at the 1993 Annual Meeting of the American Public Health Association, San Francisco.

Bellah, R. N., Madsen, R., Sullivan, W. M., Swidler, A., & Tipton, S. M. (1985). *Habits of the heart: Individualism and commitment in American life.* New York: Harper & Row.

Bellah, R. N., Madsen, R., Sullivan, W. M., Swidler, A., & Tipton, S. M. (1991). *The good society.* New York: Alfred A. Knopf.

Bennett, J. (1981). *Oral history and delinquency: The rhetoric of criminology.* Chicago: University of Chicago Press.

Berger, J. (1972). *Ways of seeing.* London: British Broadcasting Corporation and Penguin Books.

Berk, M. L., Bernstein, A. B., & Taylor, A. K. (1983, Winter). Use and availability of medical care in federally designated health manpower shortage areas. *Inquiry, 20,* 369-380.

Bernard, H. R. (1988). *Research methods in cultural anthropology.* Newbury Park, CA: Sage.

Berry, W. (1972). *A continuous harmony: Essays cultural and agricultural.* San Diego: Harcourt Brace Jovanovich.

Bibace, R., & Walsh, M. (1980). Development of children's concepts of illness. *Pediatrics, 66,* 912-917.

Bird, J., & Cohen-Cole, S. A. (1990). The three function model of the medical interview: An educational device. In M. Hale (Ed.), *Methods in teaching consultation liaison psychiatry* (pp. 65-88). Basel, Switzerland: Karger.

Blumer, H. (1946). *An appraisal of Thomas and Znaniecki's "The Polish Peasant in Europe and America."* New York: Social Science Research Council.

Bogdan, R. C. (1972). *Participant observation: Theory and practice.* Syracuse, NY: Syracuse University Press.

Bogdewic, S. P. (1987). *On becoming a family physician: The stages and characteristics of identity formation in family medicine residency training.* Doctoral dissertation, University of North Carolina, Chapel Hill.

Bogdewic, S. P. (1992). Participant observation. In B. Crabtree & W. Miller (Eds.), *Doing qualitative research* (pp. 45-70). Newbury Park, CA: Sage.

Borkan, J. M., Neher, J. O., Anson, O., & Smoker, B. (1993). *Referrals of alternative health care.* Submitted for publication.

Borkan, J. M., Quirk, M., & Sullivan, M. (1991). Finding meaning after the fall: Injury narratives from elderly hip fracture patients. *Social Science and Medicine, 33,* 947-957.

Borrero, M. G., Schensul, J., & Garcia, R. (1982). Research based training for organizational change. *Urban Anthropology, 11*(1), 129-153.

Brody, H. (1990). A policy imperative for primary care: Reflections on Keystone II. *Family Medicine, 1,* 42-45.

Brown, G. W. (1985). Statistics and the medical journal [editorial]. *American Journal of Diseases of Children, 139,* 226-228.

Brown, K. M. (1992, April 15). Writing about "the Other." *Chronicle of Higher Education,* p. A56.

Brueggemann, W. (1991). *Interpretation and obedience: From faithful reading to faithful living.* Minneapolis: Fortress Press.

Brueggemann, W. (1993). *Texts under negotiation: The Bible and postmodern imagination.* Minneapolis: Fortress Press.

Bruner, J. (1990). *Acts of meaning.* Cambridge, MA: Harvard University Press.

Buck, C., & Donner, A. (1982). The design of controlled experiments in the evaluation of non-therapeutic interventions. *Journal of Chronic Disease, 35,* 531-538.

Bulpitt, C. (1983). *Randomized clinical trials.* The Hague: Marinus Nijhoff.

Burke, J. (1978). *Connections.* Boston: Little, Brown.

Calinescu, M. (1987). *Five faces of modernity: Modernism, avant-garde, decadence, kitsch and postmodernism.* Durham, NC: Duke University Press.

Campbell, D. (1969). Ethnocentrism of disciplines and the fish-scale model of omniscience. In M. Sherif & C. W. Sherif (Eds.), *Interdisciplinary relationships in the social sciences* (pp. 328-348). Chicago: Aldine.

Campbell, D., & Fiske, D. (1959). Convergent and discriminant validation by the multi-trait-multimethod matrix. *Psychological Bulletin, 56*(2), 81-105.

Caputo, J. (1987). *Radical hermeneutics: Repetition, deconstruction and the hermeneutic project.* Bloomington: University of Indiana Press.

Carey, J. W. (1993). Linking qualitative and quantitative methods: Integrating cultural factors into public health. *Qualitative Health Research, 3*(3), 298-318.

Carter, W. B., Beach, L. R., & Inui, T. S. (1986). The flu-shot study: Using multiattribute utility theory to design a vaccination intervention. *Organizational Behavior and Human Decision Processes, 38,* 378-391.

Chassin, M. R., Kosecoff, J., Park, R. E., Winslow, C. M., Kahn, K. L., Merrick, N. J., Keesey, J., Fink, A., Solomon, D. H., & Brook, R. H. (1979). Does inappropriate use explain geographic variations in the use of health care services? A study of three procedures. *Journal of the American Medical Association, 258,* 2533-2537.

Cheney, C., & Ramsdell, J. W. (1987). Effect of medical records' checklists on the implementation of periodic health measures. *American Journal of Medicine, 83,* 129-136.

Chesla, C. A. (1992). When qualitative and quantitative findings do not converge. *Western Journal of Nursing Research, 14,* 681-685.

Cho, J. H. (1987). *A social phenomenological understanding of family violence in Korea.* Unpublished doctoral dissertation, University of Illinois, Urbana.

Cho, J. H. (1993). *Violence in the Korean family.* New York: Aldine.

Christoffel, K., Binns, H., Stockman, J., McGuire, P., Poncher, J., Unti, S., Typlin, B., Lasin, G., Siegel, W., & Pediatric Practice Research Group. (1988). Practice-based research: Opportunities and obstacles. *Pediatrics, 82* (part 2), 399-406.

Clifford, J. (1983). Power and dialogue in ethnography: Marcel Griaule's initiation. In G. Stocking (Ed.), *Observers observed* (pp. 121-156). Madison: University of Wisconsin Press.

Clifford, J., & Marcus, G. (Eds.). (1986). *Writing culture: The poetics and politics of ethnography.* Berkeley: University of California Press.

Clinton, J. J. (1990). The Agency for Health Care Policy and Research: Relevance for primary care research. In J. Mayfield & M. L. Grady (Eds.), *Primary care research: An agenda for the 90's* (pp. 41-44). Rockville, MD: Agency for Health Care Policy and Research.

Cohen, J. (1990). Things I have learned (so far). *American Psychologist, 45,* 1304-1312.

Cohen, S. J. (1983). Potential barriers to diabetes care. *Diabetes Care, 6,* 499-500.

Cohen-Cole, S. A. (1991). *The medical interview: The three function approach.* St. Louis: Mosby.

Cohen-Cole, S. A., & Bird, J. (1985). Interviewing the cardiac patient II: A practical guide for helping patients cope with their emotions. *Quality of Life and Cardiovascular Care, 2,* 7-12.

Commission on Health Research for Development. (1990). *Health research: Essential link to equity in development.* Oxford, U.K.: Oxford University Press.

Connor, E., & Mullan, F. (Eds.). (1982). *Community oriented primary care.* Washington, DC: National Academy Press.

Cook, T. (1985). Postpositivist critical multiplism. In R. Shotland & M. Mark (Eds.), *Social science and social policy* (pp. 21-64). Beverly Hills, CA: Sage.

Cooper, H. M. (1987). *Integrating research: A guide for literature reviews* (2nd ed.). Newbury Park, CA: Sage.

Coughlin, E. (1992, June 10). Mother love and infant death in a Brazilian shantytown. *Chronicle of Higher Education,* pp. A7-A9.

Coward, D. D. (1990). Critical multiplism: A research strategy for nursing science. *Image: Journal of Nursing Scholarship, 22*(3), 163-167.

Crabtree, B. F., & Miller, W. L. (1992). A qualitative approach to primary care research: The long interview. *Family Medicine, 23*(2), 145-151.

Craik, K. H. (1986). Personality research methods: An historical perspective. *Journal of Personality, 54,* 18-51.

Crane, D. (1975). Decisions to treat critically ill patients: A comparison of social versus medical considerations. *Milbank Quarterly, 53*(1), 1-33.

Crocker, L. M., & Algina, J. (1986). Introduction to classical and modern test theory. New York: Holt, Rinehart, & Winston.

Cronbach, L. J., & Meehl, P. E. (1955). Construct validity in psychological tests. *Psychological Bulletin, 52,* 281-302.

Culpepper, L. (1991). Family medicine research: Major needs. *Family Medicine, 23*(1), 10-14.

Cummings, S. R., Coates, T. J., Richard, R. J., Hansen, B., Zahnd, E. G., VanderMartin, R., Duncan, C., Gerbert, B., Martin, A., & Stein, M. J. (1989). Training physicians in counseling about smoking cessation: A randomized trial of the "Quit for Life" program. *Academic and Clinic, 110*(8), 640-647.

Cummings, S. R., Richard, R. J., Duncan, C. L., Hansen, B., VanderMartin, R., Gebert, B., & Coates, T. (1989). Training physicians about smoking cessation. *Journal of General Internal Medicine, 4,* 482-489.

Cunningham, J. B. (1993). *Action research and organizational development.* Westport, CT: Praeger.

Davidoff, F., Goodspeed, R., & Clive, J. (1989). Changing test ordering behavior. *Medical Care, 27*(1), 45-58.

Davis, K., & Russell, L. (1972). The substitution of hospital outpatient care for inpatient care. *Review of Economics and Statistics, 54*(2), 109-120.

Delbecq, A. L., Van de Ven, A. H., & Gustafson, D. H. (1975). *Group techniques for program planning: A guide to nominal group and Delphi processes.* Glenview, IL: Scott-Foresman.

Deleuze, G. (1992). What is a dispotif? In T. Armstrong (Ed. and Trans.), *Michel Foucault, philosopher* (pp. 159-168). New York: Routledge.

Deleuze, G., & Guattari, F. (1983). *On the line* (J. Johnston, Trans.). New York: Semiotext(e).

Delvecchio-Good, M. J. (1992). Qualitative designs: A discussion. In F. Tudiver, M. J. Bass, E. Z. Dunn, T. G. Norton, & M. Stewart (Eds.), *Research methods for primary care* (Vol. 4, pp. 96-105). Newbury Park, CA: Sage.

Deming, W. E. (1986). *Out of the crisis.* Cambridge: MIT Press.

Denzin, N. K. (1970). *Sociological methods: A sourcebook.* Chicago: Aldine.

Denzin, N. K. (1984). *On understanding emotion.* San Francisco: Jossey-Bass.

Denzin, N. K. (1987a). *The alcoholic self.* Newbury Park, CA: Sage.

Denzin, N. K. (1987b). *The recovering alcoholic.* Newbury Park, CA: Sage.

Denzin, N. K. (1988). The natural history of a university employee assistance program. *Journal of Drug Issues, 10,* 33-52.

Denzin, N. K. (1989). *Interpretive interactionism.* Newbury Park, CA: Sage.

Denzin, N. K. (1994). The art and politics of interpretation. In N. Denzin & Y. Lincoln (Eds.), *Handbook of qualitative research* (pp. 500-515). Thousand Oaks, CA: Sage.

Denzin, N. K. (in press). Living and dying in an EAP. *Journal of Drug Issues, 16.*

DePoy, E., & Gitlin, L. N. (1993). *Introduction to research: Multiple strategies for health and human services.* St. Louis: Mosby.

Deutch, F., & Murphy, W. F. (1954). *The clinical interview: Vol 1. Diagnosis: A method of teaching associative exploration.* New York: International University Press.

Devall, B. (1988). *Simple in means, rich in ends: Practicing deep ecology.* Salt Lake City: Peregrine Smith.

DeWalt, B. R. (1985). Anthropology, sociology and farming systems research. *Human Organization, 44*(2), 106-114.

DeWalt, B. R., & Pelto, P. J. (1985). Micro and macro levels of analysis in anthropology: Issues in theory and research. Boulder, CO: Westview.

Deyo, R. A., Loeser, J. D., & Bigos, S. J. (1990). Herniated lumbar intervertebral disc. *Annals of Internal Medicine, 112,* 598-603.

DiGuiseppi, C. G., Rivara, F. P., Koepsel, T. D., & Polisar, L. (1989). Bicycle helmet use by children: Evaluation of a community-wide helmet campaign. *Journal of the American Medical Association, 262,* 2256-2261.

Dilthey, W. L. (1900/1976). *Selected writings.* Cambridge, U.K.: Cambridge University Press.

Dingwall, R. (1977). Atrocity stories and professional relationships. *Sociology of Work and Occupations, 4,* 371-396.

Dobyns, L. (1990, August). Ed Deming wants big changes, and he wants them fast. *Smithsonian,* pp. 74-83.

Donaldson, M. S., & Povar, G. J. (1985). Improving the master problem list: A case study in changing clinician behavior. *Quality Review Bulletin, 11,* 327-333.

Draper, N. R., & Smith, H. (1966). *Applied regression analysis.* New York: John Wiley.

Duff, R. S., & Hollingshead, A. B. (1968). *Sickness and society.* New York: Harper & Row.

Duffy, M. (1987). Methodological triangulation: A vehicle for merging quantitative and qualitative research methods. *Image: Journal of Nursing Scholarship, 19*(3), 130-133.

Duggan, A. K., Starfield, B., & DeAngelis, C. (1990). Structured encounter form: The impact on provider performance and recording of well child care. *Pediatrics, 85*(1), 104-112.

Dzurec, L. C. (1989). The necessity for and evolution of multiple paradigms for nursing research: A poststructuralist perspective. *Advances in Nursing Science, 11*(4), 69-77.

Dzurec, L. C., & Abraham, I. L. (1993). The nature of inquiry: Linking quantitative and qualitative research. *Advances in Nursing Science, 16*(1), 73-79.

Early, F., & Seifert, M. (1981). *Starting your own patient advisory council.* Spring Park, MN: M.D. Publishing.

Easton, D., & Schilling, C. (Eds.). (1991). *Divided knowledge: Across disciplines, across cultures.* Newbury Park, CA: Sage.

Eddy, D. M. (1984). Variations in physician practice: The role of uncertainty. *Health Affairs, 3,* 74-84.

Eisenberg, J. M. (1979). Sociologic influences on decision-making by clinicians. *Annals of Internal Medicine, 90,* 957-964.

Eisenberg, J. M. (1985). Physician utilization: The state of research about physicians' practice patterns. *Medical Care, 23,* 461-483.

Eisenberg, J. M. (1986). *Doctors' decisions and the cost of medical care.* Ann Arbor, MI: Health Administration Press.

Eisenberg, J. M., Schwartz, J. S., McCaslin, F. C., & Kaufman, R. (1990). Substituting diagnostic services: New tests only partly replace older ones. *Journal of the American Medical Association, 263*(13), 1767-1768.

Eisenberg, J. M., & Williams, S. V. (1981). Cost containment and changing physicians' practice behavior. *Journal of the American Medical Association, 246,* 2195-2201.

Eisler, R. (1987). *The chalice and the blade.* New York: Harper Collins.

Ellen, R. F. (1984). *Ethnographic research: A guide to general conduct.* New York: Academic Press.

Elstein, A. S., Holzman, G. B., Ravitch, M. M., & Metheny, W. (1986). Comparison of physicians' decisions regarding estrogen replacement therapy for menopausal women and decisions derived from a decision analytic model. *American Journal of Medicine, 80*(2), 246-258.

Engel, G. (1977). The need for a new medical model: A challenge for biomedicine. *Science, 196,* 129-136.

Engel, G. L. (1988). How much longer must medicine's science be bound by a seventeenth century world view? In K. White (Ed.), *The task of medicine: Dialog at Wickenburg* (pp. 113-136). Menlo Park, CA: Kaiser Family Foundation.

Engel, G. (1992). How much longer must medicine's science be bound by a seventeenth century world view? *Family Systems Medicine, 10,* 333-346.

Epstein, A. M., Begg, C. B., & McNeil, B. J. (1986). The use of ambulatory testing in prepaid and fee-for-service practices: Relation to perceived profitability. *New England Journal of Medicine, 314,* 1089-1094.

Epstein, P. E. (1990). Cassandra and the clinician: Are clinical prediction rules changing the practice of medicine? *Annals of Internal Medicine, 113,* 636-647.

Erickson, F. (1982). Audiovisual records as a primary data source. *Sociological Methods and Research, 11*(2), 213-232.

Erikson, E. H. (1975). *Life history and the historical moment.* New York: Norton.

Evans, R. G. (1973). Supplier-induced demand: Some empirical evidence and implications. In M. Perlman (Ed.), *The economics of health and medical care* (pp. 162-173). London: Macmillan.

Everett, G. D., deBlois, S., Chang, P. F., & Holets, T. (1983). Effect of cost education, cost audits, and faculty chart review on the use of laboratory services. *Archives of Internal Medicine, 143,* 942-944.

Fay, B. (1987). *Critical social science.* Ithaca, NY: Cornell University Press.

Feinstein, A. (1985). The "chagrin factor" and qualitative decision analysis? *Archives of Internal Medicine, 145,* 1257-1259.

Feldstein, M. S. (1970, May). The rising price of physicians' services. *Review of Economics and Statistics, 52,* 121-133.

Feldstein, P. J. (1973). *Financing dental care: An economic analysis.* Lexington, MA: Lexington.

Ferguson, C. E. (1993). *The man question: Feminist visions of subjectivity in feminist theory.* Berkeley: University of California Press.

Fielding, N. G., & Fielding, J. L. (1986). *Linking data.* Beverly Hills, CA: Sage.

Filmer, P., Phillipson, M., Silverman, D., & Walsh, D. (1972). *New directions in sociological theory.* Cambridge, MA: MIT Press.

Fine, A. (1986). *The shaky game: Einstein, realism and the quantum theory.* Chicago: University of Chicago Press.

Fine, M. (1992). *Disruptive voices: The possibilities of feminist research.* Ann Arbor: University of Michigan Press.

Fiske, D. W. (1978). *Measuring the concepts of personality.* Chicago: Aldine.

Fiske, D., & Shweder, R. (Eds.). (1986). *Metatheory in social science: Pluralisms and subjectivities.* Chicago: University of Chicago Press.

Folland, S., Goodman, A., & Stano, M. (1993). *The economics of health and health care.* New York: Macmillan.

Foucault, M. (1980). *Power/knowledge: Selected interviews and other writings, 1972-1977* (C. Gordon, Ed.; C. Gordon, L. Marshall, J. Mepham, & K. Soper, Trans.). New York: Pantheon.

Francis, V., Korsch, B. M., & Morris, M. J. (1969). Gaps in doctor-patient communication: Patients' response to medical advice. *New England Journal of Medicine, 280,* 535-540.

Frankel, R. M., & Beckman, H. B. (1989a, February). *Communication aspects of medical malpractice.* Paper presented at the Mid-Winter Meetings of the International Communication Association, Monterey, CA.

Frankel, R. M., & Beckman, H. B. (1989b). Conversation and compliance with treatment recommendations: An application of microinteractional analysis in medicine. In B. Dervin, L. Grossberg, B. J. O'Keefe, & E. Wartella (Eds.), *Rethinking communication: Vol. 2. Paradigm exemplars* (pp. 60-74). Newbury Park, CA: Sage.

Franks, P., & Clancy, C. M. (1993). Physician gender bias in clinical decision making: Screening for cancer in primary care. *Medical Care, 31,* 213-218.

Franks, P., Clancy, C. M., & Nutting, P. A. (1992). Gatekeeping revisited—Protecting patients from overtreatment. *New England Journal of Medicine, 327*(6), 424-427.

Frenk, J. (1992). Balancing relevance and excellence: Organizational responses to link research with decision making. *Social Science and Medicine, 35*(11), 1397-1404.

Friedrichs, J., & Ludtke, H. (1974). *Participant observation: Theory and practice.* Westmead, UK: Saxon House.

Frymoyer, J. W., & Cats-Baril, W. L. (1991). An overview of the incidences and costs of low back pain. *Orthopedic Clinics of North America, 22,* 263-271.

Fuchs, V. R. (1986). *The health economy.* Cambridge, MA: Harvard University Press.

Fuchs, V., & Kramer, M. (1973). *Determinants of expenditures for physicians' services in the United States, 1948-1968.* Occasional Paper 117. New York: National Bureau of Economic Research.

Gadamer, H. G. (1975). *Truth and method.* London: Sheed & Ward.

Game, A. (1991). *Undoing the social: Towards a deconstructive sociology.* Toronto: University of Toronto Press.

Geertz, C. (1983). *Local knowledge.* New York: Basic Books.

Gemson, D. H., Colombotos, J., Elinson, J., Fordyce, J., Hynes, M., & Stoneburner, R. (1991). Acquired immunodeficiency syndrome prevention. *Archives of Internal Medicine, 151,* 1102-1108.

Gilgun, J. F., Daly, K., & Handel, G. (Eds.). (1992). *Qualitative methods in family research.* Newbury Park, CA: Sage.

Gilligan, C. (1982). *In a different voice.* Cambridge, MA: Harvard University Press.

Gilliss, C., Gortner, S., Hauck, W., Shinn, J., Sparacino, P., & Tompkins, C. (1993). A randomized clinical trial of nursing care for recovery from cardiac surgery. *Heart & Lung, 22*(2), 125-133.

Gilliss, C., Lewis, C., Holaday, B., & Pantell, R. (1989). A health education program for day care centers: An educational program. *Maternal Child Nursing, 14*(4), 266-268.

Gladwin, T. (1964). Culture and logical process. In W. Goodenough (Ed.), *Explorations in cultural anthropology: Essays in honor of George Peter Murdock* (pp. 167-177). New York: McGraw-Hill.

Glaser, B. C., & Strauss, A. L. (1967). *The discovery of grounded theory: Strategies for qualitative research.* New York: Aldine.

Glover, J. A. (1938). The incidence of tonsillectomy in school children. *Proceedings of the Royal Society of Medicine, 31,* 1219-1236.

Goetz, J. P., & LeCompte, M. D. (1984). *Ethnography and qualitative design in educational research.* New York: Academic Press.

Goleman, D. (1991, November 13). All too often the doctor isn't listening, studies show. *New York Times,* pp. C1, C15.

Good, M. D. V. (1992). Local knowledge: Research capacity building in international health. *Social Science and Medicine, 35*(11), 1359-1367.

Good, M. J. D., Good, B., & Cleary, P. D. (1987). Do patient attitudes influence physician recognition of psychosocial problems in primary care? *Journal of Family Practice, 25*(1), 53-59.

Goodale, F. (1984). Academic credibility: Can your department of family medicine meet the challenge? *Journal of Family Practice, 18*(3), 471-476.

Goodwin, L. D., & Goodwin, W. L. (1984). Qualitative vs. quantitative research or qualitative and quantitative research? *Nursing Research, 33*(6), 378-380.

Gorenberg, B. (1983). The research tradition of nursing: An emerging issue. *Nursing Research, 32*(6), 347-349.

Gortner, S., Gilliss, C., Shinn, J., Sparacino, P., Rankin, S., Leavitt, M., Price, M., & Hudes, M. (1988). Improving recovery following cardiac surgery: A randomized clinical trial. *Journal of Advanced Nursing, 13,* 649-661.

Gottlieb, L. K., Margolis, C. Z., & Schoenbaum, S. C. (1990). Clinical practice guidelines at an HMO: Development and implementation in a quality improvement model. *Quality Review Bulletin 16*(2), 80-86.

Gouldner, A. (1970). *The coming crisis of Western sociology.* New York: Basic Books.

Gramsci, A. (1971). *Selections from the Prison Notebooks of Antonio Gramsci.* (Q. Hoare & G. Smith, Ed. & Trans.). New York: International Publishers.

Gray, B. H. (1992). The legislative battle over health services research. *Health Affairs* (Millwood), *11*(4), 38-66.

Greco, P. J., & Eisenberg, J. M. (1993). Changing physicians' practices. *New England Journal of Medicine, 329,* 1271-1274.

Greenfield, S., Kaplan, S. H., & Ware, J. E., Jr. (1985a). Expanding patient involvement in care: Effects on blood pressure control. *Proceedings of National Conference on High Blood Pressure Control.*

Greenfield, S., Kaplan, S. H., & Ware, J. E., Jr. (1985b). Expanding patient involvement in care: Effects on patient outcomes. *Annals of Internal Medicine, 102*(4), 520-528.

Greenfield, S., Kaplan, S. H., Ware, J. E., Martin, E., Yano, E. M., & Frank. J. (1988). Patient participation in medical care: Effects on blood sugar control and quality of life in diabetes. *Journal of General Internal Medicine, 3,* 448-457.

Greenfield, S., Nelson, E., Zubkoff, M., & Manning, W. (1992, March). Variations in resource utilization among medical specialties and systems of care. *Journal of the American Medical Association, 267,* 1624-1630.

Grilli, R., Apolone, G., Marsoni, S., Nicolucci, A., Zola, P., & Liberati, A. (1991). The impact of patient management guidelines on the care of breast, colorectal, and ovarian cancer patients in Italy. *Medical Care, 29,* 50-63.

Grossberg, L., Nelson, C., & Treichler, P. (Eds.). (1992). *Cultural studies.* New York: Routledge.

Grossman, M. (1972). *The demand for health.* New York: Columbia University Press.

Grosz, E. (1989). *Sexual subversions: Three French feminists.* Sydney: Allen & Unwin.

Guba, E. (1990a). *The paradigm dialog.* Newbury Park, CA: Sage.

Guba, E. G. (1990b). Subjectivity and objectivity. In E. Eisner & A. Peshkin (Eds.), *Qualitative inquiry in education: The continuing debate* (pp. 74-91). New York: Teachers College Press.

Guba, E., & Lincoln, Y. (1989). *Fourth generation evaluation.* Newbury Park, CA: Sage.

Gubrium, J. F. (1986a). *Oldtimers and Alzheimer's.* Greenwich, CT: JAI.

Gubrium, J. F. (1986b). The social preservation of mind. *Symbolic Interaction, 9,* 37-51.

Gubrium, J. F. (1988a). *Analyzing field reality.* Newbury Park, CA: Sage.

Gubrium, J. F. (1988b). Family responsibility and caregiving in the qualitative analysis of the Alzheimer's disease experience. *Journal of Marriage and the Family, 50,* 197-207.

Gubrium, J. F. (1992). *The mosaic of care.* New York: Springer.

Gubrium, J. F. (1993a). *Speaking of life: Horizons of meaning for nursing home residents.* Hawthorne, NY: Aldine.

Gubrium, J. F. (1993b). Voice and context in a new gerontology. In T. Cole, W. A. Achenbaum, P. L. Jakobi, & R. Kastenbaum (Eds.), *Voices and visions of aging* (pp. 46-63). New York: Springer.

Habermas, J. (1971a). *Knowledge and human interests* (J. Shapiro, Trans.). Boston: Beacon. (Original work published 1968)

Habermas, J. (1971b). *Theory and practice* (J. Biertel, Trans.). Boston: Viking.

Habermas, J. (1975). *Legitimation crisis* (T. McCarthy, Trans.). Boston: Beacon.

Habermas, J. (1987). *The philosophical discourse of modernism* (F. Lawrence, Trans.). Cambridge: MIT Press.

Hall, D. (1991). The research imperative and bureaucratic control: The case of clinical research. *Social Science and Medicine, 32*(3), 333-342.

Haraway, D. J. (1991). *Simians, cyborgs, and women: The reinvention of nature.* New York: Routledge.

Harding, S. (Ed.). (1987). *Feminism and methodology.* Bloomington: Indiana University Press.

Harding, S. (1991). *Whose science? Whose knowledge? Thinking from women's lives.* Ithaca, NY: Cornell University Press.

Harris, C. M. (1989). Seeing sunflowers. *Journal of the Royal College of General Practitioners, 39,* 313-319.

Harris, J. S. (1990). Why doctors do what they do: Determinants of physician behavior. *Journal of Occupational Medicine, 32*(12), 1207-1220.

Hartwig, F., & Dearing, B. E. (1980). *Exploratory data analysis.* Beverly Hills: Sage.

Hauck, W., Gilliss, C., Donner, A., & Gortner, S. (1990). Randomization by cluster. *Nursing Research, 40*(6), 356-358.

Haygarth, J. (1800). *Of the imagination, as a cause and as a cure of disorders of the body: Exemplified by fictitious tractors, and epidemical convulsions.* Bath, UK: R. Cruttwell.

Headache Study Group of the University of Western Ontario (1986). Predictors of outcome in headache patients presenting to family physicians—A one year prospective study. *Headache, 6,* 285-294.

Heckerling, P. S., Tape, T. G., & Wigton, R. S. (1992). Relation of physicians' predicted probabilities of pneumonia to their utilities for ordering chest x-rays to detect pneumonia. *Medical Decision Making, 12*(1), 32-38.

Hedges, L. V., & Olkin, I. (1985). *Statistical methods for meta-analysis.* New York: Academic Press.

Heidegger, M. (1962). *Being and time.* New York: Harper & Row. (Original work published 1927)

Heider, K. (1988). The Rashomon effect: When ethnographers disagree. *American Anthropologist, 90,* 73-81.

Heller, D. (1991). *Growing up isn't hard to do if you start out as a kid: Children's candid views of everyday life.* New York: Villard.

Henige, D. P. (1982). *Oral historiography.* New York: Longman.

Herbst, A. L., Ulfelder, H., & Poskanzer, D. C. (1971). Adenocarcinoma of the vagina. Association of maternal stilbestrol therapy with tumor appearance in young women. *New England Journal of Medicine, 284*(15), 878-881.

Herriott, R. E. (1982). Tensions in research design and implementation: The Rural Experimental Schools Study. *American Behavioral Scientist, 26,* 23-44.

Higginbotham, N. H. (1992). Developing a social science component within the International Clinical Epidemiology Network (INCLEN). *Social Science and Medicine, 35,* 1325-1327.

Hillman, A. L., Pauly, M. V., & Kerstein, J. J. (1989). How do financial incentives affect physicians' clinical decisions and the financial performance of health maintenance organizations? *New England Journal of Medicine, 321*(2), 86-92.

Hired, G. S. (1991). Culture tales: A narrative approach to thinking, cross-cultural psychology, and psychotherapy. *American Psychologist, 46,* 187-197.

Hollingshead, A. B., & Redligh, F. C. (1958). *Social class and mental illness.* New York: John Wiley.

Houts, A., Cook, T., & Shadish, W. (1986). The person-situation debate: A critical multiplist perspective. *Journal of Personality, 54*(1), 53-107.

Hsiao, W. C., Braun, P., Dunn, D., Becker, E. R., DeNicola, M., & Ketcham, T. R. (1988). Results and policy implications of the resource-based relative-value study. *New England Journal of Medicine, 319,* 881-888.

Huberman, A. M., & Crandall, D. P. (1982). Fitting words to numbers: Multisite/multimethod research in educational dissemination. *American Behavioral Scientist, 26,* 62-83.

Hulley, S., & Cummings, S. (Eds.). (1988). *Designing clinical research.* Baltimore: Williams & Wilkins.

Hurwitz, E. S., Barrett, M. J., Bregman, D., Gunn, W. J., Schonberger, L. E., Fairweather, W. R., Drage, J. S., La Montagne, J. R., Kaslow, R. A., & Burlington, D. B. (1985). Public Health Service study on Reye's syndrome and medications. Report of the pilot phase. *New England Journal of Medicine, 313*(14), 849-857.

Husserl, E. (1962). *Ideas.* New York: Collier. (Original work published 1913)

Hutcheon, L. (1988). *A poetics of postmodernism: History, theory, fiction.* New York: Routledge.

Institute of Medicine. (1978). *A manpower policy for primary health care.* Washington, DC: National Academy of Sciences Press.

Inui, T. S., & Carter, W. B. (1985). Problems and prospects for health services research on provider-patient communication. *Medical Care, 23,* 521-538.

Inui, T. S., & Carter, W. B. (1988). Design issues in research on doctor-patient communication. In M. Stewart & D. Roter (Eds.), *Communicating with medical patients* (pp. 197-210). Newbury Park, CA: Sage.

Johnson, J. C. (1990). Selecting ethnographic informants. Newbury Park, CA: Sage.

Jorgensen, D. L. (1989). *Participant observation: A methodology for human studies.* Newbury Park, CA: Sage.

Kaplan, S. H., Greenfield, S., & Ware, J. E., Jr. (1989a). Assessing the effects of physician-patient interaction on the outcomes of chronic disease. *Medical Care, 27*(suppl), s110-s127.

Kaplan, S. H., Greenfield, S., & Ware, J. E., Jr. (1989b). Implications of doctor-patient relationships for patients' health outcomes. In M. Stewart & D. L. Roter (Eds.), *Communicating with medical patients* (pp. 228-245). Newbury Park, CA: Sage.

Kaplan, S. H., & Ware, J. E., Jr. (1989). The patient's role in health care and quality assessment. In D. Nash & N. Goldfield (Eds.), *Assessing the quality of care* (pp. 25-68). Philadelphia: American College of Physicians.

Katerndahl, D. A., & Cohen, P. A. (1987). Quantitatively reviewing the literature: The application of meta-analysis. *Family Practice Research Journal, 6,* 123-129.

Katz, P. (1985). How surgeons make decisions. In R. Hahn & A. Gaines (Eds.), *Physicians of Western medicine* (pp. 155-175). Dordrecht, the Netherlands: D. Reidell.

Kelsey, J. L., Thompson, W. D., & Evans, A. S. (1986). *Methods in observational epidemiology.* New York: Oxford University Press.

Kennedy, P. (1989). *A guide to econometrics* (2nd ed.). Cambridge: MIT Press.

Kmenta, J. (1986). *Elements of econometrics* (2nd ed.). New York: Macmillan.

Korsch, B. M., Gozzi, E., & Francis, B. (1968). Gaps in doctor-patient communication, I: Doctor-patient interaction and patient satisfaction. *Pediatrics, 42,* 855-871.

Kosecoff, J., Kanouse, D. E., Rogers, W. H., McCloskey, L., Winslow, C. M., & Brook, R. H. (1987). Effects of the National Institutes of Health consensus development program on physician practice. *Journal of the American Medical Association, 258,* 2708-2713.

Kravitz, R. L., Greenfield, S., Rogers, W., and Manning, W. (1992). Differences in the mix of patients among medical specialties and among systems of care. *Journal of the American Medical Association, 267,* 1617-1623.

Kritchevsky, S. B., & Simmons, B. P. (1991). Continuous quality improvement: Concepts and applications for physician care. *Journal of the American Medical Association, 266*(13), 1817-1823.

Kroker, A., & Cook, D. (1986). *The postmodern scene: Excremental culture and hyper-aesthetics.* New York: St. Martin's.

Kushman, J., et al. (1978, Fall). Nonsolo dental practice: Incentives and returns to size. *Journal of Economics and Business, 31,* 29-39.

Kuzel, A. J. (1992). Sampling in qualitative inquiry. In B. Crabtree & W. Miller (Eds.), *Doing qualitative research* (pp. 31-44). Newbury Park, CA: Sage.

Langwell, K. (1980, Spring). Real returns to career decisions: The physician's specialty and location choices. *Journal of Human Resources, 15,* 278-286.

Lather, P. (1986a). Issues of validity in openly ideological research: Between a rock and a soft place. *Interchange, 17*(4), 63-84.

Lather, P. (1986b). Research as praxis. *Harvard Educational Review, 56*(3), 257-277.

Lather, P. (1991). *Getting smart: Feminist research and pedagogy with/in the postmodern.* New York: Routledge.

Lather, P. (1992, October). *Feminism, methodology and the crisis of representation: Researching the lives of women with HIV/AIDS.* Paper presented at the Annual Conference of the Journal of Curriculum Theorizing, Dayton, OH.

Lather, P. (1993). Fertile obsession: Validity after poststructuralism. *Sociological Quarterly, 34*(4).

Lau, J., Antman, E. M., Jimenez-Silva, J., Kopelnick, B., Mosteller, F., & Chalmers, T. C. (1992). Cumulative meta-analysis of therapeutic trials for myocardial infarction. *New England Journal of Medicine, 327,* 248-254.

Lazare, A. (1987). Shame and humiliation in the medical encounter. *Archives of Internal Medicine, 147,* 1653-1658.

Lazare, A. (1989). Three functions of the interview. In A. Lazare (Ed.), *Outpatient psychiatry: Diagnosis and treatment* (pp. 153-157). Baltimore: Williams & Wilkins.

Lecercle, J.-J. (1990). *The violence of language.* London: Routledge.

LeCourt, D. (1975). *Marxism and epistemology.* London: National Labor Board.

Lee, P. R. (1985). Health promotion and disease prevention for children and the elderly. *Health Services Research, 19,* 783-792.

Lewis, C., Knopf, D., Chastain-Lorber, K., Ablin, A., Zoger, S., Matthay, K., Glasser, M., & Pantell, R. (1988). Patient, parent, and physician perspectives on pediatric oncology rounds. *Journal of Pediatrics, 112*(3), 378-384.

Lewis, C. C., Pantell, R. H., & Sharp, L. (1991). Increasing patient knowledge, satisfaction, and involvement: Randomized trial of a communication intervention. *Pediatrics, 88*(2), 351-358.

Lewis, C. E., Racheleefsky, G., Lewis, M. A., de la Sota, A., & Kaplan, M. (1984). A randomized trial of A.C.T. (asthma care training) for kids. *Pediatrics, 74,* 478-486.

Lewis, M. A., Salas, I., de la Sota, A., Chiofalo, N., & Leake, B. (1990). Randomized trial of a program to enhance the competencies of children with epilepsy. *Epilepsia, 31*(1), 101-109.

Lewis-Beck, M. S. (1980). *Applied regression: An introduction.* Beverly Hills, CA: Sage.

Light, R. J., & Pillemer, D. B. (1982). Numbers and narratives: Combining their strengths in research reviews. *Harvard Educational Review, 52*(1), 1-23.

Light, R. J., & Pillemer, D. B. (1984). *Summing up: The science of reviewing research.* Cambridge, MA: Harvard University Press.

Like, R. C., Breckenridge, M. B., Swee, D. E., & Lieberman, III, J. A. (1993). Family health science and the new generalist practitioner. *Family Systems Medicine, 11*(2), 149-161.

Lincoln, Y. S. (1991). The arts and sciences of program evaluation. *Evaluation Practice, 12,* 1-7.

Lincoln, Y., & Guba, E. (1985). *Naturalistic inquiry.* Newbury Park, CA: Sage.

Lind, J. (1953). A treatise of the scurvy. In C. P. Stewart & D. Guthrie (Eds.), *Lind's treatise on scurvy.* Edinburgh: Edinburgh University Press. (Original work published 1753)

Lindemann, E. C. (1924). *Social discovery.* New York: Republic.

Lipid Research Clinics Program. (1984). The Lipid Research Clinics Coronary Primary Prevention Trial results. I. Reduction in incidence of coronary heart disease. *Journal of the American Medical Association, 251,* 351-364.

Lipkin, M., Jr. (1987). The medical interview and related skills. In W. T. Branch (Ed.), *The office practice of medicine* (pp. 1287-1306). Philadelphia: W. B. Saunders.

Lipton, H. L., & Svarstad, B. L. (1977). Sources in variation in clinician communication to parents about mental retardation. *American Journal of Mental Deficiency, 82,* 155-161.

Lomas, J. (1991). Words without action? The production, dissemination, and impact of consensus recommendations. *Annual Review of Public Health, 12,* 41-65.

Lomas, J., Anderson, G. M., Domnick-Pierre, K., Vayda, E., Enkin, M. W., & Hannah, W. J. (1989). Do practice guidelines guide practice? The effect of a consensus statement on the practice of physicians. *New England Journal of Medicine, 321,* 1306-1310.

Lomas, J., Enkin, M., Anderson, G. M., Hannah, W. J., Vayda, E., & Singer, J. (1991). Opinion leaders vs. audit and feedback to implement practice guidelines. *Journal of the American Medical Association, 265,* 2202-2207.

Louis, K. S. (1982a). Multisite/multimethod studies: An introduction. *American Behavioral Science, 26,* 6-22.

Louis, K. S. (1982b). Sociologist as sleuth: Integrating methods in the RDU study. *American Behavioral Scientist, 26,* 101-120.

Luft, H. S. (1986). Economic incentives and constraints in clinical practice. In L. H. Aiken & D. Mechanic (Eds.), *Applications of social science to clinical medicine and health policy* (pp. 500-518). New Brunswick, NJ: Rutgers University Press.

Lynch, K. (1976). *Managing the sense of a region.* Boston: MIT Press.

Lyotard, J. (1984). The postmodern condition: A report on knowledge (G. Bennington & B. Massumi, Trans.). Minneapolis: University of Minnesota Press.

Magraw, R. M. (1966). *Ferment in medicine.* Philadelphia: W. B. Saunders.

Majchrzak, A. (1984). *Methods for policy research.* Beverly Hills, CA: Sage.

Makiya, K. (1993). *Cruelty and silence.* New York: Norton.

Malinowski, B. (1961). *Argonauts of the western Pacific.* New York: E. P. Dutton.

Manning, W. G., et al. (1987, June). Health insurance and the demand for medical care: Evidence from a randomized experiment. *American Economic Review, 77,* 251-277.

Margolis, C. Z., Warshawsky, S. S., Goldman, L., Dagan, O., Wirtschafter, O., & Pliskin, J. S. (1992). Computerized algorithms and pediatricians' management of common problems in a community clinic. *Academic Medicine, 67,* 282-284.

Marienthal, P. (1992). *The dissertation as praxis: An encounter with liberatory methodologies and the emergence of an educator.* Unpublished doctoral dissertation, Ohio State University.

Marquis, D. (1983). Leaving therapy to chance: An impact in the ethics of randomized clinical trials. *Hastings Center Report, 13*(4), 40-46.

Mauksch, L. B., & Leahy, D. (1993). Collaboration between primary care medicine and mental health in an HMO. *Family Systems Medicine, 11*(2), 121-135.

May, J. J. (1975). Symposium: The policy uses of research: Introduction. *Inquiry, 12,* 228.

Maynard, D. (1989). Notes on the delivering and reception of diagnostic news regarding mental disabilities. In D. Helm, W. Anderson, & A. Rawls (Eds.), *The interactional order: New directions in the study of social order* (pp. 54-67). New York: Irvington.

Maynard, D. (1991). Bearing bad news in clinical settings. In B. Dervin (Ed.), *Progress in communication sciences* (Vol. 10, pp. 143-172). Norwood, NJ: Ablex.

Maynard, D. (1992). On co-implicating recipients in the delivering of diagnostic news. In P. Drew & J. Heritage (Eds.), *Talk at work: Social interaction in institutional settings* (pp. 331-358). Cambridge, UK: Cambridge University Press.

McCall, R. B. (1977). Challenges to a science of developmental psychology. *Child Development, 48,* 333-344.

McClelland, M., & Sands, R. G. (1993). The missing voice in interdisciplinary communication. *Qualitative Health Research, 3*(1), 74-90.

McDermott, J. (1990). Some heartland farmers just say no to chemicals. *Smithsonian, 21*(1), 114-127.

McKinlay, J. B. (1993). The promotion of health through planned sociopolitical change: Challenges for research and policy. *Social Science and Medicine, 36*(2), 109-117.

McPhee, S. J., Bird, J. A., Jenkins, N. H., & Fordham, D. (1989). Promoting cancer screening. *Archives of Internal Medicine, 149,* 1866-1872.

McWilliam, E. (1992a). *Educative research in pre-service teacher education: Postpositivist possibilities.* Unpublished manuscript.

McWilliam, E. (1992b). *In broken images: A postpositivist analysis of student needs talk in pre-service teacher education.* Unpublished doctoral dissertation, University of Queensland, Australia.

Meinert, C. L. (1986). *Clinical trials: Design, conduct, and analysis.* Oxford, UK: Oxford University Press.

Merleau-Ponty, M. (1964). *The primacy of perception* (W. Cobb, Trans.). Evanston, IL: Northwestern University Press.

Miles, M. B. (1982). A mini-cross-site analysis. *American Behavioral Scientist, 26,* 121-132.

Miller, W. L., & Crabtree, B. F. (1992). Primary care research: A multimethod typology and qualitative road map. In B. Crabtree & W. Miller (Eds.), *Doing qualitative research* (pp. 3-28). Newbury Park, CA: Sage.

Miller, W. L., & Crabtree, B. F. (1994). Clinical research. In N. Denzin & Y. Lincoln (Eds.), *Handbook of qualitative research* (pp. 340-352). Thousand Oaks, CA: Sage.

Mills, C. W. (1959). *The sociological imagination.* New York: Oxford University Press.

Mishler, E. (1979). Meaning in context: Is there any other kind? *Harvard Educational Review, 49*(1), 1-19.

Mishler, E. (1990). Validation in inquiry-guided research: The role of exemplars in narrative studies. *Harvard Educational Review, 60*(4), 415-442.

Misztal, B., & Moss, D. (1990). *Action on AIDS: National policies in comparative perspective.* New York: Greenwood.

Mitchell, E. (1986). Multiple triangulation: A methodology for nursing science. *Advances in Nursing Science, 8*(3), 18-26.

Mitchell, J. M., & Sunshine, J. H. (1992). Consequences of physicians' ownership of health care facilities—Joint ventures in radiation therapy. *New England Journal of Medicine, 327,* 1497-1501.

Mittman, B. S., Tonesk, X., & Jacobson, P. D. (1992, October). Implementing clinical practice guidelines: Social influence strategies and practitioner behavior change. *Quarterly Review Bulletin, 18,* 413-422.

Mizrahi, T. (1986). *Getting rid of patients: Contradictions in the socialization of physicians.* New Brunswick, NJ: Rutgers University Press.

Modic, M. T., & Ross, J. F. (1991). Magnetic resonance imaging in the evaluation of L.B.P. *Orthopedic Clinics of North America, 22,* 283-301.

Montuori, A., & Conti, I. (1993). *From power to partnership: Creating the future of love, work, and community.* San Francisco: Harper & Row.

Morgan, D. L. (Ed.). (1993). *Successful focus groups.* Newbury Park, CA: Sage.

Morse, J. M. (1991). Approaches to qualitative-quantitative methodological triangulation. *Nursing Research, 40*(1), 120-123.

Moser, C. A. (1958). *Survey methods in social investigation.* London: Heinemann.

Moses, L. E. (1985). Statistical concepts fundamental to investigations. *New England Journal of Medicine, 312,* 890-897.

Moustakas, C. (1990). *Heuristic research.* Newbury Park, CA: Sage.

Mueller, C. D., & Monheit, A. (1988). Insurance coverage and the demand for dental care: Results for nonaged white adults. *Journal of Health Economics, 7,* 59-72.

Muller, J. H. (1992, December). Participant observation, one approach to primary care research. *Society of Teachers of Family Medicine Research News,* pp. 32-37.

Murrey, K. O., Gottlieb, L. K., & Schoenbaum, S. C. (1992, December). Implementing clinical guidelines: A quality management approach to reminder systems. *Quarterly Review Bulletin, 18,* 423-433.

Myers, S. A., & Gleicher, N. (1991). A successful program to reduce cesarean section rates: Friendly persuasion. *Quarterly Review Bulletin, 17*(5), 162-166.

Nagle, L. M., & Mitchell, G. J. (1991). Theoretic diversity: Evolving paradigmatic issues in research and practice. *Advances in Nursing Science, 14*(1), 17-25.

National Asthma Education Program Office of Prevention, Education, and Control; National Heart, Lung, and Blood Institute; National Institutes of Health. (1991, June). *Executive summary: Guidelines for the diagnosis and management of asthma.* Bethesda, MD: Author. (Publication No. 91-3042A)

Newhouse, J. P. (1987, May). Health economics and econometrics. *American Economic Review, 77,* 269-273.

Newhouse, J. P., et al. (1982). *Some interim results from a controlled trial of cost sharing in health insurance.* Santa Monica, CA: Rand Corporation.

Nichter, M., & Kendall, C. (1991). Beyond child survival: Anthropology and international health in the 1990's. *Medical Anthropology Quarterly, 5,* 195-203.

Novich, M., Gillis, L., & Tauber, A. I. (1985). The laboratory test justified. *American Journal of Clinical Pathology, 84,* 756-759.

Nutting, P. A. (Ed.). (1987). *Community oriented primary care: From principles to practice.* Washington, DC: U.S. Government Printing Office.

Nutting, P. (Ed.). (1990). Community-oriented primary care: From principles to practice. Albuquerque: University of New Mexico Press.

Nutting, P. A. (1991). A research agenda for primary care: Summary report of a conference. Rockville, MD: Agency for Health Care Policy and Research.

Nutting, P., & Connor, E. (1986). Community-oriented primary care: An integrated model for practice, research, and education. *American Journal of Preventive Medicine, 2*(3), 140-147.

Oakley, A. (1981). Interviewing women: A contradiction in terms. In H. Roberts (Ed.), *Doing feminist research* (pp. 30-61). London: Routledge.

O'Brien, K. (1993). Improving survey questionnaires through focus groups. In D. Morgan (Ed.), *Successful focus groups*. Newbury Park, CA: Sage.

O'Brien, P. C. (1993). Meta-analysis [editorial]. *Mayo Clinic Proceedings, 68,* 91-93.

Ormiston, G. (1990). Postmodern differends. In A. Dalery & C. Scott (Eds.), *Crisis in continental philosophy* (pp. 235-283). Albany: State University of New York Press.

Palmer, R. H., Louis, T. A., Hsu, L. N., Peterson, H. F., Rothrock, J. K., Strain, R., Thompson, M. S., & Wright, E. A. (1985). A randomized controlled trial of quality assurance in sixteen ambulatory care practices. *Medical Care, 23,* 751-770.

Palmer, R. H., Strain, R., Maurer, V. W., Rothrock, J. K., & Thompson, M. S. (1984). Quality assurance in eight adult medicine group practices. *Medical Care, 22*(suppl), 632-643.

Pantell, R. H., & Goodman, B. W., Jr. (1983). Adolescent chest pain: A prospective study. *Pediatrics, 71,* 881-887.

Pantell, R. H., & Lewis, C. C. (1986). Physician communication with pediatric patients: A theoretical and empirical analysis. *Advances in Developmental and Behavioral Pediatrics, 7,* 65-119.

Pantell, R. H., & Lewis, C. C. (1992). *Talking with children: How to improve the process and outcome of medical care.* Unpublished manuscript.

Pantell, R., Lewis, C., & Sharp, L. (1989). Improving outcomes in asthmatic patients: Results of a randomized trial. *American Journal of Diseases of Children, 143,* 433.

Pantell, R. H., Stewart, T. J., Dias, J. K., Wells, P., & Ross, A. W. (1982). Physician communication with children and parents. *Pediatrics, 70,* 396-402.

Patton, M. Q. (1990). *Qualitative evaluation and research methods* (2nd ed.). Newbury Park, CA: Sage.

Paul, B. (Ed.). (1955). *Health, culture and community.* New York: Russell Sage Foundation.

Payer, L. (1988). *Medicine and culture: Varieties of treatment in the United States, England, West Germany, and France.* New York: Henry Holt.

Pearlin, L. (1992, March). Structure and meaning in medical sociology. *Journal of Health and Social Behavior, 33,* 1-9.

Peck, M. S. (1987). *The different drum: Community making and peace.* New York: Simon & Schuster.

Pelto, P., & Pelto, G. H. (1992). Developing applied medical anthropology in Third World countries: Problems and actions. *Social Science and Medicine, 35,* 1389-1395.

Perrin, E. C., & Gerrity, S. (1981). There's a demon in your belly: Children's understanding of illness. *Pediatrics, 67,* 841-849.

Perrin, E. C., & Gerrity, S. (1983). There's a demon in your belly: Children's understanding of illness. *American Journal of Diseases of Children, 137,* 874-878.

Perrin, E. C., & Perrin, J. M. (1983). Clinicians' assessments of children's understanding of illness. *American Journal of Diseases of Children, 137,* 874-878.

Pheysey, D. C. (1993). *Organizational cultures: Types and transformations.* New York: Routledge.

Philips, D. (1990). Postpositivistic science: Myths and realities. In E. Guba (Ed.), *The paradigm dialog* (pp. 31-45). Newbury Park, CA: Sage.

Pies, C. (1993). *Creating ethical reproductive health care policy: Views and values concerning Norplant: Bringing many voices to the policy discussion.* San Jose, CA: Education Programs Associates.

Poggie, J. (1972). Toward quality control in key informant data. *Human Organization, 31,* 23-30.

Polanyi, M. (1966). *The tacit dimension.* New York: Doubleday.

Polit, D., & Hungler, B. (1989). *Nursing research: Principles and methods* (4th ed.). Philadelphia: J. B. Lippincott.

Popper, K. R. (1959). *The logic of scientific discovery.* New York: Basic Books.

Poster, M. (1989). *Critical theory and poststructuralism: In search of a context.* Ithaca, NY: Cornell University Press.

Poster, M. (1990). *The mode of information: Poststructuralism and social context.* Chicago: University of Chicago Press.

Priester, R. (1992). *Taking values seriously: A values framework for the U.S. health care system.* Minneapolis: University of Minnesota, Center for Biomedical Ethics.

Quantz, R. A. (1992). On critical ethnography (with some postmodern considerations). In M. D. LeCompte, W. L. Millroy, & J. Preissle (Eds.), *The handbook of qualitative research in education* (pp. 447-506). New York: Academic Press.

Quinby, L. (1991). *Freedom, Foucault, and the subject of America.* Boston: Northeastern University Press.

Rabinow, P. (1977). *Reflections on fieldwork in Morocco.* Berkeley: University of California Press.

Ramsey, C. J. (Ed.). (1989). *Family systems in medicine.* New York: Guilford.

Reason, P. (1994). Three approaches to participative inquiry (pp. 324-339). In Denzin, N. & Lincoln, Y. Newbury Park, CA: Sage.

Reason, P. (Ed.). (1988). *Human inquiry in action: Developments in new paradigm research.* London: Sage.

Reinhardt, U. (1975). *Physician productivity and the demand for health manpower.* Cambridge, MA: Ballinger.

Reis, S., Borkan, J., & Hermoni, D. (1992). Low back pain: More than anatomy. *Journal of Family Practice, 35*(5), 509-510.

Rhoades, R., & Booth, R. (1982). Farmer-back-to-farmer: A model for generating acceptable agricultural technology. *Agricultural Administration, 11,* 127-137.

Richardson, L. (1992). The consequences of poetic representation: Writing the other, rewriting the self. In C. Ellis & M. Flaherty (Eds.), *Windows on lived experience* (pp. 125-140). Newbury Park, CA: Sage.

Riegelman, R. K. (1981). *Studying a study and testing a test.* Boston: Little, Brown.

Riesenberg, D., & Glass, R. M. (1989). The Medical Outcomes Study. *Journal of the American Medical Association, 262,* 943.

Riley, D. (1988). *"Am I that name?" Feminism and the category of "women" in history.* Minneapolis: University of Minnesota Press.

Rioch, M. J. (1970). The work of Wilfred Bion on groups. *Psychiatry, 33*(1), 56-66.

Rodnick, J. E. (1987). Research in family medicine: Counterculture continued. *Family Medicine, 19*(4), 251-252, 305-307.

Roman, L. G., & Apple, M. (1990). Is naturalism a move away from positivism? In E. Eisner & A. Peshkin (Eds.), *Qualitative inquiry in education: The continuing debate* (pp. 38-73). New York: Teachers College Press.

Romney, K., Weller, S., & Batchelder, W. H. (1988). Culture as consensus: A theory of culture and informant accuracy. *American Anthropology, 88,* 313-338.

Rorty, R. (Ed.). (1967). *The linguistic turn: Recent essays in philosophical method.* Chicago: University of Chicago Press.

Rosenau, P. (1992). *Post-modernism and the social sciences: Insights, inroads, and intrusions.* NJ: Princeton University Press.

Rosenfield, P. L. (1992). The potential of transdisciplinary research for sustaining and extending linkages between the health and social sciences. *Social Science and Medicine, 35*(11), 1343-1357.

Rosenthal, R. (1984). *Meta-analytic procedures for social science research.* Beverly Hills, CA: Sage.

Rossiter, L. F., & Wilensky, G. R. (1983, Summer). A reexamination of the use of physician services: The role of physician-initiated demand. *Inquiry, 20,* 162-172.

Rossiter, L. F., & Wilensky, G. R. (1987). Health economist induced demand for theories of physician-induced demand. *Journal of Human Resources, 22*(4), 624-627.

Rossman, G. B., & Wilson, B. L. (1985). Numbers and words: Combining quantitative and qualitative methods in a single large-scale evaluation study. *Evaluation Review, 9*(5), 627-643.

Rost, K., & Frankel, R. M. (1993). The introduction of the older patient's problems in the medical visit. *Journal of Health and Aging, 5*(2), 387-401.

Rost, K. M., Flavin, K. S., Cole, K., & McGill, J. B. (1991). Change in metabolic control and functional status after hospitalization: Impact of patient activation intervention in diabetic patients. *Diabetic Care, 14*(10), 881-889.

Roter, D. L. (1977). Patient participation in the provider-patient interaction: The effect of patient question asking on the quality of the interaction, satisfaction and compliance. *Health Education Monographs, 5,* 281-315.

Roter, D. L., & Frankel, R. M. (1992). Quantitative and qualitative approaches to the evaluation of the medical dialog. *Social Science and Medicine, 34*(20), 1097-1103.

Rushton, J. P., Brainerd, C. J., & Pressley, M. (1983). Behavioral development and construct validity: The principle of aggregation. *Psychological Bulletin, 94,* 18-38.

Sacks, H. (1972). *Adjacency pair organization.* Unpublished lecture notes. University of California, Irvine.

Sacks, H. S., Berrier, J., Reitman, D., Ancora-Berk, V. A., & Chalmers, T. C. (1987). Meta-analysis of randomized controlled trials. *New England Journal of Medicine 316,* 450-455.

Sale, K. (1991). *Dwellers in the land: The bioregional vision.* Philadelphia: New Society.

Salomon, G. (1991). Transcending the qualitative-quantitative debate: The analytic and systematic approaches to educational research. *Educational Research, 20,* 10-18.

Scheler, M. (1961). *Ressentiment.* New York: Free Press. (Original work published 1912)

Schensul, S., & Schensul, J. (1982). Advocacy and applied anthropology. In G. Weber & G. McCall (Eds.), *Social scientists as advocates.* Beverly Hills, CA: Sage.

Scheper-Hughes, N. (1992). *Death without weeping: The violence of everyday life in Brazil.* Berkeley: University of California Press.

Schlesinger, M., Cleary, P. D., & Blumenthal, D. (1989). The ownership of health facilities and clinical decision making. *Medical Care, 27*(2), 244-257.

Schlesselman, J. J. (1982). *Case-control studies: Design, conduct, analysis.* New York: Oxford University Press.

Schmookler, A. B. (1984). *The parable of the tribes: The problem of power in social evolution.* Berkeley: University of California Press.

Schmookler, A. B. (1988). *Out of weakness: Healing the wounds that drive us to war.* New York: Bantam.

Schroeder, S. A., Myers, L. P., McPhee, S. J., Showstack, J. A., Simborg, D. W., Chapman, S. A., & Leong, J. K. (1984). The failure of physician education as a cost containment strategy. Report of a prospective controlled trial at a university hospital. *Journal of the American Medical Association, 252*(2), 225-230.

Schur, C. L., Berk, M. L., & Schoenman, J. (1992, June). *The costs and distributional implications of alternative Medicare prescription drug benefits.* Paper presented at the Annual Meetings of the Association for Health Services Research, Chicago, Illinois.

Schwandt, T. (1990). Paths to inquiry in the social disciplines: Scientific, constructivist, and critical theory methodologies. In E. Guba (Ed.), *The paradigm dialog* (pp. 258-276). Newbury Park, CA: Sage.

Schwartz, J. S., & Cohen, S. J. (1990). Changing provider behavior. In J. Mayfield & M. Grady (Eds.), *Primary care research: An agenda for the 90s* (pp. 45-53). Washington, DC: U.S. Department of Health and Human Services, Public Health Service, Agency for Health Care Policy. (DHHS Publication No. 903460)

Sechrest, L. (1963). Incremental validity: A recommendation. *Educational and Psychological Measurement, 23,* 153-158.

Sechrest, L. (1992). Roots: Back to our first generations. *Evaluation Practice, 13,* 1-7.

Seifert, M. H. (1982a). The patient advisory council concept. In E. Connor & F. Mullan (Eds.), *Community oriented primary care* (pp. 307-312). Washington, DC: National Academy Press.

Seifert, M. H. (1982b). Research in family practice: A blueprint for the eighties. *Family Practice Research Journal, 1*(4), 211-223.

Seifert, M. H. (1987). An incremental patient participation model. In P. Nutting (Ed.), *Community oriented primary care: From principle to practice* (pp. 379-383). Washington, DC: U.S. Government Printing Office.

Seifert, M. (1992). Qualitative designs for assessing interventions in primary care: Examples from medical practice. In F. Tudiver, M. J. Bass, E. Z. Dunn, T. G. Norton, & M. Stewart (Eds.), *Research methods for primary care* (Vol. 4, pp. 89-95). Newbury Park, CA: Sage.

Selltiz, C., Jahoda, M., Deutsch, M., & Cook, S. (1959). Research methods in social relations. New York: Henry Holt.

Sewell, W. H. (1989). Some reflections on the golden age of interdisciplinary social psychology. *Annual Review of Sociology, 15,* 1-16.

Sharp, L., Pantell, R. H., Murphy, L. O., & Lewis, C. C. (1992). Psychosocial problems during child health supervision visits: Eliciting, then what? *Pediatrics, 89,* 619-623.

Shavelson, R. J., & Webb, N. M. (1991). *Generalizability theory: A primer.* Newbury Park, CA: Sage.

Shavelson, R. J., Webb, N. M., & Rowley, G. L. (1989). Generalizability theory. *American Psychologist, 44,* 922-932.

Sherif, M., & Sherif, C. W. (Eds.). (1969). *Interdisciplinary relationships in the social sciences.* Chicago: Aldine.

Sieber, S. D. (1973, Spring). The integration of field methods and survey research. *American Journal of Sociology, 78,* 1335-1359.

Silverman, D. (1985). *Qualitative methodology and sociology.* Brookfield, VT: Gower.

Silverman, D. (1987). *Communication and medical practice.* London: Sage.

Smith, A. G., & Robbins, A. E. (1982). Structured ethnography: The study of parental involvement. *American Behavioral Scientist, 26,* 45-61.

Smith, M. L., & Glass, G. V. (1977). Meta-analysis of psychotherapy outcome studies. *American Psychologist, 32,* 752-760.

Soule, M. (1985). What is conservation biology? *Bioscience, 35,* 727-734.

Soumerai, S. B., & Avorn, J. (1990). Principles of educational outreach ("academic detailing") to improved clinical decision-making. *Journal of the American Medical Association, 263,* 549-556.

Soumerai, S. B., McLaughlin, T. J., & Avorn, J. (1989). Improving drug prescribing in primary care: A critical analysis of the literature. *Milbank Quarterly, 67*(2), 268-317.

Sox, H. C. (1979). Quality of patient care by nurse practitioners and physician's assistants: A ten-year perspective. *Annals of Internal Medicine, 91,* 459-468.

Spilker, B. (1991). *A guide to clinical trials.* New York: Raven.

Spitzer, W. V. (1977, July). The intellectual worthiness of family medicine. *Pharos,* pp. 2-12.

Spodick, D. H. (1975). Numerators without denominators: There is no FDA for the surgeon. *Journal of the American Medical Association, 232,* 35-36.

Spodick, D. H. (1982). Randomized controlled clinical trials. *Journal of the American Medical Association, 247*(16), 2258-2260.

Stake, R. (1986). The case-study method of social inquiry. *Educational Researcher, 7,* 5-8.

Stanfield, II, J. H. (1993). In the archives. In J. Stanfield & D. Rutledge (Eds.), *Race and ethnicity in research methods.* Newbury Park, CA: Sage.

Stanfield, II, J. H. (1994). Ethnic modeling in qualitative research methods. In N. Denzin & Y. Lincoln (Eds.), *Handbook of qualitative research* (pp. 175-188). Newbury Park, CA: Sage.

Stanfield, II, J. H., & Rutledge, D. (Eds.). (1993). *Race and ethnicity in research methods.* Newbury Park, CA: Sage.

Stange, K. C., Miller, W. L., Crabtree, B. F., O'Connor, P. J., & Zyzanski, S. J. (1994). Multimethod research: Approaches for integrating qualitative and quantitative methods. *Journal of General Internal Medicine, 9,* 278-282.

Stange, K. C., & Zyzanski, S. J. (1989). Integrating qualitative and quantitative research methods. *Family Medicine, 21*(6), 449-451.

Starfield, B. (1992). *Primary care: Concept, evaluation, and policy.* New York: Oxford University Press.

Starfield, B., Steinwachs, D., Morris, I., Dause, G., Siedert, S., & Westin, C. (1979). Patient-doctor agreement about problems needing follow-up. *Journal of the American Medical Association, 242,* 344-346.

Starfield, B., Wray, C., Hess, K., Gross, R., Birk, T. P. S., & D'Lugoff, B. C. (1981). The influence of patient-practitioner agreement on outcome of care. *American Journal of Public Health, 71*(2), 127-132.

Steckler, A., McLeroy, K. R., Goodman, R. M., Bird, S. T., & McCormick, L. (1992). Toward integrating qualitative and quantitative methods: An introduction. *Health Education Quarterly, 19*(1), 1-8.

Steele, D. J., Jackson, T. C., & Guttman, M. C. (1990). Have you been taking your pills? The adherence monitoring sequence in the medical interview. *Journal of Family Practice, 20,* 294-299.

Stein, R. E. K., & Jessop, D. J. (1988). Thoughts on interdisciplinary research. *Journal of Clinical Epidemiology, 41*(9), 813-815.

Stephens, G. G. (1989). Family medicine as counterculture. *Family Medicine, 21*(2), 103-109.

Stewart, A. L., Greenfield, S., Hayes, R., & Wells, K. (1989, August). Functional status and well-being of patients with chronic conditions. *Journal of the American Medical Association, 262,* 907-913.

Stiles, W. (1989). Evaluating medical interview process components: Null correlations with outcomes may be misleading. *Medical Care, 27,* 212-220.

Stiles, W. B. (1992). *Describing talk: A taxonomy of verbal response modes.* Newbury Park, CA: Sage.

Stoeckle, J. D., & Billings, J. A. (1987). A history of historytaking: The medical interview. *Journal of General Internal Medicine, 2,* 119-127.

Strauss, A. (1975). *Chronic illness and the quality of life.* St. Louis: Mosby.

Strauss, A. (1987). *Qualitative analysis for social scientists.* New York: Cambridge University Press.

Sudnow, D. (1967). *Passing on.* Englewood Cliffs, NJ: Prentice Hall.

Sullivan, W. (1983). Beyond policy science. In N. Haan, R. Bellah, P. Rabinow, & W. Sullivan (Eds.), *Social science as moral inquiry* (pp. 297-319). New York: Columbia University Press.

Svarstad, B. (1974). *The patient-physician encounter: An observational study of communication and outcome.* Unpublished doctoral dissertation, University of Wisconsin.

Svarstad, B., & Lipton, H. L. (1977). Informing patients about mental retardation: A study of professional communication and patient acceptance. *Social Science and Medicine, 11,* 645-651.

Swedlow, A., Johnson, G., Smithline, N., & Milstein, A. (1992). Increased costs and rates of use in the California Workers' Compensation system as a result of self-referral by physicians. *New England Journal of Medicine, 327,* 1502-1506.

Tarlov, A. R., Ware, J., Greenfield, S., & Nelson, E. (1989). The Medical Outcomes Study. *Journal of the American Medical Association, 262,* 925-930.

Tax, S. (1958). The Fox Project. *Human Organization, 17,* 17-19.

Thompson, P. (1978). *Voices of the past.* Oxford, U.K.: Oxford University Press.

Tomlinson, H. (1990). After truth: Post-modernism and the rhetoric of science. In H. Lawson & L. Appignanesi (Eds.), *Dismantling truth: Reality in the post-modern world* (pp. 43-57). New York: St. Martin's.

Tonkin, E. (1992). *Narrating our pasts: The social construction of oral history.* Cambridge, UK: Cambridge University Press.

Topf, M. (1990). Increasing the validity of research results with a blend of laboratory and clinical strategies. *Image: Journal of Nursing Scholarship, 22*(2), 121-123.

Trend, M. (1978). On the reconciliation of quantitative and qualitative analyses. *Human Organization, 37,* 345-354.

Trend, M. G. (1979). On the reconciliation of qualitative and quantitative analysis: A case study. In T. Cook & C. Reichardt (Eds.), *Quantitative and qualitative methods in evaluation research* (pp. 68-86). Beverly Hills, CA: Sage.

Turner, B. J., Day, S. C., & Borenstein, B. (1989). A controlled trial to improve delivery of preventive care: Physician or patient reminders? *Journal of General Internal Medicine, 4,* 403-409.

Turner, F. J. (1932). *The significance of sections in American history.* New York: Henry Holt.

University of Minnesota. Department of Family Practice. (1993). *Report of the Task Force on Building Capacity for Research in Primary Care: Putting research into practice.* Minneapolis: Author.

Van der Geest, S., Speckmann, J. D., & Streefland, P. (1990). Primary health care in a multi-level perspective: Towards a research agenda. *Social Science and Medicine, 30*(9), 1025-1034.

Van Maanen, J. (1988). *Tales of the field: On writing ethnography.* Chicago: University of Chicago Press.

Van Newkirk, A. (1975). Bioregions: Towards bioregional strategies for human culture. *Environmental Conservation, 2,* 108-109.

Volk, L. A. (1992). Review and analysis of ambulatory care claims: 1985-1992. *Forum: Risk Management Foundation of the Harvard Medical Institutions, 13*(2), 2-5.

Waddell, G. (1987). A new clinical model for the treatment of low back pain. *Spine, 12,* 532-644.

Webb, E., Campbell, D., Schwartz, R., & Sechrest, L. (1966). *Unobtrusive measures: Nonreactive research in the social sciences.* Chicago: Rand McNally.

Webb, E., Campbell, D. T., Schwartz, R. D., Sechrest, L., & Grove, J. (1981). *Nonreactive measures in the social sciences.* Boston: Houghton-Mifflin.

Weller, S. C., & Romney, A. K. (1990). *Metric scaling correspondence analysis.* Newbury Park, CA: Sage.

Wennberg, J. E. (1984). Dealing with medical practice variations: A proposal for action. *Health Affairs* (Millwood), *3,* 6-32.

Wennberg, J., & Gittelson, A. (1973). Small area variations in health care delivery. *Science, 182,* 1102-1108.

Wennberg, J. E., & Gittelson, A. (1982). Variations in medical care among small areas. *Scientific American, 246,* 120-133.

White, K. L. (1988). *The task of medicine.* Menlo Park, CA: Henry J. Kaiser Family Foundation.

White, K. L. (1991). *Healing the schism: Epidemiology, medicine, and the public's health.* New York: Springer.

White House Domestic Policy Council. (1993). *The President's Health Security Plan.* New York: Times Books.

Whitford, M. (1991). *Luce Irigaray: Philosophy in the feminine.* London: Routledge.

Whyte, W. F. (Ed.). (1991). *Participatory action research.* Newbury Park, CA: Sage.

Wilder, A. (1983). Story and story-world. *Interpretation, 37,* 353-364.

Witherell, C., & Noddings, N. (1991). Prologue: An invitation to our readers. In C. Witherell & N. Noddings (Eds.), *Stories lives tell: Narrative and dialogue in education* (pp. 101-195). New York: Teachers College Press.

Wohlwill, J. F. (1973). *The study of behavioral development.* New York: Academic Press.

Wonnacott, T. H., & Wonnacott, R. J. (1977). *Introductory statistics for business and economics* (2nd ed.). New York: John Wiley.

Woodbrooks, C. (1991). *The construction of identity through the presentation of self: Black women candidates interviewing for administrative positions at a research university.* Unpublished doctoral dissertation, Ohio State University.

World Health Organization. (1978). *Primary health care: Report of the International Conference on Primary Health Care,* Alma-Ata, USSR, 6-12 September, 1978. Geneva: World Health Organization.

Yin, R. K. (1989). *Case study research* (rev. ed.). Newbury Park, CA: Sage.

Zemke, R. (1989). The continua of scientific research designs. *American Journal of Occupational Therapy, 43*(8), 551-553.

INDEX

ABOUT THE CONTRIBUTORS

Richard B. Addison is Assistant Clinical Professor in the Department of Family and Community Medicine at the University of California, San Francisco, and a core faculty member of the Family Practice Residency Program at Community Hospital of Sonoma County in Santa Rosa, California. He leads ongoing support/personal and professional development groups for resident-physicians and other health care workers. He also maintains a private practice as a clinical psychologist specializing in seeing physicians and their families. His research interests include the professional socialization of family physicians, physician stress and impairment, support services for residents, physicians caring for dying patients and their families, and most passionately, interpretive and hermeneutic approaches to naturalistic and other qualitative research. He is coeditor of *Entering the Circle: Hermeneutic Investigation in Psychology.*

David A. Bergman is Vice President for Health Care Practices and Quality of Care at Lucille Packard Children's Hospital at Stanford University and Clinical Associate Professor of Pediatrics at Stanford University School of Medicine. He did his undergraduate training at Yale University, his medical training at the University of Illinois, and a residency in pediatrics at Rochester-Strong Memorial Hospital and Stanford University Hospital. He has been actively involved in the area of practice guideline development and outcomes assessment. He currently serves as the Chairman of the American Academy of Pediatrics Committee on Quality Improvement and has been involved in the development and assessment of practice guidelines with the California Children's Hospital Association. He has published numerous articles in this area and is actively involved in research projects concerning practice pattern analysis and outcomes assessment.

Jane Bernzweig is Assistant Research Psychologist in the Division of General Pediatrics at the University of California, San Francisco. She did her undergraduate training at the University of Rochester and her graduate training at the University of California at Berkeley. Her postdoctoral training in prevention research with children was at Arizona State University. She has conducted research in primary prevention with children and families as well as studies of physician-patient communication.

Stephen P. Bogdewic is Associate Professor and Vice Chair in the Department of Family Medicine as well as Assistant Dean for Primary Care Education at Indiana University. His scholarly interests include the professional socialization of medical trainees, faculty development, and general methodological issues in qualitative research. His publications have appeared in such journals as *Academic Medicine, Family Medicine,* and *Health Care Management Review.* He received his Ph.D. from the University of North Carolina at Chapel Hill.

Jeffrey Borkan is Assistant Professor of Family and Community Medicine at the University of Massachusetts Medical Center, Director of Research in Family Medicine at Ben-Gurion University in Israel, a Lecturer in Behavioral Science, and the Coordinator of the Israeli Family Practice Research Network. He is a medical anthropologist and practicing rural family physician who, for the last decade, has straddled two fields and two continents. His academic training has taken him from the University of Michigan and Hebrew University to Case Western Reserve, the University of Washington, and Harvard. His areas of interest include qualitative research, narrative analysis, health beliefs, hip fractures, and lower back pain.

Kate Brown is Associate Professor at the Creighton University's Center for Health Policy and Ethics, where she directs a required course on the "ethics of service" with second-year medical students. Her doctorate in sociomedical sciences from Columbia University combined study in cultural anthropology and public health policy. Her research and teaching bring cross-cultural and feminist perspectives to bioethics and health policy.

Carolyn Clancy is Director of the Division of Primary Care at the Agency for Health Care Policy and Research. She is a general internist with research interests in the impact of financial incentives on physicians' decisions, women's health, and physicians' use of preventive services. She attended the University of Massachusetts Medical School (M.D. 1979), did a residency in internal medicine at Worcester Memorial Hospital (M.A.), and was a Kaiser Fellow in General Internal Medicine at the University of Pennsylvania from 1982 to 1984. From 1984 through 1990 she was an Assistant Professor in the Department of Medicine at the Medical College of Virginia in Richmond. She joined

AHCPR in the Division of Primary Care in November 1990 and was appointed Director in April 1993. While at AHCPR she developed the curriculum for the Public Health Service Primary Care Policy Fellowship, for which she is now Codirector, and has published a number of papers on primary care and the effects of financing on access to care. She holds a clinical appointment in the Department of Health Care Sciences at George Washington University.

Benjamin F. Crabtree is a medical anthropologist serving as Research Director in the Department of Family Practice at the University of Nebraska Medical Center. He has written numerous methodological articles and chapters on diverse topics ranging from time series analysis and log-linear modeling to in-depth interviewing and approaches to qualitative data analysis. He is coeditor of *Doing Qualitative Research,* which explores the use of qualitative research in primary health care.

Norman K. Denzin is Professor of Sociology, Communications, and Humanities at the University of Illinois, Urbana-Champaign. He is the author of numerous books, including *The Handbook of Qualitative Methods* (coedited with Yvonna Lincoln), *The Research Act, Interpretive Interactionism, Images of Postmodern Society, The Recovering Alcoholic,* and *The Alcoholic Self,* which won the Coley Award from the Society of the Study of Symbolic Interaction in 1988. He is the editor of *Studies in Symbolic Interaction: A Research Annual,* and *The Sociological Quarterly.*

Richard M. Frankel is Associate Professor of Medicine at the University of Rochester School of Medicine and Dentistry and is Codirector of the Internal Medicine Residency Program at Highland Hospital in Rochester, New York. In addition, he directs the Department of Medicine's Center for Human Interaction. After completing his Ph.D. in sociology at the Graduate School and University Center of the City University of New York, he was a postdoctoral fellow in qualitative approaches to mental health research at Boston University. In 1986, he was a Fulbright Senior Research Fellow in sociolinguistics and social medicine at the University of Uppsala in Sweden. He has also held visiting professorships in Holland, Great Britain, and the United States. He has lectured and published widely on face-to-face communication in a number of contexts, including developmental disabilities, airline cockpit crews, and a range of medical encounters.

Valerie J. Gilchrist is Associate Professor of Family Medicine at Northeastern Ohio University's College of Medicine. A graduate of the University of Toronto Medical School and Family Medicine Residency, she completed a Fellowship in Family Medicine at the University of North Carolina. She has been teaching and practicing in northeast Ohio for more than 10 years. Her writing and research interests are the doctor-patient relationship, health promotion and disease prevention, women's health issues, and feminist theory.

Catherine L. Gilliss is Professor and Chair in the Department of Family Health Care Nursing, School of Nursing, University of California, San Francisco. She serves as Director of the Family Nurse Practitioner Program and Coordinator of a cross-departmental core curriculum in primary care for nurse practitioners and nurse midwives. A nurse practitioner herself, Dr. Gilliss has developed and operates a school-based health service for non-English-speaking teens. Her research addresses outcomes of health care intervention, including care that is focused on the family.

Jaber F. Gubrium is Professor in the Department of Sociology at the University of Florida. He has conducted research on the social organization of care in diverse treatment settings, from nursing homes and physical rehabilitation to counseling centers and family therapy. His continuing fieldwork on the organizational embeddedness of social forms serves as a basis for an interpretive comparative ethnography. He is the editor of *Journal of Aging Studies* and the author of *Living and Dying at Murray Manor* (1975), *Oldtimers and Alzheimer's* (1986), *Analyzing Field Reality* (1988), *The Mosaic of Care* (1991), and *Speaking of Life* (1993). His recently coauthored text *What Is Family?* (1990) and new book *Constructing the Life Course* (1994), both with J. Holstein, present social constructionist approaches to domestic order and life change.

Morgan Jackson is the Associate Administrator for Minority Health, Agency for Health Care Policy and Research, United States Public Health Service. He earned his A.B. and M.D. degrees from Harvard University and an M.P.H. while a Robert Wood Johnson Foundation Clinical Scholar at the University of Washington. His clinical background in primary care and his experiences in HIV/AIDS, health policy, and technology assessment are the basis for his current work in minority health at AHCPR.

P. K. Jamison received her Ph.D. in instructional technology and curriculum studies from Indiana University and is currently an educational cosultant at the Indiana University School of Medicine. A feminist educator and philosopher, she is the author of several publications that examine the ideology of instructional technology and its impact on education. Her current work includes critical and qualitative explorations of teaching, media, instructional development, and social/organizational change.

Valerie Janesick is Associate Professor of Curriculum and Instruction at the University of Kansas, Lawrence. She teaches classes in qualitative research methods, curriculum theory, curriculum planning and evaluation, and developing intercultural awareness in education. She holds a courtesy appointment in the Department of Russian and East European Studies, which allows her to organize numerous faculty and student exchanges between Moscow, St. Petersburg, and Izhevsk, Russia, and Lawrence. Her research interests include qualitative research methods, ethics in research, and comparative curriculum issues in Russian, Japanese, and Chinese schools. As a dancer, arts educator, and researcher on teaching, she has focused on international perspectives and cultural use of languages in the educational setting. Her writings have been published in *Curriculum Inquiry, Anthropology and Education Quarterly,* and various education journals. She is currently working on a text on understanding ethical issues in fieldwork through qualitative case studies. She is currently planning to do a documentary on Japanese arts education programs as a result of her recent Fulbright study in Japan.

David A. Katerndahl is Associate Professor and the Director of Research and Education in the Department of Family Practice at the University of Texas Health Science Center in San Antonio. He graduated in 1980 from the Family Practice Residency Program of Ohio State University and received his Masters in Education in 1981. Since joining the Department of Family Practice in 1984, he has coordinated faculty development and has chaired committees for the North American Primary Care Research Group and the Texas Academy of Family Physicians. In 1985, he founded the Primary Care Research Methods and Statistics Conference, which is now in its eighth year. He is widely published in the areas of panic disorder and meta-analysis.

Anton J. Kuzel is Associate Professor, Department of Family Practice, at the Medical College of Virginia, Richmond. After completing his undergraduate, graduate, and postgraduate training at the University of Illinois, he served as Associate Director of the Fairfax Family Practice Program in Fairfax, Virginia, and is now Coordinator of Graduate Programs and Faculty Development in the Department of Family Practice at MCV-VCU. His research interests include the practical applications of qualitative inquiry to family medicine research, with particular emphasis on the doctor-patient relationship, preventive care, and chemical dependency.

Patti Lather is Associate Professor of Educational Policy and Leadership at Ohio State University, where she teaches qualitative research and feminist pedagogy. Her work includes *Getting Smart: Feminist Research and Pedagogy With/in the Postmodern* (1991) and *Within/Against Feminist Research in Education* (1991). She has an essay in *After Postmodernism,* edited by Herbert Simons and Michael Billig (Sage, 1994), and her current work is on researching the lives of women with HIV/AIDS.

Robert McCall is Professor of Psychology and Codirector of the University of Pittsburgh Office of Child Development and its Policy and Evaluation Project. His scholarly interests focus on longitudinal research design and analyses, and he is the author of a leading undergraduate statistics text and several scholarly articles and chapters on this topic. In addition, as part of his responsibilities in codirecting the Policy and Evaluation Project, he guides an interdisciplinary group of program evaluators who, working collaboratively with faculty at the university and service professionals in the community, are evaluating a variety of health, education, welfare, and mental health community-based prevention and treatment service demonstration programs. In addition to having written about methodology and statistics, Dr. McCall is widely published in the areas of mental development in infants, developmental change in mental performance through the lifespan, the communication of science to the general public through the mass media, and underachieving students.

William L. Miller is a physician-anthropologist who has recently moved to Lehigh Valley Hospital in Allentown, Pennsylvania, where he is Vice Chair and Program Director of a newly formed family medicine residency program. He has been active in an effort to make qualitative research more accessible to health care clinicians and researchers. He has contributed book chapters and articles detailing step-by-step applications of qualitative methods, including the book *Doing Qualitative Research,* which he coedited with Benjamin Crabtree. His research interests center on the role of the patient-physician relationship in health care, on physician and patient understanding of pain, and on hypertension.

Curt D. Mueller is Senior Research Director at the Project HOPE Center for Health Affairs in Bethesda, Maryland, where he specializes in health economics and health policy. He has had extensive experience in managing and conducting economic analyses for the private and public sectors on the demand for medical care and pharmaceutical products, physician behavior and supply in rural areas, and impacts of health technology. Prior to joining

Project HOPE, he was a Senior Analyst with the Physician Payment Review Commission, Washington, D.C., where he was responsible for overseeing development of resource-based relative value scales to measure physician practice costs. He also served as an economist with the Agency for Health Care Policy and Research and as a member of the faculty of the Department of Public Administration, the Maxwell School, Syracuse University. He earned his Ph.D. in economics at the University of North Carolina, Chapel Hill.

Thomas B. Newman is Associate Professor of Laboratory Medicine, Pediatrics, and Epidemiology and Biostatistics at the University of California, San Francisco, Director of the UCSF Clinical Database Research Program, and Associate Director of the Robert Wood Johnson Clinical Scholars training program at UCSF. He did his undergraduate training at the University of California, Santa Cruz, his medical training at the University of California, San Diego, his residency in pediatrics at UCSF, and a clinical epidemiology fellowship at UCSF and UC Berkeley. He has a longstanding interest in retrospective clinical research studies and has published such studies on a wide range of topics, from the long-term effects of the military draft on mortality to the evaluation and treatment of jaundice in newborn babies.

Robert H. Pantell is Professor of Pediatrics and Director of the Division of General Pediatrics at the University of California, San Francisco. He did his undergraduate training at Columbia University, his medical training at Boston University, a residency in pediatrics at the University of North Carolina at Chapel Hill, and a fellowship in health services research at Stanford University. He is coauthor of the best-selling *Taking Care of Your Child,* a winner of the American Medical Writers Association Award, and author of numerous publications in health services research and behavioral pediatrics.

Louis F. Rossiter is Professor of Health Economics in the Department of Health Administration at the Medical College of Virginia, Virginia Commonwealth University. He teaches in the graduate program in health administration. He is also Director of the Office of Health Care Policy and Research in the Office of the Vice President for Health Sciences on the MCV Campus. Founding Director of the Williamson Institute for Health Studies at the Medical College of Virginia, he conducted numerous research projects on the financing and delivery of health care. One major project was the National Medicare Competition Evaluation, which examined the costs, service use, and quality of care under health maintenance organization enrollment for Medicare beneficiaries. He also studied the costs of new Medicaid managed care programs on an evaluation of experiments in California, Missouri, New Jersey, New York, and Minnesota. From 1989 to 1991 he took a leave of absence to serve as Senior Policy Advisor to the Administrator of the Health Care Financing Administration, Department of Health and Human Services. During that period he dealt with prospective payment for the costs of capital for hospitals, physician payment reform, provider taxes and donation schemes under Medicaid, PRO reform, and managed care issues for Medicare and Medicaid.

Lee Sechrest is Professor of Psychology at the University of Arizona and also head of the Evaluation Group for Analysis of Data. He works primarily in the areas of research methodology and program evaluation, with special emphasis on health services. Prior to coming to Arizona, he was Director of the Center for Research on the Utilization of Scientific Knowledge at the University of Michigan, where he also held appointments as Professor of Public Health and of Psychology. He has had other faculty positions at Florida State University, Northwestern University, and Pennsylvania State University. His Ph.D. in clinical psychology is from Ohio State University.

Milton Seifert, Jr., has been a family physician in full-time general practice in Excelsior, Minnesota, since 1961. He has had academic appointments as Clinical Associate Professor, Department of Family Practice and Community Health, University of Minnesota, and Assistant Clinical Professor, Department of Family Medicine and Practice, University of Wisconsin. He and his associates have developed the Eagle Medical Model with the help of the Family Health Foundation of America, the Robert Wood Johnson Foundation, the Management Medicine Foundation, and a Small Business Innovative Research grant from the National Institutes of Health. He has served as the Chair of the Research Committee of the Minnesota Academy of Family Physicians from 1969 to 1989 and was named the 1990 Minnesota Family Physician of the Year. He is also a member of the Ambulatory Sentinel Practice Network, the Society of Teachers of Family Medicine, and the North American Primary Care Research Group. His primary interest is practice-based research.

Souraya Sidani is currently a doctoral candidate in Nursing at the University of Arizona and expects to complete her work in 1994. She received a B.S. degree in nursing and a teaching diploma in health education at the American University of Beirut, Lebanon. She subsequently worked as a clinical instructor at the School of Nursing there and later as a continuing education program coordinator at Makassed General Hospital in Beirut.

John H. Stanfield, II, is Professor of African-American and African Studies and Professor of Sociology at the University of California, Davis. He is a historical sociologist of knowledge, sciences, and racial inequality. He has published several books on race and the history of human science and on methods as ethnic cultural products.